Philosophy and the Jewish Question

Philosophy and the Jewish Question

Mendelssohn, Rosenzweig, and Beyond

Bruce Rosenstock

FORDHAM UNIVERSITY PRESS
NEW YORK 2010

Copyright © 2010 Fordham University Press

All rights reserved. No part of this publication may be reproduced, stored in a retrieval system, or transmitted in any form or by any means—electronic, mechanical, photocopy, recording, or any other—except for brief quotations in printed reviews, without the prior permission of the publisher.

Fordham University Press has no responsibility for the persistence or accuracy of URLs for external or third-party Internet websites referred to in this publication and does not guarantee that any content on such websites is, or will remain, accurate or appropriate.

Library of Congress Cataloging-in-Publication Data

Rosenstock, Bruce (Bruce Benjamin)
 Philosophy and the Jewish question : Mendelssohn, Rosenzweig, and beyond / Bruce Rosenstock.
    p. cm.
 Includes bibliographical references and index.
 ISBN 978-0-8232-3129-4 (cloth : alk. paper)
 1. Judaism and philosophy. 2. Philosophy, Jewish. 3. Judaism and Politics. 4. Judaism—Doctrines. 5. Mendelssohn, Moses, 1729–1786. 6. Rosenzweig, Franz, 1886–1929. 7. Arendt, Hannah, 1906–1975. 8. Cavell, Stanley, 1926– I. Title.
 B5800.R675 2010
 181′.06—dc22

2009021916

Printed in the United States of America
12 11 10   5 4 3 2 1
First edition

For

Bertold Rosenstock
1916–1944

May his memory be for a blessing.

CONTENTS

List of Abbreviations   ix

Acknowledgments   xiii

Introduction: Mendelssohn and Rosenzweig Beyond 1800   1
   1800 • Rosenzweig and Mendelssohn • The Plan of the Book

1. Performing Reason: Mendelssohn on Judaism and Enlightenment   28
   Introduction • Jewish "Civil Improvement" • *Jerusalem*: Philosophy against Despotism • Mendelssohn's Expressivism • Writing and Mendelssohn's Dialectic of Enlightenment • Mendelssohn and Wittgenstein's Private Language Argument • Mendelssohn's Defense of Jewish Interiority • Mendelssohn on Judaism as a "Living Script"

2. Jacobi and Mendelssohn: The Tragedy of a Messianic Friendship   79
   Introduction: Background to the Spinoza Quarrel • Jacobi's Gnostic Turn • Jacobi vs. "the Jews of Speculative Reason" • Mendelssohn's Response to Jacobi

3. In the Year of the Lord 1800: Rosenzweig and the Spinoza Quarrel   123
   Introduction: Mendelssohn and Jacobi on Revelation • The Hebrew Bible and Paganism • Christianity and Paganism: 1800 • Language as the Site of Revelation • Conclusion: Rosenzweig and Jacobi

4. Reinhold and Kant: The Quest for a New Religion of Reason 162
   Overview: Reinhold, Kant, and Hegel Before 1800 •
   Reinhold: Hebrew Mysteries Unveiled • Kant's Religion of
   Sublimity

5. Beautiful Life: Mendelssohn, Hegel, and Rosenzweig 205
   Introduction: Reading through Hegel • Infinite Life,
   Judaism, and Christian Fate • The Last Supper Once More
   • Hegel's Children • Rosenzweig's Children • Art and Hope:
   The Sorrows of Christian Life

6. Mendelssohn, Rosenzweig, and Political Theology: Beyond
   Sovereign Violence 244
   Overview • Rosenzweig and Schmitt on the Political •
   Arendt contra Schmitt: Natality vs. Violence •
   Mendelssohn's Political Theology

7. Beyond 1800: An Immigrant Rosenzweig 276
   Introduction • Rosenzweig and Cavell on Revelation •
   Festive Existence: Rosenzweig and Cavell on Redemption •
   Conclusion

Epilogue: *Pirates of the Caribbean* Once More 309

Notes 325

Bibliography 357

Index 367

ABBREVIATIONS

Fragment G. W. F. Hegel, *Systemfragment von 1800* (*Fragment of a System from 1800*). The German text is found in Hegel 1907: 343–51. The English translation is found in Hegel 1948: 309–19. Citations are to the English translation and the German text.

Golgotha J. G. Hamann, *Golgotha und Scheblimini!* (1784) (*Golgotha and Scheblimini!*). The German text is found in Hamann 1949–57, 3:291–320. The English translation is found in Dunning 1979. Citations are to the English translation and the German text.

Hebrew Mysteries K. L. Reinhold, *Die Hebräischen Mysterien, oder die älteste religiöse Freymaurerey* (1786) (*The Hebrew Mysteries, or the Oldest Religious Freemasonry*). The German text is found in Reinhold 2006. Translations are mine throughout.

Hegel-Staat F. Rosenzweig, *Hegel und der Staat* (1920) (*Hegel and the State*), 2 vols., reprinted in Rosenzweig 1962. Translations are mine throughout.

Improvement C. W. Dohm, *Ueber die bürgerliche Verbesserung der Juden* (*On the Civil Improvement of the Jews*). The German text is found in Dohm 1781–83. References without a volume number refer to Dohm's text (1781) in vol. 1; those given in vol. 2 refer to Johann David Michaelis's 1783 "Beurtheilung" ("Response"). Translations are mine throughout.

Jacobi to Fichte F. H. Jacobi, *Jacobi an Fichte* (1799) (*Jacobi to Fichte*). The German text is found in Jacobi 1812–25: 3: 1–57.

ix

x   *Abbreviations*

	The English translation is found in Jacobi 1994: 496–536. Citations are to the English translation and the German text.
Jerusalem	M. Mendelssohn, *Jerusalem, oder über religiöse Macht und Judentum* (1783) (*Jerusalem, or, On Religious Power and Judaism*). The German text is reprinted in three versions: *JubA* 8: 99–204; Mendelssohn 2001; and Mendelssohn 2005. The English translation is found in Mendelssohn 1983. Citations are to the English translation and the 1783 German original (pages noted at the head of the *JubA* reprint and marginally in the Mendelssohn 2001 reprint).
JubA	M. Mendelssohn, *Gesammelte Schriften Jubiläumsausgabe* (*Collected Works Jubilee Edition*). For publication details, see Mendelssohn 1971–90.
Kant Letters	K. L. Reinhold, *Briefe über die kantische Philosophie* (1786–87) (*Letters on the Kantian Philosophy*). The English translation is found in Reinhold 2005.
Little Book	F. Rosensweig, *Büchlein vom gesunden und kranken Menschenverstand* (*Little Book Concerning the Healthy and the Sick Common Sense*). The English translation is found in Rosenzweig 1999.
Morning Hours	M. Mendelssohn, *Morgenstunden; oder Vorlesungen über das Daseyn Gottes* (1785) (*Morning Hours, or, Lectures on the Existence of God*). The German text is reprinted in *JubA* 3.2:1–175 and is also available online at http://www.zeno.org/Philosophie/M/Mendelssohn,+Moses. Translations are mine throughout. Citations are to the chapters and pages in *JubA* 3.2.
On Things Divine	F. H. Jacobi, *Über göttliche Dinge und ihre Offenbarung* (1811) (*On Things Divine and their Revelation*). The German text is found in Jacobi 1812–25: 3:245–460. Translations are mine throughout.
PI	L. Wittgenstein, *Philosophische Untersuchungen* (1953) (*Philosophical Investigations*). The English translation is found in Wittgenstein 1958.

Religion-Reason	I. Kant, *Die Religion innerhalb der Grenzen der blossen Vernunft* (1793) (*Religion within the Boundaries of Mere Reason*). The English translation is found in Kant 1998. Citations are to the English translation and the German Academy edition.
Spinoza-Letters	F. H. Jacobi, *Über die Lehre des Spinoza in Briefen an den Herrn Moses Mendelssohn* (1785) (*Concerning the Doctrine of Spinoza in Letters to Herr Moses Mendelssohn*). The English translation is found in Jacobi 1994: 173–251. The German text of all editions published in Jacobi's lifetime is found in Jacobi 2000. Citations are to the English translation and the German text.
Spirit-Fate	G. W. F. Hegel, *Der Geist des Christentums und sein Schicksal* (unpublished ms., dated to 1799) (*The Spirit of Christianity and its Fate*). The German text is found in Hegel 1907: 243–342. The English translation is found in Hegel 1948: 182–301. Citations are to the English translation and the German text.
Star	F. Rosenzweig, *Der Stern der Erlösung* (1921) (*The Star of Redemption*). The German text of 1921 is reprinted, with original pagination retained, in three versions: Rosenzweig 1976, band 2; Rosenzweig 1988; and online (http://publikationen.ub.uni-frankfurt.de/volltexte/2005/1932/). The English translation is found in Rosenzweig 2005. Citations are to the English translation and the German text.
Vorrede	M. Mendelssohn, *Vorrede . . . zu des Hrn. Kriegsraths Dohm Abhandlung: Ueber die bürgerliche Verbesserung der Juden* (1782) (*Preface . . . to Dohm's Treatise: On the Civil Improvement of the Jews*). The German text is found in *JubA* 8:1–96. Translations throughout are mine.

ACKNOWLEDGMENTS

I owe a debt of gratitude to the Illinois Program for Research in the Humanities for providing me a fellowship in 2005–6 that allowed me to take a semester off from teaching and work entirely on this book. The fellows who met weekly to discuss ongoing projects offered immense support. In particular, I would like to thank Professor Matti Bunzl, then the director of the IPRH, for his ongoing encouragement. I would like to thank Professor Robert McKim, chair of the Department of Religion at the University of Illinois at Urbana-Champaign, who generously provided me with teaching reduction in the fall semester of 2006. Professor Gary Porton of the Department of Religion at Illinois was extraordinarily supportive throughout the writing of this book. Without his faith in my project, I could not have brought this book to completion.

My daughters Penelope and Sissela were lovingly tolerant of my self-absorption during the writing of this book, and I sincerely beg their forgiveness for the many, many times that "just a minute" extended into hours. I owe them big time.

I could not have written this book without the help of my wife, Harriet Murav. She and I talked though nearly every chapter more than once, and her critical advice has vastly improved this book. But above all else, Harriet teaches me how to make every day *yontovdik*. I am still only a beginner in the lessons, but her love and faith in me draw me forward step by step.

Finally, I would like to say a word about Bertold Rosenstock, the person to whom this book is dedicated. From the age of three, he grew up with his older brother Georg, my father, in the Jewish Orphanage in Frankfurt am Main. Declining the opportunity to emigrate with his brother to America in 1938 after Kristalnacht, Bertold joined the Hehalutz Zionist youth movement centered in Berlin where he served as a teacher in the Youth Aliyah school. Later, he directed the Youth Aliyah Hachsharah training camp in Hummelo, Netherlands. There he helped young Jews to acquire the agricultural skills required for emigration to Palestine. Bertold was arrested by the Gestapo on April 10, 1943. He perished in Auschwitz the following year.

Philosophy and the Jewish Question

INTRODUCTION

Mendelssohn and Rosenzweig Beyond 1800

> No Jewish philosopher of religion in Germany until Rosenzweig followed Mendelssohn's lead entirely ... This is a remarkable fact: it seems as if German-Jewish philosophy went full circle to return to its point of origin.
>
> AMOS FUNKENSTEIN, *Perceptions of Jewish History* (228)

> Seldom can the historian indicate the beginning and end of a movement with such a precision as in the case of German-Jewish philosophy. It started with Mendelssohn's *Jerusalem* (1783) and ended with Rosenzweig's *Stern der Erlösung* (1921).
>
> FUNKENSTEIN, *Perceptions of Jewish History* (257)

1800

The year 1800 marks a moment when, according to Rosenzweig, history takes a false turn. The generation living around the year 1800, having witnessed an unprecedented popular revolution in France, sensed that they stood on the cusp of a new and glorious future. Rosenzweig finds this sense of nearly messianic expectancy in a verse from Friedrich Hölderlin's poem of 1800, "To the Germans" ("An die Deutschen"), which he uses as an epigraph to his book *Hegel und der Staat* (1920):

> Aber kömmt, wie der Strahl aus dem Gewölke kömmt,
> Aus Gedanken vielleicht, geistig und reif die Tat?
> Folgt die Frucht, wie des Haines
> Dunklem Blatte, der stillen Schrift?

> (But as lightning from clouds, out of mere thoughts perhaps,
> Will the deed in the end, lucid, mature, leap out?

As from dark orchard leaves, from
Quiet scripts does the fruit ensue?")[1]

In the British tradition, the well-known lines of William Wordsworth convey the same sense of a generation's new hope:

> Bliss was it in that dawn to be alive,
> But to be young was very heaven; . . .
> Not favour'd spots alone, but the whole earth
> The beauty wore of promise, that which sets,
> To take an image which was felt, no doubt,
> Among the bowers of paradise itself,
> The budding rose above the rose full blown.
> (*The Prelude* [1805] 10.693–706)

The year 1800 thus represents a moment of world-renewing hopefulness, but the hope was not fulfilled. After initially waging its battles in defense of liberty, it seemed to many that the French revolutionary army was corrupted by a lust for conquest. But the hope of the youthful German generation of 1800 was not entirely abandoned. Rather, it was transferred to the world of speculative thought, the world of Spirit. Near the conclusion of *Glauben und Wissen* (*Faith and Knowledge*) (1802), G. W. F. Hegel (1770–1831) declares that a "speculative Good Friday" will soon take the place of the "historic Good Friday" (Hegel 1977: 191). After quoting Hegel's statement that his speculative philosophy marks an "important epoch in time, a time of ferment, when the Spirit has made an about-face, shed its prior form, and acquired a new one," Rosenzweig continues:

> Thus is the self-consciousness of the thinker swollen to bursting. He stands eye to eye with his time. Even more: he speaks to it and it speaks to him. He is actually ready and able to enter into it, "to be" it. He has stepped beyond what Dante called the middle of our life's way. The stations of life have for him become the epochs of the world. The stream of thought has crested its banks and waters the thirsty acres of time. (*Hegel-Staat* 1:220–21.)

According to Rosenzweig, the messianic hope of the German generation of 1800 was betrayed when that generation took refuge in a world built by speculative philosophy. Speculative philosophy, Rosenzweig explains as he traces the development of Hegel's thought in the decades after 1800, ultimately made common cause with the brutality and violence of history when

Hegel proclaimed that "what is rational, is actual; and what is actual, is rational [was vernünftig ist, das ist wirklich; und was wirklich ist, das ist vernünftig]."[2] The messianic hope of 1800 was replaced by an unholy alliance of philosophy and the German state. A thinker had dared to become one with his time,[3] to fuse his life with world history, but in doing so he had managed only to "water the thirsty acres" of his own Prussian state. "One can say that Hegel was the philosopher of the Prussian state," Rosenzweig says, "but one can equally well say that the Prussian state of 1820 is a thought of the Hegelian philosophy. One statement is just as true, and just as false, as the other" (*Hegel-Staat* 2:169).

Rosenzweig conceived of his philosophy as making it possible for the messianic hopes of the epochal moment of 1800 finally to be realized.[4] Having begun his magnum opus, *Der Stern der Erlösung* (*The Star of Redemption*) in 1918 while serving on the Balkan front, Rosenzweig completed it in 1919 and published it two years later, in 1921.[5] Rosenzweig wrote *The Star of Redemption* in order to release the redemptive spring that was drawn into tension but also held in check by 1800. Rosenzweig believed that on the other side of 1800 there was a hope for the redemption of the world that could, if reawakened, break through the alliance of philosophy and the state. This alliance, in Rosenzweig's view, was a modern paganism that only the redemptive force of revelation itself could shatter.

Rosenzweig did not view the hope for world redemption as a hope for a political revolution, but for the renewal of the power of revelation in the world. Rosenzweig believed that the hope of the young German generation of 1800, although fanned by the events of the revolution in France, had its deepest roots in an earlier, bloodless revolution, the "Copernican revolution" of Kant's *Critique of Pure Reason* (1781). Because their messianic fervor sprang from a philosophical revolution, it could be fulfilled through one as well.

Kant's work overthrew no king, but it did overthrow the God of the German Enlightenment, the Necessary Being who providentially governed the world without ever disturbing its perfect clockwork mechanism with even a single miracle or word of revealed speech. Kant's work inspired the hope that a path towards a nondogmatic recuperation of miracle and revelation might be discovered. This was to be a revelation not based upon a blind faith in the authority of the scriptures, but one that emerged from the inward freedom of the individual. To be sure, Rosenzweig does not want to resurrect the Kantian faith in the regulative Ideas of God and the Immortality of the Soul. Rather, he wants to release the redemptive force that Kant's assault on the Enlightenment's sterile rationalism had begun to unleash until it was derailed by speculative philosophy. Rosenzweig's *The Star of Redemption* sets out to show that the "in-itself" reality of God, of Man, and of the World that Kant had placed beyond speculative reason's grasp could be rediscovered on the common ground of revelation. To do this, Rosenzweig had first to demolish the pagan synthesis of God, Man, World, and State that Hegel's philosophy had constructed.

Opposed, then, to the pagan forces of Hegelian philosophy and the state, according to Rosenzweig, stands the messianic hopefulness associated with revelation. The year 1800 marks the point when the path towards revelation opened by Kant had been blocked by speculative philosophy. Rosenzweig had come to believe that the terrible cataclysm of the Great War had realigned the forces that checked the messianic expectancy of 1800 and held in abeyance the growth of the force of revelation. The Great War had dealt the pagan fusion of philosophy and the state its deathblow, and revelation was prepared to spring forth into history. *The Star of Redemption* undertook the work of clearing away the last traces of paganism. It aimed at nothing less than finally breaking the spell of 1800.

I take Rosenzweig's interpretation of the meaning of the year 1800 very seriously. Like him, I believe that 1800 marks in German history an epochal moment involving the transformation of philosophy, the state, and what Rosenzweig calls "revelation." But the messianic potential of this epochal moment was not sprung free by *The Star of Redemption*. Nor was it sprung free even by the word of revelation itself, at least as it came to expression in the new Buber-Rosenzweig Bible translation. Rosenzweig conceived of the translation of the Hebrew Bible as another assault on the historical forces still blocking access to the messianic force held in check on the other side of 1800. Yet Rosenzweig's attempt to break through the paganism of philosophy and the state was cut short with his death in 1929 after a seven-year heroic battle waged, with the support of his wife Edith, against the increasing ravages of amyotrophic lateral sclerosis ("Lou Gehrig's Disease"). In any case, the future of any project dedicated to dismantling the forces of paganism in Germany seemed already to be doomed. Rosenzweig's project remains incomplete.

This book is written in the belief that today Rosenzweig's project—to allow revelation to enter history in order to end the idolatry of the state—remains of critical importance. The path I will follow in picking up the thread of this project is one suggested by Amos Funkenstein, whom I quote in the epigraph to this introduction. I will argue that by bringing Mendelssohn and Rosenzweig into conversation across the divide of 1800, we may close the circle of the never-completed German-Jewish philosophical project that, as Funkenstein says, begins with Mendelssohn's *Jerusalem, or On Religious Power and Judaism* (1783)[6] and ends with *The Star of Redemption* (1921). Closing this circle means envisioning a democratic, redemptive politics that joins Rosenzweig's philosophy of revelation with Mendelssohn's political philosophy. In other words, closing the circle of German-Jewish philosophy means rethinking the relationship between revelation and the state.

This is the first book-length study devoted to Mendelssohn and Rosenzweig together. I do not claim to offer exhaustive treatments of either thinker's work. Although I devote separate chapters to each figure, I also interweave explorations of various aspects of their philosophies in every chapter. Leora Batnitzky's discussion of Mendelssohn in her book on Rosenzweig, *Idolatry and Representation*, makes an important contribution towards the subject of Rosenzweig's relation to Mendelssohn, but much more remains to be done.[7] In what follows, I will describe the path my book will follow in exploring the Mendelssohn-Rosenzweig connection. It may be useful to begin by explaining what seems to have discouraged others from linking Mendelssohn and Rosenzweig. I am referring to Rosenzweig's own reflections about Mendelssohn.

Rosenzweig and Mendelssohn

Rosenzweig did not have a great deal to say about Moses Mendelssohn. His most extensive discussion of Mendelssohn comes in the essay entitled "'The Eternal': Mendelssohn and the Name of God."[8] Rosenzweig's rather negative portrait of Mendelssohn, which I will describe in a moment, would certainly discourage anyone who might think to draw Rosenzweig's philosophy into conversation with Mendelssohn's. But Rosenzweig's critique of Mendelssohn raises certain questions that call for deeper reflection. Far from discouraging the search for the commonalities joining Mendelssohn's and Rosenzweig's philosophical projects, I read this essay as an incitement to undertake the search.

In the essay, Rosenzweig discusses Mendelssohn's decision to translate the name of God, the tetragrammaton YHWH, as "the Eternal [der ewige]" or "the Eternal Being [das ewige Wesen]" in his new rendering of the Five Books of Moses into German. As Rosenzweig explains, Mendelssohn justifies his translation of the tetragrammaton as "the Eternal Being" in his commentary on the biblical pericope in which God reveals his name to Moses at the burning bush (Ex 3:12–14). In that passage, God responds to Moses's question about how he should refer to "the God of your fathers" when speaking with the Israelites. Rosenzweig first offers the version of the answer as it appears in his and Buber's new German translation of the Jewish Bible:

> Gott aber sprach zu Mosche:
> Ich werde dasein, als der ich dasein werde.
> Und sprach:
> So sollst du zu den Söhnen Jisraels sprechen:
> ICH BIN DA schickt mich zu euch.⁹
>
> (Now God said to Moshe:
> I will be-there howsoever I will be-there.
> And said:
> Thus shall you say to the Sons of Israel:
> I AM THERE sends me to you.)¹⁰

Mendelssohn's translation, however, offered:

> Gott sprach zu Mosche: Ich bin das Wesen, welches ewig ist. Er sprach nämlich: So sollst du zu den Kindern Jisraels sprechen, "Das ewige Wesen welches nennt sich 'Ich bin ewig' hat mich zu euch gesendet."¹¹
>
> (God spoke to Moshe: "I am the being that is eternal." He said further: "Thus should you speak to the children of Israel, "The Eternal Being which calls itself 'I am eternal' has sent me to you.")

Mendelssohn in his commentary explains that the tetragrammaton, whose root letters show a connection with the verb *to be* that is inflected in this passage in what is differently translated as "I am there" or "I am eternal," expresses "perfection in respect of existence and providence." It is the first of these attributes of perfection, the perfection of existence (i.e., necessary existence), that Mendelssohn says he hopes to capture with the translation of tetragrammaton as "the eternal being." Rosenzweig explains that "in the classic eighteenth-century beliefs was a belief in the possibility of a rational theology, and in such a theology ... the notion of a being necessarily existent might inevitably imply the notion of a providential one" (104). Rosenzweig concludes that, for Mendelssohn, "the God of prayerful petition" has become a "deduction" of rational theology.

Rosenzweig praises Mendelssohn for turning to the Exodus pericope in order find a translation for the tetragrammaton. But Rosenzweig believes that Mendelssohn's decision to translate the tetragrammaton with "the eternal being" is terribly wrong. This translation, he explains, completely obscures the fact that revelation takes place between a speaking subject uttering the pronoun *I* in relation to a listener, a *You*. For Rosenzweig, the import of God's self-revelation at the burning bush consists not in his informing Moses that he is a "perfectly existing" being who names himself "I am eternal," but rather in God's declaration that he is an *I* who calls out to a *You*. "I am there" does not name a philosophical postulate but "the personal God of immediate experience" (108).

Rosenzweig's essay foregrounds what he believes is the distance separating his own philosophy of revelation from the "rational theology" of Mendelssohn. He says that Mendelssohn's "attenuated belief" in the German Enlightenment's Necessary Being is "no longer possible for us after the work of Kant the Crusher, to use Mendelssohn's phrase for him" (104). Thus, Rosenzweig seems to set Mendelssohn on the far side of 1800, before the redemptive forces of miracle and revelation began to be unleashed by the critical work of "Kant the Crusher." But Rosenzweig not only places himself on the other side of the Kantian divide, he also shows us in this essay which post-Kantian voice he is listening to when he claims to hear the rumblings of a new outbreak of revelation around 1800. That voice is certainly not Hegel's. Invoking the importance of the *I-You* relation of direct speech against Mendelssohn's rationalistic deduction of God's personhood from his necessary being, Rosenzweig is repeating in nearly identical terms the critique leveled against Moses Mendelssohn in Mendelssohn's own day by Friedrich Heinrich Jacobi (1743–1819). Jacobi was the first to introduce the idea that divine revelation was connected with the dialogical encounter between an *I* and a *You*.[12]

There is a tremendous irony in the fact that Rosenzweig stands on the side of Jacobi against Mendelssohn. The dispute between Mendelssohn and Jacobi about rational theology and its relationship to the personal revelation of God as a *You*, a dispute that came to be known as the "Spinoza Quarrel" (Spinozastreit), marked a decisive turning point in the history of the German Enlightenment. Indeed, the dispute can be said to have been decisive in creating the conditions for what Rosenzweig identifies as the epochal transformation in German philosophy marked by the year 1800. The dispute, carried on in private letters between Mendelssohn and Jacobi for nearly two years, broke out publicly in 1785 when Jacobi released the correspondence in *Über die Lehre des Spinoza in Briefen an den Herrn Moses Mendelssohn* (*Concerning the Doctrine of Spinoza in Letters to Herr Moses Mendelssohn*).[13] The dispute seemed to define in the sharpest possible terms the cultural and philosophical tensions within the German Enlightenment. On one side stood Mendelssohn as the representative of rational theology. On the other side stood Jacobi and men like Johann Caspar Lavater (1741–1801) and Johann Georg Hamann (1730–88) who, from different angles to be sure, defended the suprarational revelation of Christianity. Jacobi argued that the Enlightenment's rational theology and its supporting Leibnizian-Wolffian metaphysics (of which Mendelssohn was the foremost exponent), descended from Spinoza. Jacobi contended that Spinoza alone had the courage to draw out the consequence of basing one's theology on an idea of God as a perfectly necessary being, namely, that neither God nor humans have any actual freedom. Without freedom, one can at best have an "intellectual" love of God, as Spinoza calls it, but a love that is neither rational nor planned—a love between divine and human persons who address one another as *I* and *You*—seems excluded. A necessary being cannot love a contingent human being and certainly cannot be revealed in the flesh of such a being.

At the center of Jacobi's assault against Enlightenment rational theology are two Jews—Spinoza and Mendelssohn—who are portrayed as responsible for the suborning of Christian revelation. Jacobi argued that Spinoza and Mendelssohn had managed to insinuate their abstract, hyper-rationalistic, Jewish God into the very heart of Christian Germany. It is therefore tremendously ironic that Rosenzweig will return to Jacobi's concept of revelation precisely in order to recover the living power of the *Jewish* Bible in his and Buber's new translation.

Rosenzweig's essay on Mendelssohn's decision to translate the tetragrammaton as "the eternal being" thus leads directly back to the moment when philosophy in Germany awakens to discover that it has become *Judaized*. Rosenzweig, at the end of the history of German-Jewish philosophy, returns to the scene of a struggle over whether the Jewish God—and therefore Judaism and the Jewish people—has a rightful place in Germany. Whatever Rosenzweig may say about his break with Mendelssohn's name for God, he certainly stands with Mendelssohn against those who see their task to be the de-Judaization of German culture. There were some months in Rosenzweig's life, during the late summer of 1913, when he came close to believing that the revelation held in abeyance on the other side of 1800 was a solely Christian revelation. But his wavering on this issue ceased and was replaced with the conviction that the life of the Jewish people is one way that revelation enters into history and that the life of the Christian church is another way.[14]

Amos Funkenstein, as we have seen, claimed that Mendelssohn and Rosenzweig stand not only as the first and last Jewish philosophers in Germany, but that with Rosenzweig German-Jewish philosophy "went full circle to its point of origin." What Funkenstein is pointing to when he connects Mendelssohn and Rosenzweig is certainly not their understanding of how YHWH reveals Himself as a speaking *I*, but rather how both thinkers understand the way that this revelation unfolds in history. Both Mendelssohn and Rosenzweig see revelation's entrance into history to be, first of all, embodied in the life of the Jewish people. Both men view the life of the Jewish people to be a living sign system, the unfolding in a people's life practices of the written revelation of the Hebrew Bible. Although Rosenzweig and Mendelssohn differ about the translation of the tetragrammaton, they agree on something far more fundamental. They agree that the Jewish people are the living translation of God's word. In articulating this claim, both men turn the Jewish Question (Does the Jewish God have a place in the German state?) back upon the questioner: Does the living word of God have a place in the German state?

Although Funkenstein points us in the direction of discovering the deep affinity between Mendelssohn and Rosenzweig, it is Leora Batnitzky, in her work on Rosenzweig's philosophy, *Idolatry and Representation*, who articulates the relationship most clearly. Batnitzky, emphasizing Mendelssohn's notion that Judaism is a living sign system, what he calls a "living script," points out that what this sign system signifies is neither a theological creed nor, as it was for Philo for example, an allegorized moral code. Indeed, the living sign system of the Jewish people points to no "positivity," as Mendelssohn's contemporaries would call it, but rather points to the limit of all sign systems in relation to God. In his *Jerusalem*, Mendelssohn argues that God's nature cannot be transcribed into a fixed arrangement of signs, whether they be iconic (hieroglyphs) or abstract (alphabetic). God's nature is infinite and every fixed representation of that nature is necessarily finite and therefore partial. There is, therefore, an insuperable obstacle confronting humans when they think about God. They can use the word *infinite* to describe God, but they can form no representation of an infinite being.

According to the story Mendelssohn tells in *Jerusalem*, the insuperable obstacle posed to the finite mind in its inevitable attempt to represent the infinite became, as human civilization progressed, a stumbling block and barrier to humanity's natural capacity to acknowledge God as the infinite, providential Creator of all finite beings. Human civilization cannot make any progress unless it employs a sign system, initially imagistic and later more abstract, to pass on its experience from one generation to another. But together with the use of hieroglyphic signs to represent living speech, there came the temptation to imagine that the signs themselves represent God: "The images lost their value as signs," Mendelssohn explains. "The spirit of truth, which was to have been preserved in them, evaporated, and the empty vehicle that remained behind turned into a pernicious poison" (*Jerusalem* 115; 2:88). This temptation manifested itself in antiquity in the idolatrous fetishization of images of God, but the tendency to idolatry is present even when the sign system is as abstract as the numbers used by the Pythagoreans to represent the nature of God: "One believed, or at least made others believe, that all the mysteries of nature and of the Deity were concealed in these numbers; one ascribed miraculous power to them . . ." (*Jerusalem* 117; 2:92). And finally, the tendency to idolatry is also present in the theological effort to create creedal definitions of God.

Mendelssohn argues that God revealed written and oral laws to the Israelites in order to show the world that no fixed script can ever represent God.

> The forefathers of our nation, Abraham, Isaac, and Jacob, remained faithful to the Eternal, and sought to preserve among their families and descendents pure

concepts of religion, far removed from idolatry. And now their descendents were chosen by Providence to be a priestly nation; that is, a nation which, through its establishment and constitution, through its laws, actions, vicissitudes, and changes was continually to call attention to sound and unadulterated ideas of God and his attributes. It was incessantly to teach, to proclaim, preach,[15] and to endeavor to preserve these ideas among the nations, by means of its mere existence, as it were. (*Jerusalem* 117–18; 2:93–94)

The actions of the Jewish people in fulfillment of the laws revealed at Mt. Sinai constituted a new kind of sign system, one devised by God specifically to resist the inherent tendency to fetishize signs. "Man's actions," Mendelssohn states, "are transitory; there is nothing lasting, nothing enduring about them that, like hieroglyphic script, could lead to idolatry through abuse or misunderstanding" (*Jerusalem* 119; 2:96). And while the actions enjoined by the laws were intended for the "felicity" of the Israelite nation, they also bore a message to all humanity in their nature as action signs, namely, that God cannot be captured once and for all in any unchanging representation. The Jewish community witnesses against idolatry "by means of its mere existence [durch ihr bloßes Dasein]" as Mendelssohn puts it in a striking phrase that Rosenzweig will repeat in a 1919 essay on the role of the Jewish people in history.[16] Furthermore, the unending process of interpreting God's will by carrying on an orally transmitted conversation about the written law—a process to which and by which the Jewish people have covenanted themselves to God in every generation—also attests to the impossibility of fixing God's nature in a finite set of words. In every aspect of their corporate existence, the Jewish people reveal the limits imposed upon finite beings, despite their inevitable temptation to fix in a permanent representation the infinite being of God.

Leora Batnitzky sees Mendelssohn's concept of the Jewish people as the living embodiment of the injunction against idolatry to be the most important precursor of Rosenzweig's view of the Jewish people as challenging the greatest of all idolatries in the modern world, the idolatry of the state. This is how German-Jewish philosophy comes "full circle" with Rosenzweig. Rosenzweig disagrees with what he perceives to be Mendelssohn's rational theology and favors Jacobi's side of the Spinoza Quarrel, but he fully embraces Mendelssohn's conception of the Jewish people as the living embodiment of revelation in history, a revelation that opposes what Rosenzweig calls the "false eternity" of the state.

I have tried so far to suggest why, despite the appearance of a vast difference between Mendelssohn's and Rosenzweig's philosophies, it is worthwhile to seek the commonalities that join them. I have argued that Rosenzweig's essay on Mendelssohn's translation of the tetragrammaton opens onto the scene of a profoundly consequential struggle between Mendelssohn and Jacobi, the Spinoza Quarrel, in which the most fundamental questions about the nature of the Jewish God and the Jewish people's role in history were broached. At one level, Rosenzweig seems to side with Jacobi against Mendelssohn, but this is not the end of the story. Mendelssohn and Rosenzweig agree that the life practices of the Jewish people translate the word of God into history. But this convergence is also not the end of the story. Mendelssohn and Rosenzweig have entirely different interpretations of how the Jewish people relate to the state. Their political theologies are as distinct as are the ways they translate the name of God. Mendelssohn's *Jerusalem* not only argues for the full integration of the Jewish people into the civic life of the state, it proposes a novel interpretation of the relationship of church and state that would radically transform not only the relationship between the state and the Jewish people, but also the relationship between the state and Christianity. No less significantly, Mendelssohn's political theology would radically transform the ecclesial power structures sustaining the authority of both Judaism and Christianity. Rosenzweig's political theology, on the other hand, would undo what Mendelssohn proposes.

Mendelssohn's goal in *Jerusalem* is to show that the state should be the sustaining framework for the noncoercive associations of its citizens into communities of worship, each with its own specific cultural life practices. In an essay entitled "Mendelssohn and the State," Willi Goetschel has argued that Mendelssohn "articulates a critical alternative to the sovereign-based theory of the state" (Goetschel 2007: 476). Sharply disagreeing with Hobbes that the state's laws are the expression of a monolithic sovereign power, Mendelssohn, according to Goetschel, sees the state as "a part of civil society which provides the framework for the individual's civil and political rights and obligations" (480). Goetschel draws attention to the longest footnote in *Jerusalem*, in which Mendelssohn proposes the creation of state-supported, secular educational institutions that would provide the opportunity for children of Jewish and Christian parents to be taught in a religiously neutral environment. Mendelssohn argues that the state must allow Jewish and Christian parents to divorce when either partner decides that the marriage is incompatible with his or her religious commitments, but that the state should also make it possible for them to fulfill their joint obligations to educate their children. The specific case that the footnote addresses is that of a Jewish father who has converted to Christianity and will not divorce his wife. She finds it impossible to live as a Jew with him, and the state refuses her request for a civil divorce on grounds of its religious neutrality. Mendelssohn sees this as a surreptitious reintroduction of religious coercion under cover of neutrality. The state's neutrality should never curtail the freedom of religious expression among its citizens. The state provides the legal and institutional matrix for the flourishing of the worshiping communities within it.

Although Mendelssohn believes that the state is theoretically separable from religion, in reality it is impossible, as Goetschel puts it, "to divide the scope of human existence between the two spheres" (Goetschel 2007: 484). Just as Mendelssohn opposes Hobbes's view of the state as the "mortal god" that entirely embodies God's sovereignty in this world, Mendelssohn also opposes Locke's view that religion is an entirely private matter of conscience that has nothing to do with the goals of the state. The freedom of religion that Mendelssohn defends is a freedom that supports the fullest expression of religion as an interlacing network of voluntarily assumed commitments and shared life practices. As such, religion cannot and should not be severed from the civil realm of the state. Willi Goetschel puts the point most clearly in his analysis of Mendelssohn's *Jerusalem* in *Spinoza's Modernity*, a book that does much to recover the importance of Mendelssohn's unique contribution to Enlightenment political theory:

> For Mendelssohn, as for Spinoza, the state is no longer understood as the fundament onto which civil life is grafted. Analyzed as "mechanical deeds [todte Handlungen]" and "works without spirit [Werke ohne Geist]," the state provides a neutral framework that needs to be filled with spirit (Geist) in order to fulfill its function. And this is the point where religion receives its specific role. Mendelssohn does not imagine the relationship between state and religion to be a clear-cut coordination of two equal institutions. Rather, he argues that their cooperation is to be understood in terms of a framework based on the concept of the political that takes human nature into account in its undiminished complexity . . . Mendelssohn's conception of the political underlines the point that the state is not to be reduced to a detached, formalized machine simply running on its own.

By emphasizing the equally fundamental spiritual and religious aspects in the genesis of civil society, he formulates a theory of the state which recognizes that religion and individual spiritual happiness are intimately linked to the definition and legitimation of political institutions. (Goetschel 2004: 155–56)

In the next chapter, I will explain in greater detail Mendelssohn's argument about the emergence of civil and religious institutions through the interlocking of what he calls, following the legal philosopher Samuel von Pufendorf (1632–94), "perfect" and "imperfect" rights. But for the moment, Goetschel's emphasis upon the intimate relationship between the state and religion may serve as a key to understanding the difference separating Mendelssohn's and Rosenzweig's political theologies.

Rosenzweig, unlike Mendelssohn, sees both Jewish and Christian worshiping communities to be in differing degrees of conflict with the state. The Jewish people stand outside history and are at the goal towards which all other peoples, with their fates tied to states, are moving. The Jewish people pose an eternal challenge to all other peoples' pretensions to having attained permanence through the state. To be sure, Christians also stand opposed to the state's claim to provide eternal life to its people. But Christians bear the burden of bending the temporal life of the state into the rhythm of eternity that is embodied in the sacred cycle of Christian holy days. For Rosenzweig, only Christian worshipping communities weave their life practices into the life of the state, and always in opposition to the state's desire to encompass all aspects of the lives of its subjects.

When Rosenzweig discusses the nature of the state in *The Star of Redemption*, it is clear that he does not share Mendelssohn's view of it as originating in a contract among individuals who are seeking an arbitrational framework in which to resolve such disputes as will inevitably arise as they attempt, free from coercive power, to realize their diverse commitments within an intricate network of shared life practices, from marriage and childrearing through work and culture. For Rosenzweig, the state is like Hobbes's mortal god, the Leviathan state, but the stress is on "mortal." Christian worshiping communities must continuously assert the eternal sovereignty of God against the state's claim to being the last instance of sovereignty in the world. According to Rosenzweig, the eternal corporate body of the diasporic Jewish people places in clearest possible light the mortality of the sovereign state.

What separates Rosenzweig from Mendelssohn's theory of the state is not so much Hobbes as it is Hegel.[17] Although I will return to this topic in a later chapter, a few words about Rosenzweig's reading of Hegel are in order here. The distance separating Rosenzweig from Mendelssohn can be described as the the distance created by the French Revolution, the ensuing revolutionary wars, and the collapse of the Holy Roman Empire. Rosenzweig reads Hegel as holding a mirror to the historical transformation that brought the modern German state into being. In that mirror, Mendelssohn's hopes for an enlightened, democratic polity, expressed in *Jerusalem*, are almost entirely driven from view.

Rosenzweig reads Hegel's theory of the state as giving expression to what every state seeks after but can never attain to, namely, unchanging actuality ("Wirklichkeit"). For Mendelssohn, the state is not a superindividual that attempts to impose permanence upon the flux of mortal life; rather, it is precisely woven out of mutually supporting threads of obligation and rights that link individuals together in patterns of association that change over time without losing their purchase on living actuality. For Hegel, however, the state must constantly justify itself through violence as an individual actor on the stage of world history, staking its very life in order to maintain its hold on actuality. "World history is the world's court of judgment" is, as Rosenzweig points out in *Hegel-Staat*, the "Grundsatz" of Hegel's mature thinking about the state. The state's sovereign power is legitimate only so long as it has the power to create history or, better put, to remain on the winning side of history.[18]

According to Rosenzweig, Hegel quickly became disillusioned with the revolutionary claims of the French nation-state to embody Reason in history (see, for one example of this recurrent theme, *Hegel-Staat* 1:110). In Hegel's writings after 1800, according to Rosenzweig's account, the state was no longer seen as, first and foremost, the consummation of the ethical destiny ("Schicksal") of the individual. Rather, the state was now seen through the lens of a newly found political realism. "From out of the actual experience of the state as destiny emerges the knowledge: the state is might [der Staat ist Macht]" (*Hegel-Staat* 1:104). The state as might conforms to the ultimate judgment of the "court of history": Might is triumphant in history. It is this judgment that Hegel after 1800 will assert to be the expression of Reason in history: What is actual, is rational. This conflation of philosophy's judgment with history's judgment is, as I said above, what Rosenzweig decries as the modern form of paganism. But Rosenzweig, although he will call it paganism, does not deny that this outlook captures the truth about the state. In one of the most impassioned passages of *Hegel-Staat*, Rosenzweig describes the nature of the state as Hegel came to understand it in the years after 1800:

> Before us stands the state of the eighteenth century with its newborn will to might, with its indifference to the task of unifying all members from one end to another, with its undervaluing of national strivings and its lack of understanding for the spiritual powers that are encompassed within the life of the nation. "Might, might, and once more, might" stands written over the entrance to the edifice of this state; before the light of this sun all the inner complexity of the state's life and all the spiritual richness of its national life vanish from the bedazzled gaze of the thinker. He seems to have no intimation . . . that this so coolly dismissed richness is the heart from out of which the warm blood in the veins of the Leviathan had been able to stream forth. (*Hegel-Staat* 1:109)

Rosenzweig admits that Hegel's vision of the state still included elements of the earlier conception of the state as the guarantor of the rights of free, self-determining individuals. Might had not yet triumphed over right, and Hegel's philosophy of the state shows the contradictions within the state itself that, ultimately, will be resolved when right yields entirely to might in the future Prussian police state. "The philosopher is positioned as the faithful mirror of this ambiguous situation," Rosenzweig says about Hegel in relation to the intermingling of might and right in the state at the opening of the nineteenth century. Even though the image in the mirror is not yet clear, the future can be read in it nonetheless: "for the researcher whose gaze is cast backwards," Rosenzweig concludes, the "faithful mirror" that Hegel holds up is a "valuable witness" to the "inner workings of the time" (*Hegel-Staat* 1:110).

The modern state, Rosenzweig will say in *The Star of Redemption*, is power. In its essence, it is pagan. To get past Hegel, philosophy must no longer justify the power of the state as rational. Philosophy must view the state through the lens of revelation rather than reason. In making this claim, Rosenzweig is following the lead of Hegel's final reflections about the relationship between the state and religion, between the human and the divine perspectives on history.[19] Hegel could not entirely reduce history to the pure expression of might. Rosenzweig explains in *Hegel-Staat* that Hegel eventually came to believe that the judgment of world history had the last word only on all things "in the world," but another realm, the spiritual realm whose consummation is found in Christianity, holds jurisdiction over history as a whole. There will always be sovereign states that come and go, but the gathered worshipping community ("Kirchengemeinde") of the invisible church will never pass away. Hegel's concept of the church, Rosenzweig writes, is constructed "in the strictly Protestant sense as an inward and supramundane one" whose community is "a community of saints or the faithful" (*Hegel-Staat* 2:184). The invisible church dwells within the state, but its life is woven into the state's temporal fabric with only the slimmest of threads, ready to be cut as the mortal body of the state dies. Transcending the legal order of each individual state, the church provides a society of peoples ("Völkergemeinschaft") that constitutes the "fourth kingdom" about which Daniel spoke, the kingdom of the "saints of the Most High" that will go on without end. In summarizing what he calls Hegel's "metaphysics of the state [Metaphysik des Staats]," Rosenzweig adumbrates his own view of the relationship between Christianity and the state in *The Star of Redemption*:

> Out of his deep and fundamental commitment to the eternal worth of Christianity, although to be sure not basing his argument upon it, Hegel has arrived at a kind of superstate society of peoples without any state-like form of organization. He has arrived at a Church, if one wants, whose invisible overseer is the law of world history, the "World Spirit" . . . But Hegel has come to this conclusion along the route of strictly individuating states; the invisible law that encompasses this invisible society of peoples, the law of world history, is the same law that eternally divides visible peoples. Only out of the oppositions of independent states does history grow, and only history is the band that ties together these independent peoples. And therefore it was with good reason that we hesitated to call the society of peoples a "Church." It would have nearly been ironic to call it "invisible."[20] And yet this is the name Hegel has given it. He wants in this way to indicate that there is a moral law for humanity that exists beyond the individual state; he wants to rob the unconditional relation between the single individual and his state of its unconditionality. Therefore he constructs his concept of the church in the strictly Protestant sense as a purely inward and supramundane one that recognizes the only society to be the society of saints or the faithful. The unseverable relations that bind this church to the world are mediated only through the single soul. (*Hegel-Staat* 2:184).

Rosenzweig accepts the fundamental structure of Hegel's vision of the relation of state and church. The state preserves itself as an individual actor in world history through might and violence; the individual Christian relates to world history as a "single soul" within the churchly "society of peoples" that transcends the conflicts of separate states. As for the Jewish people, and this takes Rosenzweig well beyond Hegel, they live in a realm that has fully shed the state's mortal body in order to possess an eternal body, regenerating itself anew in every generation. With this Hegelian conceptuality (at least as regards Christianity and the state) firmly in place, Rosenzweig cannot envision the integral relationship between state and religion that Mendelssohn had argued for. He cannot envision a democratic, redemptive political praxis.

More than anything else, then, it is Hegel who stands in the way of reconciling Rosenzweig's and Mendelssohn's political theologies. If Rosenzweig's adoption of Jacobi's side in the Spinoza Quarrel is the first irony we encounter in studying Rosenzweig's relation to Mendelssohn, here is a second irony at the heart of German-Jewish philosophy, for Hegel, as I will argue in Chapter 5, fashioned his conception of the relation between Christianity and the state very much in opposition to Mendelssohn's *Jerusalem*. Hence, Rosenzweig seems once more to stand on the side of Mendelssohn's opponents. Rosenzweig sought to break the alliance of philosophy and the state that Hegel had fashioned, but he left Hegel's state in place as he dismantled the philosophical edifice that seemed to support it. The state is thus voided of all possible intrinsic worth in relation to the newly released power of revelation in history. It is the mortal body in which Christian revelation will grow, much like a chrysalis in its cocoon. Mendelssohn's state, however, possesses the same goal as that of revelation, namely, to make it possible for individuals to perfect the world and thereby to enhance its beauty. The state is a humanly constructed instrument that does not function as a superindividual highest instance of power but rather offers a contractual framework for the shared commitments through which human life is transformed into beautiful life. Rosenzweig, although he separates religion from the state, agrees with Mendelssohn that beauty is what is produced when individuals gather together at times of worship, lifting individuals into new choreographies of time. If we want to reconnect Mendelssohn's and Rosenzweig's political theologies, one approach that is possible, therefore, passes through their aesthetic theories. This is the approach I will take in this book. Mendelssohn's political philosophy is deeply informed by his aesthetic theory, in which beauty is defined as the product of the perfecting of the world. By emphasizing Rosenzweig's own aesthetic theory in *The Star of Redemption*, we may find a ground of commonality upon which to reconnect Mendelssohn and Rosenzweig on the plane of the political.

Perhaps one might ask what need or value there is to so neatly "close the circle" that joins Mendelssohn and Rosenzweig. Perhaps it is best to acknowledge what separates Rosenzweig and Mendelssohn and leave matters at that. But I believe that more is at stake here. Peter Eli Gordon has recently pointed out that Rosenzweig's political theology, Rosenzweig's insistence on the unique ahistorical place of the Jewish people is perhaps the most serious problem confronting those who wish to inherit Rosenzweig's philosophy of revelation. One wants to find a way to claim that, although the Jewish people may model a form of embodied revelation, this does not foreclose other paths toward such a redemptive sociality, paths that may take unpredictable directions. One would like, in other words, to find a way to articulate Rosenzweig's philosophy as a basis for a democratic redemptive politics.[21] If we can put Rosenzweig's *The Star of Redemption* into conversation with Mendelssohn's *Jerusalem*, the lineaments of such a democratic political theology begin to emerge.

By reconnecting Mendelssohn and Rosenzweig, I want to clear a path for closing and thus completing the circle of German-Jewish philosophy. I want to contribute to what I understand to be the unfinished business of Rosenzweig's *The Star of Redemption*, namely, to return philosophy to a moment of hope before a certain self-induced disease, a sort of "death-in-life," overtook it. Rosenzweig names that moment 1800 and associates it primarily with Hegel's claim that the state—raised into full self-reflexive glory through the philosopher who saw "eye to eye" with his time—was the visible embodiment of God in history, a history whose violence is humanity's "slaughterbench." Rosenzweig draws from Hegel's final reflections about the supramundane, invisible church and argues that it is in constant tension with the state's pretensions to eternality. The visible but diasporic and stateless Jewish people, Rosenzweig claims, live in eternal separation from the violence of history, bearing witness to the not-yet-achieved goal of redemption. Rosenzweig's work seeks to break through the post-1800 resurgent paganism of philosophy and the state, but it remains locked within the Hegelian vision of the state as born in and sustained by violence. Rosenzweig's project of turning to revelation to break through the paganism of the state will not be complete until the messianic expectancy of 1800 is drawn into relation with Mendelssohn's conception of the state, which opens the possibility of a democratic political theology. Only then can a new rapprochement be envisioned for those worshiping communities—Jewish, Christian, and Muslim—who claim to inherit the revelation of the Hebrew Bible.

The Plan of the Book

In Chapter 1, "Performing Reason: Mendelssohn on Judaism and Enlightenment," I first of all consider the background to Mendelssohn's *Jerusalem*, namely, the debates surrounding Christian Wilhelm Dohm's work advocating Jewish emancipation, *Über die bürgerliche Verbesserung der Juden (Concerning the Civil Improvement of the Jews)* (1781). I examine the argument of *Jerusalem* as a provocation against the regnant understanding of the nature of enlightened sociality among Mendelssohn's contemporaries in Germany. According to Mendelssohn, the Jewish people can serve as a model of enlightened sociality because they are the "living script" of divine revelation, embodying a noncoercive, dogma-free social-religious bond. At the heart of Judaism is an open-ended conversation across the generations. In explicating Mendelssohn's conception of Judaism as a conversation-based sociality, I invoke its modern parallel in Wittgenstein's analysis of how meaning is constructed through language practices that are open to constant revision and reinterpretation. The Wittgenstein I present here is the one that has inspired the work of Stanley Cavell. In his many writings, from the 1960s until today, Cavell has not only offered a number of compelling readings of Wittgenstein's *Philosophical Investigations*, but he has also carried forward the Wittgensteinian tradition in a philosophical vision of "ordinary language" as the site of a human mutuality that forgoes all demands for epistemological certitudes and metaphysical guarantees, call them dogmas. Cavell's vision will guide me throughout the book as I attempt to "close the circle" linking Rosenzweig and Mendelssohn. In addition to helping me connect Mendelssohn to Wittgenstein, Cavell's conception of acknowledgment as the basis of the social contract helps me unpack the philosophical importance of Mendelssohn's discussion of oaths in *Jerusalem*. The individual's allegedly privileged access to a self-transparent interiority is, according to Cavell, mistakenly understood to ground our acknowledgment of the other's humanity. When Mendelssohn attacks the practice of requiring oaths from ecclesiastical officials, he is resisting a picture of human sociality as grounded in a commonly shared core of interiority that is somehow represented and fixed by means of one's sworn oath. Mendelssohn, as Cavell says about Shylock, wants to be acknowledged as a fellow human of flesh and blood even if his "Jewish" interiority seems to threaten the homogeneity of the body politic.

Chapter 2, "Jacobi and Mendelssohn: The Tragedy of a Messianic Friendship," deals at length with the Spinoza Quarrel and how it reflects what I take to be Jacobi's gnostic assault on the Jewish God as the true face of the abstract and lifeless God of Enlightenment Reason. The Spinoza Quarrel began when Jacobi confronted Mendelssohn with a story about Gotthold Ephraim Lessing's confession to him, shortly before his death in 1781, that he was a Spinozist (i.e., atheist). The personal animus involved in Jacobi's attempt to divide Mendelssohn from his late friend contributed to the fact that, tragically, neither could understand what the other was saying. Ironically, both Jacobi and Mendelssohn attempt to defend the claim of revelation against the excesses of Enlightenment Reason (as Mendelssohn's attack on the language philosophy undergirding the use of oaths attests), but they are unable to find any common ground of dialogue. Jacobi views Judaism through the figure of a hyper-rationalist Spinoza and he understands Mendelssohn as committed to replacing revelation with a religion of reason. For Jacobi, Jewish sociality as Mendelssohn presents it in *Jerusalem*—the "living script" of revelation—falls so far outside his Protestant understanding of the dichotomous relationship between (inward) "life" and (outward) "script" as to be nearly incomprehensible. For Mendelssohn, on the other hand, Jacobi's notion of an immediate revelation that is experienced in the individual's encounter with a radical Otherness—the personal *You* of an indwelling Godhead—is only another form of Christian fanatical "enthusiasm [Schwärmerei]." Jacobi and Mendelssohn simply cannot communicate with one another, although they are both struggling to carve out a space for a lived revelation within the bounds of finite temporality. Rosenzweig said Mendelssohn's friendship with Lessing was emblematic of the "tragedy of the Jew until today." Their friendship, he explains, was "too messianic" because it forced Mendelssohn to strip himself of his Jewish difference in order to join with Lessing on the ground of the Enlightenment religion of reason. Mendelssohn's engagement with Jacobi in the Spinoza Quarrel forced him to confront this fact. It was not only death that separated him from his friend, but also his inescapable recognition that, if he wanted to defend his and Lessing's religion of reason, he would have to do so as a Jew. But, as he also recognized, this defense was doomed from the start. Mendelssohn could show that Jewish revelation was compatible with the religion of reason, but Jacobi was forcing him to show that both were also compatible with Christian revelation. Ultimately, the "third term" of the religion of reason had to be abandoned as the common term joining Judaism and Christianity. Mendelssohn could not see that Jacobi was, actually, offering a way to do this, by severing revelation from its historical specificity and considering it to be an ever-present possibility. Mendelssohn could not recognize that Jacobi was opening a new path towards revelation, but this is exactly what drew Rosenzweig to Jacobi. Unfortunately, Rosenzweig largely accepted Jacobi's portrait of Mendelssohn as a defender of the religion of reason. A closer reading of Mendelssohn, however, along the lines that I will lay out in Chapter 1, enables us to overcome this portrait.

In Chapter 3, "In the Year of the Lord 1800: Rosenzweig and the Spinoza Quarrel," I show how Rosenzweig's philosophy of revelation can be read as laying the foundation for a new "messianic friendship," one between Mendelssohn and Jacobi. I will show how Rosenzweig inherited Jacobi's concept of experientially based revelation, but took it beyond Jacobi's gnostic anti-Judaism by offering a decidedly anti-gnostic reading of the "root words" of the Hebrew Bible in *The Star of Redemption*. Rosenzweig is at pains to show that the God of the Hebrew Bible is a person and not, as Jacobi claims Spinoza represents Him, subjectless substance. Rosenzweig can be said to have offered a posthumous resolution of the Spinoza Quarrel that respects both Mendelssohn and Jacobi in their efforts to offer philosophical recuperations of the concept of lived revelation. It is in this sense that I speak of a "messianic friendship" between Mendelssohn and Jacobi. Such a friendship was, to be sure, impossible at the time they lived, but it may at least be imagined as a possibility offered by Rosenzweig's bicovenantal model of the relationship between Judaism and Christianity. In the course of this chapter, I discuss Rosenzweig's conception of the Hebrew Bible as embodying revelation in opposition to what he calls "paganism." I go on to treat Rosenzweig's concept of 1800 as the moment when the messianic force of the Hebrew Bible's revelation was ready to spring forth once more in a renewed Christianity and a renewed Judaism. The key to Rosenzweig's vision of 1800 is a new philosophy of revelation that sees revelation as an event taking place within language itself. This new philosophy draws directly from Jacobi, but it also resonates deeply with Mendelssohn's view that Judaism, as a revealed legislation, is enacted in open-ended conversation. We can therefore understand that Rosenzweig, going back to 1800 in order to release the messianic force held in abeyance by the rise of speculative philosophy, had in fact found a way to resolve the Spinoza Quarrel that divided Jacobi and Mendelssohn. In so doing, he began the process of releasing revelation from its subsumption within the edifice of German idealism, a subsumption that was, quite against Jacobi's intentions, the philosophical fruit of the Spinoza Quarrel he initiated.[22]

Chapter 4, "Reinhold and Kant: The Quest for a New Religion of Reason," charts the efforts on the part of Karl Leonhard Reinhold (1757–1823) and Immanuel Kant (1724–1804) to construct a religion of reason that was intended to be the philosophical supersession of Christianity. They represent their philosophical supersession of Christianity as a cleansing of Christianity of all its remaining ties to Judaism. In this way, they respond to Jacobi's accusation that the religion of reason is merely a cover for the reintroduction of the abstract Jewish God in place of Christianity's personal God. Reinhold and Kant, although they did not stand on Jacobi's side of the Spinoza Quarrel, nonetheless saw that it was necessary to separate their religion of reason from any connection with Mendelssohn's Judaism. Karl Reinhold was Kant's most important "early adopter," publishing a series of articles entitled "Letters on the Kantian Philosophy" in 1786–87. Reinhold saw Kant's philosophy as answering the deepest need of the historical moment, namely, to find a way to resolve the Spinoza Quarrel. He also saw that it fully answered to what he had argued for in another work, *The Hebrew Mysteries; or, the Earliest Religious Freemasonry* (1786), namely, the public promulgation of the truth—preserved in Freemasonry through the centuries—that God is the unrepresentable One of the Egyptian mysteries, a truth that Moses, unsuccessfully, had tried to wrest from Egypt's priestly class and pass on to an entire people. Jesus had tried again to lay bare the essential truth that had been obscured by the "Hebrew mysteries" of the Jewish priests. Reinhold's exposition of Kant was intended to finally accomplish what Moses and Jesus had failed at, that is, the enlightenment of an entire people. If evidence was needed to support Rosenzweig's intuition that

Kant's *Critique of Pure Reason* inspired young Germans with messianic hopes, Karl Reinhold, twenty-four in the year of its publication, would supply it. Reinhold believed that Kant had opened the path to universal enlightenment; he had demonstrated that God is unrepresentable. But how did Kant solve the Spinoza Quarrel (even though he wrote the *Critique* nearly five years before it broke out publicly)? The problem that Jacobi had drawn attention to was that the Enlightenment's religion of reason presented a God of unfreedom. Reinhold did not want to embrace what he (together with Kant, who agreed on this point with Mendelssohn) saw as Jacobi's "Schwärmerei," his argument that revelation was based upon an immediate and incorrigible intuition of an inward divinity that opened the individual to a realm of freedom. But neither did Reinhold believe that after Kant's *Critique of Pure Reason* Mendelssohn's arguments that God's necessary being and infinite power were compatible with human freedom could be sustained. Reinhold claimed that the universally legislating voice of reason—the ground of our noumenal freedom—that Kant had described as the "practical" aspect of reason was the source of the belief in the existence of a transcendent, superhuman, commanding Being. This Being could be the object of a "rational faith," but must remain wholly unrepresented.

Kant's own *Religion within the Boundaries of Mere Reason* (1793) follows some six years after Reinhold's attempt to construct a Kantian religion of reason. Kant resists Reinhold's picture of the religion of reason as the last stage in humanity's repeated attempts, most notably undertaken by Moses and Jesus, to make public the "mystery" that the only true commanding voice is that of Reason and that God, if he exists, is unrepresentable and unknowable. Kant focuses on the ineradicable evil within the human being and argues that no progress or enlightenment can ever dissolve it. This evil is the inevitable concomitant of freedom; it is the use of freedom to enslave oneself to the unfreedom of mere *thinghood*. Kant believes that Judaism epitomizes the way that radical evil hides behind the veneer of the law. Kant's notion of groundless freedom is, as he says, the philosophical exposition of the Christian doctrine of salvation through unmerited, inexplicable grace. Kant does not want to dissolve all the mysteries, but rather to point to the one, inescapable, mystery: ultimate freedom is not self-legislating reason, but the groundless "turn" from self-imposed enslavement to nature to self-imposed freedom under the legislation of practical Reason. Kant's insistence that the "subjective ground of freedom" is inscrutable brings him close to Jacobi, although Kant himself would likely have resisted the comparison. In the freedom that is free even to enslave itself is a mystery that escapes every attempt at systematic explanation. Jacobi had claimed that the turn from self-enslavement into freedom is the awakening of the *I* by God's *You*. There is for both Kant and Jacobi something that ultimately resists all systematicity. Hegel attempts to capture this, too, within the net of speculative philosophy.

Chapter 5, "Beautiful Life: Mendelssohn, Hegel, and Rosenzweig," discusses Hegel's early theological writings, with special attention to *The Spirit of Christianity and its Fate*. Hegel considered Kant's religion of reason to be too "sublime," too far removed from the "beauty" of a this-worldly communion of worshipers who had overcome their empirical particularity not by joining a noumenal Kingdom of Ends but by loving one another. Hegel turns to Kant's *Critique of the Power of Judgment* in order to find an alternative model of how infinity and finitude can be joined in the beauty of organic form. Hegel builds his conception of Christianity as the religion of beauty against the ugliness of Judaism, a religion of lifeless, loveless individualities whose existence is premised on the worthlessness of all of nature in comparison with their abstract God. Despite Hegel's anti-Jewish polemic, which is largely directed against Mendelssohn, his connection of religion with the beauty of finite existence is of decisive importance for Rosenzweig. Hegel's exposition of how the Last Supper almost manages to transcend the fixity of an objective representational sign system in favor of a completely embodied, self-recreating ritual is, I will argue, indebted to Mendelssohn's notion of the Jewish people as a "living script" of revelation. Rosenzweig is deeply influenced by Hegel's description of the commensality of love achieved in the Last Supper, but I will contend that his recuperation of this description for how the Jewish people embody revelation is a "reading through" of Hegel to Mendelssohn, a release of Mendelssohn from the Hegelian text. I will conclude the chapter by examining Rosenzweig's inheritance of Hegel's conception of religion as the beautiful fusion of "infinite and finite Life." Rosenzweig takes this conception and reads the choreography of the Jewish sacred year as its embodiment. Rosenzweig also draws from Hegel's notion that Christianity's "fate" is to fail at this embodiment because of its "descent" into ritualized forms of worship. Rosenzweig takes up Hegel's view that it is Christianity's "fate" to be embodied within ever-recurrent rituals and fuses it with Hegel's conception of the state as ever relegitimizing its existence in its conflict with other states. Rosenzweig shows how the choreography of the Christian sacred year opens like a spiral into the temporality of the state and weaves the fabric of redemption out of the life and death of the nation state.

In the concluding chapters of the book, "Mendelssohn, Rosenzweig, and Political Theology: Beyond Sovereign Violence" (Chapter 6) and "Beyond 1800: An Immigrant Rosenzweig" (Chapter 7), I seek to close the circle linking Rosenzweig and Mendelssohn. The prior chapters show that Rosenzweig broke through the 1800 edifice of German idealism by connecting with the new opening for revelation's entrance into history. Rosenzweig returned to the sources of revelation's breakthrough into history, and hoped to restore their messianic potential by connecting these sources with a new understanding of the Hebrew Bible as the revealed Word of God, and of the Jewish people as the living expression of this word in time. What Rosenzweig accomplishes is, in this way, a release of the voice of Mendelssohn's *Jerusalem* from its silencing at the hands of Jacobi, Reinhold, Kant, and Hegel. But, as I show in Chapter 6, Rosenzweig left behind Mendelssohn's dream of a democratic sociality that would join revelation and the life of the state. In Chapter 7, "Beond 1800: An Immigrant Rosenzweig," I imagine an "immigrant Rosenzweig" who enters into conversation with two thinkers, Hannah Arendt and Stanley Cavell, who embrace America as promising a new form of democratic life that, in every generation, calls upon a people to reimagine and rededicate themselves to the covenant of "We the people."[23] Besides reading America through a biblical lens of a sociality based upon (re)covenanting, Arendt and Cavell share many of Rosenzweig's concerns: in particular, taking philosophy out of its academic professionalization and reconnecting philosophy with the "extraordinariness of ordinary life." I argue that this immigrant Rosenzweig might learn to shed his Hegelian view of the state as a superindividual that legitimates itself through violence. I show that Arendt's notion of natality, which has much in common with Rosenzweig's concept of creation in *The Star of Redemption*, is advanced precisely to counter this Hegelian view of the political as grounded in violence, a view that was most forcefully articulated in the work of Carl Schmitt. Schmitt, I suggest, lies behind Rosenzweig's discussion of the state in *The Star of Redemption*. Arendt's natality, linked to Rosenzweig's creation, can supply a new grounding for a democratic redemptive politics. I turn to Cavell's notion of remarriage as a metaphor for democratic sociality in order give flesh and bones to this redemptive politics. I argue that Rosenzweig's discussion of revelation as moving from the intimacy of soul and God into a public proclamation exactly parallels Cavell's discussion of the "creation of the new human" that is offered in the remarriage comedies of the 1930s. Finally, I argue that the hope for redemption that would guide democratic politics is one that is born when we, together, find the words to praise the beauty of our common and commonly inhabited world. Cavell treats of this redemptive praise in a discussion of a dance number in a Fred Astaire movie, *The Band Wagon*. I link this discussion to Rosenzweig's own discussion of dance as the art of redemption par excellence. In the vision of the dance, we are able to glimpse new forms of loving communality.

Philosophy's imbrication with the "Jewish Question" in Germany began with Moses Mendelssohn and ended with Franz Rosenzweig. In its beginning and its end, philosophy was understood to be something far more than an academic enterprise. Philosophy for Mendelssohn and Rosenzweig was intended to be a thinking-through of a pressing existential problem: how to live as Jews in modernity, how to live without dogmas of any kind, whether religious or philosophical. Both figures returned to the sources of Judaism in order to think beyond the dead ends of academic philosophy and of Jewish tradition. What they discovered in these sources was a conception of revelation as a commandment to take responsibility for recreating the world through speech, but never to seek to say everything once and for all, never to use language to build a tower to heaven in order to establish one human order upon the world. This is an understanding that Mendelssohn and Rosenzweig share with the figures I invoke throughout this book—Wittgenstein, Arendt, and Cavell—as partners in the ongoing conversation about "philosophy and the Jewish Question." With these thinkers, the conversation takes on existential dimensions beyond the life of Jews in modernity. But if we understand the full import of the authorial projects of both Mendelssohn and Rosenzweig, the question on which they staked their lives—how to reconcile Western philosophy to what Rosenzweig called "the possibility of experiencing wonder"[24]—was never only a Jewish question. For without the possibility of experiencing wonder, there can be no human world at all.

ONE

Performing Reason: Mendelssohn on Judaism and Enlightenment

> The civil status of a contradiction, or its status in civil life: there is the philosophical problem.
>
> LUDWIG WITTGENSTEIN, *Philosophical Investigations* §125

Introduction

In the September 1784 edition of the *Berlinische Monatschrift*, the leading Prussian journal devoted to advancing the cause of Enlightenment, Moses Mendelssohn published his response to a question posed by the editor of the journal: "Was ist Aufklärung?" or "What is Enlightenment?"[1] In December of the same year, Immanuel Kant offered his response. In his study of Kant's essay, Michel Foucault (1984) draws attention to the significance of the participation of both Mendelssohn and Kant, the two most prominent German-speaking philosophers of the day, in the *Berlinische Monatschrift*'s discussion about the meaning of Enlightenment. Foucault marks this moment as fateful for both Germans and Jews. Until this moment, Foucault says, Mendelssohn had addressed problems common to Jewish thought and German philosophy, for example, the immortality of the soul (in *Phädon; oder, Über die Unsterblichkeit der Seele*). And German authors, Lessing foremost among them, had tried "to make a place for Jewish culture within German thought." But the publication of the two response essays from Mendelssohn and Kant signals a shift from efforts at rapprochement across the German and Jewish worlds to a joint assumption of responsibility for a single historical process: "With the two texts published in the *Berlinische Monatschrift*, the German *Aufklärung* and the Jewish *Haskalah* recognize that they belong to the same history; they are seeking to identify the common processes from which they stem. And it is perhaps a way of announcing the acceptance of a common destiny—we now know to what drama that was to lead" (Foucault 1984: 33).

In this chapter I will look in detail at the way that Mendelssohn, from 1781 to his death in (the first week of) 1786, sought to persuade his readership that the Jewish and German Enlightenment projects "belonged to one history" and shared "a common destiny." When Foucault says that with the appearance of Mendelssohn's and Kant's essays in the *Berlinische Monatschrift* "the German *Aufklärung* and the Jewish *Haskalah* recognize that they belong to the same history," his language obscures the authorial agency at work behind this recognition. I will argue that what Foucault elides is the historical significance of Mendelssohn's late writings, including his response essay to the question "What is Enlightenment?" in *Berlinische Monatschrift*, but also, most importantly, his *Jerusalem, or On Religious Power and Judaism* and *Morning Hours*.[2] In *Jerusalem*, Mendelssohn calls upon his German and Jewish readership to accept their mutual interdependence in the single project of national Enlightenment. The terms in which Mendelssohn makes this call, however, challenge the dominant Enlightenment conceptions of history, Christianity, rationality, language, and truth. Mendelssohn's challenge called forth critical and on occasion vituperative responses from many readers. Perhaps the most well-known of these is J. G. Hamann's *Golgotha und Scheblimini!* (1783), one of the founding documents of the rising counter-Enlightenment.[3] Even those sympathetic to the political goal of Jewish emancipation were unwilling to accept the full revisioning of the Enlightenment paradigm of rationality and truth that underlay Mendelssohn's political views. Mendelssohn did indeed join together the Jewish and German Enlightenment projects, but the juncture was, from its very inception, the site of resistance to, and, in the end, repression of, Mendelssohn's philosophic voice.

My reading of Mendelssohn aims to show that his late work makes an important but largely overlooked contribution to philosophy, one that deserves to be placed in relation to developments in philosophy over a century later, including, perhaps most famously, Ludwig Wittgenstein's critique of "private language" in his *Philosophical Investigations*, but also Franz Rosenzweig's "speech thinking" in *The Star of Redemption*. Taking my cue from the American philosopher Stanley Cavell, one of the foremost contemporary inheritors of Wittgenstein's philosophical project, I would broadly characterize these twentieth-century developments in philosophy as attempting to offer a response to skepticism. What distinguishes the response of Wittgenstein (and, I will argue in a later chapter, Rosenzweig as well) to skepticism is his refusal to search for either metaphysical or epistemological foundations for the everyday practices of human life that skepticism calls into question. Wittgenstein appeals to "ordinary language" to provide an exit from skeptical doubt and the metaphysical errors it engenders. Ordinary language for Wittgenstein is the site of commonly shared language practices ("games") to whose relatively stable but never finally fixed arrangements our lives together bear witness, and daily reproduce. I read Mendelssohn as one of the inaugural voices in this philosophical recuperation of ordinary language, tied closely to what he calls "common sense," against the threat of skepticism. In *Morning Hours*, for example, Mendelssohn speaks about common sense ("der gemeine Menschenverstand," "der gesunde Menschenverstand," or, simply, "Gemeinsinn") as his philosophical touchstone. "As often as my speculation seems to lead too far from the imperial thoroughfare of common sense [Gemeinsinn], I stand still and attempt to orient myself," Mendelssohn writes in *Morning Hours* (10:82). "Experience has taught me," Mendelssohn continues, "that in the great majority of cases, common sense usually has right on its side, and reason must speak on behalf of speculation quite forcefully in order to make me follow it and abandon common sense."[4] Common sense, Mendelssohn claims, comes to expression in the shared linguistic practices that orient the lives of humans in their efforts to make sense of their world. When philosophical speculation departs from the realm of common sense, it removes concepts from their linguistic contexts and creates problems whose solution requires the dissolution of the problem itself, that is, understanding it as mere "verbal strife [Wortstreit]": "Language is the element in which our isolated concepts live and move. They can undergo change through an alteration of this element, but they cannot leave it without risk of giving up the ghost [den Geist aufzugeben]" (*Morning Hours* 7:61). Not only does this view about the source of philosophical problems foreshadow that of Wittgenstein, it is also the guiding principle of Franz Rosenzweig's *Büchlein vom gesunden und kranken Menschenverstand* (*Little Book Concerning the Healthy and Sick Common Sense*).[5] Mendelssohn, Rosenzweig, and Wittgenstein share a faith in the common practices of a linguistic community to restore the health of a reason sickened with skepticism, frustrated in its quest for unattainable epistemological and metaphysical certitudes.

My reading of Mendelssohn also aims to provide an etiology of philosophy's traditional resistance to ordinary language and common sense, its yearning after forms of knowledge that would provide metaphysical and epistemological certainty in the face of skeptical doubt. I will argue that Mendelssohn's late philosophy met with resistance and finally repression precisely because it blocked the metaphysical move to certainty. Rather, it demanded an acknowledgment of the irreducible heterogeneity of sign and signified at the heart of every speech act, a heterogeneity that divided the speaking subject from himself and from his auditor. This division, Mendelssohn claimed, can never be closed, but it can be crossed. The division can be crossed if partners in a conversation are willing to risk speech in the absence of certainty and without expectation of closure. Such speech is a sign of and a gesture towards a sociality that Mendelssohn finds exemplified, as we will see, in his friendship with Lessing. Mendelssohn's theory of language as the site of both risky uncertainty and promising sociality called for the acknowledgment not only of the irreducible heterogeneity of sign and signified, but also of the Jew and the Christian. Indeed, for Mendelssohn the Jew is the *sign of heterogeneity per se*. After Mendelssohn, philosophy could not make its yearned-for escape into epistemological certitude unless it first "solved" the problem of Jewish heterogeneity. As Foucault says, "We know to what drama that was to lead."

Jewish "Civil Improvement"

Mendelssohn's *Jerusalem* is a fuller development of his earlier response to Christian Wilhelm Dohm's groundbreaking work, *Ueber die bürgerliche Verbesserung der Juden* (*On the Civil Improvement of the Jews*) (1781).[6] In 1782,

Mendelssohn offered his initial response to Dohm, publishing a translation (made by his friend Marcus Herz) of Menassah ben Israel's *Vindiciae Judaeorum* (*The Salvation of the Jews*) (1656), a work that appealed to Oliver Cromwell to allow Jews once again to settle in England.[7] Mendelssohn added a preface ("Vorrede") to Menasseh ben Israel's text and published both together as an independent "appendix" ("Anhang") to Dohm's treatise. Mendelssohn's Vorrede aroused a firestorm of criticism in response to his radical claim that Judaism should not need to seek equal rights with Christianity in the state because, properly speaking, no religion has rights in the state. Mendelssohn wrote *Jerusalem* in order to defend himself against the criticisms raised against the Vorrede. But, just as he had gone far beyond the arguments of Dohm's treatise in his preface, Mendelssohn goes far beyond the Vorrede in *Jerusalem*. To trace the spiraling intensity of Mendelssohn's writing, we must begin with a brief description of Dohm's text.

The most important treatise on the Jewish Question of the time, Dohm's *On the Civil Improvement of the Jews* argued for extending civil rights to Jews in order, first of all, to bring the state into greater conformity with its own enlightened goal of confessional neutrality and, second of all, to foster both religious enlightenment and economic development among Jews themselves so that they could become "nützliche Bürger," useful citizens. The Jews, Dohm thought, could and would become "useful members of civil society" if they were granted civil rights. While not making it a precondition of their reception of civil rights, Dohm expected that Jewish religious enlightenment would accompany Jewish emancipation. Dohm supported his arguments in favor of Jewish emancipation by pointing to the fact that the Jews had once been capable of self-governance and had achieved a high culture among the kingdoms of the ancient world. "Moses wanted to found a lasting and flourishing state, and his law contains nothing that contradicts this goal," Dohm declares (*Improvement* 143). The degradation of Jewish society, the Jewish propensity for "fraud and usury" (*Improvement* 97), arose as a result of the loss of political independence, the necessity of finding livelihoods as petty tradesmen, merchants, and bankers, and the growth of the "sophistry" of rabbinic legislation (*Improvement* 96, 138). The oppressive constriction of Jewish society, brought on by intolerant legislation and outright persecution, Dohm argued, crippled the Jewish nation's religious, cultural, and economic vitality. The insecurity about the future that accompanies the mercantile trades, to which Jewish economic life was largely reduced, led Jews to concentrate their intellectual energies on "ceremonial trivialities" that were given exaggerated importance as means to secure God's blessings (*Improvement* 143). But the cultural and religious corruption of the once vibrant Jewish spirit could be overcome once new economic opportunities, especially in manufacturing and agriculture, became available to the Jews. Civil rights were, Dohm argued, a precondition to Jewish economic integration in the state.

Dohm expected that Jewish religious enlightenment would ultimately lead to the surrender of Jewish religious observances that were out of step with citizenship in an enlightened nation-state. Dohm accepted the Pauline characterization of Judaism as a religion whose laws, to the extent that they fostered the ethnic separation of Jew from gentile, had been annulled by Christ's dispensation of a new covenant between God and all of humanity. Dohm's enlightened attitude toward the Jews reveals itself precisely in his refusal to offer the typical theological characterization of the continuing Jewish allegiance to separatist laws as due to spiritual blindness or a divine curse. Rather, Dohm focuses on the historical conditions which, following the destruction of the Temple by the Romans in 70 CE and the end of the Jewish polity in Palestine, contributed to the hardening of Jewish law into the sine qua non of Jewish survival. Dohm had no desire to compel the religious changes that would allow Jews to move rapidly from "unhappy Asiatic refugees [unglückliche Asiatische Flüchtlinge]" (*Improvement* 8) into citizens with a distinct religious "confession." He expected that such changes would come as a matter of course, in three or four generations, as Jews gained access to all areas of civic life. Dohm concluded his treatise with a discussion of military service, whose inevitable breaches of Sabbath observance during times of war might seem to make Jewish participation impossible. Dohm argued that the injunction against fighting on the Sabbath was a post–70 CE development and that it would be dropped once Jews felt they had a stake in defending the nation. Given the amount of time Dohm devotes to this topic, it would seem that he understood joint military service to be the fastest route both to Jewish civic integration and also Jewish religious reform.

In offering his arguments about the original compatibility of Sabbath observance with military service, Dohm appealed to the most famous Orientalist of the day, Johann David Michaelis (1717–91), to offer his reflections about the Mosaic Sabbath commandment and its historic development.[8] Michaelis took the opportunity of responding not only to Dohm's interpretation of the Sabbath, but to the entire treatise. Michaelis represented himself as sympathetic to the enlightened political principles that guided Dohm's treatise, but he felt that Dohm had underestimated the resistance of the Jews to the religious reforms that would allow them to participate in civic life. Jews, Michaelis argued, would be very reluctant to alter their dietary laws, which made commensality with gentiles impossible, or to mitigate the demands of the Sabbath law, which stood in the way of military service. But Michaelis reserved his most trenchant remarks for an aspect of the Jewish character that Dohm had been silent about, namely, the Jewish contempt for oaths. In discussing the question of military service, Michaelis dismissed the possibility that Jews, if they were unwilling to eat with gentiles, could be organized in separate regiments. "Hardly anyone would advise making special regiments comprised of them," Michaelis continued (*Improvement* 2:50), "especially since the Jew's oath [Judeneid] is the most hole-ridden thing [häcklischste] thing in the world, and it is not one of the unjust accusations made by Eisenmenger [in his anti-Jewish work *Entdecktes Judentum*] that one can raise serious doubts whether what in our eyes is an oath is held to be such by the Jew." This passage comes after an earlier attack on the sort of Jew who has renounced his allegiance to Jewish law and publicly consumes pork "in what is really intended as an affront to his religion" (*Improvement* 2:38). Such a pork-eating Jew, Michaelis avers, demonstrates that his oaths are worthless, since "how can one know what he thinks about the oath, whether he believes that God everywhere takes cognizance of oaths and punishes the oath-breaker, whether in this world or the next?" Michaelis says that in a court of law any prosecutor could easily show the emptiness of a pork-eating Jew's testimony, but "what if this happened in the hundreds and thousands?" It would be "sheer heartlessness" against "our original oath-fearing citizens" to compel them to accept equality with "strangers whose oaths cannot be relied upon." Michaelis has here made it clear that *on no terms* will he accept Jews as civic partners. He has placed the Jews in a double bind. Both their allegiance to traditional practices and their shedding of them make them untrustworthy. At the heart of the double bind, Michaelis has identified Jewish speech as making Dohm's enlightened solution of the Jewish Question impossible. The mind of the Jew, Michaelis tells us, is never transparently represented in his speech; Jewish words do not mean what they say. Holding Christian standards of truth in contempt, the Jews must remain permanent "strangers" to society.

In 1782, one year before Michaelis's comments were published in a supplementary volume ("Zweiter Theil") of Dohm's work, Mendelssohn offered his own reply to Dohm, as I have already mentioned, in his Vorrede to Menassah ben Israel's seventeenth-century appeal for toleration of Jews in Cromwellian England. We shall see that his intervention in the debate over civil rights for the Jews will ultimately bring him into direct conflict with Michaelis, but only after his publication of *Jerusalem*. The groundwork for this conflict, however, is laid in the Vorrede. Here, despite his overwhelming approval of the enlightened spirit of Dohm's treatise, Mendelssohn raises objections against the very notion of "rights" as applied to religious or ecclesiastical bodies. Dohm had suggested that the Jewish community in Germany should be given rights to enforce theological uniformity over its members, rights also granted to other confessing communities. Dohm wrote that, "like every ecclesiastical society [kirchliche Gesellschaft]," the Jews should have the right to exclude individuals from their community "for a time or forever." If the individuals oppose the rabbis' judgment, the state should support a rabbinic edict of excommunication (*Improvement* 124). In attacking Dohm's suggestion that the Jewish community should be free to exercise a state-enforced right of excommunication, Mendelssohn advances a theory of the social contract as the basis of the state.

According to this theory, the social contract transforms an individual's "unspecified inner duties [unbestimmte innere Plichten]" towards "the human race in general [dem menschlichen Geschlechte überhaupt]" into specific outward duties toward other members of the state. This transformation, Mendelssohn says, takes "imperfect [unvollkommene]" rights and makes them "perfect [vollkommene]." Thus, in the state of nature ("der Stand der Natur") I have an imperfect duty to use my surplus goods in order to alleviate the misery of the "human race," while in the state of society ("der Stand der Geselligkeit") this duty "is more closely delimited" ("näher eingeschränkt") and thereby perfected. My imperfect, unspecified duty in the state of nature is called "inner" because its fulfillment is entirely at my discretion. However, in the state of society, the duty is "outer" because it is no longer entirely at my discretion to choose when and how to fulfill it. In addition, I can be compelled by the state to fulfill my duty if necessary. The social contract also means that the individual who finds himself in economic straits and who has, in the state of nature, only an "imperfect right" to expect from nature or humanity in general the means necessary to find happiness ("Glückseligkeit"), now has a "perfect, outer right" to demand such means from his fellow citizens. Under the terms of the social contract, then, "inner duties" and "inner rights" are transformed into outer duties and rights. To make "inner" duties and rights "outer" is to "alienate" them ("veräussern") (cf. Vorrede 20).[9]

Having established the significance of the social contract as the transformative agent of both perfecting and alienating (making "outer") natural rights and duties, Mendelssohn goes on to argue that an individual cannot alienate the "inner" natural right to use her own reason to examine her beliefs ("Meinungen") and judgments ("Urteile"). Since beliefs and judgments "do not depend directly upon our will [da sie nicht unmittelbar von unserm Willen abhängen]" (Vorrede 20), they are not in our power to alienate and place at the discretion of another person. One therefore has a natural right to use one's own reason to examine one's beliefs and judgments in order to decide whether or not to continue to hold them. This natural right is an inalienable property ("unveräußerliches Eigentum") of the individual person (Vorrede 20). Beliefs and judgments cannot, by their very nature, be placed at another's discretion. One cannot, for example, meaningfully bind oneself contractually to judge that a certain act is moral if one actually finds it to be immoral. "It is one thing to hold back from acting upon one's judgment and another thing entirely to hold back from the judgment itself. The action stands directly under the power of our will, the judgment does not" (Vorrede 20). Only one's own reason can test the truth of one's beliefs and the probity of one's judgments. The natural use of one's own reason constitutes an inner right that cannot be contracted away. Therefore no society has a right to force its members to accept certain beliefs.

Mendelssohn has an additional argument against the right of an *ecclesiastical* society to force its members to accept certain beliefs. One cannot alienate one's right to use one's reason for the same reason that one cannot alienate *any* right to an ecclesiastical society. The fundamental goal of such a society is to *inspire* free and heartfelt benevolence and not *coerce* acts of benevolence. "Its goal," Mendelssohn states, "is social uplift, the sharing of the heart's outpouring whereby we give thanks for benefits received from God and express our childlike trust in His goodness" (Vorrede 21). No religious society can consistently promote its fundamental goal of freely motivated benevolence and at the same time coerce acts of benevolence. The members of any ecclesiastical society never contract to alienate *any* inner right to it. This does not mean, however, that an ecclesiastical society does not promote the transformation of the inner duty of benevolence into outward deed, only that the individuals towards whom one ought to fulfill one's duty will not be specified by any particular social contract. These individuals remain identified as members of the human race, each equally deserving benevolence. King Solomon, Mendelssohn explains, decreed that any stranger ("Fremder") should be free to pray at the Temple in Jerusalem. The rabbis state that idolaters and criminal Israelites must be permitted to offer sacrifice at the Temple because "no one should be denied the opportunity to improve" (Vorrede 22). Every ecclesiastical society, Mendelssohn claims, is a purely voluntary, noncontractual gathering of individuals who seek to encourage one another in the display of benevolence towards humanity as a whole.

Mendelssohn concludes his Vorrede with an appeal to the contemporary Jewish communal leaders. In line with his view that the ecclesiastical society is noncoercive in its promotion of benevolence, Mendelssohn calls specifically upon the rabbis of his day to give up the use of excommunication. Comparing the outlook of King Solomon and the rabbis to that of the contemporary Jewish leadership, Mendelssohn writes: "Thus did they judge at a time when they had a somewhat greater right and authority to be exclusive in matters of divine worship, and *we*, would we not be ashamed to exclude dissidents from our own barely tolerated ecclesiastical gatherings?" (Vorrede 22). Although Mendelssohn concludes his Vorrede with an appeal to his fellow Jews to display "love of one's fellow [Bruderliebe]" in order to turn the hatred of the nations against them into love, one can also hear within his words a challenge to his Christian readers to renounce their own exclusivism and intolerance.

These are the arguments in the Vorrede that provoked a firestorm of criticism. Even warmly sympathetic reviews of the Vorrede's impassioned call for an end to prejudice and hatred against the Jews were critical of Mendelssohn's rejection of ecclesiastical rights. "What a gentle voice of wisdom and humanity speaks in it," declares J. G. Herder in a review from 1782. "And how exact, how thoughtfully chosen, are all the words of this dear voice . . . I think it is Pascal who remarked upon how pleasant it is when one hears in a published work not an author, but a human being."[10] Herder, however, like most other readers, found Mendelssohn's rejection of ecclesiastical rights to be entirely unacceptable. One anonymous author (it was August Friedrich Cranz, an admirer of Mendelssohn who worried that his reputation for satire would lead Mendelssohn to dismiss his remarks) claimed that by attacking ecclesiastical rights Mendelssohn was, at the very least, demonstrating that Jewish law was no longer binding upon him.[11] A law without sanctions, with no power to punish infractions, cannot be a viable law. Cranz was not really interested in the truth or falsity of Mendelssohn's claim about ecclesiastical rights, but only in pointing out the apparent inconsistency in Mendelssohn's continuing to observe a law that was, in principle, unenforceable. Cranz argued that Mendelssohn should, in all logic, abandon Jewish observance. Having recognized the nullity of Jewish law, Mendelssohn's next step should be conversion to Christianity.

Jerusalem: *Philosophy against Despotism*

Mendelssohn's defense of his observance of the Jewish law is not the first topic addressed in his *Jerusalem*. That defense comes only in section 2 of the work. In section 1 of *Jerusalem*, Mendelssohn goes over once again his arguments that "ecclesiastical right" is, like "square circle," a contradiction in terms. I have already sketched these arguments, but they deserve a somewhat fuller treatment if the rhetorical and philosophical design of *Jerusalem* is to be properly appreciated. Rehearsing the arguments will also allow us to see Mendelssohn's philosophical method in its practical application.

Mendelssohn approaches the question of whether the phrase "ecclesiastical right" makes sense by examining the way we ordinarily use the term "right." This is typical of Mendelssohn's philosophical method. Mendelssohn believes that philosophers often entrap themselves in problems whose solution demands that philosophical language be returned to language's ordinary usage and thus led out of its contradiction with everyday life. Mendelssohn's methodology is captured by Wittgenstein's remark, quoted in the opening epigraph to this chapter, about "the philosophical problem" being "the civil status of a contradiction, or its status in civil life." But the philosophical problem that Mendelssohn is addressing in *Jerusalem*, namely, the relation between civil and religious power, is not just one among a number of possible philosophical problems. It goes to the question of the meaning of "civil life" and the language by which it is constituted, the language of the so-called social contract which underwrites state power. To draw the proper distinction between the life of the individual in civil society and in religious society requires a philosophical examination of how language, the medium of human existence in any society, differently constitutes civil and religious societies.

Philosophy's task for both Mendelssohn and Wittgenstein is to uncover the contradictions in "civil life" that run the risk of voiding the meaning of the social contract, that is, the possibility of our *taking one another at our words*, trusting to the conventions that underwrite civility. The contradictions that threaten to undermine the social contract hide beneath language's surface appearance of logical coherence. On the very first page of *Jerusalem*, Mendelssohn identifies such apparent coherence as the ally of despotic power. When church and state are in agreement, Mendelssohn writes "the noblest treasure of human felicity is lost; for they seldom agree but for the purpose of banishing from their realm . . . *liberty of conscience*, which knows how to derive some advantage from their disunity" (*Jerusalem* 33; 1:4). The univocity of church and state is the end of freedom of thought. Mendelssohn continues to explain:

> Despotism has the advantage of being consistent. However burdensome its demands may be to common sense, they are, nevertheless, coherent and systematic. It has a definite answer to every question. You need not trouble yourself any more about limits; for he who has everything no longer asks, "how much?" (*Jerusalem* 34; 1:4)

The alliance of church and state is the highest form of despotism, and it maintains itself against the free conscience because, unlike the authority-questioning conscience, it "has the advantage of being consistent" and because it "has a definite answer to every question" (*Jerusalem* 34; 1:4).[12] People often are willing to relinquish the "trouble" of thinking if they have ready-made answers to all questions, if they never need to confront contradictions in life. Wittgenstein's reference to philosophy's responsibility to face squarely every "contradiction in civil life" seems not to be freighted with such political significance, but he does speak about the human temptation to seek for "crystalline purity" in thinking, a search that only creates "slippery ice where there is no friction" and "conditions [that] are ideal," but because of which "we are unable to walk" (*PI* §107). In order to walk, "we need friction," and such friction is provided by "the rough ground" of "ordinary life" (*PI* §107, 108). Both Mendelssohn and Wittgenstein attempt to reveal the problems beneath the surface calm of linguistic purity and consistency, a surface calm hiding what Wittgenstein calls "deep disquietudes" whose "significance is as great as the importance of our language" (*PI* §111). Mendelssohn speaks about despotism's coherence as a "structure" where "perfect calm reigns in all its parts." In reality, however, the calm of despotism is "only that dreadful calm which, as Montesquieu says, prevails during the evening in a fortress which is to be taken by storm during the night" (*Jerusalem* 34; 1:4). Mendelssohn is aware that the uncovering of the contradictions and "deep disquietudes" hiding beneath our language may, initially, create a situation of danger, but he also knows that no despotism offers real security, and no contradiction can long remain invisible.[13] The contradiction that in his day had broken through the surface appearance of "ideal conditions" and had offered a chance to rediscover the significance of "ordinary life" was, for Mendelssohn, the Jewish Question. To answer the question of civil rights for the Jews called upon all the resources of philosophy.

After cautioning that his work will challenge the "coherence" of the despotic alliance of church and state, Mendelssohn goes on in section 1 of *Jerusalem* to argue that church and state should not, in fact, differ in their goals, but only in the methods by which they go about achieving these goals. For both church and state, the goal is human happiness in a complete life, including the life we spend upon this earth and that unending life we may hope for beyond our death. Mendelssohn argues that distinguishing between "temporal" and "spiritual" happiness as the concerns of state and church, respectively, as he says Locke does, opens the door to a possible despotic alliance of church and state if it seems that the separate goals of each could be better achieved when both act together. To forestall this possibility, Mendelssohn rests his distinction between church and state upon the different *means* employed by each in seeking their common goal, human happiness in this life and the next. Human happiness, Mendelssohn asserts, depends upon the exercise of benevolence. In his essay "On Evidence in Metaphysical Sciences" (1763),[14] Mendelssohn argues for the role of benevolence in human happiness on the basis of the assumption that the only compelling reason for an ethically free being to act is to "bring about as much perfection, beauty, and order in the world as is possible for him." This choice aligns the free human with God: "I conform to the great final purpose of creation and become an imitator of divinity whenever I render a creature, myself or another, more perfect" ("On Evidence" 295–96). Not only is benevolence necessary to support the physical needs of all members of the community, it is necessary for a complete and full life in which one cultivates and gives expression to the inner wellspring of benevolence within the heart of every human. "Benevolence, in reality, makes us happier than selfishness; but we must, while exercising it, be aware that it springs from ourselves and is the display of our powers" (*Jerusalem* 41; 1:21). The state and the church should both seek to promote the impulse to benevolence through teaching and persuasive discourse of all forms, but only the state is empowered to use coercive means when it becomes necessary to do so for the general welfare. The state is so empowered because of the social contract that maintains it, an agreement by which the individual alienates what Mendelssohn now calls "duties of conscience [Gewissenspflichten]" to allocate for the benefit of others those of his goods that are not required for his own survival. In the Vorrede, Mendelssohn had described these duties as "unspecified" and "inner." In *Jerusalem*, he continues to identify these duties as "inner [innerlich]" (see *Jerusalem* 47; 1:32). Yet in alienating these duties of conscience, the individual lifts them out of the sphere of private discretion and into the sphere of enforceable obligations.

Expanding upon the rather brief account in his Vorrede, Mendelssohn says that the social contract transforms the possessors of "imperfect" rights and duties into possessors of "perfect" rights and duties. Imperfect rights are rights that an individual who lacks the goods necessary for survival has against the surplus goods of another. They are imperfect because, although everyone has a right to those goods that can sustain his existence, no one can make a specific claim against a certain percent of another individual's goods. The other individual has an "imperfect" duty of conscience to act benevolently and share his surplus goods with those in need, but it is within the individual's discretion (a matter of his conscience) how much of his surplus wealth he will share, and with whom he will share it. The imperfect claim to surplus goods and the imperfect duty to provide them are, in the state of nature, two inherently conflicting principles. The lack of definite and measurable *extension* that constitutes their imperfection (in what amounts, from which owners, and to which claimants, the rights and duties should be measured out) makes them stand opposed to one another as two pure *intensities* of the will (two expressions of the will to freely employ all of one's powers—one below the threshold of survival equilibrium and one above it). However, once a contract or an agreement is reached between the parties, the imperfect claim becomes a perfect (i.e., delimited and enforceable) right to another's surplus goods and the owner's imperfect duty of conscience to share his surplus goods becomes a perfect (i.e., delimited and enforceable) duty. A contract between one party with an imperfect right and another party with an imperfect duty to share certain goods (whether those goods are material or "spiritual") transforms and, one could say, *perfects* each party. The contract resolves the collision between imperfect right and imperfect duty. The contract is a declaration that both parties freely enter into in order to resolve the collision by giving their conflicting wills a measured harmonization.[15] Each party gains: The owner of surplus goods fulfills his or her imperfect duty of conscience to act benevolently; the claim holder against these surplus goods acquires what is necessary to his or her existence. The resolution of the collision of imperfect right and imperfect duty does not, however, always hold fast, and in such outbreaks of colliding wills an arbiter is called in, a "moral person" empowered by the social contract to adjudicate (recalibrate, so to speak) conflicts and enforce contractual agreements. "It is by agreements of this kind that man leaves the state of nature and enters into the state of social relations," Mendelssohn says in concluding his discussion of rights, duties, and contracts in *Jerusalem*. "His own nature impels him to enter into associations of various kinds in order to transform his fluctuating rights and duties into something definite" (*Jerusalem* 56; 1:55). Every society expresses a definite form and configuration of the impulse to perfection within the world.

It is interesting to note that Mendelssohn's exemplary contract is not for a sale or exchange of goods, or the contract between an employer and a worker. Mendelssohn does not discuss such contracts, but they can clearly be seen to be derivative of the contract by which one person promises to give some of his surplus goods to another. In effect, a contract that stipulates an exchange of equivalent goods is simply two contracts bundled as one. The worker must give the employer a certain part of his laboring capacity, once he or she enters the contract. And the employer must give the worker a certain amount of his property. Each has enforceable rights against the other. Mendelssohn, it seems, wants to stress freely given benevolence over mutual need as the basis of society. On a mutual need model, the social contract cancels out the deficits of each individual. The summative effect of the social contract is not for Mendelssohn the *zeroing out* of the weakness or negativity of each constitutive will; rather, it is the *increase* of the "perfection" of "fluctuating" and "imperfect" wills which, in the state of nature, are rich with potentiality but lack a determinate structure in which to realize it.

Hobbes is the classic political theorist of the social contract as the zeroing out of individual weakness. For him, the state of nature is a condition of war where the individual has little chance to live out his natural lifespan. The civil state offers the best chance to the individual to live out the natural term of his life. The social contract removes a negativity (the subtraction of a number of years from the likely lifespan of the individual) but it does not in any way increase the power of the individual. Mendelssohn views humanity as composed not of beings seeking to extend their lifespans, but of beings freely choosing at every moment to realize their power—which they are given by God—to perfect themselves and the world about them.[16] The realization of their potential to perfect themselves and the world can only take place in the context of civil society.

Mendelssohn's anti-Hobbesian view, as Willi Goetschel has persuasively argued in *Spinoza's Modernity*, has its source in Spinoza's political philosophy. Goetschel draws attention to the phrase in Spinoza's *Political Treatise* that declares that in the ideal civil state of the self-governing multitude, "everyone is led as if by one mind [omnes una veluti mente ducuntur]." Explaining the "as if [veluti]" construction, Goetschel writes:

> The expression "una veluti mente" does not so much establish a norm as simply highlight the intricate constitution that makes the civil state. This makes the formula resistant to instrumentalization. There is no other way, it suggests, to conceive of such *una mens* or "state spirit" other than as the democratically perfected realization of the political power of the multitude. (Goetschel 2004: 75–76)

Goetschel points out that for Spinoza and Mendelssohn alike, the task of the civil state is to allow for the actualization of the natural—Mendelssohn calls them both "natural" and "imperfect"—rights (and duties) of the individual, to "establish the framework in which those rights can be expressed and realized" (Goetschel 2004: 74). I will return to the Spinozist theory of the ideal state as the "democratically perfected realization of the political power of the multitude" in Chapter 6, where I will connect it not only to Mendelssohn's political philosophy, but also to that of Hannah Arendt. For all three thinkers, the power of democratic action is not calculable as the simple sum of the force of each individual, but is rather qualitatively distinct from the sum of its parts. And it is certainly not the cancellation of individual weaknesses or defects. As Stephen B. Smith says about Spinoza's concept of power: "Power is not simply a zero-sum game. Rather, we often increase our capacities by learning to join and cooperate with others for shared ends" (Smith 2003: 100). With the coordination of the "powerpotential" (Goetschel's rendering of Spinoza's linkage of *potestas* and *potentia*) of the individuals within a democratic state, something new comes into being, a "single mind." It is the fundamental concern of both Spinoza and Mendelssohn to make sure that the civil "single mind" or "state spirit" should not be reduced to a despotically enforced religious orthodoxy. For Arendt, the threat arises not from religious orthodoxy but from totalitarian ideology.[17] For all three thinkers, the challenge is to maintain the dynamic tension within the "single mind" of the political body, to maintain its openness to a not entirely predictable or masterable futurity.[18] But let me now return to Mendelssohn.

Once having entered into society, the individual will be taught that freely offered benevolence, the sum and substance of what God asks of us, is conducive to his felicity in this life and in the life to come. The state takes responsibility for teaching its citizens that relations among members of the state, if established on principles of benevolence, are conducive to both the general welfare and to the moral fulfillment of the individual. But if a citizen will not comply with the arrangements for mutual benevolence laid down by the state, the state has the right, deriving from the social contract, to coerce the individual to comply. Every ecclesiastical society has the responsibility to teach the citizens of the state how the felicity and welfare of society are part of God's plan for humanity and that benevolence is what God wishes for and from us.

> It is the business of the church to convince people, in the most emphatic manner, of the truth of noble principles and convictions; to show them that duties toward men are also duties toward God, the violation of which is in itself the greatest misery; that serving the state is true service of God; that charity is his most sacred will; and that true knowledge of the Creator cannot leave behind in the soul any hatred for men. To teach this is the business, duty, and vocation of religion; to preach it, the business and duty of its ministers. How, then, could it ever have occurred to men to permit religion and its ministers to preach exactly the opposite? (*Jerusalem* 43; 1:24)

The church should teach citizens that God is the model of perfect, freely offered benevolence, and that God expects nothing more or less of us than that we imitate Him. Indeed, the church will teach that God created us in His image, meaning that He wishes us to become as He is, freely offering our benevolence to our fellow humans. The state views the human as a creature whose complexly interwoven and often contradictory motives, whose flawed self-knowledge, vanity and pride, cannot be relied upon to maintain the social welfare. The church views the human as the irreplaceable and sacred instrument through which God offers His benevolent love to the world. "The state treats man as the immortal son of the earth," Mendelssohn declares in a wonderfully succinct formulation, "religion treats him as the image of his Creator" (*Jerusalem* 70; 1:84).

Mendelssohn establishes the difference between the civil and the ecclesiastical society on the basis of his theory of the social contract as the perfecting of imperfect rights and duties. Such perfecting requires an alienation of one's freedom to act (it is a determination of one's indeterminate will). Ecclesiastical society, Mendelssohn argues, is not established on the basis of any alienation of one's power of action, no enforceable and delimited exercise of one's power is agreed to, and therefore any use of coercion by ecclesiastical society against its members is illegitimate. A church is not a moral person created by the alienation of some part of our right to act from purely "inner" grounds, at our own discretion. Nor is God a party to a contract that humans make with Him by which they alienate rights to Him. One enters into the contract with the state freely when one acknowledges that through the state one fulfills (at least in part) one's duty of conscience to act benevolently. A church is not formed as the arbitrational framework for conflicting wills; a church is a gathering of individuals who encourage and promote one another's freely given benevolence. There is no limit to the extent or intensity of this benevolence, just as God does not limit His benevolence to one part of humanity or offer it with more power of His will to one person in preference to another. Any ecclesiastical society is a vessel through which pours God's infinite will to benevolence. Such a society cannot coerce benevolence because, first of all, the violent nature of coercion is opposed to benevolence and, second, any legitimate use of coercion by society involves a resolution of conflicting wills, and God's will is neither itself in conflict with human wills nor is God a "moral person" to whom the right to adjudicate collisions of rights and duties has been alienated. "God is not a being who needs our benevolence, requires our assistance, or claims any of our rights for his own use, or whose rights can ever clash or be confused with ours," Mendelssohn asserts (*Jerusalem* 57; 1:58) and a little further on he reiterates this point: "He desires no *service* from us, no sacrifice of our rights for his benefit, no renunciation of our independence for his advantage. His rights can never come into conflict and confusion with ours. He wants only what is best for us, what is best for every single individual; and this must, evidently, be self-consistent and cannot contradict itself" (*Jerusalem* 59; 1:60–61). God's will is purely benevolent and purely loving; the combined wills of those who constitute any ecclesiastical society should be the pure expression of this benevolent love. How can force be conjoined to such pure benevolence without corrupting it, or, better put, replacing it with its very opposite, with hatred? An ecclesiastical society can arrogate coercive powers to itself only if it believes that it is charged with resolving the conflict between the will of humans and the will of God, between, in other words, the natural but imperfect right of God (to be served by humans) and the natural but imperfect duty of humans (to give God their love and obedience). But imperfection exists only in the rights and duties obtaining between humans; God is in no way imperfect. From the error of ascribing to God a claim against humanity for obedience and love, Mendelssohn says, "flow all the unjust presumptions which the so-called ministers of religion have at all times permitted themselves to make in the name of the church" (*Jerusalem* 58; 1:59). Ecclesiastical leaders have arrogated to themselves the authority to fix the terms of the allegedly colliding wills of God and humans. But only human, finite wills can possibly collide, and only the humanly constructed "moral person" of the state is vested with the right to settle these collisions and sanction the settlement with threats of punishment.

Mendelssohn in section 1 of *Jerusalem* expands upon the points he made in the Vorrede with a discussion of the rather common practice in both Germany and England of requiring entrants to ecclesiastical offices to swear an oath that they agree to the truth of the church's creed as laid out in summary propositions. In England, the case that Mendelssohn specifically mentions, there were thirty-nine such creedal propositions to which members of the clerical establishment of the Church of England needed to swear before taking their office. Such oaths, Mendelssohn argues, offer the prestige and economic enticements of church office as bait to bring the individual's conscience into conformity with the church, and thus the church is using means that are inconsistent with its fundamental principles. The church has no right to punish its members' failures to fulfill the duties prescribed by their consciences, and neither can the church seek to seduce the consciences of its officers with monetary or other rewards. Mendelssohn goes so far as to say that the church should not even pay its ministers and teachers, but rather they should be recompensed for their time by the state. Mendelssohn adds that the church has no right to refuse membership to someone who does not agree with its creed, or who will not comply with its teachings. Such expulsion or excommunication exercises an illegitimate power over the conscience, bringing fear of social disgrace or economic ruin to threaten the conscience.

The discussion of the illegitimacy of oaths, of payment for religious teaching by the church, and of excommunication of church members for dissent brings section 1 of *Jerusalem* to a close. At this point in the text, Mendelssohn seems to have undermined all the traditional foundations of ecclesiastical authority. It is as if he has deliberately pushed his critique of ecclesiastical rights to its farthest limit in order to bring into the sharpest possible relief his defense of his continuing allegiance to Jewish law. That defense will occupy section 2 of *Jerusalem*. In defending his acceptance of the obligations of Jewish law, Mendelssohn must show how Judaism defines a unique society, neither purely ecclesiastical (differentiated from other ecclesiastical societies only by its creed) nor purely civil (with coercive power to compel compliance to its laws). In other words, Mendelssohn must argue that Judaism is neither a church nor a state. Judaism is, he will argue, the exemplary constitution for a human society in which the performance of the law is the uncoerced enactment of God's benevolent will. The idea that God's election of the Jewish people is for the purpose of creating an exemplary particularity that embodies the universal human ideal is given one of its first and most powerful expressions in Mendelssohn's *Jerusalem*. Jewish exemplarity, Mendelssohn argues, reveals the ideal human society in which the ecclesiastical and civil dimensions find their perfect conjoined expression. The interrelation of Jewish election and Jewish exemplarity as it plays out in Rosenzweig and Derrida has recently been examined by Dana Hollander in *Exemplarity and Chosenness* (2008). My discussion of Mendelssohn seeks to situate him within the problematic of exemplary particularity whose centrality for both Rosenzweig and Derrida Hollander has ably demonstrated.

To understand Mendelssohn's notion of the exemplarity of the Jewish people, it is necessary to explore the logic of the church-state relationship that Mendelssohn advances in *Jerusalem*. Jeffrey Librett has drawn attention to a conceptual aporia at the heart of Mendelssohn's analysis of church-state relations in *Jerusalem*. Librett points out that Mendelssohn begins *Jerusalem* by arguing that the linkage of church and state as it has taken shape in the past is sheer despotism (the use of state power to maintain one religious creed above others), but Mendelssohn does not want to privatize religion (the route taken by Locke in defending religious toleration). Thus, Mendelssohn must imagine a different way for church and state to interrelate, and by the end of section 1 we can perhaps catch a glimpse of the answer: The church, as the noncoercive vehicle for perfecting divine benevolence in the world, is what the state strives to become. The church is the realization of the state's potential. If ever church and state were to be unified, it would mean the qualitative transformation of the state into its perfection as a noncoercive society and the qualitative transformation of the church into its perfection as noncoercive law. Such a church-state unity would be the fully enlightened society, where obedience to the law is achieved entirely through rational persuasion. This unification of church and state, the qualitative transformation of both into a single society of individuals coming together to freely obey noncoercive laws (laws not sanctioned by any threat of punishment, in other words), is not a vague, future ideal. It has already come into being. It is Judaism.

Judaism is not the religion of a church, nor is it the constitution of a state. As Jeffrey Librett puts it, "Judaism is neither a revealed religion nor a politics because it is *both*" (Librett 2000: 64). Because Judaism is the unity of both church and state, it is qualitatively distinct from either one. Although Mendelssohn cannot count himself a citizen of the Prussian state, he is a citizen of the ideal, enlightened church-state. If the Prussian state will not grant him citizenship, this only reflects upon its lack of enlightenment.

Before discussing section 2 and offering a fuller development of these points, I need to spend some time examining the philosophy of language that underlies Mendelssohn's critique of oaths in section 1. This philosophy will be deployed in section 2 in the defense of Jewish law as a form of performative speech. Only after we understand Mendelssohn's philosophy of language in *Jerusalem* can we properly appreciate the force of his defense of Jewish law.

Mendelssohn's Expressivism

The theory of the social contract that Mendelssohn advances in *Jerusalem* depends upon the notion that language has the power to alter the world, to perfect it. John Austin, in *How to Do Things with Words*, will call this language's "illocutionary power," and both Austin and Mendelssohn focus on the promise as a signal case of this power. When one makes a promise to another, one enters into a contract in which the other's imperfect right to the promiser's goods becomes perfect rights to those goods. The goods in question can consist of movable or immovable property, or intangible goods (talents, creative capacities, even rights themselves). A promise to another individual cedes some of these goods or some use of these goods to the other. The promise requires some form of external declaration ("Willenserklärung"): "In reality, everything depends solely upon this declaration of will, and even the actual transfer of movable goods is valid only insofar as it is taken to be a sign of a sufficient declaration of will" (*Jerusalem* 54; 1:49). The promise itself effects the transfer of property: "It is, therefore, possible to cede and relinquish to others one's right to immovable or even intangible goods by means of sufficiently intelligible signs" (*Jerusalem* 54; 1:50). A contract is not voided if one "keeps one's fingers crossed" in some internal mental space. Nor is a contract valid because it is tethered to an internal mental space where the promise's intention resides securely. Signs alone suffice to make a contract valid, and their intelligibility depends on their ability to be interpreted by other signs, their possibility of being disambiguated at least to the point of allowing for a resolution in a court of law about the contract's terms.

Mendelssohn's expressivism does not posit a perfect match between the intention to make a promise and the speech act of promising. Since the promise is made through signs, there is always room for further interpretation. I will talk in the next section about some further implications of this view of language, but in this section I want to underscore Mendelssohn's view that language expresses a human's participation in and construction of a social world. Language is not a mirror of internal states. When Mendelssohn spoke about the "liberty of conscience" that is under threat when state and church agree, he was talking about not only an internal space of freedom—Hobbes, he says, had granted this much freedom to subjects of his sovereign state—but more significantly about the freedom to use language expressively without first demonstrating to some authority that one is trustworthy enough to speak, that one's words correspond to one's inner intentions. Every citizen makes a promise when entering into the social contract that creates the moral person of the state. The state is built up out of promises; it cannot call them into question without undermining its legitimacy.

Mendelssohn's theory of language runs counter to the dominant picture in Enlightenment philosophy of how meanings are attached to words. It was Amos Funkenstein who initially drew attention to the significance of Mendelssohn's distinctive theory of language (and language's written representation) for any understanding of the larger goals of Mendelssohn's *Jerusalem* (Funkenstein 1993: 18ff.). More recently, David Martyn, in his "Nachwort" to his edition of *Jerusalem*, has argued persuasively that Mendelssohn's theory of language is not only new within the context of the German Enlightenment, it is new for Mendelssohn as well (Mendelssohn 2001: 147ff.). Martyn focuses upon Mendelssohn's claim that there is no escape from the use of signs to understand signs—in other words, that there is no direct access to what has been called a "master signified" that could serve as a touchstone to determine the truth or falsity of speech. In what follows, I will pursue Martyn's lead, but I will not draw a Derridean lesson from this theory of the sign as Martyn does (see Martyn 2002: 71).[19] Or, better put, the Derridean lesson I would draw is not one that focuses on the radical play of the signifier, but one that foregrounds the performativity underwriting every sign, what Derrida speaks of as the "I promise a language" that every utterance, spoken or written, implies. Every utterance is a promise to realize language itself as an address to another, as a responsibility to hear and respond. This is a Derridean lesson that draws him quite close to Wittgenstein.[20]

What is at stake in the conflict between Mendelssohn's theory of language and that of his contemporaries is perhaps most saliently brought out in the response of the Orientalist Michaelis to *Jerusalem*. I have previously discussed Michaelis's comments about the Jewish oath. Mendelssohn's denial of the validity of ecclesiastical oaths in both his Vorrede and *Jerusalem* will elicit from the Orientalist Michaelis a critical response to *Jerusalem* in which he brands Mendelssohn as nothing more than an apologist for the Jewish contempt for oaths.[21] We will see that Michaelis is not altogether wrong to say that Mendelssohn holds oaths in contempt. The difference between Michaelis and Mendelssohn over the question of the value of oaths rests ultimately in their different answers to the question, posed to Jesus by Pontius Pilate, that stands at the origin of the fateful struggle over the political and religious meanings of the name "Jerusalem": "What is truth?"

The difference between Michaelis and Mendelssohn goes to the heart of what each believes about how words represent the truth. Michaelis had written a treatise in 1759, entitled *On the Influence of Languages on the Opinions of Men* (*Über den Einfluss der Sprachen auf die Meinungen der Menschen*). Mendelssohn, it happens, penned a rather critical review of this treatise in the journal he published with Lessing and Friedrich Nicolai, *Briefe, die neueste Literatur betreffend* (*Letters concerning the Most Recent Literature*, 1759). The treatise, which won the Prussian Royal Academy Prize for a competition set on the topic, can serve as an example of the reigning Enlightenment conception of language. In the treatise, Michaelis argues that the etymologies of words prove on occasion to be "archives" of scientifically valuable information about the world, but in other cases they are evidence of ignorance and superstition. Michaelis does not argue for the creation of a logically "transparent" language where words are unambiguous signifiers of clear and distinct concepts. Rather, he seeks to show how language can be purified of its grossest errors and directed on a path of scientifically informed evolution. Michaelis begins his treatise by comparing different languages' names for plants and, showing the paucity of such names in general usage, he recommends that European languages should seek to attain a more accurate representation of the botanical world by making use of as many regional words for plants as possible, and insuring their conformity to the taxonomic categories of contemporary botany. Every national language should seek to become more accurate in its word usage, but Michaelis admits that this cannot be done by the fiat of a group of scholars who would coin new words or redefine current words in light of the best scientific and philosophical attainments of the day. Languages, Michaelis says, are too "democratic" for such imposition of norms from above. The best method for bringing a language into conformity with the truth is rather to rely upon great national poets (Michaelis calls them "classical writers") who are also either versed in science or are themselves scientists. "No person can assume to himself the authority of a classical author, . . . yet is every reformer of sciences to cultivate his language with as much application as if he really aimed at that distinction. Here it is that divine poetry triumphs most signally: blending itself with the serious sciences, it imparts to them a new degree of perfection" (Michaelis 1771:76).

Michaelis understands the dynamic and "democratic" nature of language, but he nonetheless measures language by the standard of a scientific regime of truth. Michaelis says that he would never try to extirpate from language expressions such as "the sun sets in Berlin at such and such an hour" that are, strictly speaking, scientifically false (it is the motion of the earth and not the sun that causes the change from day to night). Michaelis knows that no amount of effort could make the true representation of the facts, "Berlin sets at such and such an hour," acceptable to people. Sometimes, ineradicable sensory illusions determine how people actually experience the world (Michaelis 1771: 2). But even with his recognition of the limits of accuracy in language, Michaelis still adheres to an ideal of scientific truth.

Mendelssohn breaks with the Enlightenment ideal of scientific accuracy that dominates Michaelis's conception of language. The opening chapter of Mendelssohn's *Morning Hours* (1785) is entitled "What is Truth?" In this chapter, Mendelssohn launches into a critique of the theory that truth is the agreement of word, concept, and object. Mendelssohn explains that according to the theory, things serve as "originals" of which concepts and thoughts are the "copies." Words, as copies of copies, are merely "silhouettes" ("Schattenrisse") of the thoughts. The problem with this theory is that "there is no means to compare thoughts with objects, that is, copies to originals. We have only copies before us and it is by means of them alone that we can judge of the originals" (*Morning Hours* 1:10). Language for Mendelssohn is not first and foremost a medium to convey information whose content is "the opinions of people and the point of view in which objects appear to them," as Michaelis puts it in his treatise (Michaelis 1771: 2). Later in *Morning Hours*, Mendelssohn describes the view, advanced by the contemporary French philosopher Helvétius, that human knowledge could be best advanced if words could be "empty signs and symbols" that would function like "numbers in the art of calculating," so that the truth of a proposition might be established in as certain and simple a manner as summing a column of figures. Associated with each word would be a number. "Accordingly," Mendelssohn writes, "the entirety of human language would be a mere collection of empty, algebraic signs that we position and bind together according to certain rules." Mendelssohn counters that this reduction of each word in the language to an empty sign representing a single sensation that in turn is connected to one type of object would mean that "we would remain as cold and indifferent at the performance of the most admirable playwright or during the reading of a poem or speech as we are when we do an algebraic calculation" (*Morning Hours* 4:42).

Rather than being "a tool for thinking and constructing a rational discourse" (*Morning Hours* 4:41), language for Mendelssohn is one among many ways that humans bring their social and creaturely being to expression. Mendelssohn's philosophy of language is part of what Charles Taylor calls the "expressivist" alternative to the dominant Enlightenment rationalist-utilitarian paradigm. According to the expressivist view,

> men are expressive beings in virtue of belonging to a culture; and a culture is sustained, nourished and handed down in a community. The community has itself on its own level an expressive unity. It is . . . a travesty and a distortion to see it as simply an instrument which individuals set up (or ought ideally to set up) to fulfill their individual goals, as it was for the atomist and utilitarian strand of the Enlightenment. (Taylor 1979: 2)

In the expressivist view, which Mendelssohn developed along with his contemporary Herder, language's truth should not be measured by its scientific accuracy, but by the degree to which it expresses or distorts the authentic human relationship to one's fellows, the world, and God. Frequently, science and philosophy distort this truth. Thus, Mendelssohn describes the prereflective attitude toward the world of the "simple man" as one that has not yet been corrupted by skeptical doubts:

> The man who lives simply has not yet devised the objections which so greatly confuse the sophist. For him the word *nature*, the mere sound, has not yet become a being that seeks to supplant the Deity. He still knows little of the difference between direct and indirect causality; and he hears and sees instead the all-vivifying power of the Deity everywhere—in every sunrise, in every rain that falls, in every flower that blossoms and in every lamb that grazes in the

meadow and rejoices in its own existence. This mode of conceiving things has in it something defective, but it leads directly to the recognition of an invisible, omnipotent being, to whom we owe all the good we enjoy. (*Jerusalem* 95; 2:42–43)

One can see in this description of the originary meaning of "nature" the outlines of Mendelssohn's philosophical anthropology, which serves him as the grounding of his philosophy of language. This philosophical anthropology is directly opposed to that of Hobbes. Mendelssohn views the human as dependent upon others' benevolence and as moved to benevolence once his or her survival needs have been met; the human senses the world to be a gift, not a collection of ownerless things to be appropriated through the exercise of his power. The human acknowledges God as the benevolent giver of life and the world. Language, according to Mendelssohn, can either express or distort these human truths. Language is not a calculus designed to transparently mirror the world. It is the way that humans in a community bring a world of shared meanings into being.

Writing and Mendelssohn's Dialectic of Enlightenment

Language can distort these human truths, but not because of its inaccuracies. Rather, language distorts the truth because, as long as it remains unassisted by some mnemonic tool or prosthesis, its power to express the truth is temporally limited to the moment of utterance. When one speaks to another with the aim of expressing one's gratitude, or requesting help, or of offering counsel, the words may affect the listener to act in a certain way, or to respond in turn with more speech, but this living exchange cannot, unless repeated countless times in the same words and between many people, become part of the wider culture. For many ancient cultures, this meant that poetry, myth, wisdom sayings, and folklore were entirely dependent upon oral transmission and face-to-face teaching. Mendelssohn sees great advantages with oral instruction: It can "keep pace with all changes of time and circumstances, and can be varied and fashioned according to a pupil's needs, ability, and power of comprehension" (*Jerusalem* 102; 2:59). But orality's limitation is that cultural memory resides in only a few tradents and cannot be shared easily among all who desire access to its full heritage.

To this end, "visible signs" are necessary. That is, a writing system must serve to disseminate culture. With writing, human culture is extended and, as a consequence, enhanced through the contribution of many who had no previous access to it. But culture is also threatened with rigidification as language ceases "to keep pace with all changes of time and circumstance" and as certain symbols acquire sacrosanct authority.

> It seems to me that the change that has occurred in different periods of culture with regard to written characters has had, at all times, a very important part in the revolutions of human knowledge in general, and in the various modifications of men's opinions and ideas about religious matters, in particular. (*Jerusalem* 104; 2:64)

Writing, the visible representation of speech, can supplant speech itself. Truth as that which comes to expression in direct and responsive speech is replaced with truth as that which can be represented in fixed propositions. Religions develop dogmas.

The introduction of writing transforms culture. Words are abstracted from their living contexts and subjected to philosophical examination. *Nature*, for example, no longer expresses the human response to the world as the gift of a powerful and benevolent being, but it becomes a philosophical abstraction, the collection of potential pieces of property, of objects that one can grasp either physically or mentally, in the form of sense impressions. If the world is defined as what is graspable by the senses or the mind, we are led to philosophical skepticism. We are led to ask whether the sensible or mental representation corresponds to the reality of the object. We are led to Hume's skepticism about the objective grounds for our representation of cause-and-effect relations between any two objects, and, as a consequence, we are led to question whether God created the world. Hume's skepticism about God's causal agency undermines the grateful attitude toward nature that Mendelssohn attributes to the "simple man," but it also opens the possibility of recuperating the moral tenor of this attitude in a less naive way. Mendelssohn says that "as soon as an Epicurus or Lucretius or Helvétius or Hume criticizes the inadequacy of this mode of conceiving things and (which is to be charged to human weakness) strays too far in the other direction, and wants to carry on a deceptive game with the word *nature*, Providence again raises up other men among the people who separate prejudice from truth, correct the exaggerations on both sides, and show that truth can endure even if prejudice is rejected" (*Jerusalem* 95; 2:43). Critical thinking will raise skeptical doubts that challenge accepted truths, but the response should not be to cling to prior dogmas. One must recover the truth in a form that acknowledges the force of the criticism but also trusts in the expressive truth within everyday language.

This dialectic—simplicity of expressive truth, followed by its written representation and the consequent reification of the sign and rigidification of thought, followed in turn by skeptical criticism of the rigidified truth, and then finally a return to a new form of expressive truth—is inherent in the life of every language and the life of every culture. Mendelssohn does not think that this dialectic can be escaped, or that on the whole humanity is moving forward in its capacity to express the truth of its social and creaturely nature. Precisely because Mendelssohn has broken with the Enlightenment model of scientific truth as the measure of a language's truth, he cannot find in the progress of science any proof that humanity is making *moral* progress. Influenced by his reading of Rousseau's *Essay on the Origin of Inequality*, Mendelssohn divides moral from scientific or technological progress. Unlike Rousseau, however, he does not see history as a steady corruption of humanity, but as the ever-repeated dialectic of corruption and return to health. "Now, as far as the human race as a whole is concerned, you will find no steady progress in its development that brings it ever closer to perfection. Rather do we see the human race in its totality slightly oscillate; it never took a few steps forward without soon afterwards, and with redoubled speed, sliding back to its previous position" (*Jerusalem* 96; 2:47).[22] Despite the oscillation that characterizes humanity's history, each individual is equipped to move forward beyond superstition to a rational comprehension of God, the world, and his or her place within the scheme of creation. "Progress," Mendelssohn declares, "is for the individual man" (*Jerusalem* 96; 2:45).

Mendelssohn describes his theory of the oscillating history of critical enlightenment and dogmatic rigidification as one that contrasts with the progressive view of human history advanced by his friend Gotthold Ephraim Lessing (see *Jerusalem* 95; 2:44). Although he is critical of Lessing's progressivist view of history, Mendelssohn seems to have adopted his theory about writing and orality from him. In the last years of his life, Lessing put considerable effort into laying out a theory of human history that was based upon Freemasonry. In *Ernst and Falk: Dialogues for Freemasons*

(1778) and *The Education of the Human Race* (1777–80),[23] Lessing explains that the final stage of human enlightenment will see both Judaism and Christianity superseded by the religion of reason, what Lessing called "the religion of Christ," as distinct from the "Christian religion." The dialogues of *Ernst and Falk* make it clear that one of the sources of Lessing's theory of enlightenment was Freemasonry. Freemasonry, while its historic roots date to long before the eighteenth century, began to spread among the intelligentsia of both Europe and the American colonies after the foundation of the Grand Lodge of England in 1717. Freemasonry offered its members a purely rational religion that it declared was based upon an age-old teaching about the *pan kai hen*, the "All and One," the cosmos and the indwelling spirit of its divine Architect, venerated in the Egyptian mystery cult of Isis, transmitted to the Greeks as the teachings of Hermes Trismegistus, and passed down in the traditions of the Kabbalah. Lessing made the case in *Ernst and Falk* for the existence throughout history of a brotherhood of enlightened individuals who had worked, without publicizing their aims, for the tempering of political and religious divisions within humanity, modeling in their "deeds *ad extra*" the principles of a universal religion of reason whose truths are unable to be finalized as a written creed.[24] Members of this brotherhood owe their highest allegiance to no single state or religion, but to humanity itself. They pursue their aims outside the institutional frameworks of state and church. In his day, Lessing said, many members of this brotherhood called themselves Freemasons. Explaining how Freemasons draw new members to themselves without availing themselves of any written media, Lessing declares that "they allow good men and youths whom they consider worthy of their company to divine and guess at their deeds—to see them, in so far as they can be seen" (Lessing 2005: 187). The orality of Freemasonic tradition was not only a means to assure its secrecy; Lessing explains in *Ernst and Falk* that all written expressions of the truth harden into dogmas, and dogmas are precisely what the enlighteners aim to destroy. The lack of fixity in the expression of Freemasonic beliefs extends even to the name "Freemason." The name "Freemason" was not always associated with this brotherhood, nor was there always an institutional framework within which the brotherhood could find true fellowship—the members were often at odds with their unenlightened contemporaries—or plan concerted action. For much of history, the enlightened brotherhood was more an idea in each member's mind than an actual group of self-selected men who met in secret to reinforce one another's otherwise lonely paths as world enlighteners.

Mendelssohn never shared Lessing's faith in the existence of such a band of enlighteners in every generation, and in *Jerusalem* we read why he could not share this faith. First, the progressive unfolding of enlightenment in history meant to Lessing that Judaism was superseded by Christianity on the path of enlightenment, and that Christianity in turn would be replaced by one universal "religion of reason." Above all, Lessing in *Ernst and Falk* hoped for an end to religious differences among humans. Mendelssohn would have none of this. In the final pages of *Jerusalem*, Mendelssohn inveighs against those who would try to unite all faiths so as to overcome religious strife and persecution. It is not entirely clear whom Mendelssohn has in mind, but Lessing's *Ernst and Falk* shows clearly that Lessing's goal in promoting Freemasonry was the supersession of all religious strife and persecution by advancing a universal religion of reason. Therefore, Mendelssohn could not insist upon the right of Judaism to continue its existence without framing its continuing existence within an alternative theory of human history. Hence Mendelssohn constructs his theory of the oscillating movement between enlightenment and dogmatism within each nation's history, with different nations moving at different rates of change.

It is not that Mendelssohn thought that enlightenment is simply replaced by some constantly recurring mental blindness, with history being one step forward followed by one step backward in enlightenment. Enlightenment does move forward on the whole, but never on a straight path. The oscillating swing between enlightenment and dogmatism meant that Lessing's dream of one universal religion was unachievable, since it would mean that all humanity would agree to never again adopt a religious dogma, or, differently put, to frame religious truths as fixed propositions whose truth was held to be unquestionable. As Mendelssohn says near the conclusion of *Jerusalem*, the effort to rid the world of all religious differences in favor of one universally accepted religion of reason is more likely a cover for the growth of a new form of "fanaticism" which, having lost its hold when operating under the banner of one faith, now adopts the banner of a "union of faiths" to achieve its "bloodthirsty purposes" (*Jerusalem* 136; 2:134–35).

But Mendelssohn does not merely dismiss Lessing's bold dream of a final triumph of the brotherhood of enlighteners over the dark forces of dogmatism as perhaps the most advanced form under which fanaticism might hide.

Mendelssohn's most daring move is to embrace Lessing's concept of a brotherhood of enlighteners who refuse to put their beliefs into written form because the truth which they embrace is, in the final analysis, a radical rejection of all forms of written dogma. Their truth is that God's nature cannot be represented in physical shapes—whether they be sculpted shapes or the shapes of letters—without falsifying God's nature. All dogmatism is idolatry. Lessing had in *Ernst and Falk* described human history as the slow rejection of all forms of idolatry in favor of a more and more refined, spiritualized, and rational conception of God. The brotherhood of enlighteners was composed of those in every generation who had aspired to this refined interpretation of God's unrepresentability. Mendelssohn adopts this conception of the band of enlighteners and makes it the historical task of the Jewish people: to convey in their every action the rejection of idolatry, the refusal to fix God's nature in any form, whether imagistic or textual. I will talk about Mendelssohn's theory of Judaism as a "living script" that resists rigidification into idolatrous dogma shortly, but before I turn to this I want to consider one further facet of Mendelssohn's expressivist theory of language, namely, its rejection of a private interiority as the site of meaning.

Mendelssohn and Wittgenstein's Private-Language Argument

We have already seen that Mendelssohn breaks with the Enlightenment ideal of linguistic accuracy measured by a scientific regime of truth. Words are expressive, according to Mendelssohn, of the human's relation to the world, to God, and to one's fellows. One's moral commitments are expressed in all one's speech acts as acts of truth telling, they are not a set of propositions that exist in one's mind. More generally put, the meaning of a word does not reside somewhere inside one's head like an object one pins a word to. This notion, that words attach to meanings on the basis of some mental act of binding one to the other, is very much a part of the Enlightenment model of language as ideally a tool for the accurate and unambiguous representation of the truth. According to this model, language improves when speakers connect their words to scientifically refined meanings. Michaelis understands that one cannot attach a word to a meaning by fiat of a committee of experts. In order for the meaning to be tied to the word, the word must be used with its new meaning by a "classical" poet-scientist and then come into common speech with this precedent behind it. But despite the necessity of the public use of the word by the poet, it is clear that Michaelis imagines that a word's meaning is given to it by an internal mental act. This is the picture that Mendelssohn contests.

Mendelssohn argues that the meaning of a word is not learned by affixing the word either to a concept or to a thing that supposedly is an instance of that concept, but by connecting the word to other words. Conveying meaning through speech is not a matter of communicating inner presentations through the medium of words. One can never be sure that the concepts one person may have associated with certain words are the same as the concepts of another person using the same words, and one cannot even be sure that a word we use fully matches the concept we have. In a brilliant turn of phrase, Peter Fenves has described Mendelssohn's skepticism about language's capacity to communicate meaning in a trustworthy manner as leading Mendelssohn "into a sphere where he is in danger of ex-communicating himself" (Fenves 2001: 83). In other words, Mendelssohn's critique of the idea that words are anchored to meanings that can be accessed extralinguistically places him in danger of what Plato in the *Phaedo* (89d1) called "misology," the hatred of language as a betrayer of communication rather than its facilitator.

How does Mendelssohn avoid the danger of misology? How does he account for the possibility of communication, of knowing what another person means? Mendelssohn assumes that meanings are never clearly and precisely conveyed, but that we clarify them through verbal exchanges that lead from one word to another and another until, at last, we seem to using the same words in the same ways, although this agreement in usage does not foreclose the possibility of further disagreement at a later date about the meaning of these same words. Given the significance of Mendelssohn's critique of the mentalist picture of meaning for the entire project of *Jerusalem*, it is useful to quote it in its entirety. The passage is part of Mendelssohn's attack on the legitimacy of demanding oaths as a condition of assuming either a civil or ecclesiastical office.

> The perceptions of the internal sense are rarely so palpable that the mind is able to retain them securely and to give them expression as often as it may be desired. They will slip away from it at times, just when it thinks it has taken hold of them. I may feel sure of something right now, but a moment later, some slight doubt of its certainty may sneak or steal its way into a corner of my soul and lurk there,

without my being aware of its presence. Many things for which I would suffer martyrdom today may perhaps appear problematic to me tomorrow. If, in addition, I must put these internal perceptions into words and signs, or swear to words and signs which other men lay before me, the uncertainty will be still greater. *My neighbor and I cannot possibly connect the very same words with the very same internal sensations, for we cannot compare them, liken them to one another and correct them without again resorting to words. We cannot illustrate the words by things, but must again have recourse to signs and words, and finally, to metaphors; because, with the help of this artifice, we reduce, as it were, the concepts of the internal sense to external sensory perceptions.* But, given this fact, how much confusion and indistinctiveness are bound to remain in the signification of words, and how greatly must the ideas differ which different men, in different ages and centuries, connect with the same external signs and words. (*Jerusalem* 66; 1:76–77; italics mine)

Mendelssohn argues that it simply makes no sense to speak of a sign whose relation to one's internal consciousness is fixed through time or which is identically represented in two different consciousnesses. His argument is quite innovative, and is based upon a consideration of how language represents, or fails to represent, inner states of consciousness. He is saying that one cannot swear that one believes a certain statement because (1) one may retain certain doubts about the truth of the statement "in a corner" of one's soul; (2) one cannot be certain that one will never come to entertain such doubts; (3) one cannot be certain that what one understands the words of the statement to mean are what the words are taken to mean by the oath giver. The last point is the most damaging to the idea of religious oaths. It seems to be the center of this passage's critique of oaths, and it deserves some further explanation.

Mendelssohn argues that words cannot be connected to some internal mental state that can be compared with the internal mental state of another. Mendelssohn is arguing that one cannot assert that two internal mental states are the same except on the basis of signs, and there is no way to affix a sign to an internal state, to make it point at it, so to speak. Even though I can be certain of the truth of the statement "I feel the pain of a toothache," for example, I cannot be certain that it is the *same* pain as I felt a year ago. It may *seem* to be the same pain, but I have no way of checking whether this is true. I may use the same word to describe it (*toothache*), but I cannot be certain that the word corresponds to the identical feeling. What is true about my inability to compare two distinct internal mental states is true for two different people as well. "My neighbor and I cannot possibly connect the very same words with the same internal sensations, for we cannot compare them, liken them to one another and correct them, without resorting to words" (*Jerusalem* 66; 1:76).[25]

Mendelssohn's argument is remarkably similar to the argument that Wittgenstein advances in his *Philosophical Investigations* against the idea that one can name one's sensations through an internal mental act.

> Let us imagine the following case. I want to keep a diary about the recurrence of a certain sensation. To this end I associate it with the sign "S" and write this sign in a calendar for every day on which I have the sensation.—I will remark first of all that a definition of the sign cannot be formulated.—But still I can give myself a kind of ostensive definition.—How? Can I point to the sensation? Not in the ordinary sense. But I speak, or write the sign down, and at the same time concentrate my attention on the sensation—and so, as it were, point to it inwardly.—But what is this ceremony for? for that is all it seems to be! A definition surely serves to establish the meaning of a sign.—Well, that is done precisely by the concentration of my attention; for in this way I impress on myself the connexion between the sign and the sensation.—But "I impress it on myself" can only mean: this process brings it about that I remember the connexion *right* in the future. But in the present case I have no criterion of correctness. One would like to say: whatever is going to seem right to me is right. And that only means that here we can't talk about "right." (*PI* §258)

Wittgenstein's argument here is one of the mainstays of his critique of what he calls "private language." The British philosopher Daniel Hutto summarizes Wittgenstein's critique in a single, succinct sentence: "It cannot be a condition of our ability to use and understand language successfully that we are able to grasp absolutely determinate 'meanings'" (Hutto 2003: 161). Hutto calls this the "intellectualist picture" of language, and it is the target of both Mendelssohn's and Wittgenstein's arguments against the way words attach to meanings by some internal act of focused consciousness. Although Wittgenstein seems uninterested in the political ramifications of the intellectualist picture of language, for Mendelssohn this picture was the mainstay of despotism. As Peter Fenves puts it, Mendelssohn's attack on the intellectualist picture of meaning aims to show that the soul "has a geometry of its own; convictions and doubts cannot be determined in the same way as the world available to outer sense; and therefore the conditions under which one is supposed to swear in the name of the Eternal about the time-bound complexities of one's own soul are always artificial, forced and violent" (Fenves 2001: 85–86). Michaelis had relied upon the intellectualist picture to justify his claim that the oaths of Jews cannot be trusted, that the Jewish "geometry of the soul," we might say, does not conform to the homogeneous space of the Cartesian grid upon which, allegedly, all possible "soul-points" can be plotted. The Jewish soul, Michaelis is suggesting, is incommensurate with the space of humanity. Mendelssohn does not set out to plot the Jewish soul on some universal geometry of the human soul. Rather, he argues that every soul has its own geometry which is never able to be mapped (projected) perfectly onto ordinary language. As Fenves has argued, the spatial dissymetries that divide one soul's geometry from another's are only able to be overcome *in time*, that is, in the patient address and response of conversation. I will explain this temporalization of communication in the next section.

Mendelssohn's Defense of Jewish Interiority

In Mendelssohn's critique of language as requiring identical internal sensations among language users we see clearly the moral context of this critique. We see that it has to do with getting the reader to be tolerant of his fellow in matters of the deepest import, namely, beliefs about God and salvation. We should not admit or refuse to admit our fellow into our society on the basis of a commonly held belief to whose truth one must swear beforehand. Our sociality grows out of the shared commitment to conversation about such beliefs and is based upon our acknowledgment that no fixed proposition can represent a truth that can compel our assent forever. We cannot know with certainty our own minds, and we therefore cannot demand to know the minds of our fellows. In Wittgenstein, the moral context of his argument against private language is not so apparent. It has been the burden of Stanley Cavell's writing on Wittgenstein to demonstrate that the moral context is never far from the surface.[26] In a paragraph not too far from the one about naming sensations, Wittgenstein begins "What gives us *so much as the idea* that living beings, things, can feel?" (*PI*283). Cavell shows that this question, the very heart of the skeptic's doubt, has profound moral implications. It suggests that one's ability to respond to another as a fellow human being is grounded in one's acknowledgment of the other *in the absence of any knowledge of the other's mind or interiority.*

Perhaps the aptest and most relevant passage I can adduce in which Cavell develops the moral dimension of Wittgenstein's philosophy of language comes in his analysis of the famous speech in which Shylock declares: "I am a Jew. Hath not a Jew eyes?" The speech ends: "The villainy you teach me I will execute, and it shall go hard but I will better the instruction" (*Merchant of Venice* 3.1.50–69). Cavell says that when one requires certitude about the other's internal "sentience" and does not acknowledge the humanity of the other without such proof in spite of all the outward marks of the other's humanity, one is precisely denying the other's humanity. Shylock's speech, Cavell argues, is a protest against the idea that a Jew may be *analogically similar* to a human being in all external respects, but because he lacks an inward "Christian sentience," he is not only *different* but, to the Christian, *different from the human* as such. To "prove" his humanity, Shylock in effect says, according to Cavell, "I will take upon myself your sentience," that is, I will convert to "Christian humility," which Shylock understands to be nothing more than, as Cavell says, "vengeance disguised with passiveness." Therefore, in taking his pound of flesh as revenge, Shylock

> is telling us that he perceives Antonio's refusal of acknowledgment as mutilation—the denial, the destruction, of his intactness. His revenge thus speaks: You think my sentience can be at best merely like yours; you hedge mine. I'll show you that you can have exactly mine. And there is also the suggestion: There is no proof for you that I am a man, that I am flesh, until you know that you are flesh. For you to learn this will be my better instruction. (Cavell 1979: 478–79)

Mendelssohn, like Shylock, wants to counter the requirement to "prove" the Jew's humanity by somehow demonstrating the Jew's identical interiority to that of the Christian. Mendelssohn knows that this is a proof that the Jew can never provide. To be sure, no one can provide proof that his or her interiority is identical to that of another, but the Jew cannot even *seem* to do so. We have seen that Michaelis forecloses the possibility of accepting any proof of the Jew's truthful representation of his or her interiority.

The intellectualist picture of language in which a mental act somehow cements words to sensations acquires its philosophical attraction from its apparent refutation of the skeptical claim (advanced by Hume) that sign and signified are only related through associative mental habits that lack any firm foundation in reality. But Mendelssohn and Wittgenstein show that skepticism cannot be overthrown through a philosophy of language that anchors words to meanings by internal mental acts. Such anchoring cannot generate knowledge that is rationally verifiable by reference to external sensory evidence. Skepticism is, in fact, never simply overthrown. It is *accepted* as the very condition of our tolerant, humane sociality. Cavell reads Wittgenstein as making a case for *living with skepticism* by accepting that ordinary language is epistemologically and metaphysically foundationless. Learning to live with skepticism is, according to Cavell, the beginning of the moral life. Cavell's reading of Wittgenstein draws some of its textual support from several passages in the *Philosophical Investigations* that seem to carry a moral weight, as when Wittgenstein says that one's attitude to another human being is not based upon a belief about the other, as, for example, that the other "is not an automaton"; rather, "my attitude towards him is an attitude towards a soul. I am not of the *opinion* that he has a soul" (*PI* II.iv, 178e).

The claim that Wittgenstein is making in this last remark captures very well the entire moral thrust of Mendelssohn's philosophy of language in *Jerusalem*, namely, that sociality becomes fully human only when we do not base it upon commonly accepted beliefs, but upon a commonly shared condition of embodied, creaturely finitude. Mendelssohn attacks the philosophical presupposition underlying oath taking. This presupposition states that attaching meaning to words is an internal mental act, something like a focusing of the mind on an object residing within it. Mendelssohn says that one does not establish the meaning of words by an act of focusing one's mind on its contents and declaring, for example, "I believe that *God* refers to the Trinity of Father, Son, and Holy Spirit." The content of one's belief about a word's meaning can only be expressed by using other words, and their meanings can only be expressed in different words. The process is endless, and if two people ever come to agreement about the meaning of a disputed word, it is an agreement that will always be tested as new contexts arise where the word has not previously been used and new questions arise about how to apply the word in these contexts. No meaning is final. But while this might seem to lead to radical skepticism about all communication, Mendelssohn draws another moral from the inescapable necessity of multiplying words upon words: Instead of leading one to skepticism, the endlessness of talk holds the promise of human fellowship in tolerance and friendship. Immediately after the long paragraph I quoted above in which he argues against the intellectualist picture of how words acquire their meanings, Mendelssohn continues:

> Dear reader, whoever you may be, do not accuse me of skepticism or of employing some evil ruse in order to turn you into a skeptic. I am perhaps one of those who are furthest removed from that disease of the soul, and who most ardently wish to be able to cure all their fellow men of it. But precisely because I have so often performed this cure on myself, and tried it on others, I have become aware of how difficult it is, and what little hope one has of success. With my best friend [no doubt Lessing is meant], whom I believed to be ever so much in accord with me, I have very often failed to come to terms about certain truths of philosophy and religion . . . Nevertheless, our ideas had to rub against each other for a long time before they could be made to fit themselves to one another, and before we could say with any assurance: Here we agree! Oh! I should not like to have for a friend anyone who has had this experience in his lifetime, and can still be intolerant, and can still hate his neighbor because he does not think or express himself on religious matters in the same way as he does; for he has divested himself of all humanity. (*Jerusalem* 66–7; 1:77–78)

To recognize that one does not know one's own mind with certainty allows one to acknowledge the other in all his or her heterogeneity. If we accept the fact that we are strangers to ourselves, we cannot hate the strangers outside ourselves. The beginning of tolerance is the acceptance of the unbridgeable gap separating words from fixed meanings, the unclosable chasm between sign and signified. The joint participation in conversation with one's friend in the unfolding of a tentative agreement about the meaning of one's words is the model for how a tolerant and enlightened society should work. Again, this society is not envisioned as a vague, future ideal. It precisely brings to expression the ideal unity of church of state. It is Judaism. Peter Fenves describes Judaism's ceremonial laws as enjoining an ongoing "Feier" ("solemn celebration") that is also an ongoing conversation: "Judaism makes it possible for the longevity of conversations about the nature of the Eternal to come into line with the swiftness of occasions consecrated in and by the divine name" (Fenves 2001: 89). I will explain Judaism's temporality of the "Feier" in greater detail in the next section.

Mendelssohn on Judaism as a "Living Script"

I have argued that Mendelssohn's critique of how meanings attach to words is based upon a thought experiment—attempting to identify two internal sensations as the same by an act of internal naming—that is repeated in Wittgenstein's *Philosophical Investigations*. Wittgenstein wants to replace the idea of meaning as an internal mental act of naming with the more flexible concept of "language game" in which the use of words is governed by criteria that are never given as fixed rules, but are rather clarified as "moves" that are made and contested; that is, as words are transferred into new contexts and new meanings—new "metaphors" as Mendelssohn would say—those contexts and meanings become part of the word's signification. Another way that Wittgenstein says that criteria are made explicit is when the game is taught: "One learns the game by watching how others play. But we say that it is played according to such-and-such rules because an observer can read these rules off from the practice of the game . . ." (*PI* §54). Learning a game requires that it be played; understanding a word means making it one's own by making new moves with it, sometimes successfully and sometimes not. Wittgenstein, like Mendelssohn before him, is not frightened by the possibility that a word's meaning will always have a measure of "confusion and indistinctiveness." Wittgenstein writes: "One might say that the concept 'game' is a concept with blurred edges" (*PI* §71). For Mendelssohn, acknowledging this confusion is the very possibility of tolerance and friendship.

In her *Life of the Mind* (1978), Hannah Arendt takes Wittgenstein's embrace of "language games" to be another way of saying that thinking happens in language and not in a single vision or intuition of the truth (see 100ff.). And she further understands Wittgenstein's notion of the game-like nature of language to capture something fundamental about thinking, namely, that it is not designed to serve a purpose beyond itself, as if it were a sort of tool. Games end after a certain defined point is reached, but the play is not the *means* towards this end. If thinking is a language game, its purpose is found within itself, and if it is an open-ended game that never ends, then the point is to keep it going. Arendt, very much like Mendelssohn, says that "language is entirely metaphorical" and, also like Mendelssohn, that the metaphor "bridges the gulf between the visible and the invisible" (123), the gulf between the world we share and the inner world of our thoughts. The problem for Arendt is to find a metaphor for thinking itself that does not freeze the open-endedness of language in a fixed image that reifies the thinking process. The metaphor of game can capture something about the noninstrumental aspect of the thinking process, but it does not serve well to capture its open-ended nature. "The quest for meaning,"

Arendt says, "produces no end result that will survive the activity, that will make sense after the activity has come to an end . . . The only possible metaphor one may conceive of for the life of the mind is the sensation of being alive. *Without the breath of life the human body is a corpse; without thinking the human mind is dead*" (123). For Arendt, thinking is *the life of the mind*. This suggests that language as open-ended conversational sociality is the medium in which human life comes most fully to expression. I think this is a view that Wittgenstein would share. It is certainly at the heart of Mendelssohn's philosophy of language. But, as we have seen, this philosophy of language is advanced within the context of an argument that the Jewish people should be admitted as equals to civil society without having to prove that their interiority is identical to that of their Christian neighbors. But we may ask if Mendelssohn is perhaps offering his readers not only a critical argument about the legitimate demands we may make as a condition of entrance into civil society, but also a positive evaluation of Judaism as the very embodiment of an ideal, noncoercive, tolerant sociality. We will find support for this as we now turn to Mendelssohn's discussion of Judaism in section 2 of *Jerusalem*. We will see that for Mendelssohn the Jewish people, preeminently among all nations, embody what Arendt calls "the life of the mind," the unending conversation that expresses our task as humans. The Jewish people embody the life of the mind in their performance of the ceremonial laws, and it is for this reason that Mendelssohn can find no higher expression of his philosophical identity than his conformity to the Jewish law. This will constitute his answer to Cranz, whose challenge to Mendelssohn's theory of the noncoercive nature of religion sparked the writing of *Jerusalem*. Arnold Eisen has written that Mendelssohn's theory of Jewish people as a "living script" is "the most intrinsically interesting section" of all of *Jerusalem* (Eisen 1990: 240). I hope in what follows to show the foundations of this judgment

We have seen that Mendelssohn believes that every society must eventually make use of writing in order to represent what had previously been the living, face-to-face transmission of culture through oral teaching. And writing, as I discussed in the section above on the "dialectic of enlightenment," inevitably leads to the reification of the sign over the signified.[27] The signified, the thought represented by the sign, never was fixed in one's mind permanently, but was always open to question, doubt, and further clarification. The sign, however, seemed to give the thought a certain permanence, and seemed therefore to render it *beyond question*. The sign made further thinking unnecessary. According to Mendelssohn's review of human history, for the large majority of people, a superstitious belief in the sanctity of the sign answered all doubts and replaced the need to think. For those in power, such superstition suited their interest in maintaining the people in a state of ignorance. In fact, the more the signs were disconnected from the thoughts they originally conveyed, the more powerful and mysterious they seemed in themselves. Efforts to reconnect signs and thoughts, to demystify the signs, were met with resistance, or were simply made into new opportunities to endow a new set of signs with mysterious power. The Pythagoreans, Mendelssohn explains, tried to use signs of such abstraction—numbers—that no one could take them as meaningful in themselves. But the effort was foiled when people began to look for "a secret power in the numbers themselves" which only led, once more, to "folly," the idolatrous worship of numbers as gods (*Jerusalem* 117; 2:92–93). Later Greek philosophers criticized this number mysticism, but their abstractions in turn fell prey to the human tendency to reify signs.

If we connect this "dialectic of enlightenment" with what Mendelssohn says about the necessity of adding words to words in order to come to a tentative agreement about meanings, we can see that taking an oath is like reifying a sign. When a group insists upon having its members swear an oath to certain beliefs, they are, in effect, claiming that a certain arrangement of words can represent God so perfectly and with such precision that future refinements are impossible. But no finite arrangement of words can represent the infinite God. Swearing an oath to a dogma is the worship of idols.

It is therefore of critical importance for any religion that seeks to avoid idolatry that it not put its beliefs into writing. An ecclesiastical society, as Mendelssohn explained in section 1 of *Jerusalem*, should only seek to promote benevolence through benevolence, i.e., through noncoercive means. The most seductive form of coercion, because it is not the sheer exercise of force, is coercion through words. The written word is, by its very nature, coercive. It seems more permanent and therefore more true than speech. But how can an ecclesiastical society be formed that is not based upon the written word? Mendelssohn believes that no writing is necessary for a free, rational human to come to a basic understanding of the nature of God as the benevolent Creator of the world. It would therefore be true to say that all of humanity constitutes a single ecclesiastical society. Because this society cannot coerce obedience, it can only be formed out of the free acceptance of the debt one owes to the infinitely benevolent God. This debt, Mendelssohn says, can only be repaid by freely offering benevolence to one's fellow human, the only duty we owe to God. And thus religious society points back to civil society, and ought to be indistinguishable from civil society *in its ideal form of noncoerced mutual benevolence*: "serving the state is the true service of God" (*Jerusalem* 43; 1:24). I have previously referred to Jeffrey Librett's discussion of the aporia at the heart of *Jerusalem*, namely, how to unify church and state without creating a despotic religious power. I suggested that Mendelssohn offers Judaism as a model for resolving this aporia. Mendelssohn is aware that Judaism in any of its historical configurations is not the perfect instantiation of the union of church and state. Rather, Judaism serves as what might be called a critical ideal. The best that can be hoped for in history is that the drive to the idolatry of the sign—to one or another form of religious despotism—be checked by a counter-drive to demystify the sign. This is the function of Judaism in history.

Judaism's legislation creates both a religious and a civil society. As the ideal interweaving of religion and civil realms, there is no creed distinguishing those who are members of the community (i.e., those consenting to the creed) from those outside the community. Judaism, Mendelssohn insists, possesses no special religious dogmas but relies entirely on the free exercise of reason to provide such knowledge of God as any human is capable of. And the laws by which Jewish society is created are both oral and written, making it impossible to fix them once and for all in writing. The "Mosaic constitution" of ancient Israel consisted of laws commanded by God; these were partly disseminated in writing as preserved in the legal portions of the first five books of Moses, but were mostly shared in orally transmitted teachings. The authority of these laws did not rest upon a coercive human power, but upon the miraculous speech of God at Mt. Sinai to the assembled people, and God's continuing revelation of the law to Moses during the forty days and nights he remained on Mt. Sinai and then throughout the forty years of wandering in the desert. Mendelssohn admits that the divine origin of the law is not something that can be rationally demonstrated, but neither is it an article of a creed to which each Jew must swear. It is, to be sure, believed to be true on faith, but the belief itself is not commanded by God, and the very term *faith* should not be interpreted as equivalent to *belief*. Mendelssohn explains that the term translated commonly as *faith* (der Glauben) in the Hebrew Bible is "in most cases, *trust, confidence*, and firm reliance on pledge or promise" (*Jerusalem* 100; 2:54). When the Jewish people accept on faith the divine origin of their law, this is not based upon an epistemic act consisting of believing a certain proposition to be true. Rather, they are responding with trust and confidence to an orally transmitted tradition, offered by one generation to the next in fulfillment of the promise and pledge made at Mt. Sinai that "we will do and we will obey." To place one's trust in this tradition is to accept the obligation to abide by the laws and to teach them to the next generation.

The legislation revealed to Moses at Mt. Sinai is received by Israel as a gift of divine benevolence, and this is its entire sanction. The laws of the Mosaic constitution, unlike those of all other civil societies, including the Israelite kingdom under the Davidic monarchy, do not demand any alienation of the rights of conscience—the imperfect duties to offer benevolence to the human race—to a higher, coercive power. Mendelssohn goes so far as to argue that infractions of the laws of the original Mosaic constitution *are not, strictly speaking, punished*. When a civil law is transgressed, the punishment meted out by the state reflects the failure of the state in this instance to elicit free and benevolent (nonselfish) action from the citizen. The punishment is not intended to elicit such benevolence, and is not therefore itself an act of benevolence. Mendelssohn is very clear that state power is invoked when loving persuasion and teaching has failed to elicit its desired response. But in the Mosaic constitution, the punishment meted out to those who willingly reject the sanction of the law, divine benevolence, is itself an act of divine benevolence. Mendelssohn declares that it is "a quality of divine love that for man nothing is allowed to go entirely unpunished" (*Jerusalem* 123; 2:105).

It may be difficult to accept Mendelssohn's interpretation of the death penalty that was handed down for breaking the Sabbath law as an act of divine love. Mendelssohn is himself aware that this may at first seem special pleading on behalf of the uniqueness of Jewish law, so he spends considerable time explaining his point. Mendelssohn says that in ancient Israel, if corporal punishment or the death penalty were to be handed down, "the criminal had *to have acknowledged the punishment in express words*" and then in the presence of witnesses the criminal must then have "*committed the crime immediately afterwards*" (*Jerusalem* 129; 2:119). In other words, the criminal must first demonstrate that his action springs from a complete rejection of the benevolence of God, and the infliction of the punishment becomes his own freely accepted subjection to the law. "In the state of this paternal ruler, the transgressor suffers no other punishment than the one he himself must wish to suffer were he to see its effects and consequences in their true light" (*Jerusalem* 124; 2:108). Even the death penalty, which one might imagine would make impossible any such recognition of God's love in the punishment, falls under this principle. If the transgressor does not acknowledge before his death that the punishment he is about to receive is what he himself would have wished for, he will ultimately acknowledge this after his death. Mendelssohn rejects the possibility of an infinitely extended punishment in the afterlife, or of a divinely sanctioned punishment in this life that is not aimed at bringing about repentance. The divine law, Mendelssohn insists, has no element of coercion within it and is not supposed to be obeyed out of fear.

Judaism, then, is not a religion (with a creed) but is rather a "revealed legislation" that models the ideal interweaving of civil and religious spheres as one unified expression of divine benevolence in human life. "In the original constitution," Mendelssohn declares, "state and religion were not conjoined [vereiniget], but *one* [eins]" (*Jerusalem* 128; 2:117). Having denied that Judaism contains doctrines to which allegiance must be sworn as a condition of membership in the Jewish religious society, Mendelssohn has opened himself to the objection, raised by the August Cranz in his pamphlet *Das Forschen nach Licht und Recht*, that in order to be truly free of coercion, the Jew should abandon the ceremonial laws that seem to lack all basis in reason and have no coercive force over the Jew. Mendelssohn counters this objection by arguing, as we have just seen, that the absence of coercive force is a sign of the presence of divine love and benevolence towards the Jewish people. Mendelssohn is clearly conscious of the Christian attack on the Jewish law as an expression of divine wrath, which was supplanted by divine love with the dispensation of the new covenant in Christ. No, says Mendelssohn, divine love is what is at work in Jewish law, even in its punishments. But this argument addresses only one arm of the objection raised by Cranz against him. Why, if love is revealed in Jewish legislation, should the Jew find it necessary to maintain his commitment to the law if a more direct, and more rational, expression of divine love is found in the teaching of Jesus in the New Testament? Is not *imitatio Christi* an advance upon Jewish ritual performance?

Mendelssohn's reply to the question of why the New Testament's offer of divine love in Christ should not draw the Jew away from the law is not intended to challenge Christianity directly, but it cannot help but do so. Mendelssohn defends the rationality of Jewish ritual performance on the basis of the argument that every visible or written sign inevitably devolves into an idol that stands in place of the signified reality. Jewish ritual performance, on the other hand, is a living sign system that cannot be reified into one fixed symbol. Jewish performativity, if I may be permitted to call it this, does not translate into action the written laws of the Hebrew Bible, but rather it expresses the conversational sociality that is constituted as speech partners seek together to interpret the meanings of the words they use. As I have explained, this conversational sociality is the living expression of language's open-endedness, the process whereby "living, spiritual instruction" creates and is in turn sustained by a community of tolerant friends. The revealed legislation of the Hebrew Bible, accompanied by an oral interpretation that was not supposed to be written down, is rational because such a revelation provides its own built-in prophylactic against the idolization of the sign over the signified, of the image over the original. We can now see that Mendelssohn's critique of the Enlightenment model of language is intimately connected to a critique of the claim that Christ has supplanted the law. Mendelssohn says that if divine love is to be revealed in history, it makes most sense that it be revealed as a law whose performance is a "kind of living script, rousing the mind and heart, full of meaning, never ceasing to inspire contemplation and to provide the occasion and opportunity for oral instruction" (*Jerusalem* 102–3; 2:60).[28] To fix revelation in a single image of divine love is to invite idolatry, whether of the image itself or of some doctrinal interpretation of how the image incarnates divine love. Thus, the letter of the ceremonial law of Judaism is alive, whereas the alleged consummation and overcoming of the law in Christ threatens death, or at least can be used to threaten death when it becomes fixed as religious dogma whose criticism is *heresy*. The living power of the letter of the law—its transmission across the generations through its incitement to conversation—is aptly described in Goetschel's characterization of it as "an imaginative and consistent resource for tradition to constantly regenerate" (Goetschel 2004: 163).

It should be clear now why Mendelssohn believes that without Judaism's emphasis upon the observance of the law, Judaism would be left with nothing that ties it to its origin in the covenant at Mt. Sinai, and nothing that can provide for its continuing life. Judaism has no creedal doctrines that could serve to bind together its religious society. After the destruction of the second Temple in 70 CE, "the civil bonds of the nation were dissolved; religious offenses were no longer crimes against the state; and the religion, as religion, knows of no punishment, no other penalty than the one the remorseful sinner *voluntarily* imposes upon himself. It knows of no coercion, uses only the staff [called] *gentleness*, and affects only mind and heart" (*Jerusalem* 130; 2:122). What Mendelssohn is saying here is that through the loss of its civil society, the Jewish people have become the most perfect representatives of what a religious society should be, the voluntary association of those who acknowledge God's benevolent love and lovingly respond to this divine gift. This response is enacted when one fulfills the commandment, "Love thy neighbor as thyself." Judaism binds its society together through a shared trusting response to the commanding voice of God in its laws. Judaism has nothing more to teach about the nature of God than what any human could grasp with unaided reason. God has, therefore, revealed Himself to humanity in two ways: to human reason, which is capable of grasping that God is "the necessary, independent being, omnipotent and omniscient, that recompenses men in a future life according their deeds" (*Jerusalem* 97; 2:48), and to the Jewish people, in the gift of laws which guide their society towards felicity in this life and in the next. The first is a universal revelation, and the second is a historical embodiment of this universal truth. The first, Mendelssohn will say, is the "universal religion of mankind," and the second is "revealed legislation," and is not, in the common meaning of the term, a *religion* at all. Judaism is a "living script" whose goal is to arouse questions in the minds of those who behold its performative enactment: "What a student himself did and saw being done morning till night pointed to religious doctrines and convictions and spurred him on to follow his teacher, to watch him, to observe all his actions, and to obtain the instruction which he is capable of acquiring by means of his talents of which he had rendered himself worthy by his conduct" (*Jerusalem* 103; 2:60). The questioning mind of the youth is not focused upon doctrinal propositions, but upon the actions that are taken to be signs of divine benevolence. The exemplary figure of the rabbi is the embodiment of the written and the oral law, and he is meant to be *read*. The performative script that is the living law-observant Jew cannot be given one final reading. In contrast with "visible signs" that are reified into fixed truths, the living script of the Jewish people must be reinterpreted in every generation, and thus the survival of the Jewish people is guaranteed precisely because no generation can bring its interpretive history to a close. In living the law out of the moral force based upon trust in the covenant, the speech-acts of the Jewish people display how language is, in its ideal form, *covenantal performance*.

It is not the case that, according to Mendelssohn, Judaism has never been seduced by the written word to put the sign before the signified. In his own day, Mendelssohn admits that there are many Jews who would dispute his interpretation of the noncoercive, open-ended nature of the law. But Judaism has largely managed to triumph over the seduction of writing because what the written text of the Hebrew Bible reveals is not a set of propositions about God, but a set of commandments, unenactable without oral interpretation, aimed at eliciting actions that in turn are aimed at opening questions about the meaning of these actions. The written laws are not declarative or constative affirmations that are either true or false. They are voiced in the Hebrew Bible as perlocutionary utterances whose *truth*, if we may use this term (I would suggest *felicity* if this did not threaten to raise unnecessary confusion between Austin's and Mendelssohn's use of this term), lies in their being embodied in living practice. Their performance, to be sure, is related to a belief in the divine origin of the voice commanding them, but the belief emerges out of their performance: The performance of the laws "guide[s] the inquiring intelligence to divine truths, partly to eternal and partly to historical truths upon which the religion of this people was founded" (*Jerusalem* 128; 2:116). In a succinct summary of the relationship between the inquiring intelligence and the life in which it is embodied, Mendelssohn says that "the ceremonial law was the bond which was to connect action with contemplation, life with theory" (*Jerusalem* 128; 2:116).

By the end of *Jerusalem*, the reader should be led to the view that Judaism's foundation in a noncoercive, orthodoxy-free association brings it closer to being a rational form of religious community than Christianity. Willi Goetschel has said that if Mendelssohn had carried out an explicit comparison of Judaism and Christianity in regard to their relative compatibility with the religion of reason, the result "would come out to the latter's [i.e., Christianity's] disadvantage" (Goetschel 2004: 124).[29] Mendelssohn argues that orthodoxy—a creed that members of the religious community must swear to accept as true—is inherently contradictory and therefore irrational. Mendelssohn has pushed his claims so far as to call into question the rationality of any civil society that will not make a place for the Jewish people as equals. Further, he has left Christian theology without any justifiable claim to represent the revealed truth. The only truth about God is one that is consonant with reason and is available to all humans universally. Finally, Mendelssohn's attack upon all visible signs as ultimately degenerating into idolatry can only suggest to a perceptive reader that the image of Christ is inevitably the close ally of religious despotism. In the end, one may wonder what Mendelssohn would suggest a non-Jew should do to participate in a religious society. Mendelssohn answers this question in his response essay in the *Berlinische Monatschrift*, "On the Question: What Does 'To Enlighten' Mean?" (Mendelssohn 1997: 313–17). Just as Judaism is the bond of theory and life in a single "living script," Mendelssohn will define *Bildung* ("education") as the conjunction of theory (*Aufklärung* or "enlightenment") and practice (*Kultur*) in the nation. Thus, *Bildung* is offered in the essay as doing for the nation what Judaism does for the Jewish people. It aligns the life practices of a people with an enlightened, critical rationality that checks any nascent idolatry within the society.

The Jewish people embody "what it means 'to enlighten.'" As I have mentioned earlier, Mendelssohn sees the Jewish people as acting in the role that Lessing had assigned to the hidden band of enlighteners in every society who live by no fixed creed and who do hidden works of benevolence. Because the Jewish people are the living words of the historical revelation of God, when they enter as equals into civil society, God may be said to dwell in the society's midst. In effect, the Jewish people, as long as they maintain their ceremonial law, render each nation in which they live into a new, terrestrial Jerusalem, the site of God's presence. This is the reason, I venture to suggest, that Mendelssohn has titled his book *Jerusalem*. Willi Goetschel has persuasively argued that the title alludes to the prophecy of the prophet Zechariah (8:22) that "many great peoples and the multitude of nations shall come to seek the LORD of hosts in Jerusalem" (New JPS trans.). Mendelssohn twice in *Jerusalem* refers to the words of the prophet "love peace and truth": once in a note (*Jerusalem* 101; 2:57) and also in the final line of the book. These words from Zechariah come immediately before the verses that predict that Jerusalem will become the center of the world's worship of God. Goetschel interprets the reference to Jerusalem as Mendelssohn's rejoinder to the Christian hermeneutic of the church as the "new" Jerusalem. Mendelssohn counters this by stressing the Jewish understanding of Jerusalem as both particular to the Jewish people and also universally accessible to all nations. "Jerusalem," Goetschel states, "symbolizes the universal in the shape of a locality, history, and particular religion" (2004: 148). I agree with Goetschel, but I would stress that Mendelssohn identifies the particular Jerusalem where God is worshipped as *the living script enacted by the Jewish people*. Jerusalem *lives* in the in the midst of the nations. If the nations truly "love peace and truth," they cannot fail to recognize the Jewish people as God's indwelling presence in their midst.

Not only is there no way for a nonrational divine revelation to manifest itself in the nation other than in the living performance of the Jewish law, there is no other way to protect the freedom of reason itself from despotism—Mendelssohn in the first pages of *Jerusalem* had argued that Hobbes sacrificed the freedom of conscience to the despotism of sovereign power—than by respecting the heterogeneity of the Jewish law, its irreducibility to any proposed rational system of truths. Suppose, says Mendelssohn, that a consensus about religious truth could be reached, would this be desirable? Given the inability of humans to find agreement about any but tautological logical truths, a unification of religions would be merely verbal. "Oh, if this universal hypocrisy shall have any purpose whatsoever, I fear it would be intended as a first step again to confine within narrow bounds the now liberated spirit of man" (*Jerusalem* 137; 2:137–38). Against all efforts to resolve religious conflicts in the name of a single unified church of humanity, Judaism raises its dissident voice in the name of the ineradicable heterogeneity in the very heart of humanity. The fact that "God has stamped everyone, not without reason, with his own facial features" is a sign that to seek after unanimity of expressed belief and transparency of interior intentionality as social ideals is "deliberately to contravene our calling, our vocation [Bestimmung] in this life and the next" (*Jerusalem* 138; 2:139).[30]

According to *Jerusalem*, humanity's vocation requires an acknowledgment of human diversity. It requires that one call into question the reified idolatry of the sign in whatever form this may assume. We can conclude from this that the Jewish people, insofar as their religious practice shows that revelation cannot be truthfully represented except in the "living script" of covenantal performance, bear the responsibility of displaying how a nation should fulfill the "calling and vocation" of humanity itself. The Jewish people model the ideal of enlightened sociality, and their resistance to the hegemony of a single regime of truth is an inescapable element of their enlightened condition. Mendelssohn has, unlike Dohm, offered an account of why admission of the Jews into civil equality with Christians is necessary on the grounds that the Christian nation cannot reach enlightenment without the Jews. An enlightened nation is tested by how well it reads the "living script" of the Jewish people. Mendelssohn's stress upon the enlightened society being one where heterogeneity is accepted and where, to the greatest extent possible, the state dispenses with coercive measures to guarantee acts of benevolence, was perhaps idealistic. In his somewhat ambiguous praise of the utopian vision of *Jerusalem*, J. G. Herder wrote in a letter to Mendelssohn that "in the Jerusalem above us or that will come in the future, I grant that no one there would doubt the truth of your theory" (Mendelssohn 1979: 193).

If the Jews themselves have obscured the clarity of their script by routinizing the law into fixed prescriptions, Mendelssohn will take it upon himself to bear the burden of Jewish writing. In effect, Mendelssohn offers himself as a Jew who must be read if enlightenment is to be realized in Germany's civil society. His writing poses challenges to both Christians and Jews: Can Christian Germans read this Jew or will they turn away from him, as Michaelis does, as someone who threatens the truths and the oaths that guarantee their social coherence? Will Jews in Germany respond to his call to them to fulfill their task as a distinct people? This is the challenge Mendelssohn poses to his readers, whether Christian or Jewish, who wish to create an enlightened nation together.

TWO

Jacobi and Mendelssohn: The Tragedy of a Messianic Friendship

> Vielleicht erleben wir es noch, daß über den Leichnam des Spinoza sich ein Streit erhebt, wie jener über den Leichnam Moses zwischen dem Erzengel und Satanas.
>
> (Perhaps we shall live to witness a battle over the corpse of Spinoza like that former one between the Archangel and Satan over the corpse of Moses.)
>
> Letter of Friedrich Heinrich Jacobi to Moses Mendelssohn, April 26, 1785

> Tragödie des Juden bis heute: Mendelssohn und Lessing ... Die Freundschaft von Mendelssohn und Lessing war zu messianisch.
>
> (The tragedy of the Jew until today: Mendelssohn and Lessing ... The friendship of Mendelssohn and Lessing was too messianic.)
>
> FRANZ ROSENZWEIG, "Lessings Nathan"[1]

Introduction: Background to the Spinoza Quarrel

For nearly two years, from November, 1783 until October, 1785, Moses Mendelssohn and Friedrich Heinrich Jacobi engaged in an exchange of letters that proved to be of overwhelming significance for the future of philosophy. Jacobi published the narrative of this epistolary philosophical quarrel, with full texts of his own letters and excerpts or summaries of Mendelssohn's, in a work entitled *Über die Lehre des Spinoza in Briefen an den Herrn Moses Mendelssohn* (*Concerning the Doctrine of Spinoza in Letters to Herr Moses Mendelssohn*).[2] Jacobi's central claim in his *Spinoza-Letters* was that Germany's most famous spokesperson for the Enlightenment vision of a religiously tolerant society, Gotthold Ephraim Lessing, was a "decided Spinozist." In his first letter to Mendelssohn (of November, 1783), Jacobi reported the details of conversations about Spinoza that he had had with Lessing in the summer of 1780, six months before Lessing's death on February 15, 1781.[3]

In those conversations, according to Jacobi, Lessing revealed himself to be a believer in the *hen kai pan*, the "One and All," which he identified with the infinite, all-encompassing God of Spinoza, a God indistinguishable from the infinitude of Nature itself. The "One and All" has neither temporal beginning nor end, and no greater importance attaches to any single point or possibility within it than to any other. All things are equal insofar as they are the finite and evanescent manifestations of the one divine substance that underlies them all. The "One and All" does not give pride of place to human beings, with their hopes and aspirations; seen from the perspective of the unchanging reality of God, there is no freedom of the will and no capacity to alter the inexorable and infinitely extended chain of causes and effects in which the human subject is enmeshed. Nature is merely the endless shadow-play of coming to be and passing away, lacking design or moral purpose. George di Giovanni nicely summarizes the argument that Jacobi claimed to have had with Lessing:[4]

> If one is to believe Jacobi's report of his 1779 conversation with Lessing,[5] the point he had been arguing with him was that the philosophers, driven by their enthusiasm for explanation, are given to mistaking conditions of explanation for conditions of existence, and hence to assuming that reality conforms to the abstractions that philosophers have created. Since such abstractions leave behind the individuality of actual human beings, and since, however, it is only as individuals that these beings can be the subjects of action, it follows that the philosophers' view of reality does not allow for genuine action. As Jacobi famously put it, in a world such as the philosophers conceive it, one should not say that Raphael painted the *School of Athens*, but rather that an anonymous efficacy has made its way across the world and had resulted in something that we call the *School of Athens* and associate with the name of Raphael. That, according to Jacobi, was the ultimate implication of the Spinozist formula of the *hen kai pan* ("one and all"). (di Giovanni 2005: 13)

Jacobi's target is the idea that for every existing thing, there must be an explanation for why it is the thing it is, i.e. why it exists with exactly the set of properties it has and why all other possible sets of properties were not actualized. Confusing conditions of explanation with conditions of existence,[6] philosophers then seek for a single cause of each thing's existence. Since each source calls in turn for explanation, philosophers look for a single source for the existence of *all* things. Spinozism, at least as Jacobi interprets it, is the position that there can only be one ultimate source for all objects and that nothing exists independently of this one source. According to this position, each finite object is a dependent part of an infinite whole. The identity and existence of the part is entirely determined by the whole. Self-determination is a chimera. Philosophy thus begins by trying to explain the unique, individual identities of things and, with Spinoza, it ends by denying the independent existence of any individual. Put differently, explanation cancels *free* existence.[7]

In this chapter I will discuss in detail the profoundly significant ramifications of Jacobi's arguments against Spinozism, which he first developed in *Spinoza-Letters* in reported conversations with a Spinozist-leaning Lessing and in letters with Mendelssohn, a defender of rationalist philosophy if not of Spinozism as such. In the next section I will argue that Jacobi's critique of Spinozism is, to put it in a word, *gnostic*. Jacobi shares with ancient gnosticism a fundamental rejection of the Jewish God in favor of a higher divinity who reveals himself in a special form of knowledge (*gnosis*) to select individuals. In the subsequent section, I will offer a more detailed account of Jacobi's critique of the Enlightenment's "religion of reason," of which Mendelssohn had been the most prominent exponent in the 1780s when Jacobi launched his gnostic assault against the Jewish God who, Jacobi argued, was the projection of "degenerate reason" (*Spinoza-Letters* 232; 166). This account of Jacobi's assault on the Jewish God of "degenerate reason" will take me beyond his *Spinoza-Letters* to several of his other works, published from 1789 to 1815. In the fourth section of the chapter, I will turn to Mendelssohn's response to Jacobi's gnostic assault against the Jewish God. I will discuss the transition from Mendelssohn's defense of the religion of reason on its own terms in *Morning Hours* (published in 1785, with *Spinoza-Letters* released quickly afterwards as a counter to the work) to his aggressive posture in his last work, *To the Friends of Lessing* (1786), where Mendelssohn champions Judaism and the religion of reason as the Enlightenment's best defenses against what Mendelssohn takes to be Jacobi's Christian "fanaticism" ("Schwärmerei").

I have subtitled this chapter "The Tragedy of a Messianic Friendship." Rosenzweig, as I will presently explain, thought that the friendship between Mendelssohn and Lessing was "too messianic," and I believe that Jacobi sensed this as well. When Jacobi wrote to Mendelssohn about Lessing's Spinozistic atheism, he was attempting to do two things that might, on the face of it, seem contradictory. First, he wanted to shock Mendelssohn and make him feel that he, Jacobi, in but a matter of weeks, had been taken into Lessing's intimate trust, whereas Mendelssohn had been held at arm's length over the course of his decades-long friendship with Lessing. Jacobi even wrote to Mendelssohn about Lessing's motive for this reserve, saying that Lessing told him that he wanted to spare Mendelssohn's more religious sensibility. Second, Jacobi wanted to paint both Lessing and Mendelssohn with the same brush of hyper-rationalistic atheism. Jacobi seems, in other words, to have wanted to claim Lessing for himself, but then to attack Lessing and Mendelssohn as if they were one persona. The contradiction is partially resolved if we understand Jacobi to be attacking the cultural image that Mendelssohn and Lessing had forged, that of a Christian and Jew who had found a way to live together in friendship beyond their religious differences. Jacobi would not be content until he had destroyed both the reality of this friendship (by making Mendelssohn feel that Lessing had never revealed himself completely to him), and the public image of Jewish-Christian enlightened tolerance that this friendship had come to assume. Jacobi sensed that Mendelssohn and Lessing were pushing humanity towards a resolution of the conflict between Christianity and Judaism that would, in effect, reduce Christianity to (Spinozistic) Judaism.

Rosenzweig, like Jacobi, saw the Mendelssohn-Lessing friendship as one based upon a neutralization of both Christianity and Judaism. Unlike Jacobi, Rosenzweig envisioned a different sort of "friendship" between Christian and Jew that would allow each in their separate performances of revelation to participate in the work of the redemption of the world. I think that Mendelssohn sought just this kind of messianic friendship, but Lessing was not capable of joining him. Jacobi forced Mendelssohn to confront this truth. Jacobi forced Mendelssohn to recognize that even his best friend, however tolerant of Jewish difference, nonetheless fundamentally agreed with Spinoza that Judaism's rituals had no reason to exist in an enlightened society. I argued in Chapter 1 that Mendelssohn in *Jerusalem* sought to counter Lessing's progressivist view of history, while at the same time embracing Lessing as an ideal conversational partner. Jacobi forced Mendelssohn to recognize that his disagreement with Lessing could not be resolved by "agreeing to disagree" about Judaism, by stressing Lessing's broad tolerance for religious difference over his views about history's progress. To achieve resolution, Mendelssohn would have to show that the God of Israel was not only his God, but Lessing's God as well, even though Lessing might name Him the "One and All." In the end, Mendelssohn's struggle to reconcile the God of Israel with Lessing's God exceeded his powers.

While Franz Rosenzweig may not have directly intended in his philosophy of revelation to resolve the quarrel between Mendelssohn and Jacobi, he did see his task in the history of German-Jewish relations to be the renewal of the conditions of possibility of a reconfigured Mendelssohn-Lessing friendship. He wrote: "The friendship of Mendelssohn and Lessing was too messianic. What it lacked was the blood of presentness. Can it only be like this? In any case: the basis for it has not been maintained. Today, it could be reclaimed by us [Jews], but no longer by the best of Christians, by the Lessings. Therefore they must be produced anew" (Rosenzweig 1984: 451). A messianic friendship between Jew and Christian that would have "the blood of presentness" in it would be one that allowed each to acknowledge the *difference* of the other, not their bloodless similarity on the plane of the "religion of reason" where, Rosenzweig explains, "Mendelssohn and Lessing . . . found one another on the basis of their common abstraction from their positive religions." Put differently, a properly present messianic friendship (and Rosenzweig attempted it with Eugen Rosenstock) would mean renewing the Mendelssohn-Lessing friendship as a Mendelssohn-Jacobi friendship, with each party holding fast to his own revelation. Without ever quite expressing it in those precise terms, Rosenzweig certainly conceived of his historic task as both philosopher and Jew to be the renewal of the possibility for such a messianic friendship. In the next chapter I will show how Rosenzweig achieved a reconciliation of Mendelssohn and Jacobi in a philosophy of revelation grounded in language and focusing on the Hebrew Bible as the historical embodiment of the language of revelation. This philosophy of revelation takes the gnostic sting out of Jacobi's emphasis upon the personal experience of revelation both by demonstrating the historical indispensability of the Hebrew Bible for Christianity and by setting the experience of personal revelation into the context of its worldly performance, the love of one's neighbor. Rosenzweig's philosophy of revelation, then, restores the "positivity" of both Judaism and Christianity.

Jacobi's Gnostic Turn

Let me now turn to a closer look at Jacobi's *Spinoza-Letters*. By telling the world that Lessing was a Spinozist, Jacobi hoped to show that Lessing's vaunted ideal of religious enlightenment was incompatible with faith in the personal God of biblical revelation, the God who freely brought forth his creation *ex nihilo* and fashioned humanity in His own image, that is, a humanity also capable of free creative action. Jacobi himself was far from being an orthodox Christian, but he shared the orthodox contempt for the "natural religion," purified of miracles and other "superstitious" dross, that the Enlightenment offered as a rationally acceptable interpretation of scriptural revelation. According to Jacobi, the God of the Enlightenment was nothing other than the philosophers' self-deifying Reason. The Enlightenment's so-called religion of reason (Vernunftreligion) was just that: the worship of Reason. Jacobi did not want to defend the historical truth of scriptural revelation; rather, he was waging a battle against the Enlightenment's religion of reason in order to make room for the lived experience of the revelation of the personhood of God as the fundament of a revived Christian faith. While Jacobi discounted the historicity of the miracles recorded in the scriptures, he stood firmly on the side of the miraculousness of life itself, its power to renew itself *ex nihilo*, out of nothing except the divine force dwelling within it. For Jacobi, the Enlightenment's religion of reason was a cold and lifeless affair, and concealed behind its pious veneration of a rational deity who supervised the world from afar was the stark reality of a God whose allegedly human face was but a hollow death mask.

Jacobi wanted to break through the Enlightenment's veneer of piety in order to recover the original source of religious faith, the divine "life-principle" dwelling within every individual. Jacobi believed that access to this indwelling divine principle was provided through an immediate "intellectual intuition" of one's authentic being, experienced whenever one uses one's will in order to take a new course of action in accordance with one's vision of a more perfect future. The human will shares in the divine power of beginning something new without predetermining conditions, the power of creation *ex nihilo*. In experiencing the will's freedom to act, one intuits one's inner divine life force. Jacobi declares that this experience is a revelation with a power of conviction greater than all the rational proofs of God's existence offered by the defenders of natural religion: "the occasional occurrence in the soul of even one aspiration for the better, for the future and the perfect, is a better proof of the Divinity than any geometric proof" (*Spinoza-Letters* 214; 109). Although it is the will that provides the source of the revelation of the divine, Jacobi stresses that this revelation is also a form of *knowledge*, a higher form of knowledge than that of "earthly things." Jacobi claims that his philosophy of the revelation of God in the human will is simply restating what "all men of wisdom" have said throughout history, namely, "that the *knowledge which has only earthly things for its objects is not worthy of its name*" (*Spinoza-Letters* 242; 194). Jacobi's higher knowledge of the inner divinity arises when the understanding is grounded in the will: "man's understanding is formed through his will, which is like a spark from the eternal and pure light, and a force from the Almighty. Whoever walks in this light and acts by this power, will walk in purity from light to light; he will experience his origin and his destination" (*Spinoza-Letters* 248–49; 209).

When Jacobi speaks of a "spark from the eternal and pure light" that dwells within the human soul and that provides a source of knowledge beyond "earthly things," he is expressing what can best be described as a form of gnosticism. Jacobi, I will argue, is quite clearly a part of what the scholar Cyril O'Regan has called a "gnostic return in modernity" (2001). Modern gnosticism, like its ancient precursor, posits a two-tiered vision of the world, with the lower tier ruled over by a tyrannical deity who holds humans captive to the illusion that no other world exists and that they live to serve him and him alone. The upper tier is the realm of the true deity, the one who offers redemption from enslavement to the false god of the lower realm. In order to gain redemption, all that is necessary is to recall one's authentic identity, to remember that one's home is in the higher realm of freedom, life, and light. The gnostic redeemer brings the knowledge (*gnosis*) necessary to shatter the illusions of this world, a knowledge that is really a reawakening of one's own inner power, one's inner divinity. In Jacobi's interpretation of Christianity, Christ is the gnostic redeemer figure. As Jacobi says in *Spinoza-Letters*:

> The religion of the Christians instructs man how to take on qualities through which he can make progress in his existence and propel himself to a higher life—and with this life to a higher consciousness, in this consciousness to a higher cognition [note the stress on a new consciousness and cognition, typical gnostic motifs]. Whoever accepts this promise and faithfully walks the way to its fulfillment, he has the faith that brings blessedness. Therefore the sublime teacher of this faith, in whom all promises were already fulfilled, could with truth say:
> I am the way, the truth, and the life: whoever accepts the will that is within me, he will experience that my faith is true, that it is from God. (*Spinoza-Letters* 231; 164)

Jacobi's Christ did not bring salvation through his suffering and death on the Cross, but through his teaching, a teaching that awakens one to the reality of the divine will within oneself. In contrast with this gnostic Christ, the Enlightenment's God, hiding behind the benign face that the illusion of the religion of reason provides, is in truth the inhuman "One and All" of Spinoza. To be sure, it is reason itself that has enslaved so-called enlightened humanity to this tyrannizing illusion, but the hold of this illusion upon its victims is no less powerful for being self-inflicted.

One salient characteristic of ancient gnosticism, no less significant than its offer of salvation through a redemptive knowledge of one's authentic identity, is its identification of the tyrannical God of the lower tier of reality with the God venerated by the Jews. Jacobi's gnostic reinterpretation of Christianity was built upon the identification of Spinoza's system as the philosophical revisioning of the inner core of Judaism, its veneration of an utterly abstract and infinitely remote God, a God who has nothing to do with humanity, who can never be approached by any finite, living being, and who did not create the world *ex nihilo*.

Such an image of the God of the Jews may seem rather far-fetched if one recalls the story of creation in Genesis. Certainly, Spinoza seems to have completely broken with the idea of the creator God of Genesis. Yet Jacobi could and did argue for the connection between Spinoza's God and the Jewish God on the basis of the esoteric teachings of Judaism in the Kabbalah. The Kabbalah taught that God's true nature was only hinted at in the stories of the Bible, and only in the ecstatic visions of the prophet Ezekiel and of a small coterie of rabbis had the mysteries of the Godhead been more fully revealed. The Kabbalah's most profound teaching was that God was truly unknowable and infinitely distant from this world, that He was in His essence only able to be designated as *Eyn-sof*, the Infinite. According to the very influential sixteenth-century Kabbalist R. Isaac Luria, the spiritual and material worlds were the ever more distant emanations of the divine Light into the emptiness opened up by the Infinite's self-contraction (*zimzum*) into an infinitely small point. When Jacobi in *Spinoza-Letters* revealed Lessing to be a Spinozist, he spoke of him as a Kabbalistic Spinozist, a sort of "crypto-Jew" worshiping in secret the Infinite God whose self-contraction allowed finite human beings to momentarily occupy his place. Jacobi reported that Lessing would even joke that perhaps he himself was God, at least on that day and for that moment.⁸ Jacobi explicated Spinozism to Lessing in their initial conversation as being "nothing other than the ancient *a nihilo nihil fit* . . ., but with more abstract concepts than the philosophers of the cabbala or others before him" (*Spinoza-Letters* 187; 14). In place of the Kabbalah's *Eyn-sof*, Jacobi goes on to explain, Spinoza "only posited an *immanent* one, an indwelling cause of the universe eternally unalterable *within itself*, One and the same with all its consequences" (*Spinoza-Letters* 188; 14).

Jacobi's identification of Spinoza's God as the God of the Kabbalah allowed him to identify the hidden face of the Enlightenment God as that of the God of (esoteric) Judaism. Jacobi's gnosticizing Christianity thus provided a full-fledged re-emergence of all the essential themes of ancient gnosticism, including its attack on the Jewish God. I want to make it clear that I am not claiming that Jacobi deliberately drew from ancient gnosticism in order to construct his system. Rather, what we see in Jacobi is the reappearance of a number of common gnostic motifs at an historic moment where the dominant religious world picture mirrored that of Greco-Roman antiquity, the matrix in which gnosticism first arose. Specifically, the world pictures of both the Greco-Roman period and the Enlightenment pushed God into the extramundane distance and left nature to be governed by inexorable laws—Fate—that offered little room for human agency. The gnostic rebellion in both antiquity and the Enlightenment took place in order to discover a path towards freedom and away from fatalism. It aimed at a recovery of humanity's original "home" in a realm governed by a loving and saving God. In the name of freedom and homecoming, gnosticism posits a saving knowledge that will lift the human beyond nature, and perhaps even lift nature itself beyond its mechanized unfreedom, to a realm of Spirit. And in both antiquity and the Enlightenment, the gnostic rebellion was launched against a God who stood apart from the world and commanded its inhabitants to obey his laws, a God unlike the pagan deities but very much like the God of the Jews. In antiquity, gnosticism flourished within Christianity as the major alternative to orthodoxy, and likewise in the Enlightenment, the gnostic worldview offered a way to recuperate Christianity's message of salvation from the "principalities of this world" without returning to what was considered to be an outworn Christian orthodoxy.

The influence of Jacobi's *Spinoza-Letters* upon the younger generation of philosophers, theologians, and writers, men like Hegel, Hölderlin, Schelling, Fichte, and Schleiermacher, can hardly be overestimated, but it was not exactly what Jacobi had wished for.[9] Jacobi hoped to expose Spinozism as the hidden face of the Enlightenment's religion of reason, but the younger generation turned to Spinozism, now given the imprimatur of Lessing himself, with a vengeance, seeing it as offering the key to solving the problem that Jacobi himself had helped to expose: How can humans transcend their finitude, their existence as mere puppets within the shadow-play of nature, and recover their infinite worth as free, self-determining beings? For this younger generation, the *Spinoza-Letters* came at a propitious moment. It brought before the world a revelation of Lessing's "One and All" Spinozistic pantheism four years after Kant had published his *Critique of Pure Reason* in 1781. Kant's work had demolished the Enlightenment's pretense of offering rationally persuasive proofs for the existence of God, the immortality of the soul, and the freedom of the will. These proofs had been the mainstay of the Enlightenment's religion of reason. Jacobi's Lessing seemed to have understood even before Kant the baselessness of the religion of reason, and to have concluded that God did not exist apart from Nature, that the human soul was not immortal, and that there was no freedom of the will. But, the younger generation asked, perhaps Lessing was mistaken about his interpretation of the meaning of pantheistic Spinozism? And perhaps Jacobi had been wrong to think that pantheistic Spinozism was simply the ultimate expression of reason's self-deifying impulse, showing in the starkest terms how the impersonal *Eyn-sof* was hiding all along behind the mask of the Enlightenment's rational deism? Jacobi talked about the living, creative divinity within each individual; could this life-principle not be the infinite God sustaining all things? Was God perhaps awaiting this historic moment for humanity to recognize its own divinity and raise up the divine sparks from their entrapment in blind Nature? Far from turning the younger generation away from the God of Spinoza and the Kabbalah, Jacobi had made this immanent God striving to know itself in and free itself through humanity seem the only recourse after Kant had demonstrated that the Enlightenment's religion of reason had all along been resting upon unsound foundations.

Kant himself had offered a vastly different account of the relationship between human finitude and divine infinity. Kant sundered reality into two unbridgeable realms, that of natural phenomena, where inexorable causality held sway, and that of the "thing in itself," which experience could never penetrate. Split between these two irreconcilable realms, the finite human existed on the one side as the puppet of all-determining natural causes, but beyond this, on the side of the "thing in itself," the human was the free moral agent, a being of infinite worth. The post-Kantian generation hoped that if these two realms could be reconstructed as a living unity, as an all-embracing divine reality modeled on the "One and All" of Lessing's Spinozism, then perhaps a new path for both philosophy and religion could be opened up. To be sure, the new "One and All" would not compel human finitude to be submerged within its impersonal and purposeless infinitude, as Jacobi had thought was the case with Lessing's "One and All." A more dynamic relationship between finitude and infinity would need to be worked out, and it fell to Fichte to be the first to attempt a systematic reconciliation of Kantianism and Spinozism. Jacobi wrote what is probably his most impassioned work, his *Letter to Fichte* (1799),[10] denouncing this resurrection of Spinoza, but Jacobi could not stem the tide of what he saw as just another manifestation of philosophy's tendency to deify Reason above the personal God directly encountered in living experience. Jacobi, it seems, was Rosenzweig's precursor in identifying 1800 as a historic wrong turn away from the power of revelation that was released with Kant's demolition of the Enlightenment's religion of reason in the *Critique of Pure Reason*. Jacobi believed that he was the true heir of Kant, that he, Jacobi, alone respected the Kantian insistence upon distinguishing between the outer world of deterministic laws and the inner world of freedom, the site of God's revelation. As we will see, Jacobi saw Fichte's resurrection of Spinozism to be the ultimate expression of self-deifying Reason. Rosenzweig will associate 1800 with Hegel rather than Fichte, but the point is the same.

Despite the fact that the younger generation of philosophers turned to pantheistic Spinozism against all Jacobi's intentions, there are several things that they share with Jacobi. The younger generation rightly saw in Jacobi an ally in their assault on Enlightenment philosophy's pious pretension to have discovered a rational religion that could bring together all humans under a single God. Like Jacobi, these men did not accept Christian orthodoxy or the historical truth of the scriptural revelation. Like Jacobi, they saw the God of the Enlightenment as nothing more than the designer of a mechanistic, impersonal universe in which human freedom was an illusion. Jacobi had tried to identify the God of the Enlightenment as nothing more than a cover for the God of Spinoza, the dead, depersonalized God of radical fatalism. While the younger generation did not follow Jacobi in making this identification, they nonetheless accepted his identification of the God of the Enlightenment as the God of the Jews. In sum, the younger generation was drawn to Jacobi's gnostic rebellion against the Jewish God. By joining in this gnostic rebellion, they could claim to bring to completion the most radical thrust of the earliest gnostic Christianity, the rejection of the naive faith in the flesh-and-blood materiality of the Savior in favor of the redemptive power of *knowledge*.[11] And, to recall the historical context in which Fichte and his contemporaries were writing, we can see that these men were drawn to a gnostic rebellion against the Enlightenment God because it was under this God's banner that the French revolutionary armies were marching across Europe. Unable to effect a political transformation of Germany without betraying her to her French overlords, the younger generation found an outlet for their revolutionary energies in the gnostic rebellion against the Jewish God, a rebellion that could be achieved through a new *gnosis* rather than through new political institutions.[12]

I am certainly not the first to identify the gnostic strain in Jacobi's later inheritors. Karl Marx is the most perceptive critic of the gnostic turn in German philosophy. He explicitly speaks of the "gnostic Feuerbach" in his *German Ideology* (opening to part 3, "Saint Max," in Marx and Engels 1998: 128), and in the first of his *Theses on Feuerbach* Marx refers to Feuerbach's contrast between the "theoretical attitude" (read, *gnosis*) which Feuerbach claims as "the only genuinely human attitude" with "practice" that is "defined only in its dirty-Jewish form of appearance" (Marx and Engels 1998: 569). We should not hear the anti-Jewish slur as Marx's own judgment, but as his ironic critique of the gnostic disdain for everyday reality and for any engagement in practices that might transform it. Marx recognized that the gnostic strain of German idealism derived from the political impotence of the German intelligentsia, and he devoted hundreds of pages detailing and satirizing the gnostic "church" of the young German left-Hegelians, Saint Bruno (Bauer) and Saint Max (Stirner), in the *German Ideology*.

Jacobi stands as a major source of the powerful link between post-Kantian philosophy and the resurgence of gnosticism. This link is apparent in post-Kantian literature as well. Studies of both German and English Romanticism, more or less contemporaneous in its inception with Jacobi's philosophical interventions against hyper-rational Spinozism from 1785 to 1815, have long noted the presence of gnostic motifs. Northrop Frye, in his magisterial study of William Blake in *Fearful Symmetry*, points to Blake's gnostic sensibility, his belief that "all the works of civilization, all the improvements of the state of nature that man has made, prove that man's creative power is literally supernatural" (41). The faith that "man's creative power is literally supernatural" is something that Jacobi proclaims in all his writings, and it may even be taken as their motto. According to Jacobi, this supernatural creative power is the only means by which a human can be free of mechanized nature. A human being is free, Jacobi declares in a representative passage, "only in so far as he *does not belong to nature* with one part of his being, is not arisen from it and has not been borne by it; uses it and masters it, cuts himself lose from it and overcomes its mechanics with his free faculty, and makes use of it."[13]

Along the same lines as Frye's interpretation of Blake, E. S. Shaffer has studied what she calls Coleridge's "modern gnosticism" in "Kubla Khan," tracing it back to the appropriation of Christian Kabbalah. Coleridge was also deeply influenced by the new pantheistic Spinozism coming out of Germany. Coleridge maintained the connection between Spinozism and the Kabbalah that Jacobi had foregrounded. Coleridge, according to Shaffer, was seeking for a higher religious truth beyond both Judaism and Christianity in a gnostic-kabbalistic syncretism of both faiths (Shaffer 1975: 150ff.). In his classic study of Coleridge's debt to German philosophy, *Coleridge and the Pantheist Tradition*, Thomas McFarland has traced in great detail the development of the Romantic turn to Spinozism, Kabbalah, and pantheism that began with Jacobi's *Spinoza-Letters* (McFarland 1969).

Before turning to the next section and a closer examination of Jacobi's gnostic philosophizing, let me briefly restate the argument to this point. Although the emergence of a gnostic turn in philosophy cannot be entirely attributed to Jacobi, his influence upon Schleiermacher, Hölderlin, Schelling, and Hegel in Germany, and Coleridge and some of his contemporaries in England, is unquestionable. While Jacobi was critical of Kabbalistic pantheism, his own appropriation of a gnostic form of Christianity was an early and influential expression of a wider rejection of the Enlightenment world picture of a distant and impersonal God who governs through the intricate nexus of causes and effects that make up the mechanical necessity of nature. Jacobi revealed to the world that Lessing, long thought to be an advocate of the Enlightenment religion of reason, had privately abandoned it in favor of a Kabbalistically inspired pantheistic interpretation of Spinozism. Jacobi argued that Lessing's Spinozism was nothing more than the true face of the religion of reason. Jacobi wanted to launch a gnostic rebellion against the Enlightenment's God as the latest mask behind which the Jewish God had disguised Himself. As we will see, Jacobi views the Jewish God as the creation of "degenerate reason." The younger generation of philosophers and poets sought to fuse together Jacobi's new version of gnostic Christianity and the Spinozistic pantheism he despised. The forms which the later philosophical gnosticism took were varied, but they all shared a fundamental rejection of human finitude and its radical separation from a transcendent divine infinity. The aim of all later philosophical gnosticism was to close the breach between finitude and infinity through gnosis, which in Jacobi and Fichte, who follows Jacobi in this respect, is identified as a form of "immediate intellectual intuition" of the divine infinitude. Hegel will offer a different, historicized gnosis to close the breach between finitude and infinity, but in the end it too leaves finitude behind in order to sublate it within the infinite Self-knowledge of the Absolute. In the opening pages of *The Star of Redemption*, Rosenzweig speaks of this as the attempt to transcend mortality through the "cognition of the All." Rosenzweig's task in breaking through 1800 requires him both to shatter the "All" of idealism's gnosis and to recuperate a place in history for the Jewish God.

Jacobi vs. "the Jews of Speculative Reason"

I have noted in the previous section how Jacobi's *Spinoza-Letters* helped to bring about a gnostic rejection of the "Jewish God" of Enlightenment rational theology and a turn to pantheistic Spinozism among Germany's younger generation of thinkers. The work also shifted the terms in which the Jewish Question was to be posed in the future. The Jewish Question will be reinterpreted as the *Spinoza* Question: Is Judaism at its heart the same as Spinozism, the deification of formal and mechanical Reason? Jacobi offered a resounding *Yes* to this question. Jacobi accused post-Kantian philosophers like Fichte and Schelling of having succumbed to this Jewish God. Jacobi's challenge required of any thinker who wished to embrace a Spinozist system that he show that his philosophy was not tainted by Judaism. Until Spinoza had, as it were, been baptized in the Spirit of a *Christian* Reason, no one could be free of the taint of "Judaizing."[14] In order to understand how the God of Judaism came to be identified as the God of a mechanical universe of unfreedom, I need to explain the background of Jacobi's attack on Lessing's Spinozism, in particular the Kabbalistic interpretation of Spinoza that had influenced both Jacobi and Lessing. After explaining the linkage between pantheistic Spinozism and the Kabbalah, I will go on to detail Jacobi's critique of both Spinozism and the Kabbalah as reason's deification of itself.

Jacobi's presentation of Spinoza drew its inspiration from a work, Johann Georg Wachter's *Der Spinozismus in Jüdenthumb* (1699), that had identified the Kabbalah as the source of atheistic Spinozism. I have been so far speaking of a pantheistic reading of Spinoza, one that Lessing seems to have favored and that became widely influential in the following decades. But the more common interpretation of Spinoza was that he had simply denied the existence of God altogether. This view was developed in Wachter's book. Further, Wachter linked Spinoza's atheism to the esoteric doctrines of the Kabbalah. Wachter argued that the intricate speculation of Kabbalah about how the world was the emanation of the *Eyn-sof* was merely a corruption of reason's natural understanding of God as the transcendent Creator and providential guide of the universe. Wachter claimed, and Jacobi would follow him in this, that reason had taken the wrong path when it deemed it to be logically impossible that God had created the world out of nothing: The doctrine of *ex nihilo nihil fit* ("from nothing arises nothing") is the source of all the Kabbalah's errors. Because of this error, the Kabbalah, and also ancient Neoplatonic philosophy, which fell victim to the same mistake, replaced the Creator God with the Infinite source from out of which the world was eternally and continually recreated.

Wachter was an early Enlightenment defender of the religion of reason, or at least he began as one. Wachter hoped to defend the religion of reason by attacking Kabbalah as the distorted root of both Judaism and Christianity, with Spinoza being the latest and most consistent exponent of the Kabbalistic conflation of God and world. Like the Kabbalah, Spinoza too had fallen victim to the error of denying *creatio ex nihilo*. In Wachter's version of the religion of reason, the existence of a transcendent Creator who was outside of time required that the universe be created out of nothing rather than exist eternally alongside God, or, worse, within God. Wachter himself later recanted his position and denied that Kabbalistic Spinozism was atheistic. Rather, he said, Spinozism and the Kabbalah are pantheistic systems offering a vision of the underlying divine reality—Kabbalah's *Eyn-sof*, Spinoza's Infinite substance—from out which our world emerged and by virtue of which it maintains its being. Wachter came to believe that creation from nothing was indeed incompatible with reason, and that God was the infinite and eternal source of a continuous creation without temporal beginning or end. According to Wachter's new way of thinking, the Kabbalah offers a revealed truth that lies behind both Judaism and Christianity and is therefore the "true religion."[15]

As I have already mentioned, Jacobi reported in his *Spinoza-Letters* that Lessing before his death had revealed himself to be a pantheistic, Kabbalistic Spinozist. Jacobi further reported that he had tried, unsuccessfully, to persuade Lessing that the only coherent interpretation of Spinoza is that he is an atheist. In effect, Jacobi was reviving the anti-Jewish and anti-Spinoza Wachter of *Der Spinozismus in Jüdenthumb* against Lessing, who was defending the views of the post-recantation Wachter. In reporting his conversations with Lessing to Mendelssohn, Jacobi was forcing Mendelssohn to choose between two equally unappealing alternative characterizations of Spinoza: Spinoza the hyper-rational atheist or Spinoza the Kabbalistic pantheist. If Spinoza, as Wachter had argued, brought to expression the inner truth of Judaism, then these alternatives offered no place for Mendelssohn's Judaism as he presented it in *Jerusalem*.

This is the battleground on which the contest for Spinoza's body was being waged, as Jacobi refers to it in one of his letters to Mendelssohn in a passage that serves as the epigraph to this chapter. On the side of hyper-rational atheism stood Satan; on the side of Kabbalistic pantheism was the Archangel. Jacobi told Mendelssohn that "those of the party of the Archangel are illuminated by the *Elucidarius Cabalisticus* of Wachter," that is, the second, recantation work of Wachter (*JubA* 13, letter 690). Jacobi stood on the side of Satan. He was willing to help Satan claim Spinoza for his own because he wanted to consign to damnation not only atheistic Spinozism, but the false God of pantheism on whose behalf the "party of the Archangel" was battling. When the body of Spinoza had been dragged away by Satan, nothing would be left for the party of the Archangel but the emptiness of their own Kabbalistic fantasies. It can hardly be accidental that Jacobi's friend, J. G. Hamann, had only months before alluded to this very conflict between Satan and the Archangel over the body of Moses in his attack on Mendelssohn's *Jerusalem* in *Golgotha und Scheblimini!* The reference to the battle over the body of Moses is in the New Testament's Epistle of Jude (v. 9), and Hamann interpreted the "body of Moses" in the epistle to be the dead body of the Jewish law (*Golgotha* 227; 315). Jacobi's use of this reference carries with it, therefore, suggestions that he is hoping to see not only the end the reign of the Jewish hyper-rational God, but also of the position of Mendelssohn as spokesperson of an enlightened and tolerant legal order.[16] Jeffrey Librett has described the rhetorical thrust of Jacobi's invocation of the "battle over the body of Spinoza" that he is waging with Mendelssohn in stark but appropriate terms: "Jacobi conflates the corpus of Spinoza, the bad Jew whose thought epitomizes Enlightenment, with the corpse of Moses, the law as rotting carcass, and he does this while addressing himself in polemic to Moses himself—Moses Mendelssohn. He thereby says to Mendelssohn: reason is the letter, the Jew is the dead body of language. You, reason, are the Jew as death itself" (Librett 1999: 236). Jewish Law, Jewish Emancipation, Enlightenment Reason, Death: Jacobi's (and Hamann's) four horsemen of the apocalypse.

What did Jacobi hope would replace the body of Spinoza? Mendelssohn imagined that Jacobi wanted to consign Spinoza to damnation in order to proclaim the risen Christ, and he was not entirely mistaken. However, as I have argued in the previous section, Jacobi's risen Christ is not the Christ of orthodox Christianity, but the inner life-force of the individual, a felt reality of the will's living capacity to break free of the mechanical necessity of the hyper-rational, godless universe.

Jacobi's gnostic Christianity, like its precursor in antiquity, focuses its critical assault against a world of unfreedom tyrannized by a ruling power falsely believed to be the highest and only divinity. According to Jacobi, unfreedom stems from the determinism that followed from philosophy's denial of the possibility of creation out of nothing. If every event is explicable and conditioned by a prior cause, then there is no room for freedom. The God of this deterministic world was venerated by what he called in his 1799 text, the open letter of *Jacobi to Fichte*, "the Jews of speculative reason."[17] While these "Jews" include Leibniz, Wolff, and Fichte, they all descend from Spinoza. They all subscribe to the fundamental metaphysical principle that God is created in *my* image: "I am myself this so called being, in virtue of my selfhood, and my first and highest command is that *I shall not have other Gods outside Me*, i.e., outside that selfhood" (*Jacobi to Fichte*

524; 49). The Jews of speculative reason have taken the first commandment of the God of the Jews as their philosophical foundation. These Jews are circumcised according to what Jacobi calls the "letter of the absolutely universal law of reason" (*Jacobi to Fichte* 503; 6).[18]

In a later text, *Über den Göttlichen Dingen und ihren Offenbarung* (*On Things Divine and Their Revelation*) (1811),[19] Jacobi once again compares modern philosophers with the Jews. He describes these Jew-philosophers as offering a "wisdom" that would "slay the human being on the cross of doubt-ridden un-knowledge [Unwissenheit]" in order to free him from "the evil of error" and "to reconcile him forever with himself." After putting the human to death on the cross of skepticism, he is "resurrected with a transfigured body made of a pure logical enthusiasm that would also serve as his soul." This soul that now replaces the once-living human is only a "sickening specter that can only blink out of a hollow skull—nothingness and more nothingness." The metaphorical equation of Jews and idealist philosophers continues, but it outruns itself, losing its metaphorical force and becoming a literal indictment of the Jews themselves. The wisdom of the philosophers, Jacobi goes on,

> wants to proclaim that it is All in All, that its boneyard figure of Death is the father of the spirits, the creator of all things; that its "stick-figure gods" [Jacobi quotes a Latin phrase of Cicero, "*dii monogrammi*," reporting what Epicurus called his gods, the star constellations] are the heavenly powers that brought us out of Egyptian servitude and out of the blind paganism of all previous teaching into the blessed purity and clarity of its own teaching—and that it is leading us with a mighty hand into a promised land, where there is only metaknowledge [Erkenntniß des Erkenntnisses] but where neither milk nor honey nor any other impurities flow—a land of which we will take possession without running the risk of experiencing a fate similar to that of the Jews who, having lost sight of their horror of superstition, became a byword for gullibility and a cause for laughter among the nations on account of their superstitions and their wildly fantastical fairy tales. (*On Things Divine* 334–35)

Jacobi ends his extended comparison between the philosophers and the Jews by attacking the Jews for their superstitious gullibility and "fairy tales," by which he means to refer either to the midrashim he could have been familiar with or to the intricate theosophy of the Kabbalah, or both. He grants that at its inception, Israelite religion stood opposed to superstitious idolatry.

But Jacobi certainly does not agree with Mendelssohn that, however different rabbinic Judaism may be from the original Mosaic dispensation, the rejection of idolatry remains a constant in Jewish history. The masses of the Jews have fallen prey to superstitious fairy tales, and the elite have embraced the deification of Reason itself. Between superstition and rationalism, however, there is a deep affinity, or so Jacobi is arguing. The whole edifice of idealist philosophy rests upon the primary symbols of superstition: the skull and the skeletal representation of Death. These are the images hiding being the invisible visage of the Jewish God who declares, "You shall have no other gods before me." What I think we are entitled to say on the basis of this passage is that the pretension of philosophy to bring us into a promised land of "metaknowledge" and the pretension of the Jews to possess a true knowledge of God are, for Jacobi, identical at their root. Both pretensions spring from a rejection of the authentic and living divinity encountered within the human, and a claim to have no other God except the *I* of self-deifying conceit. This *I* is in reality nothingness and its "purity and clarity" are just a cover for the "sickening specter" of death itself.[20] This Jewish-philosophical God is what Jacobi in all his philosophical writings will seek to expose.

Jacobi held out as the only hope for human freedom a renunciation of reason's pretensions to explain everything systematically and an embrace of what Jacobi called "faith." In his first letter to Mendelssohn in the *Spinoza-Letters*, Jacobi explains that he is searching for the "boundary" between reason and what lies beyond it, a boundary that separates what can be explained from "the unanalyzable, the immediate, the simple" (*Spinoza-Letters* 194; 32). What lies on the other side of the boundary was never made clear by Jacobi, as indeed he says it cannot be explained or analyzed, but he does suggest that it is the sheer existence of the "particular and individual actuality" of both the human being and God (*Spinoza-Letters* 190; 21). This boundary, Jacobi says, was what Spinoza's philosophy showed had to be leapt across in what Jacobi called a "*salto mortale*" ("mortal leap") if one were to escape from Spinoza's deterministic fatalism:

> I love Spinoza, because he, more than any other philosopher, has led me to the perfect conviction that certain things admit of no explication: one must not therefore keep one's eyes shut to them, but must take them as one finds them. I have no concept more intimate than that of the final cause; no conviction more vital than that *I do what I think*, and not, *that I should think what I do*. Truly

therefore, I must assume a source of thought and action that remains completely inexplicable to me. (*Spinoza-Letters* 193; 29)

Jacobi had no patience for the work of reconstructing philosophy. Jacobi's philosophical skills seem to find their outlet only in exposing the inherent atheism and ultimate "nihilism" (Jacobi invented the term) of any philosophical system that attempts to carry forward the Cartesian project of using reason to defeat skepticism. In this critical task, Jacobi stands unsurpassed in the history of modern philosophy. Kierkegaard and Nietzsche equip themselves from his critical arsenal. One of the clearest expositions of how philosophical reason leads to nihilism comes from an 1815 work, Jacobi's Vorrede (preface) to the second edition of *David Hume über den Glauben* (*David Hume on Faith*).[21] Jacobi describes the progression from idealism to nihilism this way:

> The moment man sought to establish scientifically the veracity of our representations of the material world that exists beyond them, and independently of them, at that very moment the object that the demonstrators wanted to ground disappeared before their eyes. They were left with mere subjectivity, with *sensation*. And thus they discovered idealism. The moment man sought to prove scientifically the veracity of our representations of an immaterial world that exists beyond them, to prove the substantiality of the human spirit, and of a free Author of this universe who is however distinct from it, of a Providence conscious of its rule, i.e. a *personal* Providence, the only one that would be *truly* Providence—the moment he tried this, the object likewise disappeared before the eyes of the demonstrators. They were left with merely logical phantoms. And in this way they discovered nihilism. (*David Hume* Vorrede 583; 108)

Descartes was the first to engage in radical doubt about the existence of the world and God as the beginning of philosophy. Descartes sought to recover the world and God on a more secure basis using the only remaining trustworthy piece of evidence left to him after his doubt had removed the world and God: the consciousness of his doubt. Upon this consciousness, using his reason alone, Descartes attempted to prove the existence of God and the external world. But the world cannot be remade by reason. The God that Descartes rediscovered was a postulate of reason but not a *person* who communicated with the individual. The rational reconstruction of the world replaced a world of persons with a world of "logical phantoms."

How did human reason fall prey to the drive to nihilism? Jacobi spent considerable energy addressing this question. The central point of his analysis of reason's drive to nihilism has to do with the distinction between the dead machine and the living organism. Nihilism reduces the organism to the machine. Providential deism is no better than nihilism because it merely constructs an impersonal God to watch over the machine; pantheism places this impersonal God inside the machine as the "Soul of the All," in Lessing's words; Spinoza alone consistently acknowledges the machinal nature of this All.

According to Jacobi, Descartes and then Spinoza brought to expression a constituent aspect of reason, namely, its drive to reduce life to a mechanism, one that is within its power to construct. This drive to mechanize life on the part of a living, rational being seemed, as Jacobi said, "on the face of it an absurd undertaking." And yet, Jacobi continues, "this is precisely what we undertake to do whenever we strive to make nature into something that we can comprehend, that is, reduce it to a *purely natural existence*, and uncover the principle of mechanism."[22] These words come from the second edition of the *Spinoza-Letters*, published in 1789 with seven long supplementary sections. In supplement 7, from which the passage I just quoted is taken, Jacobi attempts to answer the question of why human reason seems compelled to take a path towards nihilism, towards the reduction of life to a machine. His remarks in this 1789 text are a condensation of a longer attempt he made at explaining what he called the "hereditary flaw of mankind, its primordial cancer" in his 1787 work *David Hume über den Glauben*, whose full title included the explanatory phrase *oder Idealismus und Realismus: Ein Gespräch* (or Idealism and Realism: A Dialogue). In the book, Jacobi attempts to defend his philosophy as a form of "realism." Jacobi argues that there is a direct "perception of the actuality" of indivisibly extended objects in the external world and of an indivisibly enduring selfhood in time.[23] This direct perception, which Jacobi insists can legitimately be called both "faith" ("Glaube") and "revelation" ("Offenbarung"), is how every living being encounters the world, as a spatial and temporal continuity rather than a mere mechanical assemblage of distinct parts. Indeed, subject and object are continuous with one another, coming into being as each acts upon the other. This means that reality is not reducible to a collection of mechanically juxtaposed parts, and also that the *I* is conscious of itself only as it acts upon and responds to a *Thou*. Reason can either base itself upon the direct "perception of the actual" (i.e., faith and revelation) or it can cast this perception into skeptical doubt and then lose itself in forms of explanation and analysis that dissolve the living continuity of the world into mechanical parts.[24]

David Hume on Faith is written as a dialogue between an unnamed "He" who comes to visit Jacobi, sick at home with a chill, and Jacobi's "I." *David Hume on Faith* was written as a rejoinder to the criticism leveled at him after Mendelssohn's death that he was nothing more than a dogmatic Christian religious fanatic (Schwärmer).[25] It is possible that Jacobi portrays himself as sick with influenza as a sly jab at those who accused him of causing Mendelssohn's death from complications of the same disease. *David Hume on Faith* was Jacobi's first effort at clarifying some of the more controversial points in his *Spinoza-Letters*, especially his reference to "faith" as a counter to atheistic Spinozism. Jacobi is at pains to explain why he is not rejecting reason when he invokes faith, and in order to make his case he must offer an account of how reason contains both the possibility of nihilistic atheism and its opposite, revelation. It is in showing us reason's revelatory power that Jacobi falters, as I have said.

Jacobi compares reason's self-deluded sense of the world as a machine to a dream state. In dreams we imagine a world that seems to actually exist outside of us, but its lack of reality is demonstrated by the fact the objects within this dream world are only mechanical juxtapositions of images, linked together by subjective associative connections, without any organic coherence to them. The difference between the delusion of the dream as real and our sense of reality in the waking state lies precisely in the difference between mechanical and living beings. Mechanical beings, Jacobi claims, have no inner life principle that unifies the operation of their parts; there is nothing there that exceeds the mere sum of their parts. A living being is more than the sum of its parts. That excess of life over machine is the unifying principle that brings the parts of the organism into a whole.

> Whenever we dream, we are in some state of madness. The principle of all cognition, of all feeling of truth, of every correct combination, *the perception of the actual*, abandons us, and the moment it forsakes us, or ceases to dominate, we can make things (i.e. the representation that we take as things, as happens in dreams) rhyme in the wildest fashion. For we can never make objective sense out of things except according to the objective determination of the order they appear to us, and the objective order in which they appear to us in a dream is mainly the result of merely *subjective* determinations. (*David Hume* 304; 137)

How do we distinguish waking from dreaming? Jacobi identifies the "perception of the actual" as the perception or consciousness of one's own life, the perception that one is not merely a mechanical assemblage of parts, and he insists that this sense of "our being . . . joined together in a pure unity which we call our 'I'" is only revealed to us when we are aware of another being outside us, of another *individual*: "The object contributes just as much to the perception of the consciousness as the consciousness does to the perception of the object. I experience that I am, and that there is something outside me, in one and the same indivisible moment; and at that moment my soul is no more passive with respect to the object than it is towards itself. There is no representation, no inference, that mediates this twofold revelation" (*David Hume* 277; 64). My sense of being alive is given to me when I encounter another being that is in excess of my imaginative power to represent it as a collection of parts.[26] The excess of life or "immanent activity" (*David Hume* 295; 117) over the mere assemblage of external parts in the object reveals to me in my perception of the object that I am both acting and being acted upon by the object. I confront another "self-revelatory being" (*David Hume* 296; 118) when I sense that the other being resists being "analyzed" into its parts. It opposes my will with its own will, or immanent power. This originary "two-fold revelation" is the center point of all revelation for Jacobi: "collect your being at the point of a simple perception," Jacobi says to his imaginary interlocutor in *David Hume on Faith*, "so that you might become once and for all (and be unshakingly convinced for your whole life) that the *I* and the *Thou*, the internal consciousness and the external object, must be present both at once in the soul even in the most primordial and simple perceptions" (*David Hume* 277; 65).

Someone who doubts the reality of the external world because all he possesses are sensations and all sensations are subjective (unlike "perceptions" which are of "the actual") has already lost the only proof of the world that is possible: the sense of the world's *otherness*, its *having a life* outside me. The skeptic has lost his sense of the world as occupied by living beings because he has withdrawn his will from the world. Freud would later call this the withdrawal of libido that is characteristic of the narcissist and the melancholic. Jacobi calls this withdrawal of the will "the will to will nothing" (*Jacobi to Fichte* 516; 33). It is the characteristic of the individual who, in order to overcome skepticism, seeks to establish the existence of the world and other humans on the pure principles of a rational system. In order to overcome skepticism, the individual annihilates the world:

> So if a being is to become for us a *fully* comprehended object, we must cancel it in thought as as something *objective, as standing on its own*; we must annihilate it in order to let it become something *subjective*, our own creation, *a mere schema*. Nothing must remain in it, and constitute an essential part of its concept, which is not our activity, *now* just a display of our productive imagination. (*Jacobi to Fichte* 508; 16)

The skeptic, one could say, has lost his will to live. He no longer has the will to live in a world where other, *unknowable*, beings live. Rather, he wants only to live in a world of his own creation, a world of which he has, or seems to have, *perfect* knowledge. "Psyche now knows the mystery that so long and so unbearably tortured her curiosity. Now she knows it, and she is *blessed!* Everything outside her is nothing, and she is itself a *phantom*—not just a phantom of something, but a *phantom in itself*, a real nothingness, a nothingness of reality" (*Jacobi to Fichte* 512; 25–26). Reason's inherent desire to find explanations and causes ultimately turns the self and the world into mere phantoms. To escape this descent into what Jacobi calls nihilism, reason must return to its faith in the revelation of the otherness of the world in the "simple perception" of the living separateness of the "Thou."

But Jacobi cannot explain how the return to revelation is accomplished. His anger at the world created by the "Jews of speculative reason" overcomes him, and leads him to a sort of counter-nihilism. We may see Jacobi's own nihilist impulse most clearly in a passage from *Jacobi to Fichte*. Fichte, of course, is the prophet of the *I* that produces the world from out of itself, and Jacobi declares that Fichte's self-generating *I* possesses a "will that wills nothing" (*Jacobi to Fichte* 515; 32). But Fichte is not the only target of Jacobi's attack. Jacobi considers the "good will" of Kant to be such a "will that wills nothing" because it wills only what universal reason gives it as a law, the categorical imperative, but it wills nothing concrete and particular. When Jacobi declares war against this nihilistic will, he reveals the deepest problem of his concept of the divine will as the unconditioned cause that brings life out of nothingness: In the name of this life-giving will, Jacobi would destroy everything rather than accept the "will that wills nothing" in its stead:

> I . . . admit that I do not know the *good in itself*, I declare that I become furious whenever they want to impose on me *the will that wills nothing* in its stead, this

hollow shell of self-subsistence and freedom in the absolute indeterminate, and accuse me of atheism, of true and genuine *Godlessness*, if I resist accepting it in exchange. Yea, I am the atheist and the Godless one, who, against the *will that wills nothing*, will tell lies, just as Desdemona did when she lay dying; the one that will lie and defraud, just as Pylades did when he passed himself off for Orestes; will murder, as Timoleon did; or break law and oath, like Epaminondas, or John de Witt; commit suicide like Otho . . . (*Jacobi to Fichte* 516; 32)

Here we find clearly expressed the world-destroying impulse buried within Jacobi's gnosticism.[27] He has identified the "will to will nothing" behind the speculative constructions of philosophical reason, but his own reclamation of the will seems fixed upon annihilation rather than creation. Jacobi's will to live has itself been infected by a loss of faith that *this* ordinary world is really full of other living beings. The revelation of the world's otherness is the revelation of *another* world, a higher world. In the 1815 Vorrede to *David Hume on Faith*, Jacobi sums up his answer to the nihilist reduction of everything alive to mechanical automatism:

> We could abide this claim if man were only sense and reflective understanding. There lives in man, however, a spirit immediately from God. This spirit constitutes his being proper, and through it alone does his understanding first begin to understand, i.e. become a *human* understanding. Just as this spirit is present to man in his highest, deepest, and innermost consciousness, so also is the Giver of it, *God*, present to him—more present to him through his heart than nature is to him through his external senses . . . Hence we may well have the courage of our audacious language: we believe in God because we see him; though he cannot be seen with the eye of the body, he appears none the less to us in every upright man. (*David Hume* Vorrede 588; 119–20)

The vision of God in the everyday world is given to us through our recognition that humanity—exemplified in the "upright man"—is capable of transcending itself in "virtuous action" and "true genius," as Jacobi goes on to explain. Virtue and genius are rare signs of the breakthrough of the Spirit into the otherwise dead mechanism of the cosmos. These signs are miracles that point to a realm above this world.

I do not believe that, in the end, Jacobi can help the skeptic return to faith in the living reality of the common world. Jacobi is too committed to a concept of the inner Spirit that enlivens the individual—call it his inheritance of Protestant pietism—to acknowledge how the skeptic's recovery of the common life-world cannot be a solitary experience. The world reappears in a human togetherness beyond the guarantees of knowledge. This world is what Wordsworth describes in the final pages of *The Prelude*. Wordsworth certainly shares much in common with Jacobi, and is possibly even familiar with Jacobi through conversations with his friend Coleridge, who certainly knew Jacobi's writings. But Wordsworth shows nothing of Jacobi's gnostic strain that emphasizes the inwardness of God's revelation. The following passage, although it employs terms that remind one very much of Jacobi, nevertheless provides a good example of Wordsworth's insistence that the only world worth loving is *this* common world:

> Long time in search of knowledge desperate,
> I was benighted heart and mind; but now
> On all sides day began to reappear,
> And it was proved indeed that not in vain
> I had been taught to reverence a Power
> That is the very quality and shape
> And image of right reason, that matures
> Her processes by steadfast laws, gives birth
> To no impatient or fallacious hopes,
> No heat of passion or excessive zeal,
> No vain conceits, provokes to no quick turns
> Of self-applauding intellect, but lifts
> The Being into magnanimity;
> Holds up before the mind, intoxicate
> With present objects and the busy dance
> Of things that pass away, a temperate shew
> Of objects that endure, and by this course,
> Disposes her, when over-fondly set
> On leaving her incumbrances behind
> To seek in Man, and in the frame of life,
> Social and individual, what there is
> Desirable, affecting, good or fair
> Of kindred permanence, the gifts divine
> And universal, the pervading grace
> That hath been, is, and shall be. Above all
> Did Nature bring again that wiser mood
> More deeply re-established in my soul,
> Which, seeing little worthy or sublime

> In what we blazon with the pompous names
> Of power and action, early tutor'd me
> To look with feelings of fraternal love
> Upon those unassuming things, that hold
> A silent station in this beauteous world.
> *(The Prelude* [1905] 12.20–52)

Wordsworth, like Jacobi, repudiates the hopes of a "self-applauding intellect" that seeks a "knowledge desperate." But unlike Jacobi, Wordsworth rediscovers that the "Power" of "right reason" leads him to "seek in Man" what is "desirable" in life. And also unlike Jacobi, Wordsworth's revelation opens him once again to feel the attraction of "those unassuming things, that hold / A silent station in this beauteous world." These words are utterly un-Jacobian.

Jacobi's critique of philosophic reason aims at showing that reason's project of recovering the world after having brought its existence into radical skeptical doubt is doomed to failure. His critique is astute. But Jacobi's quest to get around reason, or redirect it, through an "immediate intuition" of the life-principle in the exercise of the will seems also doomed to failure. The world cannot be *actively* recovered because it was never possessed in the first place. As Stanley Cavell has often stressed, our relation to the world is one of *reception*, in the sense of holding oneself in open readiness for an unexpected visitation. The skeptic loses the world "with the effort to *make* it present."[28] "The world," Cavell says simply, "is to be *accepted*" ("The Avoidance of Love," 324). To become receptive to the world does not mean to renounce all action, but rather to renounce the desire for *mastery*. It is not skepticism as such that must be overcome, but the *will to overcome it*. In renouncing this will, the world presents itself like a revelation, or like a homecoming. Jacobi fully understood what drives the skeptic to drastic lengths, even to the "will to will nothing," in order to recover the world, and he knew that reason passed off counterfeit currency in place of the world's authentic revelation. But Jacobi never found his way back to *this*, commonplace and ordinary, world as the site of revelation ("Offenbarung"). Part of the reason he could not find his way back to the ordinary world was that, in his estimation, it had been overrun by the "Jews of speculative reason." Mendelssohn, for his part, sensed that Jacobi was not so much targeting the nihilistic impulse in Reason, but the claim of a Jew to philosophize.

As I will now explain, Mendelssohn, not without some justification, took Jacobi's *Spinoza-Letters* as a personal assault upon him.[29] This made him unable to read Jacobi as anything more than a Christian "Schwärmer," a "fanatic."

Mendelssohn's Response to Jacobi

Mendelssohn, although he died before he could read the full exposition of Jacobi's rejection of the Enlightenment's religion of reason in works like *David Hume on Faith, Jacobi to Fichte*, and *On Things Divine and their Revelation*, understood quite well that Jacobi intended to overturn the Enlightenment's religion of reason by identifying it as atheistic Spinozism and by linking Spinozism with Judaism. He understood that this was Jacobi's strategy because Jacobi had explicitly informed him that he intended to bring to conclusion the battle over the body of Spinoza that Wachter, with whom Mendelssohn was quite familiar, that had begun earlier in the century. Jacobi said that he was on the side of the first, pre-recantation, anti-Jewish, anti-Spinoza Wachter, and he hoped to position Mendelssohn on the side of the "party of the Archangel," those who wanted to save Spinoza by interpreting him as a Kabbalistically inspired pantheist. As I have pointed out in the previous section, Jacobi's strategy placed Mendelssohn in the position of having to choose between two unappealing representations of Judaism as they were constructed by Wachter in his pre- and post-recantation works: either as atheism or as mystical Schwärmerei.[30] Mendelssohn faced a choice in how to respond to Jacobi's resurrection of Wachter in his attack on the Enlightenment religion of reason. Mendelssohn could either defend the religion of reason on its own terms without directly referring to its linkage with Judaism, or he could defend it by representing its relation to Judaism as an advantage rather than a liability. Mendelssohn begins with the first line of defense and then turns to the second. The turn happens after Jacobi publishes his *Spinoza-Letters*. In this section I want to trace in more detail Mendelssohn's two responses to Jacobi, *Morning Hours* and *To the Friends of Lessing*.

Mendelssohn's initial response to Jacobi was, as I have just said, to defend the religion of reason without reference to Judaism. This was what he undertook in his *Morning Hours* (1785).[31] When Jacobi published his *Spinoza-Letters* soon afterwards, Mendelssohn adopted the second route of defense for his religion of reason, openly acknowledging the relationship between the religion of reason and Judaism. This is the strategy of his final work, *To the Friends of Lessing*. Taking this second route of defense, Mendelssohn in effect offered *himself* as proof against Jacobi's imputation that the Enlightenment's religion of reason and Judaism were both fundamentally atheistic. Mendelssohn, in other words, finally responds to Jacobi by placing his own Jewish and enlightened identity on prominent display. Mendelssohn's strategy was to allow the reading public to judge whether he was an atheist hiding behind the mask of a believing Jew. In placing himself before the public this way, he portrayed Jacobi as not only his accuser, but the fanatical persecutor of all Jews.

Mendelssohn seeks to compel the world to judge between himself, a Jew who sought nothing more than enlightened coexistence with his Christian neighbors, and a Christian, Jacobi, who wanted to raise the specter of a philosophical Inquisition against the Jews. The stakes of this strategy are quite high. If it works, it will strike a decisive blow against anti-Jewish resistance to Mendelssohn's vision of an enlightened German society that he advanced in *Jerusalem*. If it fails, it will mean a tremendous setback for his cause. Perhaps not surprisingly, Mendelssohn's strategy plays directly into Jacobi's hands. Mendelssohn ends up linking the Enlightenment and Judaism too closely. Jacobi was arguing that it was necessary to find a new Christology removed as far as possible from both deism and Judaism, and Mendelssohn's Jewish self-display seems only to reinforce Jacobi's point. By 1800, both Mendelssohn's Judaism and the Enlightenment's religion of reason had been superseded by the new idealist project of fashioning a unified whole out of subject and object, Spirit and Substance, Kant and Spinoza. By 1800, the voices of both Mendelssohn and Jacobi could no longer be heard.

I begin the account of Mendelssohn's response to Jacobi with his *Morning Hours*. This work, as I have said, seeks to do battle with Jacobi on the neutral ground of a philosophical defense of the religion of reason. Mendelssohn decided to write this work directly after he received Jacobi's first letter detailing his conversations with Lessing in which Lessing had revealed his attraction for a Kabbalistic and pantheistic Spinoza. A year and a half after receiving this letter, Mendelssohn's *Morning Hours* was published. Since Jacobi had argued that the religion of reason, if carried to its logical conclusion, was simply atheistic Spinozism, Mendelssohn offered another interpretation of Spinozism, what he called "purified" or "refined" ("geläuterte") Spinozism, that was in effect a pantheistic variant of the religion of reason. In the center of the work Mendelssohn dealt with Lessing, attributing to him the pantheist version of the religion of reason. Mendelssohn defends Lessing's purified Spinozism as being completely compatible with a theistic religion of reason and with its affirmation of the moral purposiveness guiding the universe. Lessing, Mendelssohn claimed, had purified Spinozism of its greatest flaw, namely, its rejection of any objective distinction between good and evil. Mendelssohn hoped to preemptively take the sting out of the charge, not yet made public by Jacobi, that Lessing had been a Spinozist. Mendelssohn makes no reference to Jacobi in *Morning Hours*. Instead, Mendelssohn's strategy is to defend his own version of the religion of reason and offer a possible argument in favor of purified Spinozism, portraying this argument as one that Lessing himself had advanced.

While the philosophical strategy of *Morning Hours* makes it much less dramatic reading than Mendelssohn's second work, *To the Friends of Lessing*, it is worth spending a little time rehearsing what I regard as the central argument of the book, the one advanced in defense of purified Spinozism. What I hope will emerge from attending to this argument is Mendelssohn's belief that the irreducible reality of finite human subjectivity must be the starting point of any philosophy or philosophical theology. Quite ironically, Mendelssohn and Jacobi stand together in recognizing the inescapable finitude of human subjectivity, and post-Kantian German idealism stands in opposition to both of them in its quest to overcome the limitations of finite subjectivity once and for all. In his study of the role of the Mendelssohn-Jacobi quarrel in the formation of Leo Strauss's views about reason and revelation, Benjamin Lazier puts the essence of the quarrel quite well when writes that "Jacobi needed to keep the divine infinite free from worldly finitude" (2008: 97). Lazier shows how Leo Strauss's analysis of Mendelssohn's similar need to maintain the separation of divine infinitude and human finitude took the side of Jacobi against Mendelssohn (106–10). I hope to show in what follows and in the first section of Chapter 3 ("Introduction: Mendelssohn and Jacobi on Revelation") that Mendelssohn and Jacobi have more in common than is apparent at first sight.

Mendelssohn's defense of purified Spinozism begins with an analysis of self-consciousness. Mendelssohn argues that accompanying every sensation and thought is a reflexive awareness of its placement within an infinitely extended continuum of intensity. When one sees a bright object, for example, one is aware that the brightness one perceives is located on a graded scale of brightness, in other words, one is aware that there are increasingly brighter objects and less bright objects. No sighted human can directly and immediately sense the most intense brightness or the complete absence of brightness, since these sensations stand at the limits of an infinitely extensible continuum and human sensation is finite. "No being has an immediate conception of a greater reality than it itself possesses" (*Morning Hours* 14:119). No sighted person, Mendelssohn claims, can truly imagine what someone who is blind from birth experiences. Blindness is not merely the weakening of sight; as the sheer absence of any sense of brightness, it is the unreachable lower limit of brightness for anyone with sight.[32]

Mendelssohn takes the limitation of consciousness (and the consciousness of limitation) to be inescapable for us as finite beings. It is also what proves that we are not merely thoughts within the infinite mind of God. God may have a thought whose content is, for example, the sensation of brightness I have when I look at a fire, but God's thought cannot also include my consciousness of the placement of this sensation within an infinite continuum whose extremes I can never reach. From God's perspective, the sensation of brightness is located on a continuum of which God has a direct and immediate grasp, since God's consciousness is infinite. God can as little experience the limitation of my consciousness as the sighted person can experience the absence of sight. God, says Mendelssohn, cannot "alienate" ("entäussern") Himself from the infinitude of His consciousness in order to assume a finite consciousness. A sighted person can imagine blindness as the lessening of sight, and in this way God can imagine "a limited grade of His reality, with all the weaknesses and incapacities that follow upon this limitation." However, just as the sighted individual cannot actually alienate Himself from sight, God Himself "remains unalienated from His infinite reality" (*Morning Hours* 14:120). Therefore, even though God may imagine the thoughts and sensations of all His creatures as *objects* of His infinite mind, He cannot actually have these thoughts *as their subject*. Since I know that I have limited thoughts and sensations, I know that my thoughts are not merely thoughts within the infinite mind of God.[33] My self-consciousness of the finitude of my thoughts and sensations guarantees that I am an independently thinking being, although I am sustained in my existence by being an object within the infinite mind of God. Hence we have pantheism—

understood here as the doctrine that all things exist within God—but we also have the independent reality of finite subjectivity.

So long as pantheism acknowledges the difference between human finite subjectivity and God's infinite subjectivity, it can be counted as "purified" of the determinism of Spinoza's monistic system. The independent finite subjectivity of the human being can initiate actions in accordance with his or her finite conceptions of good and bad. God has chosen to grant independent reality to those possibilities within His infinite mind that correspond to His perfect conception of the good, and therefore this world is the best of all possible worlds, as Leibniz taught. However, the vocation of the human being is to actualize that which God's intellect sees to be the good. As we have seen in the previous chapter, Mendelssohn believes that enacting benevolence is the human's fundamental responsibility, and that in doing so the human perfects the world. The independent reality of human consciousness is part of this perfectible world, and the choices the independent human makes are not foreknown from eternity. The freedom of the human is not expressed in any act of the will whatever, but only in those acts that contribute to the perfection of the world. Such acts are expressions of the divine will, and the divine will is the free choice of what is best.

In accordance with purified Spinozism, therefore, my vocation as a human is to conform my finite conscious subjectivity, which is an object of God's infinite consciousness, to that infinite consciousness, to make choices in accordance with my awareness that I am but a part of the divine mind: "I, a human being, a thought of the divinity, will never cease to remain a thought of divinity, and I will in the endless succession of time be happy or miserable to the degree that I acknowledge my Thinker, to the degree that I love Him; to the degree that I exert myself (and Spinoza must grant exertion to this thought of God) to be similar to this Source of my being, and to love his other thoughts, as I love myself" (*Morning Hours* 14:123). If one accepts this purified Spinozism, "morality and religion are preserved" (*Morning Hours* 14:123). While Mendelssohn himself adopts a somewhat more deistic philosophical theology, with God's infinite mind and finite subjectivities standing farther apart from one another than in this picture of purified pantheism, he certainly would endorse the basic picture he has sketched here of the finite thinker finding his or her happiness in the love of the infinite Thinker and "his other thoughts," that is, the other finite subjects with whom one lives in fellowship.

Mendelssohn's own religion of reason sees the human subject as achieving greater independence from the infinite Mind of God than the purified Spinozist would allow. But Mendelssohn's starting point remains the consciousness of one's finitude. In seeking to prove the existence of an independent, infinite, and self-subsisting God who is the first cause of all finite beings, Mendelssohn offers an argument that he claims "has never yet been touched upon by another philosopher" (*Morning Hours* 16:141). Mendelssohn begins his argument by offering a variant of the premise that also served for his proof of the distinction between the infinite Mind of God and the human's finite mind in purified pantheism. Here the emphasis is on the finitude of *self*-consciousness, and this is said to consist in the awareness that one never is conscious of one's entire being. Mendelssohn writes:

> Apart from the immediate sensation of my own existence which, as we have seen, is beyond all doubt, I posit the following perception as also not open to doubt: I am not reducible to what I can clearly know about myself. This amounts to the same as saying: More belongs to my existence than I have access to through my consciousness of myself. And even what I do know of myself, is, just considered by itself, able to be further developed in both clarity and comprehension beyond what I can achieve. (*Morning Hours* 16:141)

Mendelssohn argues that the inner sense, immediately given with self-consciousness, that there is more to me than whatever is the present content of my self-consciousness, cannot be mistaken; it cannot be the result of an illusion, but is every bit as incorrigible as the feeling of pain. I cannot be in doubt that I feel pain, although I may not know its cause. Mendelssohn now adds, I cannot be in doubt that I do not know all there is to know about myself. That sense of "more" is simply unimpeachable. Mendelssohn, relying upon the further premise that everything which is actual must be thinkable, argues that the "more" of self-consciousness requires the existence of a thinker capable of apprehending the "more" of the finite self in all its reticulations, both in the direction of a deeper inwardness than consciousness can penetrate to and in the direction of a wider outward network of relations with objects and persons than consciousness can encompass.

Jacobi learned of the publication of *Morning Hours* from his friend Hamann, although Mendelssohn soon sent him a copy. Jacobi had believed, not without reason, that Mendelssohn was intending to let him read his manuscript before publishing it, and that Mendelssohn had at least tacitly agreed to a simultaneous publication of their different interpretations of Lessing's Spinozism. In a letter to Elise Raimarus written just before he published *Morning Hours*, Mendelssohn takes it upon himself to explain why he found it necessary to publish *Morning Hours* before sending Jacobi a manuscript to read. He had come to feel that he could never come to any agreement with Jacobi because, given their different philosophical "idioms," "for all eternity we would never be finished with each other" (*JubA* 13: letter 693). Jacobi's reaction upon learning that Mendelssohn had already published *Morning Hours* was swift. Without asking permission from Mendelssohn to quote from the content of his letters (Jacobi had previously given his permission to Mendelssohn to use his letters in the projected work on Lessing), Jacobi published his *Spinoza-Letters* several weeks after Mendelssohn's *Morning Hours*. One can agree with George di Giovanni's assessment that Jacobi "had good cause to feel that he had been made a fool of" (Jacobi 1994: 603n64).

Mendelssohn for his part believed that Jacobi's publication of the details of their correspondence was a dishonorable breach of privacy, and that Jacobi's revelation of conversations he had had with Lessing was simply part of a carefully planned character assassination of a man he had entrapped into making statements that were never meant to be taken seriously or to be broadcast publicly. Mendelssohn responded to Jacobi's *Spinoza-Letters* with his short work, *To the Friends of Lessing* (1786).[34] Mendelssohn fell ill after personally delivering the manuscript to his publisher on a wintry Sunday in the first week of January, 1786. The account of his death three days later by his friend and doctor Marcus Herz is given in full as part of his publisher's preface to the work. Those who had been friends of Lessing and Mendelssohn accused Jacobi of having, in effect, killed Mendelssohn.[35]

Mendelssohn in *To the Friends of Lessing* rehearses some of the same arguments in philosophical theology that had exercised him in *Morning Hours*, although now in direct contestation with the interpretive claims of Jacobi in *Spinoza-Letters*. The work is framed, however, by rather pointed and one might even say aggressive statements by Mendelssohn about his Jewish identity and about Judaism more generally. It would be wrong to say that Mendelssohn is taking a defensive posture in these passages. He is, I think it is fair to say, going on the attack against Jacobi's Christianity and even against Christianity more generally.

Early on in *To the Friends of Lessing*, Mendelssohn brings up Jacobi's attempt to identify Spinozism with Judaism. "The label 'Jew and Spinozist,'" Mendelssohn concludes after conceding that Lessing's attraction to Spinozism suggested his attraction to Judaism as well, "was very far from making as unpleasant an impression upon me as Herr Jacobi, it appears, assumed it would" (*To the Friends of Lessing* 188). Mendelssohn's defense of the religion of reason will be at the same time a defense of Judaism, since it was "the Jew Baruch Spinoza," as Mendelssohn refers to him in imitation of what he thought was Jacobi's deprecatory attitude, who was, according to Jacobi, the source of all the trouble. Mendelssohn's goal is to show that he, an exemplary Jew, can embrace both Spinoza and the religion of reason, and that he is as little an atheist as any individual who shares the common human sense that the world is the creation of a benevolent deity. If Spinoza and Mendelssohn have abandoned their faith in God for a metaphysical fiction, as Jacobi claims, then no human being has faith in God. It is not the Jew who has fallen away from an immediate and personal connection with God, but Jacobi. Let us look in more detail at how Mendelssohn seeks to pull off this reversal of roles, with the Jew on the side of the personal God and Jacobi on the side of a mechanical and rigid orthodoxy.

Near the beginning of *To the Friends of Lessing*, Mendelssohn writes: "Mr. Jacobi does not know me: according to him I might be described as reason's hireling ("Vernünftling"), as someone who defers too much to reason and not at all to faith, who so stands in the grip of delusion that he would try to set the world aright by means of metaphysical proofs, even conjure the spirits with quiddities" (196). Against this description of his complete and utter deference to reason, Mendelssohn declares that despite all the arguments and doubts he knows can be raised against it, "the obvious truth of natural religion, it seems to me, is just as brilliantly clear to any unspoilt and uncorrupted mind, just as unshakeably certain, as any proposition of geometry" (197–98). The "truths of the religion of reason," Mendelssohn goes on to say, are able to be comprehended by anyone, in "whatever life situation a human being may find himself." Mendelssohn demonstrates his point by telling a story about two men, one a Greenland Eskimo and the other a missionary, walking together one early morning:

> The argument of that Greenlander who walked about with the missionary on an ice-floe one beautiful morning was as convincing for him then, before that missionary had misguided his understanding, as it remains for me now: as he saw the

sun's first rays blaze forth over the icy peaks, he said to the pastor, "Look, brother, at the new day! How beautiful must be the one who has made this!" This argument has the same power for me as the simple and artless argument of the psalmist: "He who has made the ear, must he not surely hear? He who has fashioned the eye, must he not surely see? He, the Eternal One, who gives knowledge to the mortal man, also knows the thoughts of man" [from Ps 94:9–10]. This natural, childishly easy conclusion has for me all the clarity of a geometric axiom, and the unassailable power of an unshakeable proof. (*To the Friends of Lessing* 198)

If we map the subject positions of the argument between the Eskimo and the missionary onto those of Mendelssohn and Jacobi, Mendelssohn occupies the position of the Eskimo, and also the psalmist, and Jacobi is identified as the missionary. The missionary, attempting to teach the Eskimo the Christian catechism, is caught up short by the simple expression of wonder on the part of the Eskimo. The Eskimo does not have a name for "the one who made this," but no name needs to be given to the Creator. However, the Eskimo's simplicity of feeling might not ever rise to the level of prayer, to an address to a Creator who is a Person with a benevolent will and who can see and hear and understand the thoughts of man. This is why Mendelssohn adds the words of the psalmist. With these words, the Eskimo's awe before the beauty of the world is connected to an awareness that the Creator is approachable by a human being. The missionary is about to destroy the simple wonder of the Eskimo by teaching him to worship according to a creed. But it is not only the fact that a set of words will take the place of simple wonder that will corrupt the Eskimo, but also that he will be severed from his direct awareness of God as Creator by being taught that he cannot approach this God except through an intermediary, through Christ. Mendelssohn does not say this in so many words, but by adding the psalmist to the argument against the missionary, he shows us that the Creator is also the personal God to whom the Jew prays. In Mendelssohn's religion of reason, the Creator is attuned to humans and has no need of an intermediary in order to reach them. The words of the Hebrew Bible are an expression of this religion of reason.

The missionary distorts everything, interposing himself between the Eskimo and God, darkening the light of the morning. We will see that the light motif will recur in a similar context later in *To the Friends of Lessing*.

Mendelssohn is certainly conscious of the association between God's self-revelation and the light, especially the light of the breaking day. The psalmist's words are represented by Mendelssohn as letting us see the light directly, opening us to rather than placing themselves before God's self-revelation in the world.[36]

But there is more to be gleaned from Mendelssohn's use of the words of the psalmist. Mendelssohn must know that his readers, or at least a good number of them, would not be ignorant of the psalm from which the words come. In this psalm (Ps 94), these words are hardly the "simple and artless argument" expressing a natural man's recognition that God is like him, able to hear and see, and also to know the thoughts of men. The context, rather, is one where the psalmist accuses his persecutors and the persecutors of his people—the Lord's "heritage"—of assuming that God is deaf and blind to the workings of those who "break in pieces" his people. And it is not a general statement of the religion of reason that the psalmist makes when he says "God knows the thoughts of men," because the verse continues, "that they are vanity." For those who are not blind to the allusive significance of the psalmist's words, Mendelssohn is positioning Jacobi as the vainglorious enemy of God and God's people.

Mendelssohn's rhetorical strategy in the passage about the Greenland Eskimo and the missionary, whatever one makes of the allusive quality of the psalmist's words, is to define the subject positions of the quarrel between himself and Jacobi as, on the one hand, the Jew as the uncorrupted human and friend of God, and on the other hand, the Christian as the hardened dogmatist and, if not the enemy of God, at least an adversary of the truths of the religion of reason. As Mendelssohn puts it a little further on: "Herr Jacobi has obviously one goal: to lead his fellow man who has lost himself in the wilderness of speculation back to the level and secure path of faith" (*To the Friends of Lessing* 194). Jacobi is the missionary in the story; it is not speculative reason but Jacobi, therefore, who "misguides the understanding." The Jew is on the side of the free use of reason, of respect for the simple wonder of creation, and of direct address to a personal God. Jacobi, the Christian, stands for dogmatism and for the separation of the human from his immediate and natural relationship with God. Mendelssohn will never directly contest any of the doctrines of orthodox Christianity, but it is quite clear that his version of the religion of reason has little room for Christ: "The human whose reason has not been corrupted by sophistry need only follow his direct sense [seinem geraden Sinn] and his happiness stands secure" (*To the Friends of Lessing* 199).

Mendelssohn in *To the Friends of Lessing* will reiterate the major claim of his *Jerusalem*, that Judaism offers no "revelation of creedal doctrines or eternal truths that we are commanded to believe" and that there is not even a word for *religion* in the Hebrew language. Judaism is not a religion built upon belief in a creed as Christianity is, but rather it is, as he puts it in *Jerusalem*, a "revealed legislation" that is the "living script" in which reason is enacted. What a Jew's reason is supposed to hold to be true is nothing more or less than "the maxims and judgments of simple common sense that grasps things directly in its vision and arrives without further ado at conviction" (*To the Friends of Lessing* 197). The beliefs of the Jew are the beliefs of any human, at least as long as she trusts to her common sense and is not misled by metaphysical sophistry or religious dogmatism.

Mendelssohn returns to his defense of "purified" Spinozism in *To the Friends of Lessing*, repeating that Spinoza's error had been to fail to recognize that the actual world of finite beings could not be identical with or somehow add up to God's infinite Mind. Spinoza was not an atheist; rather, he had given *too much* reality to God and too little to finite beings. Mendelssohn makes this his main point of contention with Jacobi's interpretation of Spinoza. In Mendelssohn's first published work, *Philosophical Dialogues*, he explains that Spinoza was trying to reunite what Descartes had sundered, namely, the world of thought and the world of extended material things. Spinoza imagined that thoughts and things were matched one for one as modes of one infinite substance, but he had failed to see that God must have *chosen* just these thoughts and these things from all the possible thought-thing matches within his infinite Mind. Why, unless this were the best of all possible worlds, would just this world exist?

In *To the Friends of Lessing*, Mendelssohn reiterates this critique of Spinoza. Spinoza mistook the freedom of the will to mean making a choice among equal possibilities, a sort of unmotivated choice among things one is equally indifferent to. Spinoza found this indifferentist picture of freedom to lead to the conclusion that no choice will ever be made by a rational being calculating the options. God, perfectly rational, therefore makes no choices. According to Mendelssohn, freedom rather means being able to act in accordance with a conception of the good. Spinoza's God, on the indifferentist notion of freedom, never chooses from among all the possible worlds within himself. No world is ever allowed to become actual in Spinoza's system. Therefore, God cannot really be made equivalent to the world, whether that means reduced to nothing as the atheist interpretation of Spinoza claims, or as an indwelling divine omnipresence as the pantheist interpretation proposes. According to Mendelssohn, Spinozism can be purified of its fundamental error if one adopts what Mendelssohn calls the *perfectissimum* interpretation of freedom, where God chooses one world out of the infinitely possible worlds because it is the best world among them all. On what other basis would God have chosen?

Mendelssohn uses this argument to respond to Jacobi's challenge, resurrected from the pre-recantation Wachter, that Spinoza was expressing the esoteric pantheistic metaphysics of Kabbalistic Judaism. Mendelssohn always considered Spinoza to be, like him, a Jew seeking to deepen his knowledge of God through the exercise of reason. Spinoza, unlike Mendelssohn, found himself led away from Judaism by errors of reason, errors that were far removed from Kabbalistic or pantheistic Schwärmerei. Far from it, Mendelssohn declares. Spinoza's error led him away from any form of pantheism because Spinoza never allowed that any actual world existed. Had he been guided by the common-sense view that acting freely means acting in accordance with one's conception of what is best, Spinoza would have been led to the purified pantheism that Mendelssohn developed in *Morning Hours*. Spinoza would have accepted the irreducible reality of finite human subjectivity, and he would have seen that it "allowed itself to be very well harmonized mainly with Judaism." Indeed, had Spinoza not misunderstood the nature of "authentic Judaism" ("ächte Judenthum"), "he could have remained an orthodox Jew" (*To the Friends of Lessing* 188). As to Spinoza's objection to the continuing obligation of any Jew to follow the ceremonial laws, namely, that these laws only were binding within a state that can enforce them with threats of punishment, Mendelssohn had argued in *Jerusalem* that the Jewish law did not originally contain civil laws depending upon the coercive enforcement of the state, and did not need to contain such laws after the Jews lost their state. Jewish law, Mendelssohn argues, was and remains an ideal form of noncoercive polity whose continued existence is so far from being at odds with the state that it rather can be seen as the model for an enlightened state. Thus Mendelssohn answers Spinoza in *Jerusalem*. In his last work, *To the Friends of Lessing*, Mendelssohn returns Spinoza to the fold of the Judaism, forgiving him for his errors of reasoning and historical judgment about the nature of Jewish law. Having so vehemently argued against the right to excommunicate in Judaism, Mendelssohn now lifts the ban against Spinoza and offers him to the Jewish community as someone deluded by an error in reasoning rather than by a will to rebellion. Spinoza is indeed a Jew like me, Mendelssohn in effect tells Jacobi and the world, and if Spinoza is an atheist, then so am I. But you, Herr Jacobi, know Spinoza as little as you know me.

Throughout *To the Friends of Lessing*, Mendelssohn seeks to show that because Jacobi is opposed to the religion of reason, Jacobi is also an enemy of the common man and the Jews. As an enemy of the Jews, Jacobi is also an enemy of the entire Enlightenment project of creating a religiously tolerant state. Mendelssohn foregrounds the link between Jacobi's opposition to the Enlightenment's religion of reason and his opposition to the Jewish God. Mendelssohn expects that Jacobi's attack on Lessing's Spinozism, an attack that he couches in the abstract language of philosophy, will appear before the world as what Mendelssohn takes it to be: an attack on the entire Enlightenment project of Lessing—religious tolerance and forbearance—and an attack on both the Jews and all those of good will who, like Dohm, whose *On the Civic Improvement of the Jews* I spoke of in Chapter 1, sought to build an enlightened Germany. Near the end of *To the Friends of Lessing*, Mendelssohn draws the contrast between himself and Jacobi in the starkest possible light as a contrast between two contesting types of faith, that of the Enlightenment descending from Judaism and the other that of persecutorial tyranny descending from Christianity. Jacobi, Mendelssohn declares

> returns to the faith of his fathers, brings a muzzled reason under the yoke through the victorious power of belief, slays all emerging doubts by authority and dictate, as happens in the afterword to his text; there he "blesses and seals" his childlike return with words from the "pious, angel-pure mouth" of Lavater.
>
> I for my part remain with my Jewish lack of faith ("Unglaube"), I place my trust in no mortal's "angel-pure mouth," nor would I rely upon the authority of an "Archangel" when it came to eternal truths upon which human happiness rests, since in this matter I either stand or fall upon my own two feet. And what is more, since all of us, as H[err] J[acobi] says, are "born in belief," I therefore return to the faith of my fathers, which in accordance with the original meaning of the word, is not a faith in a teaching or an opinion, but is a trust and confidence in God's attributes. I assert with full and unqualified confidence in the omnipotence of God that He has the power to bestow upon humans the ability to recognize the truths upon which happiness is based, and I cherish the childlike

confidence in God's mercifulness, that it is His will to bestow this ability upon me. Strengthened by this unwavering faith, I seek to learn and be persuaded of as much as I can from wherever I can. And praise to the benevolence of my Creator! I *believe* that I have discovered much, and everyone can find the same, who seeks with open eyes and does not want to interpose himself before the light. (*To the Friends of Lessing* 218–19)

Mendelssohn could go no farther in making the contest between himself and Jacobi seem to be a contest between Judaism and Christianity. It would be wrong to say, as Adam Sutcliffe has claimed, that "[d]epsite his desire to normalize both Spinoza's and his own position as Jewish participants in the world of Enlightenment philosophy, the cultural pressures that stood against this were too strong for him to overcome" (Sutcliffe 2004: 179). Mendelssohn's counter-assault on Jacobi deliberately foregrounded his Judaism as offering a faith that was true to the "original meaning of the word," a faith that did not stand in the way of the light of common sense that shined from the Creator upon all humans. Mendelssohn did not seek to "normalize" Spinoza and himself as Jews, but to show that Jacobi's stance against Judaism was *abnormal*. Mendelssohn certainly felt that Jacobi was attempting to paint him and Spinoza as "faithless" Jews, but he did not feel that *qua* Jew either he or Spinoza was a questionable participant in the "world of Enlightenment philosophy." Jews did not require "normalizing" in order to enter this world; Judaism was from the start entirely consonant with the religion of reason. Indeed, Jews more than Christians were prepared for the world of Enlightenment philosophy. Jews had no theology that had to be reconciled with philosophy. Mendelssohn believed that by returning Spinoza to Judaism and by standing together with him *as Jewish witnesses to God's wish for universal human happiness* against the muzzling of reason in the name of Christianity's particularist offer of salvation through Jesus alone, he could drive Jacobi from the world of Enlightenment philosophy. Mendelssohn in effect reverses the traditional roles of "particularist" Jew and "universalist" Christian. To be sure, *To the Friends of Lessing* goes farther than any previous work of Mendelssohn's in linking the Jew and the Enlightenment, but it is not by any means a desperate defensive gesture against "cultural pressures" by which he felt overwhelmed in the end. Mendelssohn certainly misjudged the cultural pressures around him, but to the extent they represented the drive of the Enlightenment in Germany, he judged them to be ranged against *Jacobi* and not against himself.

One individual Mendelssohn probably thought he could count on for support in his quarrel with Jacobi was the theologian Friedrich Johann Zöllner, the initiator of the question "Was ist Aufklärung?" in the *Berlinische Monatschrift* to which both Kant and Mendelssohn offered response essays. Zöllner was, along with Mendelssohn and the editors of the *Berlinische Monatschrift* and a handful of other Prussian notables, a member of the Mittwochsgesellschaft (Wednesday Society), a secret group of Berlin intellectuals who constituted themselves "Friends of the Enlightenment."[37] Zöllner had been critical of Mendelssohn's position in *Jerusalem* that ecclesiastical bodies should never have recourse to oaths in order to guarantee the orthodoxy of its leaders. But Zöllner's critique was well intentioned, and was very far from the anti-Semitic attack of Michaelis we had occasion to examine in the previous chapter. But Zöllner's tolerance for Mendelssohn's views, however much he might disagree with them, was stretched to the limit with *To the Friends of Lessing*. Zöllner found himself confronted with a Mendelssohn he could not recognize, although he took pains to explain away the apparent anti-Christian tone that Mendelssohn assumed in the work. Immediately after the appearance of *To the Friends of Lessing*, Zöllner published in the *Berlinische Monatschrift* a brief article, "On a Passage in Moses Mendelssohn's *To the Friends of Lessing*" (1786: 271–75). Zöllner begins by quoting from a letter to Jacobi that Mendelssohn printed in *To the Friends of Lessing*. In the letter, Mendelssohn tells Jacobi that his "noble retreat under the banner of faith . . . is totally in the spirit of your religion which imposes on you the duty of suppressing doubt through faith. The Christian philosopher can afford the pastime of teasing the student of nature; of confronting him with puzzles which, like will-o'-the-wisps, lure him now to one corner, and now to the other, but always slip away even from his most assured grasp."[38] Zöllner comments:

> This passage, as I see it, creates a rather sensational effect, and for several reasons. On the one hand, it pains the serious friends of the truth that a great and beloved philosopher, one who had been so sincerely respected by decent Christians, could let himself be carried away to such a degree that he would write down such a worn-out jab, and at Christianity's expense. On the other hand, I hear the very same notion repeated over and over as a given, whenever someone would like to spare himself the trouble of reflection, and, by making fun of Christianity, acquire the reputation of being a martyr for reason. And a third party who really intends to follow Lavater's and Jacobi's encouragement and would try

to retreat back under the banner of his Christianity would find one more reason in this passage to strengthen his defenses against the necessity of investigating things rationally. (271–72; translation mine)

Zöllner goes on to try to exonerate Mendelssohn of outright contempt for Christianity by reading this passage as an ad hominem piece of mockery, "teasing" Jacobi with a caricaturish image of the Christian dogmatist. But the initial response of Zöllner to *To the Friends* is quite telling. He is brought to declare, almost to convince himself by the sheer force of his exclamation: "Moses Mendelssohn, without question, did not mean it, he could not have meant it!" (272). But Mendelssohn did mean it. It was a central part of his rhetorical strategy to drive as large a wedge as he possibly could between Enlightenment and Christianity.

For many reasons, Mendelssohn's strategy in *To the Friends of Lessing* was doomed to failure. Mendelssohn was not entirely unsuccessful in it, however. He thought he could count on Germany's new philosophical leading light, Immanuel Kant, to intervene on behalf of the Enlightenment goals Kant favored, and Mendelssohn wrote to him soon after Jacobi's publication of *Spinoza-Letters*, requesting that he voice an opinion about this dispute. Mendelssohn was not wrong in thinking that Kant would take his side, although he died before he could read Kant's essay in the *Berlinische Monatschrift*, entitled "What Does it Mean: To 'Orient Oneself' in Thinking?"[39] Mendelssohn was not entirely wrong to believe that his strategy of casting his quarrel with Jacobi as one between Enlightenment and Judaism on the one side, and orthodox Christianity on the other, would marginalize Jacobi and distance him from some of Germany's intellectual and cultural elites. However, the younger generation would side with Jacobi, knowing that Jacobi was by no means an orthodox believer. They would side with Jacobi's effort to recuperate a philosophical theology that stood as far as possible from both Judaism and the religion of reason. They accepted the gnostic equation of the Jewish God as the God of a lifeless, mechanical universe.

Mendelssohn never understood that Jacobi was, with admittedly insufficient clarity, seeking to salvage the possibility of the experience of revelation within the framework of finite human subjectivity. Mendelssohn did not recognize that he and Jacobi shared an emphasis on the irreducibility of human finitude and human particularity. When Jacobi said that his faith "has as its object, not eternal truths, but the finite, accidental nature of man" (*Spinoza-Letters* 231), he was very close to Mendelssohn. What divided Jacobi and Mendelssohn was, in the end, their relationship to what Mendelssohn spoke of as a "contingent" truth, the historical "fact" that Judaism, he says, does require belief in, namely, the giving of the revealed Law at Mt. Sinai. Jacobi replaced this single moment in time with his doctrine that revelation occurs continuously in time, in each individual's experience of the freedom to begin life anew, to *choose* life over death. Mendelssohn made this choice by living within the covenant, the "living script" of the Jewish people; Jacobi made it by turning toward the inner revelation of the divine within the finite particularity of the will. Neither man could understand what the other meant by *revelation* (*Offenbarung*). By 1800, the great conflict between Mendelssohn and Jacobi had been entirely superseded. The issue was no longer how to reconcile two versions of revelation, in both of which an infinite God connects with the contingent and finite realm of human existence. The issue was now how contingency and finitude could be transcended altogether. The issue was how to transform revelation into philosophical knowledge. Jacobi, more and more marginalized, drew closer to Mendelssohn, though he would never have admitted it. Rosenzweig effected the final rapprochement. The story of this rapprochement will be told in the following chapter.

THREE

In the Year of the Lord 1800: Rosenzweig and the Spinoza Quarrel

Introduction: Mendelssohn and Jacobi on Revelation

Despite all their differences, Mendelssohn and Jacobi shared a conviction, a *faith*, that God reveals himself to humanity in the contingency of a historical moment. Furthermore, this contingent revelation is made to particular individuals and is not accessible to the universalizing grasp of reason. Both Mendelssohn and Jacobi would have entirely agreed with Rosenzweig's dictum: "The essence of revelation is that it is a *fact*" ("Die Wesen der Offenbarung ist, daß sie eine *Tatsache* ist") (1984: 100). For Mendelssohn, this revelation took place once, at Mt. Sinai; for Jacobi it takes place whenever the living person feels within himself the yearning for something *more* than law-governed nature. The "supernatural" for Mendelssohn happened only once in history;[1] for Jacobi it is an ever-renewed possibility within the human spirit (Geist). In order to reconcile Mendelssohn and Jacobi, one would need to show how the revelation of God within the single person is correlated with the revelation of God in history and in the words of a historical text (the Hebrew Bible). Rosenzweig achieves this reconciliation by offering *language* as the common medium in which both personal and historical revelation takes place. In this chapter I will position Rosenzweig's philosophy within the framework of the Mendelssohn-Jacobi quarrel. I will argue that Rosenzweig, without deliberately setting out to do so, offers a path to what may be called the "messianic friendship" between Jacobi and Mendelssohn, that is, their acceptance of one another as covenantal partners on the way towards Redemption.

Let me, however, make it perfectly clear that Rosenzweig is not repeating the Hegelian gesture of *Aufhebung*. Mendelssohn and Jacobi remain worlds apart in the "messianic friendship" by which Rosenzweig reconciles them. Their worlds are not superseded by some "third" neutral zone of agreement. Their worlds cannot even be said to talk to one another. As I will show, their worlds are two works of art—two choreographies—existing within radically different temporalities. As Leora Batnitzky has cogently argued in relation to the use of Rosenzweig as a basis for Jewish-Christian dialogue, "the significance of the dialogical relation between Judaism and Christianity is that these two traditions exist in an eternally judgmental relation to one another" (Batnitzky 2000: 223). If one can speak of a "messianic friendship" between Christianity and Judaism as Rosenzweig presents them, it is a friendship between partners whose major point of agreement is that they can never allow themselves to agree with each other until the end of time. The beat to which the choreography of each moves must, as it were, remain *off*beat in relation to the other.[2]

In the next section of the chapter, "The Hebrew Bible and Paganism," I will lay out in broad terms Rosenzweig's contrast between Judaism and Christianity on the one hand, and the philosophic tradition on the other. I will show how the philosophical tradition that descends from Parmenides and reaches its culmination in German idealism is, for Rosenzweig, a form of "paganism." In the following section, "Christianity and Paganism: 1800," I will concentrate on Rosenzweig's philosophy of language in *The Star of Redemption* and its resonance with Mendelssohn's view of the Jewish people as the "living script" of revelation. Then, in the section "Language as the Site of Revelation," I will show how Rosenzweig's critique of idealist philosophy inherits the task that Jacobi left unfinished. Rosenzweig saw his philosophy as an outgrowth and overcoming of the moment in the history of the West he dubbed simply "1800." I will argue that "1800" may also name the moment when the trauma of the Mendelssohn-Jacobi quarrel was repressed. Rosenzweig's *The Star of Redemption*, without ever naming this trauma, nevertheless offers the tools for healing its wounds.[3]

Rosenzweig's philosophy of an experiential revelation involving the encounter of an *I* and a *Thou* draws significantly from Jacobi and one of Jacobi's major nineteenth-century inheritors, Ludwig Feuerbach (Kierkegaard is the other major inheritor).[4] But Rosenzweig seeks to draw the Jacobi-Feuerbach notion of an experiential revelation of a divine *Thou* into relation with his understanding of the "grammar" of the Hebrew Bible and of language more generally. In placing the disclosure of the divine *Thou* back into the linguistic texture of the Hebrew Bible, Rosenzweig overcomes the anti-Jewish gnosticism within Jacobi's attack on idealist philosophers as "the Jews of speculative reason."[5] He makes it possible for Jacobi to be read within a framework laid out by Mendelssohn. Mendelssohn argued that the enactment of the experience of revelation (for Mendelssohn this was historically circumscribed to the moment Israel stood at Mt. Sinai) took place within the "living script" of Israel as a covenantal community. Rosenzweig drew Jacobi's personal experience of revelation in the divine *Thou* within the framework of the communal *performance* of revelation. In drawing together the experiential revelation of a divine *Thou* with the Jewish people's covenantal practice, Rosenzweig manages, after more than a century, to finally find a ground of friendship between Jacobi and Mendelssohn.

Before turning to a more detailed exposition of Rosenzweig's reconciliation of Mendelssohn and Jacobi, it is useful to understand just how close Jacobi himself ultimately came to Mendelssohn's position in the battle he waged, after Mendelssohn's death, against the rising tide of German idealism. Jacobi almost appropriated Mendelssohn's own language as he pressed his claim that finitude is an inescapable feature of human consciousness, and that the gap between human finitude and divine infinitude cannot be overcome through speculative reason. But it is not only in this point that Jacobi drew close to Mendelssohn. He also came to share with Mendelssohn an understanding that revelation—and for Jacobi this meant Christianity— was essentially the opposite of idolatry, just as for Mendelssohn Judaism as revelation's "living script" stood opposed to what he referred to as the "fetishization" of mere symbols of the divine. In the following paragraphs I will explain these points of contact between Mendelssohn and Jacobi, and then I will turn an exposition of Rosenzweig's conception of the revelatory nature of language. I hope to show how this conception both builds upon the points of contact between Mendelssohn and Jacobi, and offers a reconciliation of their remaining differences.

In the previous chapter, I quoted from what Mendelssohn claimed was the basis for a proof of God's existence that no prior philosopher had ever made. The proof begins with "the immediate sensation of my own existence which, as we have seen, is beyond all doubt." So far, we are on territory that Descartes had explored with his "cogito" proof of his own existence. But now Mendelssohn takes the step that he claims is unprecedented: "I posit the following perception as also not open to doubt: I am not reducible to what I can clearly know about myself. This amounts to the same as saying: More belongs to my existence than I have access to through my consciousness of myself." Going on to argue for a Leibnizian-Wolffian metaphysics in which every virtual possibility must be the object of a representation for it to be actualized, Mendelssohn concludes that the "more" that transcends his own finite representation of himself in his self-consciousness must be the object of a representation in the infinite mind of God. I am not interested in debating the merits and faults of Mendelssohn's metaphysics.[6] What I would like to point out, rather, is how Jacobi takes over nearly the exact language Mendelssohn uses in order to argue against Fichte's metaphysical strategy of making the self-consciousness of an *I* his starting point. Jacobi writes in his cri de coeur against idealistic nihilism, *Jacobi to Fichte* (1799): "As surely as I possess reason, just as surely I do *not* posses with this human reason of mine the perfection of life, *not* the fullness of the good and the true. And as surely as I do *not* possess all this with it, *and know it*, just as certainly do I *know* that there is a *higher* being, and that I have my origin in Him. My solution too, therefore, and that of my reason is not the *I*, but the 'More than I'! the 'Better than I'!—Someone entirely Other" (Jacobi 1994: 514; 30). Jacobi, exactly like Mendelssohn, bases his knowledge of God's existence in what he calls his "not-knowledge," his self-consciousness of his lack of full self-knowledge.

Jacobi throughout his life said that the "Someone entirely Other" was the God who revealed himself in Christ: "Truly did the Holy One bear witness concerning himself: that whoever recognized him recognized the Father, and that whoever believed in him, did not believe in him, but in the one who sent him" (*On Things Divine* 426). Jacobi had no truck with

Mendelssohn's conception of a natural religion, the recognition of God as Creator that anyone could attain to, the Greenland Eskimo and philosopher alike. For Jacobi, God's only revelation took place *within* each human, as the one who redeems the individual from the laws of nature: "In so far as a human being fervently believes in an indwelling, nature-surpassing power, he believes in God; he feels Him, he experiences Him" (*On Things Divine* 426). To reject the experience of a nature-surpassing God is to be an atheist or a pagan idolater. To be open to this revelation is to be a Christian: "Christianity, conceived in its purity, is the only religion. Outside of it there is only atheism or idolatry" (*On Things Divine* 426). Jacobi has a rather expansive notion of Christianity "conceived in its purity." He claims that Socrates is a Christian because he felt the call of an inner divine voice. But what Jacobi could never admit was that God could reveal himself in *laws*, whether the natural laws governing the world or the revealed laws of the Hebrew Bible. But for Mendelssohn, it was precisely through these laws that humanity in general and the Jew in particular were related to God.

Mendelssohn and Jacobi share the idea that the experience of human finitude makes possible the acknowledgment of the existence of a transcendent God, but they develop this idea in very different ways. For Mendelssohn, the transcendent God who supports human finitude within his infinite Mind is the Creator whose will brings into reality the multiplicity of finite beings in the world. For Jacobi, the transcendent God is the Redeemer who calls upon the human to aspire to a super-natural identity. For Jacobi, this is the God spoken of in the New Testament, who sent his son into the world to draw all humans out of their enslavement to nature's laws. For Mendelssohn, however, the transcendent God revealed commandments at Mt. Sinai that turn the Jewish people into a "living script." But even here, where Mendelssohn and Jacobi seem so radically to part ways, the differences should not blind us to an even more fundamental point that they both share. We need to recall that for Mendelssohn the Jewish people enact the living script that stands opposed to any fetishization of word or image as divine. The Jewish people witness to the fact that nothing within nature is divine. Every representation is finite and points beyond itself. For Jacobi, the alternatives to Christianity are atheism and idolatry. These alternatives are not so very different, however. Atheism finds its modern form in the Spinozistic identification of God and Nature; idolatry is just a more limited form of atheism. Idolatry deifies an object within the natural world; atheism deifies the entirety of nature. Opposed to Christianity, therefore, are two forms of atheism that are, in effect, two forms of idolatry. Both Mendelssohn and Jacobi agree, then, that revelation—whether this is the living script enacted by the Jewish people or the experience of the divine Spirit within the individual—stands opposed to the immanence of the divine within nature. Both Mendelssohn and Jacobi agree that revelation stands opposed to idolatry, while each claims revelation for his religion alone. Better put, each claims that his religion is not just one among the many religions of the world. For Mendelssohn, Judaism is *not* a religion, but a revealed legislation; for Jacobi Christianity is the *only* religion because it alone is based upon the revelation of the "indwelling nature-surpassing power" of the divine Spirit.

Rosenzweig's conception of language as the site of revelation mediates between Mendelssohn and Jacobi. And his argument that Judaism and Christianity are living witnesses against idolatry—Rosenzweig calls it "paganism"—develops the most significant commonality linking Mendelssohn and Jacobi. It is perhaps easiest to begin my account of Rosenzweig's reconciliation of Mendelssohn and Jacobi with this second point, and then return to provide the philosophical grounding for Rosenzweig's "bi-covenantalism" in his discussion of language as the site of revelation.

The Hebrew Bible and Paganism

I will argue that Rosenzweig managed to reconcile Mendelssohn and Jacobi by showing how the language of the Hebrew Bible exemplifies revelation itself, enacts revelation as the coming-to-speech of God, humanity, and world, and points beyond itself to two covenantal paths, one followed by a people with the sign of the covenant in their flesh, and the other by individuals whose covenant is established through the sacrifice of Christ. Mendelssohn represents the voice of the Jewish people, Jacobi the voice of the Christian individual. Neither voice is complete in itself. Both together stand opposed to what Rosenzweig calls "paganism."

The Hebrew Bible is not the only linguistic expression of revelation, to be sure, but it is for Rosenzweig the linguistic form of this revelation that has entered into history. It is "the great historical testimony of Revelation" (*Star* 213; 221). Language that had been shaped into the words of poetry and narrative had, of course, existed before the Hebrew Bible. Indeed, the relation between poet and artwork already embodies the "categories" that Rosenzweig argues structure the configuration of God, Man, and World. These are the categories Creation, Revelation, and Redemption. Below I will say more about the way art mirrors revelation. But for now it is only important to note that, according to Rosenzweig, language as a medium that could be and had been shaped into artistic forms prepared the soil for the "historical testimony" of Revelation itself in the Hebrew Bible.

The revelatory language of the Hebrew Bible entered history, according to Rosenzweig, by calling upon a people to make its life depend upon the communal performance of this revelation. I use the term *performance* in the way one might use it to describe a drama or a dance. The Hebrew Bible is given life, Rosenzweig would say, in the choreographed movements enjoined by its commandments to Israel. Rosenzweig again and again draws a connection between the performance of the commandments and the performance of a drama or a dance. The connection between religious and artistic performance is one of the recurring themes of the *Star*, and essential to understanding Rosenzweig's conception of language as the site of revelation. For it is perhaps truer to say that it is not language *per se* but rather *language lifted into art* that is the site of revelation. The Hebrew Bible is the artistic embodiment of the revelation of God's Word, which Rosenzweig insists is also humanity's Word. The Hebrew Bible is unique as an artwork because its afterlife—its *translation*—enters history in the communal life of the Jewish people. It also enters history, but in a different way, in the communal life of the Christian *ekklesia*, the brotherhood of those whose faith is in Christ as the living embodiment of the Word of God. In these two ways, then, the Hebrew Bile gives shape to history itself—Rosenzweig speaks of it also as "orienting" history—by shaping the lives of Jews and Christians into two distinct choreographed translations of the Hebrew Bible's three moments of Creation, Revelation, and Redemption.

The Hebrew Bible, as I have said, is the artistic embodiment of revelation that provides the pattern for two choreographies of communal life. In the Hebrew Bible, the world is revealed as God's *Creation* (Genesis 1), God is revealed as the soul's *Lover* (the Song of Songs), and World, Soul, and God find their unity in Redemption, when language becomes the pure gesture of humanity's worshipful acknowledgment of the One God (Psalm 115). To show what the moments of Creation, Revelation, and Redemption might concretely mean, Rosenzweig offers an analysis of the art work in general as a microcosmic reflection of these moments. The art work is a singular, created world and not merely the mechanical fabrication of an object; within it the artist *reveals* an idea that cannot be otherwise brought to life; the work is *redeemed* by calling into being a world of spectators who are unified, despite their partial views, as they behold her work.[7] But the unfolding moments of artist, artwork, and spectator are not only a mirror of God's relation to the world and humanity. Rosenzweig also shows how the life of the Jewish people is itself a singular artwork, an ever-recreated "round-dance" of the eternal people where, as Yeats famously said, the dancer cannot be distinguished from the dance. The Jewish people themselves perform the artwork of eternal life in the rhythmic pattern of the holidays of Creation, Revelation, and Redemption. The Christian *ekklesia* has its choreography of these moments, too, but Rosenzweig will argue that, in the case of Christianity, art itself in the modern period becomes the culminating expression of the Cross. This is a profoundly *Romantic* conception of art, and we will see in the next section how Rosenzweig identifies it with the founding figure of German Romanticism, Johann Wolfgang Goethe. For the moment, let us return to the artwork at the heart of the *Star*, the Hebrew Bible.

The Hebrew Bible is a work of linguistic art in which Creation and Revelation (of God as the soul's lover) are bodied forth and Redemption is intimated in the "We" of the Psalms. While the Hebrew Bible provides the script, the law provides the choreography for the Jewish people's performance of the three inseparable moments of Creation, Revelation, and Redemption. Rosenzweig's conception of the Jewish community as an ever-recreated performance of revelation links him directly to Mendelssohn, for whom the Jewish people enacted the "living script" of the revealed legislation. For both Mendelssohn and Rosenzweig, this means that the Jewish people must remain a singular people in the midst of all the other peoples. But where Mendelssohn in *Jerusalem* spoke of the particularity of the Jewish revealed legislation as "an individual thing, which has no genus, which refuses to be stacked with anything, which cannot be put under the same rubric with anything else" (*Jerusalem* 131; 2:123), Rosenzweig situates the historical revelation at the heart of this people's life—the Hebrew Bible—as the possession of the world as a whole. Just as a linguistic artwork finds its afterlife in its translation, so too does the Hebrew Bible enter into history.

As Leora Batnitzky writes, "the act of translating the Bible" is itself an "act of revelation leading to redemption."[8] Just as each artwork draws spectators together, the Hebrew Bible draws the world together. The Hebrew Bible, when it is translated into the languages of the pagan peoples, calls each individual among the nations into a fellowship—a spectatorship—of the beauty of Israel. This beauty takes two forms: the Jewish beauty of life lived in the framework of the Law, and the Christian beauty of life lived under the sign of the Cross. Both are translations, or refractions, of the revelation of the Hebrew Bible into configurations of redemption.

By "translation" Rosenzweig means more than the sentence-by-sentence re-rendering of the Hebrew Bible. Rosenzweig speaks of the evangel of the Gospels as the translation of the narrative of the birth of Israel, with Exodus in particular figuring as the "original" upon which the birth and childhood stories of Jesus are based. The Cross is both the terminus and fulfillment of the preceding events of the life of Jesus. The giving of the Law is the fulfillment of the Exodus narrative of Israel's birth. Despite the similar pattern of the stories (from a birth narrative to a fulfilling culmination), the performance of the Hebrew Bible and its Gospel translation differ in how they are choreographed in relation to the beat of time in the world. The Christian is enjoined to make the Cross the first step of a choreographed path of suffering as the Jewish person is enjoined to follow the choreography of the law. But the Passion ends with Resurrection, and the Christian is reborn in the faith that comes to life in the emptiness of the tomb. The Christian individual's rebirth returns her to life in the time of the world in order to bear witness to the Cross, the empty tomb, and the Resurrection. Israel is born after its redemption from Egypt in order to become a people living apart from the time of the world. The Christian fellowship bends the time of the world into the choreography of ecclesiastical year and its celebration of the birth of Christ, the Passion of Christ, and the witness to his Resurrection at Pentecost. Pentecost sends the Christian back into the time of the world again in order to bear witness to all the peoples of the world in all their tongues. The Jewish year bends the time of the world into a cycle of holidays that rotate back to the beginning, from the people's birth in Exodus (Passover) to the giving of the law (Shavuot) and then to the wandering in the desert (Sukkot). The Jewish people are not sent back into the world. They remember the time of the world as the time of waiting for entrance into the promised land, this time to be possessed without threat of expulsion. They remember the time of the world, in other words, as the time of waiting for the Messiah.

Rosenzweig, like Jacobi, understood the experience of revelation within the individual to be a liberating rebirth of the individual beyond his naturally given identity. The historical revelation of the Hebrew Bible is worked out not only in the choreography of Jewish life, but also in the life and art of Christianity. For Rosenzweig, Christianity is ultimately the mediator of Revelation to the individual, just as Jacobi had claimed. We might say that Christianity allows the individual to make his life into a work of art. Thus, Judaism and Christianity open up the space for *singularities* to emerge out of the enclosed totality of the pagan cosmos, where each thing is only a part of a larger whole and never a unique and new *creation*. The singular Jewish people and the singular individuality of the Christian both witness against the totalized cosmos of paganism. Mendelssohn understood how a singular people could bear witness against paganism, and Jacobi understood how the singular individual could do so. Rosenzweig shows how both are paths deriving from the historical testimony of revelation in the Hebrew Bible.

The key to Rosenzweig's view of Judaism and Christianity as the bi-covenantal onslaught against paganism is his interpretation of the language of the Hebrew Bible as the breakthrough of revelation into history. The Hebrew Bible makes possible two choreographed paths, each bearing witness against the closed world of paganism. But paganism, according to Rosenzweig, is not limited to one historical epoch. It is an always-present existential possibility of human being-in-the-world. Revelation and paganism not only define historical formations, but are twin possibilities of living in the world. Therefore, the "word of God" cannot enter into the world with the Hebrew Bible only. Language itself must be able to be the site of the revelation of the word of God. Before I explain how language can be the site of revelation, it is useful first to understand how Rosenzweig positions his own philosophy in the history of philosophy's engagement with revelation. Rosenzweig sees his philosophy as a moment in the historic unfolding of revelation's confrontation with paganism. We need to understand the nature of this philosophical self-positioning before turning to the content of Rosenzweig's theory of language. This philosophical self-positioning pivots around the year 1800. I have spoken in the introduction about the importance of the year 1800 for Rosenzweig, and now I want to flesh out that earlier account.

Christianity and Paganism: 1800

Rosenzweig positions his philosophy in relation to an event which he refers to by the date "1800."[9] I have already briefly sketched the importance of 1800 for Rosenzweig in the opening pages of the introduction. 1800 marks an epochal shift in the conflict between Christianity as the carrier of revelation into the world and paganism, the sphere of life that resists revelation. In 1800, Christianity in two of its world-historical forms (the Petrine Church of Roman Catholicism and the Pauline Church of Protestantism) comes to an end. Paganism in the persons of Hegel and Goethe brings Christianity to this endpoint, an event of no less importance than the Christ event itself with which Christianity begins. A new beginning must be discovered if Christianity—revelation—is to have a future in history. Rosenzweig sees his own philosophy as the gateway that leads through paganism in Hegel back to language itself as the site of revelation.

The triumph of paganism in 1800 must be overcome not only in order that the historic task of Christian revelation be reinvigorated, but also in order that the Jewish people fulfill its role as the eternal "heart" of revelation. Breaking through 1800 means allowing Christianity and Judaism jointly to orient history toward redemption. In a 1919 essay entitled "Spirit and Epochs of Jewish History," Rosenzweig writes that the "Jewish spirit breaks the chains of the epochs. Because it is itself eternal and wills eternality, it rejects the omnipotence of time" (1984: 538). In the conclusion of this essay, he suggests that the achievement of Johannine Christianity is precisely to arrive at the point where the "word" of Christianity and Judaism are one (although the specific configurations of the word remain distinct). The Jew, says Rosenzweig, is through his mere existence ("durch sein bloßes Dasein") a preacher ("Prediger") of a word that "we may aptly render with a Goethean word, since in Goethe's mouth the word has a resonance that it first acquires in the language of the prophets; no Greek had ever used it this way, the word that removes from before the eyes of time the veil behind which lies eternity, the word: We bid you—to hope!" (538).[10] In this passage, Rosenzweig looks forward to his fuller description of the eternality of the Jewish people in the *Star* and to his explication of the historical role of the Johannine Christianity of hope. But Rosenzweig also uncannily hearkens back to Mendelssohn's *Jerusalem*. In the introduction (in "Rosenzweig and Mendelssohn") I quoted a passage from Mendelssohn's *Jerusalem* that declared that it was the task of the Jewish people *by means of its mere existence* ("durch ihr bloßes Dasein") "incessantly to teach, to proclaim, to preach [predige], and to endeavor to preserve" the "pure concepts of religion" among the nations (*Jerusalem* 117–18; 2:93–94). Mendelssohn would probably not have said that the Jewish people preach "hope," but both Mendelssohn and Rosenzweig agree that the Jewish people is an eternal witness and a witness to an eternality beyond the vicissitudes of history. Rosenzweig says that it is only with Johannine Christianity that the "veil" hiding eternity is removed, and the prophetic word of messianic hope can be carried to all the peoples of the world. If Rosenzweig can break through the pagan historical stasis of 1800, redemptive hope—and after the Great War such hope is precious indeed—can once again be released into history. Although he does not refer specifically to Mendelssohn as his partner in the task of releasing the force of revelation into history, Rosenzweig seems, perhaps even against his will, to bring Mendelssohn back to life in his text.[11]

Having given some indication of what is at stake in breaking through the triumphant paganism of 1800, let me return now to the question of what Rosenzweig meant by identifying the new Johannine Christianity as a Chistianity of hope whose emergence, in different and even opposing ways, is heralded by Hegel and Goethe. What sort of hope is it that Goethe's "word" offers? And how is it related to Hegel's philosophic word? To answer these questions in a single sentence, one might say that, according to Rosenzweig, Hegel must be *thought through* in order to extricate oneself from the seductive coherence of pagan reason, but that Goethe must be *lived through* in order to extricate oneself from the seductive beauty of pagan existence. In what follows I will try to explain more clearly what this means.

Hegel consummates pagan philosophy. What pagan philosophy means for Rosenzweig is not only Parmenides, Plato, and Aristotle, but the entire idealist tradition. It culminates, according to Rosenzweig, around the year 1800. In his "Urzelle to *The Star of Redemption*," Rosenzweig writes that "'1800' means an absolute end, i.e., an absolute beginning: as Hegel discovered in himself the last philosopher, so Goethe discovered in himself the first Christian" (Rosenzweig 2000: 69). In 1800, with Hegel, Christianity's battle with pagan philosophic reason is apparently lost; pagan philosophy emerges ascendant with a man who brings philosophy to its fulfillment in his own *self-consciousness*. On the other hand, with Goethe, a man *chooses* to shape his life as a classical work of art. With Goethe, the classical beauty of paganism poses an existential challenge to Christianity. Thus, Goethe, even as he embraces pagan existence, opens the possibility of a new Christian life. He is, if only *in potentia*, "the first Christian." While exactly how Goethe consummates pagan classicism remains to be further explicated, it is important to note now that Rosenzweig understands Goethe to point forward to a new form of Christian selfhood, what Rosenzweig calls "Johannine." Paganism in the figures of Hegel and Goethe brings Christianity to its "absolute end," but this end opens up a new horizon of hope, the essence of Johannine Christianity.

What is the nature of the hope that Johannine Christianity offers? We may first explain it negatively. The task of Johannine Christianity is not to go out into the pagan world with the evangel of love (the task of the Petrine, or Roman Catholic, Church), nor to lift the soul of the converted pagan into the realm of a purely spiritual faith (the task of Pauline, Protestant, Christianity). The task of the Johannine Christian—it is an individual's task and not that of an institutional church—is to make his or her life *whole*, to create out of life what Rosenzweig calls a "singularity" ("Einzelnes," *Star* 304; 318). This means, more than anything else, to transform one's "fate"—the weight of one's historical facticity—into one's "destiny." It means reconciling oneself with one's here-and-now temporal existence, a renunciation of the will to overpower time and force it to conform to one's aspirations, what Rosenzweig calls "tyrannizing over the Kingdom of heaven" (*Star* 307; 321). The transformation of fate into destiny is first accomplished, according to Rosenzweig, by Goethe. But for it to be the basis for a new Christian life, such a transformation means, as I will explain more fully in Chapter 5 (in "Rosenzweig's Children" and "Art and Hope: The Sorrows of Christian Life"), shaping one's life in relation to a nonpagan eternity, an eternity that is more than an immobilized present. It is an eternity *revealed* in the cyclical movement of the sacred holidays of the Christian year. To make this one's eternity is to live life as one's destiny, to live a life in which "man perceives his earthly eternity in the community of men" (*Star* 309; 323). It is true that the idea that Johannine Christianity opens the last of three ages in history's movement toward redemption is taken from Joachim of Fiore via Lessing's *Education of the Human Race* (2005: 238–39), a brief notice in Schelling's *Weltalter* (*Ages of the World*) and a slightly longer discussion in his *Philosophie der Offenbarung* (*Philosophy of Revelation*).[12] But that the "word" of Johannine Christianity is "hope," Rosenzweig learns from Goethe and also from the poet Hölderlin.

Rosenzweig learns that after 1800 the new Christian word is "hope" from two poetic works in particular that were composed at nearly the same moment, in the year 1803: Goethe's play *The Natural Daughter* and Hölderlin's ode *Patmos*. Both works were written under the shadow of the dismemberment of the Holy Roman Empire by the Imperial Diet in Regensburg in February, 1803.[13] Nicholas Boyle concludes the second volume of his magisterial Goethe biography with a brilliant analysis of both these poems. Boyle identifies *hope* as the leitmotif of both poems. The poems, Boyle argues, represent the painful renunciation by Goethe and Hölderlin of the glorious dream—cherished also by Schiller, Schelling, and Hegel—of a new social order founded upon a cultural synthesis of art, religion, and philosophy that would represent "fully embodied beauty." What remains after Goethe's and Hölderlin's renunciation of this dream is hope, a hope that leads to the confidence to embrace life in its everydayness: "The reward for renouncing the enjoyment of the embodied Ideal is hope that what has been glimpsed in the past, but is denied in the present, may be granted again in the future" (Boyle 2000: 787).[14]

What Boyle means by the "embodied Ideal" that Goethe and Hölderlin renounce is the restoration of a culture of classical pagan beauty. The expectation that this beauty was soon to be recovered is clearly expressed in a manuscript that Rosenzweig discovered in 1914 among Hegel's papers at the Königliche Bibliothek in Berlin. The manuscript's handwriting style dates it to around 1796 (Rosenzweig thought it was actually composed by Schelling). It describes the imminent fulfillment of all the powers of humanity—artistic, poetic, religious, philosophical—in a new "sensuous religion" embodying a "mythology of reason."[15] Rosenzweig gave the manuscript the title "The Earliest System-Program of German Idealism." The dream expressed in this manuscript is nothing less than the restoration of the grandeur of ancient Greece, but this time with a permanence guaranteed by the higher Spirit that will infuse the whole culture. As Hegel (or Schelling, if Rosenzweig is right about the authorship) writes: "No capacity will be repressed, universal freedom and equality of spirits will then reign—A higher spirit from heaven must be sent in order to establish this new religion among us, it will be the last, great work of humanity" (Rosenzweig 1984: 27). In their 1803 poems, Goethe and Hölderlin say farewell to the ecstatic vision of a revolutionary new era for humanity that will arise when philosophy leads the way beyond Christianity toward the renewal of pagan beauty. In light of the stark reality of the new political order confronting Germany, the dream of humanity's imminent "last, great work," according to Goethe and Hölderlin, must be renounced.

In place of the "great work" of cultural and social reconstruction, Goethe and Hölderlin recommend finding beauty in the commonly shared world of humanity as it is now constituted. Boyle quotes a line from *The Natural Daughter* which suggests that a more quotidian experience of beauty can hold the key to hope: "Denn, wenn ein Wunder auf der Welt geschieht; / Geschieht's durch liebevolle, treue Herzen" ("For if a miracle happens in the world, it happens through true and living hearts"; quoted in Boyle 2000: 782). The experience of such wonder depends upon a faith in the possibilities latent within time: "Das Wunder ist des Augenblicks Geschöpf" ("the miracle is a creature of the moment") (*Die Natürliche Tochter* 4.2.427).[16] These last words are spoken by a character named "Magistrate." The magistrate is a commoner who offers the noble-born heroine, appropriately named "Eugenie" ("Well-born" in Greek), his hand in marriage. Eugenie, though confronting exile as the result of a royal intrigue against her and her father, is not ready to accept the magistrate's offer of marriage to a commoner as a way to transform her fate (her suffering because of the plot of the royal intriguers) into her destiny (the life she embraces). But she also rejects the counsel of a monk to self-sacrificingly embrace exile and live the rest of her life on a remote island serving the needy and sick. She declares that she will turn to the people of the kingdom for help. In this moment her hope returns. Sitting on the shore just before she was to be transported to the island, she looks back towards her home and says:

> Dort unten hoff' ich Leben, aus dem Leben,
> Dort, wo die Masse, tätig strömend, wogt,
> Wo jedes Herz, mit wenigem befriedigt,
> Für holdes Mitleid gern sich öffnen mag.

(There below I hope to live, from the life,
There, where the common people, thronging with energy, surge,
Where every heart, content with little,
May open itself gladly with gracious sympathy.)

(4.4.633–36)

The Natural Daughter ends with the marriage of Eugenie to the magistrate, a marriage in which the heroine accepts a life lived in concealment, outside the glories of royalty to which she is entitled. In return for renouncing the immediacy of her revelation before the world in her true nobility and beauty, the "natural daughter" Eugenie wins the miracle of love that is reborn every day, in fellowship with common humanity. In this common fellowship of life lived in quotidian, middle-class marriage, there is hope that happiness may find its rebirth. As Eugenie tells her future husband, the magistrate, near the play's conclusion:

Sobald ich mich die deine nenne, lass,
Von irgend einem alten zuverläss'gen Knecht
Begleitet, mich in Hoffnung einer künft'gen
Beglückung Auferstehung mich begraben.

(As soon as I call myself yours, let me,
Accompanied by some trusted servant,
Bury myself in hope of a future resurrection of joy.)

(5.9.547–50)

Here once more is the word of hope that Rosenzweig hears on Goethe's lips, a word that rings with the expectation of resurrection within the realm of the mundane.[17]

As I have mentioned, Nicholas Boyle reads Hölderlin's *Patmos* in conjunction with *The Natural Daughter*. Hölderlin is of profound significance for Rosenzweig, as Eric Santner has amply demonstrated in *The Psychotheology of Everyday Life*. Santner in fact finds Rosenzweig to be a guide to reclaiming Hölderlin from his reception as a poet of self-abandonment before an inscrutable God. Santner rather argues that Hölderlin seeks a God who is revealed in the everyday and diurnal experience of life. Hölderlin is a poet, Santner writes, of "being-in-the-midst-of-life" (138), of "'more life' *within*" the everyday relations of our lives (142). This is the poet whom Boyle sees in *Patmos* as well. Santner does not discuss this poem, but it certainly fits his argument about the importance of Hölderlin for Rosenzweig.[18]

The Germanist Ian Cooper has recently written that *Patmos* "is, perhaps, Hölderlin's most encompassing poem: his ambitions for poetry are never broader" (2008: 34). Hölderlin's great poem of renunciation, reconciliation, and hope is named for the site where St. John the Divine (according to tradition, the same as John the Evangelist and John the Apostle), while living in exile on the island, received the vision that is recorded in the New Testament's Book of Revelation. Explicating the theme of light and darkness in the poem, Cooper describes Patmos as an island that is located "at the intersection between dusk and dawn, the point where vision is possible because there is neither encompassing darkness nor blinding light." The possibility of vision—and of receiving a vision—suggests that "intersection is . . . revelation: on Patmos we may be able to glimpse, as John did there, the end of time and the final destiny of the world, and see ourselves in relation to it" (36). We know that Rosenzweig and a number of his friends (his cousins Hans and Rudolf Ehrenberg, Eugen Rosenstock, and several others, including Karl Barth) had formed a group called "the Patmos circle" in 1915.[19] Paul Mendes-Flohr quotes a diary entry of Rosenzweig's from January, 1916 that refers to "*this* war" as finally making apparent "the Johannine transformation of the Church brought about by the Enlightenment" (quoted in Santner, 2001: 132n3; emphasis Rosenzweig's). Rosenzweig's emphasis upon "*this* war" seems to contrast with another war. Hölderlin's *Patmos*, as I have mentioned, was written in the immediate aftermath of the wars of the French Revolution. It is therefore likely, then, that Rosenzweig saw Hölderlin's *Patmos* as a lens through which to understand his own historical moment, to see himself, as Ian Cooper puts it, in relation to "the end of time and the final destiny of the world." Indeed, a note written in 1916 during Rosenzweig's early military deployment reads: "The martyrs of the Johannine church are the dead from 1792/93 and 1813" ("Die Blutzeugen der johanneischen Kirche sind die Toten von 1792/3 und 1813") (Rosenzweig 1984: 71). Rosenzweig is referring to those who fell during Germany's battles at the outset of the French Revolutionary Wars and at the close of the Napoleonic Wars. Hölderlin in *Patmos* witnesses to the birth of the new Johannine church, but also allows Rosenzweig to understand the meaning of what he is witnessing in the war. And what was it that Hölderlin allowed Rosenzweig to see?

Rosenzweig himself gives us the answer in an essay composed in Macedonia, in October 1916, "Volkschule und Reichschule" (Rosenzweig 1984: 371–411). He speaks about the dream of classical Greece that inspired German thinkers and poets like Goethe, Humboldt, Schiller, and Winckelmann before 1800, the dream of a classical beauty for which their souls yearned. But after 1800, we can no longer reach this Greece "out of the living force of our own souls." Adopting an image from the *Odyssey*, Rosenzweig says that we can only approach this Greece "if we give the shadows that stream through the portals of that world the blood of those great dead from 1800" (385), the blood of Goethe and the others. The Greece that confronts us today, Rosenzweig says, is a Greece that is lost, a Greece that has become an object of historical study. After 1800, Greece cannot be imaginatively revived "out of the living force of our own souls" as if it were a present reality. This lost Greece is one that Hölderlin glimpsed, Rosenzweig says, "before he went insane." Hölderlin's *Patmos* dates from exactly this late period in the poet's life, and it is almost certain that Rosenzweig has this poem in mind when he speaks about Hölderlin as one who glimpsed the Greece which, after 1800, is irretrievably lost. But loss is not the final word of Hölderlin's poem. There is also the holy word of expectation and hope. The opening of *Patmos* speaks of God's occultation:

Nah ist
Und schwer zu fassen der Gott.
Wo aber Gefahr ist, wächst
Das Rettende auch.

(Near
and hard to grasp is the god.
But where danger is, grows
That which saves as well.)

(ll. 1–4)

Near, but not easily grasped, is the god. The god's occultation is the greatest danger facing humanity, but it might yet "grow" into something that brings salvation. Which "god" is Hölderlin speaking about? The poet says that he spoke these words after being granted a vision of "Asia," the land of "gold-bejewelled Patroklus" and "god-built palaces." This vision comes as an answer to the poet's prayer to be granted wings with which to fly to friends ("die Liebsten") who, though they live near ("nah wohnen"), nonetheless are "growing weak on the most separated mountains" ("ermattend auf getrenntesten Bergen"), upon "peaks in time" ("Gipfel der Zeit") (ll. 5–12). The poet and these friends, we will find, come to be identified with John and the disciples. The poem is a vision of the present that is illuminated by the past. But it is not a merely allegorical or typological illumination: through the poem the light of the past illuminates the present, pointing toward "that which saves [das Rettende]."

The poet sees the plain upon which Homeric battles were fought, but he forgoes a closer approach, preferring the nearby island of Patmos, "hospitable in its poorer house." Patmos can console a shipwrecked sailor, or someone grieving for a lost friend, just as it once consoled "the god-beloved seer" John after the death of Jesus. The poet turns from Patroklus, whose death marks the turning point of the *Iliad*'s epic action, to Jesus. To renounce the dream of Greece and its gods and heroes is to confront another loss, but, as the poem's penultimate stanza proclaims, "Christ still lives." The poem thus traces the progression from grief to hope, from "danger" to "that which saves."

Though, as Hölderlin explains, Jesus told the "beloved seer"—John—and the other disciples at the Last Supper that he would return "at the right time" (a key Rosenzweigian phrase, see *Star* 290, 306; 303, 321), John and the others grieved and thought that all had been lost: "no immortal thing can be seen in heaven or upon green earth—What is the meaning of this?" The poet, who identifies himself with the grieving John, reconciles himself with the pain of the loss by reconciling himself with time:

> Denn göttliches Werk auch gleichet dem unsern.
> Nicht alles will der Höchste zumal.
>
> (Divine work is like our own.
> The Highest does not want it accomplished all at once.)
>
> (ll. 144–45)

Rosenzweig likewise speaks of the danger facing those who would hasten the endtime by "tyrannizing over the Kingdom of heaven" (*Star* 307; 321). The poet also renounces the attempt to "learn something more" than is permitted to humans to know. Instead, he turns to all that is left of the God for whom he yearns, the "firm letter" ("feste Buchstab"), the "well interpreted enduring object" ("das Bestehendes gut gedeutet"). It is this letter that poetry, "German song" ("deutscher Gesang"), must now follow (ll. 209–10). This is last line of the poem, and it returns us to the opening lines of the poem. "That which saves" ("das Rettende") is "that which endures." The poetic word must follow the enduring word of the God who revealed Himself on Patmos, and *Patmos* is the embodiment of such a following. It begins with a renunciation of Iliadic "Asia," takes the reader through the life of Jesus and his death, the grief and scattering of the disciples, and the vision on Patmos with which the entire New Testament closes. The poetic word follows the transformation of Greek epic into Greek revelation. In this poem, that which saves grows upon the soil of German song.

"Patmos" was an appropriate name for a group of friends seeking the renewal of Christianity in a war-riven world. In the poem they could find a chastened hope based upon the growth of the word of God in the soil of a more "common" life than that of ancient Greece. Hölderlin says near the center of the poem that the Son, like the sun, descends to the earth to awaken the dead like a "staff of song, downward-pointing, since nothing is common." There are many, he continues, who are waiting to be awakened by this staff. The eyes of these waiting ones "are too shy to see the light directly." ("Es warten aber / Der scheuen Augen viele Zu schauen das Licht," ll.170–71.) Renouncing the dream of beholding God face to face, these many *wait*. There is reason for hope, however, because they are able to practice opening their eyes wide in the light of the "quietly-radiant power that falls from the holy scripture" ("Stilleuchtende Kraft aus heiliger Schrift fällt," l. 177). Those "many" who wait for this "quietly-radiant power" may be the same as those who, in the first stanza of the poem, are the friends ("die Liebsten") who live near to one another ("nah wohnen") upon separate "peaks of time" and to whom the poet yearns to fly. The "near one" on the peak of time beside me, says Rosenzweig, is the one whom love alone can reach, and love, as Rosenzweig says in his discussion of the Song of Songs in the *Star*, is what is commanded in the revealed word of the scriptures. Thus *Patmos* serves as a name that reaches beyond paganism ("Patroklus") toward a life lived within the light of revelation ("Christus"). *Patmos* aptly names the group of friends who patiently await redemption while their eyes are illuminated by "the quietly-radiant power that falls from the holy scripture."

Now that we have a sense of why Rosenzweig finds in Johannine Christianity a Christianity of *hope*, we may return to discuss more fully in what way Hegel and Goethe stand at the cusp of this new Christianity, each one consummating paganism and bringing the earlier forms of Christianity to a close. Paganism is the name for a way of conceiving particularity (selfhood) as only acquiring meaning by its relation to an all-embracing totality, a "system" of particularities. With Hegel, particularity *thinks* itself as holding the totality in its self-consciousness. With Goethe, particularity *wills* itself as the "heart" of the totality. Rosenzweig quotes Goethe's epigram, "Is not the core of the world in the hearts of men?" as the summation of the "life of Goethe" ("Urzelle" 68). Rosenzweig's understanding of Goethe is more amply elaborated by his teacher, Friedrich Meinecke, in *Die Entstehung des Historismus* (*The Origin of Historicism*) (1936). Meinecke explains how Goethe's highest achievement was "to surmount both past and present in his own person, and experience them both simultaneously as symbols of the ever-creative divine nature" (Meinecke 1972: 484). Though Meinecke is writing after the *Star*, he had long seen Goethe as the most important figure in the emergence of the new historical sense for the *living unity* expressed by an entire historical epoch or by certain representative persons. Goethe possessed this sense, Meinecke believed, because he cultivated within his own life the fusion of "past and present" in an artistic, living whole.

In Hegel and Goethe, then, the totality of paganism is consummated as an immanent totality: "The conception of immanence—and what else is paganism!—which Hegel theoretically and Goethe practically led to completion, is indeed itself become *Faktum* . . ." ("Urzelle" 69). By "*Faktum*," Rosenzweig refers to the sheer, undeniable reality of something in the here and now.[20] For those who acknowledge the event of 1800, an existential challenge arises: Do I follow Hegel or Goethe (i.e., *become* a Hegel or a Goethe)? But at the moment one stands before this challenge, another path opens itself, a path that refuses *either* form of embracing one's particularity. Instead, one opens oneself to something that stands outside the "system" of pagan totality. One opens oneself to another kind of particularity in order to orient oneself. In his "Urzelle," Rosenzweig calls this opening the "word of God," a commanding word: "Do my will! Carry out my work!" (64). This command is not a Kantian imperative, a universal moral law (which Kant had called the "*Faktum* of reason"), but a *command to love*. Through love, the "particular goes step by step from one particular to the next particular, from one neighbor to the next neighbor, and forgoes love for the farthest, before it can be neighborly love" (63). With the command to love the neighbor, the pagan world system is simply refused. But it takes the epoch of 1800 to make this command—the word of revelation—audible once more in the world. Only when the particular as such (Hegel and Goethe) absorbs the totality within itself as an object of thought or of the will is the particularity of God revealed once again in the commanding word. This means, for Rosenzweig, both that once again the scriptures can be read as more than history or myth (in Hölderlin's "quietly-radiant power") and also that in language itself one can once more make audible the revelatory power of God's word (in Hölderlin's "Gesang," for example, or in the address of love across the "peaks of time").

Revelation does not become audible simply because history has passed on beyond 1800. In fact, each person must return to 1800 and stand before the existential choice posed by Hegel and Goethe in order to hear the word of God once more. What this means, in effect, is that each individual must become aware of his or her radical particularity. In the opening pages of the *Star*, Rosenzweig writes about thinkers like Kierkegaard and Nietzsche who stood before the existential choice named "1800." Rosenzweig's *Star* is written to assist everyone to return to the existential choice of 1800. It seeks to awaken in the reader a crisis of decision, and it assists the reader in recognizing the dangers posed and the hope offered by Hegel and Goethe. Much of part 1 and part 2 of the *Star* is devoted to demonstrating that Hegel as a mortal and finite particular human remains outside the system in which he imagines that his own self-consciousness as philosopher has reconciled his particularity with the totality of being. "Philosophizing reason," Rosenzweig says succinctly in the "Urzelle" letter, "grasps itself" and then, "after it is has taken up everything within itself and has proclaimed its exclusive existence, man suddenly discovers that he, who has long been philosophically digested, is still there . . . I, a completely common private-subject, I fore- and surname, I dust and ashes. I am still there" (52–53). I will have much more to say in the following sections of the chapter about Rosenzweig's argument, ultimately descending from Jacobi, that philosophical reason swallows *nothing* when it swallows itself. The seduction of pagan reason's total coherence is the seduction of self-annihilation as a response to the terror of particularity, the terror of death itself. "It is only suicide," Rosenzweig says near the beginning of the *Star*, that philosophy "would truly be able to recommend" to the individual who fears death (*Star* 9–10; 4). But before turning to Hegel as the embodiment of the seduction of self-annihilation through reason, I want to address briefly the challenge posed by Goethe in the existential choice opened up by 1800. I have suggested why Rosenzweig finds the word of hope in Goethe, but there is a grave danger associated with someone who would attempt to follow Goethe's personal model and seek to make his life into a perfect artistic whole in which every moment symbolizes the creative fusion of past and present. Goethe's seduction is the will to escape death by immortalizing oneself by making one's life an absolutely unique work of art.

Rosenzweig speaks about the dangers confronting someone who wishes to imitate Goethe in the chapter entitled "On the Possibility of Obtaining the Kingdom by Prayer" that opens the third part of the *Star*. This is the part of the book in which Rosenzweig describes the artistic shaping of time in Judaism's and Christianity's choreography of the sacred year. To enter that choreography one must avoid the temptation of Goethe, the temptation to find redemption in *the present moment alone*. To follow Goethe would require an individual to believe that at every moment of his or her life the perfection of the totality of life is realized: the Kingdom of God is *now*. Goethe's Faust staked his immortal soul on his conviction that he would *never* be able to say that any moment in his life was perfect in itself. Goethe was Faust's inversion; Goethe staked his identity on the conviction that *every* moment of his life was perfect. According to Rosenzweig, Goethe's only prayer was a prayer to his destiny: "may my life be my destiny." In this prayer, spoken not to God but to his own *daimon*, Goethe hoped to turn his life into a work of art in which every moment reflected the whole. And this life-lived-as-destiny would in turn fit within the totality of all history, reflecting the whole spectrum of human experience. The danger of following Goethe is that one is tempted to plunge into holy sinning or holy zealotry in order to "hasten" the coming of the end of time. In other words, one is tempted to plumb the depths of all experience in a Faust-like passion for an ever-greater intensity of life, or one is tempted to become fanatically devoted to a single vision of life and force the world to conform to it. These dangers stand in the way of hearing the word of revelation, the word that calls one to respond to "next one" in love. Goethe, the "great pagan," could not recognize an exteriority that his life could not encompass as one of its own facets. Only the Goethe of *renunciation*, the Goethe who, for example, speaks through *The Natural Daughter*, brings the word of hope to expression. Because he knew what it was to live the pagan dream of self-immortalization through art, Goethe in his renunciation of this dream can also be described as "the first Christian" of the era of Johannine Christianity.

Rosenzweig offers a path towards the proper imitation of Goethe in part 3 of the *Star*. One need not see every moment of one's life as perfect, but one can see a rhythm of hours and days within the sacred year as reflecting the perfection of life, as the image of the eternal life. This is what I have referred to as the "choreography of time" that shapes the Jewish and Christian years. Rosenzweig writes the third part of the *Star* specifically in answer to the challenge of Goethe, the challenge of making one's life a work of art. I will return to this in Chapter 5 when I discuss Rosenzweig's theory of art in more detail. In the remainder of this chapter I will address Rosenzweig's answer to Hegel. If his answer to Goethe is that life can be lived as a *dance*, his answer to Hegel is that to speak one's name, to say "I, fore- and surname" ("Ich Vor- und Zuname"), is already to open oneself to the word of God.

Language as the Site of Revelation

To understand Rosenzweig's theory of language, we can most fruitfully begin with the question: What is the relationship between world and language? Rosenzweig in the *Star* puts this relationship succinctly with the following formula: "where the world is, there too is language; the world is never without the word, and it exists only within the word, and without the word it would itself also not exist" (*Star* 312; 327). This may seem to be some form of language idealism, but Rosenzweig does not claim that the world is generated out of the word or language. What he means, rather, is that the world is not merely represented by words and language, but that things bear within themselves the possibility of being represented. A thing comes into being as a specific entity, that is, an entity that is one of a species or kind. All things are unlike one another, of course, "something that has never been, a beginning for itself," as Rosenzweig says (*Star* 53; 48), yet there is also an order into which they will ultimately fit. This is clearest in the case of living things that grow from single cells into reproductively mature members of a species, but Rosenzweig insists that this transformation from simple beginning point into membership in a natural kind holds true for all things. Rosenzweig speaks of this transformation as "the particular's descent upon the universal" (*Star* 55; 51). It is "the living, ever renewed flow of the phenomenon" in which each thing emerges from "a mass of undifferentiated 'givens'" and becomes "the organized world" (*Star* 55; 51). The organized world is shaped by what Rosenzweig calls the "soul of the world" or the "logos of the world," the order of natural kinds that is ever reapplied to the infinitude of the world in its becoming. The forms of the kinds may and in fact do change, to be sure, but the world never simply reverts to undifferentiated formlessness. If it did, if it lacked the possibility of finding itself represented in "logos" or "the word," it would not exist, at least not as the world. That is what Rosenzweig means with his formula "where the world is, there too is language." Rosenzweig speaks of this language-ready world as the "metalogical world."

At some point in the course of the world, a creature arises who gives phonic embodiment to the logos of the world. Things are named; relations among things are represented in sentences. This is the aspect of language that Rosenzweig calls the impersonal order of "He-She-It": "All relation finds its foothold only between third persons; the system is the world in the form of the third person; and not merely the theoretical system, but rather just as man himself becomes object to himself, just as he wants to *make* something with or of himself, he *enters into the third person*, ceases to be I (fore- and surname), he becomes 'man' (with his palm branch)" ("Urzelle" 60). The *I* is enmeshed in the "system" of "He-She-It." The emergence of the *I* that can stand in a relation to a *Thou* rather than in a systemic relation to other "third persons" is what Rosenzweig describes as revelation. Revelation breaks into the world's systematicity and puts the logos of the world out of joint. Revelation breaks the systematicity of the metalogical world.

Rosenzweig, on nearly the same grounds as Jacobi, argues that systematicity cannot account for the experience of the *Thou*.[21] But Jacobi's revelatory experience never affects the systematicity of the world; rather it opens a path to a realm "above" the world.[22] I have spoken of this as Jacobi's "gnostic" turn. Rosenzweig would likely situate Jacobi's gnostic turn as symptomatic of what he identifies as "modern life in divided reality," the last moment in the history of "old" Protestant Christianity, when "faith had quite simply forgotten the body in the spirit" and "the world had slipped away" (*Star* 299; 313). When the duality of "the purely inner reality of faith and the purely outer one of an increasingly outer world" had reached this extreme, then faith lost its connection to the everyday world and also to language (*Star* 300; 313). Jacobi placed his faith in a worldless and wordless revelation. Rosenzweig seeks to counter this separation of faith and world. He aims to restore both language and faith to the world. Restoring language to the world, however, does not mean bringing it into conformity with the logos of the "metalogical" world, but rather unsettling this logos with the language of revelation.

Rosenzweig's innovation, his break with both Jacobi and also German idealism, is to show how the systematic world of "He-She-It" is transformed by revelation. For Rosenzweig, this happens when the world reveals itself as more than the system of relations described in third-person language. Revelation first of all makes visible the contingent particularities of the world, particularities whose existence is not exhausted by their classification in a system. In other words, the world first of all reveals that side of itself in which "something that has never been" is born, where *something never before classified* can come into being. The language in which this side of the world is revealed is at first the fluid language of adjectives severed from any underlying substances. This is the language of pure phenomenality: "Just like the eye of the artist is nourished by the blue of the sky, by the green of the meadow, without, to begin with, being much interested in either the sky or the meadow. The world is only attribute, it is so from the beginning" (*Star* 139; 142). In the beginning was the Adjective. The noun, says Rosenzweig, "concretizes" the adjective. It fixes the ever-changing flux of experience into "third-person" things.[23]

What nouns do to things in space—permit their classification into a system—verbs do in time by allowing events to be fixed as having happened. This is the function of the verbal noun (the infinitive), and of the past tense. The taming of the adjective is represented mythically as the imposition of order upon chaos, and Fate replaces the miraculousness of the unforeseeable and contingent particularity of shapeshifting phenomenality. This is the revenge of the logos of the world upon the immediacy of a purely adjectival language. This revenge is what Rosenzweig calls paganism. Paganism lives in the realm of nouns and the past tense; the adjectival chaos is overcome by the order of Fate.

Paganism is the way that the world comes to speech in myth, but it is not a stable world. It contains within itself the potential of losing its worldly character, of becoming an alien habitation to the human, or at least of becoming sensed as alien. This is first of all the condition of possibility of revelation: ". . . after entering the world of Revelation, this same image of the ancient world, where one felt well before, this Platonic and Aristotelian cosmos suddenly became a world where one no longer feels at home, a disquieting world" (*Star* 237; 246). The story of how this happens is told by Rosenzweig in relation to the history of the West, and in relation to Greek antiquity more particularly, but this is not to say that this historical formation exhausts paganism.

The following paraphrase of the "disquieting" of the pagan world that Rosenzweig first traces in his "Metalogic" and "Metaethics" books (part 1, books 2 and 3 of the *Star* [49–91; 25–66] does not follow Rosenzweig's precise order of exposition. My retelling of the unsettling of the pagan world by Revelation synthesizes and in places expands upon Rosenzweig's account, but I believe it does not do it an injustice.

The story begins with the world understood to be a single cosmos, including gods, humans, and the rest of the world. This whole cosmos is alive, and self-replicating. The whole cosmos has a history that describes the emergence of its order out of chaos. Humans and their language are one natural part of the cosmos. As long as language's relation to the world remains simply a fact, the world as a whole remains also simply a given. The Greek poem that describes the origin of the cosmos, Hesiod's *Theogony*, presents itself as one artifact within the world; the poem's own creation is simply the final act in the story the poem tells. At each retelling of the poem, this "metalogical" order is therefore both affirmed and performed. The beautiful order (*kosmos*) of the poetry of the *Theogony* testifies to and is a microcosm of the ordered universe (*kosmos*) whose origin it narrates. Nothing within the metalogical cosmos points beyond the ordered cosmos of which it is a part.

Only when language is called into question as being a natural part of the world (we might call this an awareness of the arbitrariness of the sign, or of artificiality of the poetic work, however beautiful) can we also think of the world as contingently ordered, as having just *this* configuration of elements and not another. The awareness that language is a system of conventional or arbitrary signs opens the possibility of conceiving of the things of the world as not simply representatives of natural kinds, but as contingent singularities that cannot be reduced to a definable ratio of parts to a whole. The idea that language is a system of arbitrary signs reaches its high point with the Greek Sophists, who view language as a manipulable tool designed for nonrational persuasion rather than truthful representation. At about the same time that the Sophists are questioning the naturalness of language,

Greek mathematicians are exposing the nonrationality inherent even in the ideal figures of geometry. The circle is not commensurate with any polygon; there is no common measure of their perimeters or areas. They are both types of geometric figures, but they lack a "logos" or ratio to account for their being members of one genus. With the rupture of logos and world brought about by the Greek Sophists and mathematicians, the fault lines within paganism begin to emerge. Greek philosophy descending from Parmenides and Plato seeks to repair these widening fault lines and maintain the "order" that once was given with the metalogical cosmos. Revelation breaks through these fault lines in order to completely reconfigure the pagan cosmos, but the philosophy of Being (*ousia*) characterizes these fault lines as mere "semblance" (*doxa*) in order to hold fast to the self-enclosed and self-legitimizing Truth of the metalogical world.

The fault lines in paganism emerge because the "logos" of proportionality among all things fails to encompass the radical incommensurability of things, the infinitesimal remainder that separates every circle from any polygon, however many sided, or the arbitrary gap between a sign and the individual thing it names. The fault lines in paganism emerge exactly at the level of the contingent particular in its particularity. Rosenzweig says that "each particular is certainly a particular with regard to the other; but it does not regard this regard; at birth it is blind, it does nothing but be." Using the formula of the synthetic proposition, $B = A$, that represents the relation between an individual and its defining natural kind ("Socrates is a man"),[24] Rosenzweig focuses on the sheer accidentality of the B term as the "blind" being of each particular within the "metalogical" cosmos when its relation with language is severed: "According to our terminology, its symbol is B, simply B, the naked sign of individuality, without an equal sign relating to it" (*Star* 53; 49). We might say that B is the sign of the particular outside of any determinate ratio or proportion. What Rosenzweig, much like Jacobi before him, wants to recuperate is the thought of the B "as a full miracle," "as something absolutely new" (*Star* 57; 53). Much as contemporary astronomers listen for the echoes of the big bang, Rosenzweig wants to allow the adjectival fluidity of language's origin to become once again audible through the solidified nouns of paganism. Rosenzweig wants to follow the track of each thing's "descent upon" the universal back to its birth in radical singularity, back to the point where it has not yet found its assigned place in the cosmic order, where it has not yet been "attracted with a dark violence by the power of its species" (*Star* 58; 53–54). "From the most unindividual of human actions," Rosenzweig says in reference to the coupling of male and female that results in conception, "there arises a result of truly 'inexpressible,' truly unthinkable individuality" (*Star* 57; 53). It is here, at the point that Arendt will call "natality," that the fracture lines within the pagan cosmos open up. And it is precisely this "unthinkable individuality" that the philosophy of Being from Parmenides to Hegel will seek to *think away*.

It should be clear, therefore, why Rosenzweig sees his project of re-adjectivizing language and returning the B term to its natal individuality as breaking open the pagan world and thereby creating a space for Revelation, but also as breaking free of the philosophical tradition descending from Parmenides through Plato and Aristotle to Hegel. Rosenzweig tells the story of the rise of philosophy in ancient Greece as replacing the fractured totality of the mythical world with the "All" of speculative reason. Parmenides, like the other early Ionian philosophers who preceded him, understood that the logos of the world is not perfectly mirrored in myth. The logos of the world, its rationality, could not result from a god's imposition of order upon chaos, as the *Theogony* had described. Any god is just another inhabitant of the cosmos. Parmenides and the other Ionian philosophers released the infinite particularities of the world (the world's Bs) from the grip of Zeus. More than the preceding Ionian thinkers, Parmenides recognized the difficulty of asserting that $B = A$, that a particular could come to have a fixed identity. He confronted the changeful, contingent particularity of the demythologized world, but he attempts to restore the claims of a higher logos—the Logos of Being's self-same Oneness—against the disruptive force of the infinite particularities of the world. Parmenides reasserts the claims of the universal A term against the particular B term. Philosophy begins with wonder—that sense of the world as *something unforeseen*—when it frees itself from the mythic constraints of Fate, but it quickly learns to domesticate this wonder in the name of Logos. (We could say that Heraclitus was more willing to give the changeful, contingent realm of Bs their due.) Aristotle, who first acknowledged the infinitude within the finite pagan cosmos in his concept of an infinitely divisible space and time that all movement traverses, still could not acknowledge the reality of natality, of the new creation: "For his divine 'thinking of thinking,'" Rosenzweig explains, "is just thinking only of thinking; *that it might also be thinking of the unthinkable is expressly and fundamentally rejected*" (*Star* 62; 58; italics mine).

In order to counter the reassertion of metalogical systematicity in Parmenidean philosophy, where Being is defined by the unchanging self-identity of the A term, Rosenzweig reasserts the claim of one particular B term, a B term with self-consciousness and the ability to declare "B = B." Rosenzweig restores the claim of revelation against philosophy by appealing to the B term that can say "I." Such a B term can free itself from the snares of the order of the "He-She-It" and respond to the *Thou*. The sense of the world's miraculousness cannot be recuperated otherwise. Accompanying the revelation of the *Thou* is the revelation of the world in its infinitude and contingency.

Let me recapitulate the path we have so far followed in explicating Rosenzweig's reclaiming of language as the site of revelation. When logos and the world lose their common measure and their ratio, so to speak, two paths stand open to reconciling them: philosophy (Rosenzweig will also speak of it as idealism) and revelation. In idealism, the world's irrationality (the blind "thingliness" signified by B) is viewed as sheer illusion or semblance (Parmenides), or as the result of the particular's failure to perfectly instantiate the order of logos/reason (Plato), or as due to the recalcitrance of matter to the inherence of form (Aristotle), or as an emanation out of the One (Plotinus), or as generated out of the self-identical A = A of the Absolute (Hegel). In revelation, however, the world's irrationality—its contingent forms that do not merely replicate over and over an inherent logos or order—is taken as a sign of the world as a whole being contingent, of its having come into being contingently. Rather than eliminate the infinitude (for instance, the infinitesimal remainder that is left between a polygon of however many sides and the circle into which it is inscribed) that the lack of ratio opened up within the world, the path of revelation takes infinitude (or the "remainder" as Santner 2001 repeatedly names it) as its starting point. The world, in other words, is neither eternal, as is the Aristotelian cosmos, nor has it emanated or been generated from the Absolute One, as it is in idealism, but it is *created*. Creation is to the entire world what the miracle of birth is to the sheer individuality of every particular in its radical lack of "regard" of any supervening order.

But how does the individual who says "I" escape from the snares of language that seek to bring this unique B term into relation with an identity-fixing A term, some preexisting, nameable natural kind of which B would be a mere instance? How does the individual *I* resist reincorporation either into a cosmic mythic order or a philosophical Logos? For Rosenzweig, only the individual who can transform language into the very expression of his individuality can escape the reach of language's tendency to turn individuals into representatives of a class. In other words, only the individual who can acknowledge himself as *created* rather than generated out of a preexisting order can escape the "He-She-It"ness of logos and ascend to the *Thou*. However, the path from the *I* of ordinary language to the revelation of the creaturely *I* is not a direct one. Just as the metalogical world is broken open by the arbitrariness of language and the nonrationality at the heart of mathematics (although philosophy quickly steps in to close the fissures), so too must the pagan individual be brought face to face with his irreducible incommensurability with the world. Before an individual can affirm herself as an *I* who calls out to her creator, a *Thou*, she must be able to represent herself with the proposition B = B, or, in other words, "I am I, incommensurate with all other *I*s, unique and self-measuring." This is the stance of the tragic hero.

The initial resistance of the tragic hero against incorporation in the systematic nexus of Fate is not revelation, but its precursor. The formula "B = B" represents the tragic hero, what Rosenzweig calls the "metaethical man" or, simply, "Self." One of the defining declarations of Oedipus in Sophocles's *Oedipus Rex* is, simply, "Ego Oedipus," "I am Oedipus." This self-enclosed affirmation of being is the only possible expression of individuality in the enclosed "metalogical" cosmos. Oedipus's declaration is the voice of one whose actions have made him "out of proportion" with all other humans. The tragic hero is radically incommensurable with others and is his own measure, so to speak. The epic hero Achilles, in rejecting the exchange system equating military glory with booty, renders himself (his glory) commensurate only with Zeus (the glory of Zeus); the tragic hero Oedipus ends up becoming commensurate with nothing but himself. But such self-measuring uniqueness denies the difference between oneself and one's parents. It denies birth: "the day of natural birth, which is the great day for the fate of individuality, because in individuality the fate of the particular is determined by its participation in the universal, is therefore covered with darkness for the Self" (*Star* 79; 76–77). The path out of "I am I" of the tragic Self is to acknowledge oneself to have been born, to be an individual, but also, like all things that are born, mortal. This acknowledgment is already present in the conjunction of personal name and family name, "I, fore- and surname." The way out of the metaethical, tragic solitude of the affirmation "B = B" is to acknowledge one's particular name as existing within a world of proper names (rather than common nouns), to acknowledge, in other words, that it is through names that I address others and am addressed by others. With names and the language of which they are a part, I can be called out of solitude and respond to the call of the other.[25]

In his *Little Book of the Healthy and Sick Understanding*, written as a more accessible (both in style and size) version of the *Star*, Rosenzweig explains how the personal name can become the basis for a movement out of metaethical solitude towards revelation. The *Little Book* takes the example of a man and woman pledging to marry after a certain period of time. How is it that such a pledge manages to maintain itself across time, given the changes that will inevitably transform the lovers? "What is the unchangeable?" asks Rosenzweig (1999: 49). The answer, Rosenzweig says, is quite simple: the names of the lovers. It is pointless to look for some unchangeable essence (*ousia*) or interiority that remains stable across time that is the anchor point for the words of the pledge. We have seen, in discussing Mendelssohn's critique of oaths, how he and Wittgenstein agree that it is futile to take an oath that one will not change one's understanding of the meaning of certain words, like *God* or *salvation*. We use words to understand other words; we do not anchor a word to an unchanging inner intentionality. To swear that we will never change our understanding of a word is to swear that we will stop using words at all, that we will stop *thinking*. That is why Mendelssohn takes religious oaths to be tantamount to religious tyranny. So, what keeps us true to our words? What keeps us true to our pledge to marry another person?

Rosenzweig, as Hillary Putnam points out in his introduction to the *Little Book*, stands with Wittgenstein (and, I would add, Mendelssohn) in seeing language as a performance in which one enters into a community of shared language users. In the case of pledging to marry, the performance involves two humans who enter into a relationship based upon their mutual acknowledgment of how to use proper names. To call another by a proper name and to agree to be called by one's own proper name is a performance that is part of using language. To doubt that my name "really" applies to me after the course of time is to doubt that language can be used at all, that any name "means" the same thing one day after the next. Of course, we use words differently in different contexts, and we may even try to use a word in a way that it has never before been used. But we cannot do this by private *fiat*. We do this by trying to make ourselves understood, by relying upon the relatively solid ground of other words (or perhaps gestures with conventional meanings). And if someone were to declare that his pledge of marriage were no longer binding because he, though his name remains "John," is not who he was when he made the pledge, then he would not be using names the way they are used in any language. He would cease to trust that names count for anything. Perhaps he *really* has changed and no longer wishes to marry the woman to whom he pledged himself. But then *he* has changed, not the words. The words cannot prevent a person from changing and withdrawing his promise to marry, but neither can you promise to marry without using words, and you cannot marry without using a proper name. It is one thing to have a change of heart, it is another to lose faith in language entirely. If one lover changes heart, the other may *hope* for love to be renewed. If one lover loses faith in language itself, however, there is no room for hope because love cannot grow without faith that humans share a world in common when they speak. If one lover doubts the truth of any profession of love from the mouth of the other because it consists of "mere words" and demands instead certainty about the "inner essence" of the other human being, there is no room for hope. In such a case, one person applies the question "What actually is it?" to a human being, and the result, says Rosenzweig, is "the immediate disappearance of two very concrete individuals—the questioner himself and his beloved." No matter what the answer to the question of the essence behind the words, "the concrete individual is replaced by a ghost" (*Little Book* 52).

The loss of faith in language is, according to Rosenzweig, the prime symptom of the sickness of the understanding that is "idealism." "The sick reason," he writes in the *Little Book*, "rejects names as worthless, and queries actions and things. 'What are these actually?' it asks. The answer that it receives leaves everything in darkness, darkness which blurs all distinctions. There is no end here to doubt and despair" (53). The sick reason's only cure is a return to language *in faith*, in a *salto mortale* into the shared world of humanity. That the world hangs in existence not by fixed essences but by a thread made of words awakens the individual to the *miracle* of the word and the world at once. There is no refutation of doubt and skepticism. To think that there is, to think that one can penetrate to the "essence" of the world by penetrating into the essence of one's solitary selfhood, is to fall sick with idealism. This is almost exactly what Jacobi says in his critique of idealism. The difference between Jacobi and Rosenzweig is that Jacobi thought that faith lifted him to another world beyond this one, this *common* one.

In the *Star*, Rosenzweig makes the same point as he does in the *Little Book* about the sickness of idealism. He diagnoses the problem of Western philosophy as a lack of confidence in language itself. "Idealism lacks naïve trust in language," Rosenzweig writes. "To lend an ear to this voice, to answer this voice that resounds in man without apparent reason but all the more really, idealism was in no way disposed. It asked for reasons, justifications, forecasts, everything that language could not offer it" (*Star* 157; 161). To begin philosophy again requires a return to language itself as the matrix within which to discover the resources to overcome the metaphysical divide of self and world that Cartesian doubt and Humean skepticism opened up and which idealism sought to remedy but only intensified. In different ways, this return to language represented for Rosenzweig a return to the matrix in which the world is *revealed* rather than *known*. It is, as I have explained in the previous section, a return to *hope* after the self-constricting solitude of the pagan self has reached its extreme point in Hegel and Goethe.

But Hegel and Goethe, though standing at the historical limits of paganism, only reveal the existential choice between revelation and paganism that is an inescapable part of human life. Every human begins as a "natural" pagan with a child's conviction in the unbroken continuity of words and world. Every human awakens from this paganism with a disillusionment about the "mere words" of others. At this point, there are two paths out of disillusionment: revelation or idealism. To be sure, these paths run so closely beside one another that "jumping the track" is always possible. And certainly most people during most of their lives do not recognize that these paths stretch out before them. Rather, they cope with disillusionment by limiting their investments of trust in the world and settling for smaller returns. Most people back off from carrying doubt to a Cartesian extreme. But Rosenzweig is interested in exploring the limit situations where revelation and idealism are apparent in their stark difference. That is why the *Star* seeks to reveal behind the apparent forward progress of humanity after the Enlightenment the configuration of the year 1800, behind which shines the figure of the Star itself. In Chapter 5 (in the section "Art and Hope: The Sorrows of Christian Life") I will show how art can also function to awaken one from one's pagan slumbers. For the way out of our "limited trust" settlements with the world's disillusionments is by shaping our lives into works of art, into a choreography of holy days.

We might say that philosophy (idealism) and revelation have been engaged in a battle since the breakup of the mythic world of humanity's childhood, the world of a cosmos all of whose living beings—from animals to humans to gods—were ruled over by Fate, by a language of nouns and the past tense, a language of oracles and decrees. This mythic world possessed within itself the fault lines along which revelation might come to expression in language: the miraculousness of the ever-new birth of things in their radical individualities, and the emergence of a self-consciousness (represented in the tragic hero) capable of claiming this individuality as his right against all the powers of the gods and Fate. Philosophy confronts the brute particularities released with the shattering of the mythic cosmos, but it quickly seeks to repair the shattered mythic order. It replaces it with another closed world, the closure of Logos raised to the pinnacle of reality against all the competing claims of individuality. This new closed cosmos is what Rosenzweig calls the "All" of philosophy, the dream of explaining everything by deriving it from some A term. Paganism thus returns to life within philosophy. This is the key to understanding the difference between Jacobi's and Rosenzweig's critiques of idealism. For Jacobi, philosophy *judaizes* the world; for Rosenzweig, philosophy *paganizes* the world. I want in the next section to explore in more detail the contrast between Jacobi and Rosenzweig that has been one of the leitmotifs of this chapter. This will lead to some further thoughts about the significance of the year 1800 in Rosenzweig's thinking in relation to the Spinoza Quarrel.

Conclusion: Rosenzweig and Jacobi

Before the task of the Christianity of hope can be taken up by the new Johannine "first Christian" who carries forward the inheritance of Goethe by sanctifying ordinary life, the challenge of paganism in philosophy must be met. Jacobi sensed this too, but he could not find the resources to turn his critique of idealistic philosophy into a "new thinking," as Rosenzweig called his own philosophic path. Rosenzweig's "new thinking" is a philosophy that takes its lead from language itself. It is meant to show a path beyond the idealism against which Jacobi so vehemently railed in his 1799 *Jacobi to Fichte*. For Rosenzweig, the year 1800 marked an opportunity to enter a new era of Johannine Christianity, but the era could not truly be ushered in until philosophy could acknowledge the voice of revelation. Rosenzweig's language philosophy does not shrink from the contingent particularities of the world, thus allowing singularity to stand without grounding it in the systematicity of "He-She-It." This emphasis upon contingency and particularity allows for a philosophical recuperation of the experience of revelation that was so central to Jacobi. As I have said, Rosenzweig differs from Jacobi by making language the condition of possibility of revelation. The formula "B = B" expresses the tragic Self's awareness of itself as singular and unsubsumable within a genus, and from this self-awareness there opens the possible relationship between two singular persons, between *I* and *Thou*. Jacobi saw the *I-Thou* relation as precisely the particularity that would always escape reason's search for justifying and explaining all things by appeal to one underlying ground, to a universal A term. Rosenzweig shares this fundamental point with Jacobi. But Rosenzweig goes further than Jacobi when he makes the *I-Thou* relation the beginning point of his explication of the categories of Creation, Revelation, and Redemption. Rosenzweig's critique of idealist philosophy is aimed at recuperating these categories from theological dogmatics for philosophy's "new thinking."

In the section "The Hebrew Bible and Paganism" above, I related Creation, Revelation, and Redemption to Rosenzweig's interpretation of the Hebrew Bible as the literary work that carries revelation into history. I talked of how Rosenzweig saw language as the site of revelation because it broke the spell of the mythic cosmos. Now I want to return to the categories of Creation, Revelation, and Redemption and briefly describe how they are intended to break the spell of 1800, the year of German idealism's apparent triumph over revelation. What the Hebrew Bible achieved in relation to the mythic cosmos must be repeated in relation to idealist philosophy. This is the task that Rosenzweig sets for the *Star*. To the extent that he succeeds, Rosenzweig may be said to have completed Jacobi's lifelong goal of voicing the claims of revelation against the totalizing claims of philosophy.

God's creation of the world and his self-revelation to the particular self (the B = B term entering into relation with the A = A term) are for Rosenzweig two moments in the unfolding of a triadic relationship among God, the world, and humanity. This triadic relationship, Rosenzweig argues, cannot be reduced to a single monistic totality in which one of the terms serves as the underlying ground and principle of unity for the others, as post-Kantian idealistic monism had claimed. This post-Kantian idealistic monism has been ably analyzed most recently by Paul W. Franks in his book *All or Nothing* (2005), which traces the emergence of the impulse towards systemic philosophizing, largely set in motion by Jacobi's *Spinoza-Letters*, after Kant's apparent demonstration that philosophy must remain silent about the ultimate nature of the transcendent realm of the "in-itself." Franks focuses upon what he calls the "Holistic Monism" of the post-Kantian German idealists and defines it in the following terms:

> Holistic Monism may be divided into two requirements. The Holistic requirement is that, in an adequate philosophical system, empirical items must be such that all their properties are determinable only within the context of a totality composed of other items and their properties. The Monistic requirement is that, in an adequate philosophical system, the absolute first principle must be immanent within the aforementioned totality. (Franks 2005: 85)

Franks charts the German idealists' embrace of Holistic Monism after Jacobi's demonstration in his *Spinoza-Letters* that Spinoza was the first consistent Holistic Monist and that Spinoza's system is, in fact, the only "philosophically adequate system."

Of course, Jacobi hoped that his demonstration would lead to the abandonment of the attempt to construct a "philosophically adequate system" to explain how everything fits within a monistic whole. Such an attempt, Jacobi argued, would end by denying both the transcendence of God and the reality of human freedom. Both God and Man would be flattened into a single totality that excluded the possibility of what Jacobi called the "supernatural," both divine *creatio ex nihilo* and the manifestation of God within the *individual* rather than the totality. Post-Kantian idealists like Fichte, Hegel, and Schelling, quite against Jacobi's hopes, made it their goal to harmonize Kant's "Copernican revolution" with Spinozistic monism. In other words, they sought to show how the causal chain determining the existence of every empirical object has its grounding not in some unknowable, transcendental "in itself," but in an immanent principle which unifies the infinite causal chain into a single systemic whole. The endless series of causes and effects is but one aspect under which to view the universe; seen from the vantage of the "philosophically adequate system," the universe is One. For Jacobi this One is but another name for Nothing, for the emptiness of reason's dream of breaking free of all dependence upon a *transcendent* God who exists beyond the causal nexus of nature, and who manifests Himself within each person, calling her to to rise beyond mere causally determined thinghood through the exercise of her free will. No philosophic system could explain away this manifest God whose direct apprehension as transcendentally Other is given through *faith*. Such is the thrust of Jacobi's critique of idealistic monism, a critique that placed the experience of the living individual against the claims of systematic philosophizing.

While Jacobi unwittingly provided the impetus to post-Kantian thought to embrace Spinozism, the assault upon this monistic impulse in philosophy remained Jacobi's central mission, involving him in ever-deepening disputes with Fichte and then Schelling. However, he was largely unable to open a path beyond monism, though he offers tantalizing fragments that point in this direction. At the close of his epistolary novel *Edward Allwell's Collection of Letters*, for example, Jacobi says that after Kant what is called for is "a critique of language which would be a metacritique of reason" (Jacobi 1994: 496).[26] Rosenzweig, probably without being aware of Jacobi's call, answered it nonetheless in *The Star of Redemption*.

Rosenzweig in the "Urzelle to *The Star of Redemption*" makes specific reference to one of the key phrases that emerge from the Spinoza Quarrel, *salto mortale*. He describes the movement out of self-enclosed particularity (B = B) into a relation with God's particularity (A = A) as the *salto mortale* that Jacobi offered to Lessing. It is a leap out of idealism into revelation. But, unlike Jacobi's leap, this is not a leap out of nature sensed as purely mechanical into the inner world of freedom. It is a leap into community. Jacobi did not manage to find a place for the word of hope that can *grow* in this world. Jacobi, though he is centrally important for Rosenzweig, remains on the other side of 1800. In his gnostic Christianity, he remains trapped within paganism, a world-denying paganism to be sure, but paganism nonetheless.

Rosenzweig's understanding of what 1800 represented for world history—the rise of a new paganism in the form of German idealist philosophy's Holistic Monism—certainly grasps the import of the Spinoza Quarrel. And Rosenzweig's attempt to transcend this quarrel's results by restoring the claims of both Jewish and Christian covenantal lives to be the bearers of revelation witnesses to his understanding, though it was never expressed in these terms, that both Mendelssohn and Jacobi needed to be given their rights to speak once again. Rosenzweig's philosophy of revelation, we might say, returns to the scene of the Mendelssohn-Jacobi quarrel and lays the foundation for a "messianic friendship" between Mendelssohn and Jacobi.

The year 1800 marks a moment, as I have said, when a new era of Christianity emerges, according to Rosenzweig. Humanity is returned to paganism after the Enlightenment critique of miracle and superstition, but idealist philosophy cuts short the full flowering of the new Johannine Christianity that comes to transform the modern paganism following upon the Enlightenment's critique of revealed religion. Rosenzweig, like Jacobi, sought to find a way through the *I-Thou* to crack open idealist philosophy's One and All that subsumed the singular individuality of the self ($B = B$) within an encompassing universal ground ($A = A$). Rosenzweig's *Star* may be read as a multifaceted assault on paganism. It takes its stand against paganism by giving voice to three subjectivities: the human *I*, the Jewish *I*, and the Christian *I*. The voice of the human *I* opens out, insofar as it is loyal to what is revealed within it, to either the Jewish *I* or the Christian *I*. But the voice of the human *I* can only be heard if the echo chamber of philosophy's All is ruptured. What this rupturing accomplishes is the opening up of what I have called the "messianic friendship" of Jacobi and Mendelssohn. Jacobi's critique of idealism is brought to completion in Rosenzweig's philosophy of language as the site of revelation. But Mendelssohn as the voice of the Jewish *I* is also freed by the rupturing of idealist philosophy. His voice is freed from its silencing at the hands of post-Kantian philosophy.

Having told the story in this chapter of how the Mendelssohn-Jacobi quarrel finds its resolution in the philosophy of Franz Rosenzweig, I want in the next two chapters to discuss three figures who paved the way for that fateful year, 1800: Reinhold, Kant, and Hegel. These three thinkers, each in a different way, represented themselves as the philosophical expositors of a new religion of reason that would translate Christian revelation into its perfect, rational expression. Answering Jacobi's charge that any "religion of reason" must be a depersonalization and therefore a *judaization* of Christianity, Reinhold, Kant, and Hegel take it upon themselves to demonstrate that their religion of reason is radically incompatible with Judaism. Indeed, it would not be going too far to call their project the *supersession of Mendelssohn*.

FOUR

Reinhold and Kant: The Quest for a New Religion of Reason

Overview: Reinhold, Kant, and Hegel Before 1800

This chapter will focus on Reinhold and Kant, and the next will focus on Hegel. These chapters together examine how Reinhold, Kant, and Hegel search for a new version of the religion of reason that had been so central to the Enlightenment and which, they all agreed, had shown itself in need of an entirely new approach when Mendelssohn published his *Morning Hours* and Jacobi had, in response, published his *Spinoza-Letters*. Reinhold was the first to recognize that what the Mendelssohn-Jacobi quarrel had demonstrated, above all, was that a new footing for the religion of reason had to be found, one that would not be vulnerable to Jacobi's critique that hiding behind the God of Mendelssohn (and Lessing) was the Jewish God of Spinoza, a God of unfreedom.

Besides answering Jacobi, the new religion of reason would also need to respond to Mendelssohn's defense of the Jewish people as the living embodiment of the revealed legislation of the Hebrew Bible. Mendelssohn's religion of reason in *Morning Hours* was offered as the best attempt that finite minds can make at rationally comprehending the infinite mind of God. Jacobi's attack against *Morning Hours* was answered by Mendelssohn himself in *To the Friends of Lessing*. Mendelssohn argued that faith in revelation was not, in fact, incompatible with his religion of reason. He reminded Jacobi that in *Jerusalem* he, Mendelssohn, had shown that Judaism rests upon *trust* (Mendelssohn explained that the Hebrew term for *faith*—*emunah*—was better translated as *trust*) and not reason. The Jewish people trust in the historical evidence that God revealed Himself to them as a legislator at Mt. Sinai. It may seem impossible to reconcile the conception of God as infinite Mind with trust in God as the legislator of a particular law code. But Mendelssohn had claimed in *Jerusalem*, and he restated this in *To the Friends of Lessing*, that Judaism's law code not only leaves reason free to seek to understand God in the best way that any finite mind can, but it even orients reason in the right direction.[1] The revealed legislation of the Hebrew Bible is designed to keep the Jewish people ever aware of the insuperable gap between human finitude and divine infinitude. The people were to make no attempt at capturing the infinite within the finite, neither in word nor in image. They were enjoined to make the entirety of their finite lives a sign pointing beyond itself toward an infinite God.

Kant, Reinhold, and Hegel each stake a claim to be the philosophical voice of the religion of reason. Their religion of reason is offered as the universalization of the historical particularity of Christian revelation and as the completion of Christianity's supersession of Judaism. The project of constructing a new religion of reason was, as I have said, a central one for the German Enlightenment, and it was perhaps epitomized in the late text of Gotthold Ephraim Lessing, *The Education of the Human Race*, to which I will return in a moment. Kant, Reinhold, and Hegel all accepted Jacobi's argument against Lessing that speculative reason, if it dispensed with the theological category of revelation, would necessarily lead to a system that had a place only for God as (freedom-denying) Creator. The problem with retaining God as Creator and dispensing with God as Revealer was that creation was complete all at once, at the moment of creation. Whether creation was thought to be a single act preceding the existence of the world or an eternal, unchanging ground underlying the world, the relation between God and world never altered. Once creation was accounted for, there was no further need for God. Jacobi understood that this independence from a God who was believed to have revealed himself to humanity in history might at first seem to be a liberation of humanity from superstition and priestly authority, but, in truth, it reduced humanity to just one more *effect* of God's creative power. Revelation as Jacobi understood it introduced something *new* in the world, and it opened up the possibility of humanity breaking free of the causal chain (or the underlying unchanging ground) that bound all other created things to God.

Reinhold saw that Jacobi's challenge could be answered if the religion of reason could somehow sidestep God as Creator and focus entirely on God as Revealer. Jacobi demonstrated that only the God of *both* Creation and Revelation could make freedom possible; Kant had suggested that reason itself made freedom possible (in its power to command the will unconditionally, by which the will is freed from all heteronomous conditions). Reinhold concluded that the revealed God is *practical reason*, the commanding voice of Reason that lifts the individual out of the phenomenal realm of mechanical causation into the noumenal realm of self-legislating freedom. Kant basically agreed with Reinhold. At the conclusion of the *Critique of Practical Reason* (1788), Kant speaks of two objects of reverence: the "starry heavens above me and the moral law within me."[2] The vision of the starry heavens is the mind's impression of God as Creator. This vision reduces the individual to a sense of his life on earth as worthless; it "annihilates, as it were, my importance as an animal creature" (Kant 1996b: 269; AK5:162). The only recovery from this sense of worthlessness is provided by the vision of the "moral law within," a vision of oneself as a sublime moral Person in a Kingdom of Ends ruled over by a supreme moral being, God. In his *Religion within the Boundaries of Mere Reason* (1793), Kant says that this vision is the basis for a "pure religion of reason" that is "a revelation (though not an empirical one) permanently taking place within all human beings" (Kant 1998:128; AK6:122). For Kant and Reinhold, God as Creator of the "starry heavens" remained an unknowable and terrifying "in-itself," but God as the object of a "permanent revelation" is the sublime Person guiding humanity towards the "ethical community" that is its highest good. Reinhold and Kant have absorbed Jacobi's lesson that a personal God can only be encountered as a self-revealing God and not as the God of the mechanical order of the universe, but there remains for them a tremendous gap between God as

Creator and God as Revealer. Jacobi himself saw this problem in the Reinhold-Kant religion of reason, but he could only insist again and again that his God revealed his freedom in his creative and miraculous act of bringing the world into being out of nothing, and that this miraculous, creative freedom is what lives within each human being. Jacobi could not make his case within the framework of a system (nor, despite his decades-long efforts, could Schelling, who worked within the same problematic of rejoining the God of Creation with the God of Revelation). Jacobi's objections to the Reinhold-Kant "pure religion of reason" became more and more marginal to the development of post-Kantian philosophy.[3]

It fell to Hegel to absorb Jacobi's lesson about the necessity to connect God as Creator and God as Revealer and thus to provide a systematic completion of German idealism's religion of reason.[4] I will very briefly sketch Hegel's contribution here, but a fuller treatment must await the following chapter. Hegel was unhappy with the loss of God as Creator in favor of God as revealed in the commanding voice of practical reason. Agreeing with Jacobi, Hegel saw the loss of God as Creator as the loss of the *living, creative* God. Hegel attempts to show that the unity of God as Creator and as Revealer is found in the conception of God as Infinite Life, or, more precisely, God as Infinite Life "coming into self-consciousness" in a finite life. The self-consciousness of infinite life occurs first in Jesus. In approaching Hegel's religion of reason, I will rely entirely on Hegel's early theological writings, the last of which is dated September 24, 1800. The manuscripts containing Hegel's early theological writings were first published in 1907 by Herman Nohl. The writings themselves date from 1790 to 1800. The two most significant texts are *The Positivity of the Christian Religion* and *The Spirit of Christianity and its Fate*.[5] In both works, Hegel makes extensive use of Mendelssohn's *Jerusalem*, as Herman Nohl points out in his notes to *Hegel's Theologische Jugenschriften*: "The influence of this book upon Hegel, which also was important for Kant, extends throughout *Positivity* and *Spirit of Christianity*" (from Nohl's "Anhang" in Hegel 1907: 404, translation mine).

Kant's religion of reason, Hegel said, had lifted God into the realm of the sublime, leaving the particular life of the historical individual in the realm of lifeless mechanism. Hegel, agreeing with Jacobi, argued that so long as God remained in sublime, infinite distance from the here and now of the finite individual, the religion of reason was not Christianity, but a form of Judaism. According to Hegel, Reinhold and Kant failed to bear witness to the resurrection of life itself beyond the moral law in a community bound together by love. Reinhold and Kant remained trapped in the "Jewish" reverence for the law. The Christian version of the religion of reason—the Gospel according to Hegel—was the overcoming of the law by the forgiving love of a community that commemorates the resurrection of God in their midst: the forgiving love of those who know themselves to be both God-slayers (offending against the unity of life) and the slain God (as a living part of God). When a community knows itself in this way, the law is both fulfilled and transcended. Such a community, Hegel will declare in his *Spirit of Christianity and its Fate* (1799) is created in the Last Supper, but Christianity's "fate" is that this community can never be recreated in history. The ritual of the Eucharist communion supplants the lived experience of the community of love created at the Last Supper. Christianity's truth can be *known* but never *lived*. The truth of the Last Supper—that life is resurrected through love—can only be realized in what Hegel calls the "consciousness of pure life" in which subject and object are one and "spirit grasps and embraces spirit in itself" (*Spirit-Fate* 254–55). In the *Phenomenology of Spirit*, Hegel calls this "absolute knowledge."

If there is no freedom without the immediate experience of revelation, as Jacobi had argued, then Hegel attempts to show how (his) philosophy brings revelation to its secure self-possession in a living consciousness. With Hegel, as Rosenzweig had claimed in *The Star of Redemption*, philosophic reason has swallowed revelation. What began as an attempt to respond to Jacobi ends with Jacobi's nightmare: the triumph of self-absorbed Reason over God. As Jacobi wrote in 1799 in *Jacobi to Fichte*, German idealism had taken the commandment "You shall have no other gods except Me" to mean, "You shall have no other god but (the) I" (524; 49) As I will show in the next chapter, Hegel, unlike Reinhold and Kant, did attempt to respond to Jacobi's critique of the presumption of reason to be its own God, but he could not find a way to meet Jacobi's fundamental challenge, namely, to abandon the philosophic urge toward "self-divinization." As I will argue in the next chapter in elaboration of some of the themes already broached in Chapter 3, Rosenzweig reads Hegel against the grain and offers a vision of Judaism and Christianity as partners in the defeat of this philosophic "paganism" that is the idolatry of Reason.

The religion of reason constructed by Reinhold, Kant, and Hegel, in different ways, offered itself as the culmination of Christianity. As Christianity's culmination, the religion of reason finally severed Christianity from all that was Jewish within it. The new religion of reason attempts to answer not only Jacobi's charge that the Enlightenment's religion of reason had replaced the revealed God with the purely rational Creator God of a mechanical universe, but it also seeks to rebut Mendelssohn's more or less explicit claim in *Jerusalem* that Judaism was closer to the religion of reason than was Christianity. To be sure, the new religion of reason's supersession of Judaism is not undertaken in the service of traditional Christian faith. To see this, we need only recall the very different aim of J. G. Hamann's *Golgotha und Scheblimini!* (1784), the most important of the considerable number of critical responses to Mendelssohn's *Jerusalem* that appeared soon after its publication.[6] In it, Hamann undertakes a defense of Christian faith and a point by point refutation of Mendelssohn's portrait of Judaism as a "revealed legislation." Hamann, like his friend Jacobi, was not interested in a rational reconstruction of Christianity's revelation. He did not believe that Christianity needed rational reconstruction. Hamann's goal was less ambitious, though more confrontational. To understand the very different goal of men like Reinhold, Kant, and Hegel, it is useful to examine briefly Hamann's *Golgotha und Scheblimini!*

Hamann sought to counter Mendelssohn's claim that Judaism's legislation was a living education of the Jewish people in how to worship God without the tyranny of a creed or the state-enforced coercion of an established church. Mendelssohn, as I have said, argued that Judaism's revealed legislation was aimed at making the people a "living script" and teaching them in their every action how not to succumb to the idolatrous worship of reified symbols, how not to literalize the words of the Hebrew Bible into "fetishes." Hamann believed that, whatever Mendelssohn might say, Judaism's very essence was the fetishization of the Law: Describing the degeneration of the original symbolic nature of law into the dead letter of the law, Hamann writes that ". . . this earthly vehicle of a temporal, figurative, anointing, animal legislation and sacrificial worship degenerated into the corrupted and deadly creeping poison of a childish, slavish, literalistic, idolatrous superstition" (*Golgotha* 220; 305). For Hamann, the Hebrew Bible pointed allegorically beyond itself to the Incarnation. The Jewish law was designed only to maintain Israel's existence in the time of waiting between the promise contained in the covenant of the flesh and its fulfillment in the covenant of the spirit: "the promise, but no law, was given to the flesh of the righteous Abraham as the sign of the covenant" (*Golgotha* 221; 307). The circumcision of the flesh could only be justified as symbol of the promise; it lost its validity once the truth it prefigured—the circumcision of the heart—had been realized in Christ. And Jewish law, once the guarantor of a people's life, had become after Christ "the corrupted and deadly creeping poison of a . . . superstition" (*Golgotha* 220; 305).

Hamann took Mendelssohn's defense of the law—the script that enjoined freedom from creed or ecclesiastical coercion—to be evidence that the Enlightenment's critique of Christian orthodoxy would end in the *judaization* of Christianity and Christian society. "The Jews through their divine legislation, and the Naturalists through their divine reason, have seized upon a palladium for equalization: consequently, no other mediating concept remains for Christians and Nicodemuses than to believe with all their heart, with all their soul, with all their mind. For God so loved the world—This is the victory which has overcome the world, our faith" (*Golgotha* 225; 313). If the circumcision of the flesh can be harmonized with the Enlightenment's religion of reason, as Mendelssohn thought, then the religion of reason is blind to the allegorical significance of the law. The religion of reason is sheer "naturalistic, atheistic fanaticism" (*Golgotha* 227; 315). Hamann claims that Mendelssohn wants to turn the Christian and Jew into "business-brothers according to the flesh" while the Jew remains a "circumcised brother in the spirit" (*Golgotha* 226–27; 315) of the new "atheistic fanaticism." Speaking of the Jew who is "the philosophe à la Grecque"—i.e., Mendelssohn—Hamann declares that "his circumcision knife extends to everything which carries a purse [Sein Beschneidungsmesser erstreckt sich über alles, was einen Beutel trägt]" (*Golgotha* 227; 316).[7] Hamann managed to combine his critique of the judaizing tendencies of the Enlightenment with the stereotype of the money-obsessed Jew, seeking every opportunity to sever the gentile from his money. Hamann believed that the Enlightenment's religion of reason was the reversal of Christianity's supersession of Judaism, the reliteralization of circumcision. Hamann shared with Jacobi a profound suspicion that philosophical reason was the instrument of an attack on Christ in the name of the idol—God as legislator of carnal circumcision—worshiped by the Jews.

Reinhold, Kant, and Hegel stood on the side of Enlightenment and philosophical reason, although they agreed with Hamann that Mendelssohn's *Jerusalem* posed a serious challenge to Christianity. When Mendelssohn placed Judaism on the side of reason, he implied that Christianity (with its dogmatic constraints on reason and its deification of a finite human) was on the side of superstition. Reinhold, Kant, and Hegel sought to show how the religion of reason brought Christianity to fulfillment and why Judaism was on the side of superstition. Their critiques of Mendelssohn's Judaism were made in defense of their own philosophical reconstruction of Christianity. Many of their arguments are couched, sometimes explicitly and sometimes not, as responses to Mendelssohn's claim in *Jerusalem* that only Judaism, not a religion at all but rather a revealed legislation, was fully consonant with the religion of reason. We may therefore say that the new religion of reason, however differently it is formulated by Reinhold, Kant, and Hegel, is intended to respond to the twin challenges posed by Jacobi (the need for a concept of God as Revealer in order to account for humanity's freedom) and Mendelssohn (the precedence of Judaism over Christianity as an enlightened form of religion). When, therefore, Rosenzweig in the *Star* sets himself the task of breaking down the edifice of idealism's religion of reason, he is clearing the space for the return of Jacobi and Mendelssohn, as I have argued in the previous chapter. But Rosenzweig will also borrow from the building blocks of idealism's edifice in constructing his own system. One of these is the concept of sublime hope that is part of Kant's religion of reason; another is concept of the beautiful life as the fusion of divine infinitude and human finitude that is part of Hegel's philosophical reconstruction of Christianity. In future chapters I will explain these borrowings in greater detail.

In the next section of the chapter I will deal with two of Reinhold's earliest writings, *Die Hebräischen Mysterien, oder die älteste religiöse Freymaurerey* (*The Hebrew Mysteries, or the Oldest Religious Freemasonry*) and *Briefe über die kantische Philosophie* (*Letters on the Kantian Philosophy*). *Hebrew Mysteries* appeared in 1786 in two volumes of the *Journal für Freymaurer*, and *Letters on the Kantian Philosophy* (hereafter *Kant Letters*) was serialized in 1786–87 in four volumes of *Der Teutsche Merkur*.[8] I start with Reinhold rather than Kant because Reinhold chronologically precedes Kant in offering a philosophical reinterpretation of Christianity as the religion of reason. Reinhold, unlike Kant and Hegel, does not supply Rosenzweig with any building blocks for the *Star*. Whatever Reinhold's significance in the early years of post-Kantian idealism, for me he is an important historical witness to the immediate aftermath of Mendelssohn's *Jerusalem*. Reinhold shows how provocative was Mendelssohn's refiguring of Judaism, especially his depiction of its earliest form as the sui generis "Mosaic constitution" revealed to Israel at Mt. Sinai, as the exemplar of an enlightened unity of church and state. Reinhold recognized that Mendelssohn's *Jerusalem* was an explicit challenge to Lessing's late Freemasonry-inspired works, *Ernst and Falk* and *The Education of the Human Race*.[9] In both these works, Lessing laid out his ideas about the evolving enlightenment of humanity through the joint work of God and selected people who are the vehicle of God's education of all humanity. In these works, Lessing sketches the outline of a "new, eternal Gospel," a Gospel of the religion of reason. In *Ernst and Falk*, the selected people Lessing brings out into the light of history are the secret brotherhood of enlightened individuals who, in Lessing's day, are the Freemasons. In *The Education of the Human Race*, the story is told without explicit reference to this secret band, but rather the focus is on Judaism and Christianity. Examining the writing of Friedrich Schlegel, Jeffrey Librett (2000: 105ff.) has shown how consequential for the future development of German letters was Lessing's late authorship. Friedrich Schlegel, as Librett demonstrates, saw the late works of Lessing to be decisive for the future of not only philosophy and literature in Germany, but of German Christianity as well. And Librett also makes it clear that the reception and interpretation of these late works were inextricably bound up with the "Jewish Question," that is, the question of how far Germany's future depends upon acknowledging Mendelssohn's Jewish-inflected version of Lessing's inheritance in *Jerusalem*, *Morning Hours*, and *To the Friends of Lessing*.[10]

Reinhold no less than Schlegel senses the burden of Lessing's inheritance, and like Schlegel he senses the need to disentangle Lessing from Mendelssohn. Reinhold carries Lessing's project forward by, first of all, linking the symbols and rites of the Freemasons to the ancient Egyptian "lesser mysteries" involving similar rites and symbols. These lesser mysteries were transferred to the Jews by Moses who, according to Reinhold, was initiated into the Egyptian mysteries during his residence in Egypt as the pharaoh's adopted son. Second, Reinhold carries on the Lessing project by responding to Mendelssohn's anti-Lessing version of Judaism and offering in its place an anti-Mendelssohnian interpretation of Judaism as "blind faith enforced through fire and sword [blinde, durch Feuer und Schwert erzwungene Glauben]" (*Hebrew Mysteries* 43). Reinhold's continuation of Lessing's project goes beyond Lessing because he makes the Jacobi-Mendelssohn dispute over Lessing the penultimate stage in the very process of Lessing's "education of the human race." The final stage comes with Kant. The history of philosophy up to Kant now is drawn into the ambit of the history of revelation that is the concern of Lessing's "education of the human race." Reason's history is the history of religion as well, and if the new Gospel of reason that Lessing had looked forward to is not going to be the overturning of Christianity but its consummation, the continuity between Christ and Kant had to be made clear.[11] And this meant overturning Mendelssohn's account of Judaism as the signal moment in the history of revelation.

The impact of Reinhold's assault against Mendelssohn's Judaism in favor of enlightened Freemasonry is apparent in the more widely known work of Friedrich Schiller, *Die Sendung Moses* (*The Legation of Moses*) (1790), basically a condensation of Reinhold's book.[12] Jan Assmann sees Schiller's single but profoundly important innovation to have been his linkage of the aesthetic concept of sublimity (*Erhabenheit*) with the unrepresentable and unnameable One God of the Egyptian mysteries that Moses tried, unsuccessfully, to reveal to the Israelites. Assmann is right to draw attention to the significance of Schiller's move for Kant's aesthetic, but Assmann, I believe, is mistaken about Schiller as the first to have made the move. The linkage of sublimity with God's self-revelation was already a significant part of Mendelssohn's description of the difference between pagan and Jewish conceptions of God. (Assmann always overlooks Mendelssohn, quite inexplicably in light of Mendelssohn's important and highly critical appropriation of the Maimonidean theme of Jewish ceremonial law as an "accommodation" of [Egyptian] paganism.) The pagans, Mendelssohn explains, find sublimity in God's power (Macht), but Judaism finds it in God's all-goodness (Allgütigkeit). In the narrative of God's forgiving of the Israelites after the incident of the Golden Calf, Mendelssohn says that "one can no longer hesitate to regard love as being at least as sublime a pre-eminence as power" (*Jerusalem* 131; 2:100). A little later, summarizing the impact of this act of forgiveness upon the Israelites, Mendelssohn declares: "What a sublime and terrifying preparation! [Welch erhabene und schauervolle Vorbereitung!]" (*Jerusalem* 131; 2:102). The experience of having sinned and of having been forgiven is the "sublime preparation" for accepting God as not only powerful, but good. Schiller claims that the Egyptian mystery ceremonies (including circumcision) were "preparations" for accepting the "most sublime" revelation of God's unnameable Being, the "I am what is [Ich bin, was da ist]" that is found in the Temple of Isis in Egypt, and that is also the meaning of God's name as it is revealed to Moses, "I am who I am." This eternal self-identity is for Mendelssohn what reason can attain to naturally, the identity of God as "der Ewige." But for Schiller it is the essence of sublimity. Against the Jewish sublimity of *forgiving goodness*, Schiller is reclaiming the pagan sublimity of power, now understood as the power of the "the highest cause of all things, a primal strength [Urkraft] of nature, which is one and the same as the *demiourgos* of the Greek sages" (*Sendung Moses* 140). Although neither Reinhold nor Schiller will win the day with their proclamation of the new Masonic Gospel of the unnameable God of Greek wisdom and the Egyptian mysteries, their participation in the assault upon Mendelssohn's Judaism is an important part of the story I am telling in this book.

After dealing with Reinhold in the next section of the chapter, I will turn to Kant's *Religion within the Boundaries of Mere Reason* (1793).[13] In many ways, Kant's book on the religion of reason takes over Reinhold's theologico-political project in *Hebrew Mysteries* and *Kant Letters*, namely, to point the way towards a completely enlightened society. Reinhold undertook to write a history of religion and a philosophy of history in his two works in order to show that the contemporary world was entering the final stage of enlightenment, but Kant was less sanguine. For Kant, what stands in the way of enlightenment is "radical evil," the freely chosen turn away from freedom and the embrace of the motives of the empirical self above those of the transcendental self. Radical evil arises from an "inscrutable origin" within the abyss dividing the human into phenomenal and noumenal selfhoods. Radical evil attempts to close the abyss by leaping over to the phenomenal realm and attempting to make one's home there. Kant's religion of reason opens out to the Kingdom of God construed as an ethical commonwealth separated from the realm of radical evil in the same way that the noumenal realm is separated from the phenomenal realm. The ethical commonwealth lives within the horizon of a sublime hope, a hope in what cannot be empirically verified (the moral progress of the human race) but which must nonetheless guide one's actions. Kant rejected the naive faith of a Reinhold in the imminent transformation of humanity, but he believed that a *hope* for "perpetual peace" as humanity's ultimate redemption from radical evil was alone able to sustain an individual's commitment to the moral law.

Kant thought that Mendelssohn had been wrong to reject Lessing's hope for humankind's progress. In an essay entitled "On the Common Saying: That May Be Correct in Theory but It Is No Use in Practice,"[14] Kant devotes the third and final section to attacking Mendelssohn's view, discussed in Chapter 1, that humankind as a whole cannot be said to making continuous moral progress. Such a view, Kant says, makes human history into a tragedy which, after repeated tragic episodes, becomes a farce.[15] Even the "good Mendelssohn," Kant goes on, shows by his efforts on behalf of the "enlightenment and welfare of the nation to which he belonged" (i.e., the Jewish nation) that he did not consider history to be a mere farce (Kant 1996b: 306; AK8:309). In defending the position that one must act upon the hope of humankind's progress, Kant is presenting himself, as Reinhold and Schiller had previously done, as the authentic heir of Lessing's project of inaugurating a new religion of reason. Kant's vision of an ethical commonwealth of hope is given a double refraction in Rosenzweig's conception of Johannine Christianity and Judaism. The irony is that Kant considered Judaism to exemplify the realm of radical evil. This anti-Judaism, at least, he shared with Reinhold. It is time, finally, to chart in greater detail Reinhold's and Kant's versions of the religion of reason.

Reinhold: Hebrew Mysteries Unveiled

Reinhold published two works in the span of one year, 1786–87, *Hebrew Mysteries* in *Journal für Freymaurer* and *Kant Letters* in *Der Teutsche Merkur*. Both works are united in their fundamental methodology and their aim. They both offer a general historical survey of humankind's religious and philosophical development with the aim of demonstrating that the conflict between religious belief and philosophical rationality was coming to its close in the contemporary generation. In *Kant Letters*, Reinhold declares that Kant's *Critique of Pure Reason* (1781) is "just what the most pressing philosophical needs of our time call for" (16). He means, first, that the times demand a reconciliation of philosophy and faith, but he also means that the times demand a reconciliation of Mendelssohn and Jacobi. According to

Reinhold, Kant's historical significance consists in his solution of the Spinoza Quarrel before it even erupted. The Spinoza Quarrel showed the limits of two approaches to God: Mendelssohn's through reason and Jacobi's through faith. Read through the lens of the Spinoza Quarrel, Kant's *Critique of Pure Reason* shows how reason and faith can finally be reconciled.

Reinhold believes that the *Critique of Pure Reason* is not only a harbinger of a new philosophical era. A new social order is also made possible because of this revolutionary text. In this new social order, morality would no longer depend upon fear of punishment or hope of reward in the afterlife. Religion would no longer need the trappings of unintelligible ceremonies, symbols, and rituals in order to overwhelm the imagination of the masses and impress them with the supernatural power of its priests. Political authorities would no longer join forces with religious leaders in order to control a population held in the psychological and emotional bonds of superstitious awe. Reinhold's *Hebrew Mysteries* and *Kant Letters* together seek to overcome the despotism of church-state "political-theological" alliances by opening up to public gaze all the "secrets" by which these alliances are maintained, many times with those in power having themselves forgotten the real meaning or even the content of the secrets. Reinhold's uncovering in *Hebrew Mysteries* of the meaning of the Egyptian mysteries as they have been inherited by Judaism and Freemasonry is intended to respond to "the necessity of opening to view the political-theological secrets that are as old as the oldest state formations, secrets upon which reverence for the lawgiver and for the laws is based, secrets whose key was permitted to no one besides the lawgiver and his helpers" (*Hebrew Mysteries* 67). In *Kant Letters*, Reinhold's goal is to open the secrets contained in Kant's *Critique of Pure Reason*, to make it clear how Kant's work "promises for our descendents nothing less than the end of all philosophical and theological heresies" (*Kant Letters* 15).

Although both *Hebrew Mysteries* and *Kant Letters* are aimed at the uncovering of the secrets that can bring a new political-theological-philosophical era of enlightenment, they are admittedly quite different in both tone and content. *Hebrew Mysteries* offers an exposition of Jewish ceremonies, symbols, and rituals as precisely paralleling those of Freemasonry. Reinhold traced both Freemasonry and Judaism back to the Egyptian mystery religion of Isis and Osiris. He argued that the unfulfilled promise of both Judaism and Freemasonry was the open promulgation of the secret at the heart of the Egyptian mysteries: "the nullity of the popular deities [Nichtigkeit der

Volksgötter]" and "the existence of a single Ur-Being [Dasein eines einzigen Urwesen]" (*Hebrew Mysteries* 75). Where Judaism had long ago deteriorated into a despotic rule of priests, Freemasonry stood at the crossroads and could still fulfill its promise. Moses tried to build a society based upon the open knowledge that that the popular, exoteric religion of idolatrous polytheism was entirely baseless. He fashioned laws and ceremonies that corresponded to the Egyptian "lower" mysteries that were intended to draw the initiate away from the crassness and immorality of popular polytheism and prepare him or her for accepting the ultimate truth about God's unrepresentable oneness. These lower mysteries became mystifications used to sustain the power of priests, and the same thing is threatening Freemasonry, according to Reinhold. Reinhold wants to democratize Freemasonry and counter the rising tide of hierarchalization and power consolidation that was taking hold in certain lodges, especially among the "Illuminati" led by Adam Weishaupt, a radical enlightener who was willing to use despotic means to achieve his aim of a "New World Order."[16] Reinhold, we could say, wants to play the role of a latter-day Moses.

In *Kant Letters*, Reinhold argued that Kant's *Critique of Pure Reason* (1781) offered the key to interpreting the history of religion as the struggle between esoteric truth and exoteric falsehood. In the *Kant Letters*, however, Reinhold expressed this in Kantian terms as a struggle between speculative reason and sensible intuition over how to represent the unrepresentable God. Speculative reason seeks absolute certitude about the existence of a highest being through logical proofs; sensible intuition seeks to grasp the highest being in a direct and immediate manner. Kant showed that neither reason nor intuition could achieve its aim. But a "moral faith" in God was possible if we would grant a mediating role to *practical* reason. I will explain this in greater detail below, but for now it may suffice to quote from the description in the opening pages of *Hebrew Mysteries* of what the initiate into the highest mystery learned about God. This description applies to the time in the remote past when the mysteries flourished, but it provides a clear picture of what Reinhold hoped might be accomplished in his own generation:

> Initiation then was nothing less than an empty, meaningless, ceremonial formality [ein leeres sinnloses Gepräng] through which the new initiate would not have become any wiser about anything. After a period of testing, the initiate was

brought once into the sanctuary. At this point there were no more secrets, no inexplicable ceremonies, no puzzling formalities, no ambiguous hieroglyphs. Nothing here stood opposed to his reason or beyond his imaginative powers; the former was as little deceived in its expectations [to learn about God] as the latter was required to deceive itself. The Epopte [i.e., "visionary"] left the gathering neither as an indifferentist [i.e., resigned to a skeptical attitude toward God's existence] nor as a fanatic. (*Hebrew Mysteries* 16)

Reinhold insists that the highest mystery leaves reason and imagination free from illusions. The highest mystery in *Hebrew Mysteries* is that there is only one, unrepresentable God. In *Kant Letters*, Reinhold writes about the concept of God promulgated by religious elites whose words demanded blind faith just as those of the political elite demanded blind obedience. Of this religiously and politically slavish concept of God, Reinhold says that "only recently—and by far not everywhere—was one able to say aloud, without danger of being regarded an atheist, that fortunately for human beings *no object corresponds* to that concept" (*Kant Letters* 225).[17] Kant's *Critique of Pure Reason* allows the highest secret of the ancient mysteries to be openly disclosed without fear that it will lead to the "indifferentism" of the skeptic or atheist. Kant offers an idea of God that arises from our *rational* need as autonomous beings to expect that our dutiful conformity to the moral law is pleasing to a higher being. Kant shows that this higher being cannot be intuited, and therefore no mystery shrouds Kant's God from the public. Kant's *Critique of Pure Reason* is the modern form of the ancient mysteries, now made fully transparent in their rational basis. If Kant's text itself may seem mysterious and arcane to the public, Reinhold's *Kant Letters* is designed to show that this reputation is undeserved.

We could say, in light of the similarities we have so far seen between *Hebrew Mysteries* and *Kant Letters*, that Reinhold offers himself in both texts as a Moses redivivus. In *Kant Letters*, Reinhold interprets the history of reason itself, the original source of the Egyptian wisdom he uncovered in *Hebrew Mysteries*, as holding the key to the future enlightened society. Kant had shown that reason has two sides, one speculative and the other practical, whose entanglement with the receptive apparatus of human sensibility accounts for the *longue durée* of popular superstition and whose disentanglement from all sensible content accounts for historical moments of enlightenment (preserved in Egypt's mystery religion and Freemasonry).

Reinhold's self-appointed task is to reveal the underlying epistemological dynamism behind the historical conflict between philosophy and religion as speculative reason tries to disentangle its idea of God from sensibility only to be drawn once more into its ambit by the pull of practical reason to give its moral ideals an emotional power through images and representations of suprahuman beings. According to Reinhold, Kant's *Critique* signals the final triumph of reason's push for enlightenment over the abuse of human sensibility to create representations of reason's unrepresentable ideas. If in *Hebrew Mysteries* Reinhold discards Mendelssohn's living Judaism in favor of its "unveiling" as symbolizing the one and unrepresentable God of nature, in *Kant Letters* he discards Mendelssohn's own version of the religion of reason as the last gasp of speculative reason's overreaching attempt to free itself from sensibility and present a purely formal idea of God. Only practical reason—the human face of reason's power to project an ideal morality of selfless action—can cross over the Jordan into Canaan. Jesus was the first to understand that the Kingdom of God is within us, in the universal voice of morality commanding us to transcend self-love and find our true life in love for others. Kant allowed Reinhold to see that the one, unrepresentable God of the ancient mystery religions was first truly comprehended by Jesus, not by Moses. Reinhold's *Kant Letters* gives philosophical depth to the views expressed in *Hebrew Mysteries*, but it does not undo anything in *Hebrew Mysteries*. In fact, one can read the *Kant Letters* as the history of philosophy that complements *Hebrew Mysteries*' history of religion.

Hebrew Mysteries and *Kant Letters*, as I have been explaining, are united by a single, ambitious, politico-theological aim, namely, to lead German society into the promised land of Enlightenment. Together they offer a single philosophy of history as the unfolding of human enlightenment through reason's own self-cognition. In both texts, Judaism figures centrally in the history of humanity's enlightenment. In *Hebrew Mysteries*, Judaism is understood to be the corruption of Moses's revolutionary attempt to publicly promulgate the secret of the Egyptian mysteries. The problems begin with the generation of the Exodus. "The books which bear [Moses's] name are full of examples of the wearisome oscillation of the Jews between superstition and lack of belief" (*Hebrew Mysteries* 72). Judaism's priestly establishment mystified Moses's religion to maintain its despotic power over the entire society. Judaism is therefore history's first and signal example of the triumph of superstition over revolutionary enlightenment. Jews then could not but resist the revolution attempted by Jesus who, according to *Kant Letters*, tried to reveal to the world the moral truth that Moses had concealed beneath the ceremonial laws of Judaism, its "lower" mysteries. What *Hebrew Mysteries* and *Kant Letters* together accomplish is the inversion of Mendelssohn's portrait of Judaism in *Jerusalem*: Judaism for Reinhold is the paradigm case of a religion *opposed* to enlightenment. As for Mendelssohn's religion of reason in *Morning Hours*, Reinhold declares in *Kant Letters* that "with rare clarity [it] expounds ontological pseudo-arguments" and presents "the whole matter of dogmatic deism with resplendent order" (*Kant Letters* 24). Reinhold holds up *Morning Hours* as the signal example of reason's overreaching attempt to demonstrate God's existence through logical proofs. Mendelssohn's claim to model enlightenment both as a Jew and as philosopher in *Jerusalem* and *Morning Hours* has thus been superseded.

In *Hebrew Mysteries*, Reinhold makes the transformation of contemporary history dependent upon the widest possible dissemination of the ideas that comprise the "mystery" held previously in silence by Freemasons, namely, that the one "highest being" transcends every human effort to imagine or represent it. In other words, enlightenment consists in breaking down the "unholy distinction" between esoteric and exoteric that had been the basis of every mystery religion, and that was threatening to undo the democratic promise of contemporary Freemasonry. The time is right for Freemasonry to lead the world into enlightenment. Freemasonry's enlightened conception of God will triumph over the obfuscations of religious orthodoxy in all its forms. In an essay published a year before *Hebrew Mysteries*, "Gedanken über Aufklärung [Thoughts on Enlightenment]," Reinhold speaks about the ages-long resistance of ecclesiastical authorities to enlightenment:

> Judging from appearances, no one has a better grasp of the meaning of enlightenment than monks and their spiritual kin among the altar servants of every religion. These kinds of men so managed to direct their efforts against enlightenment in every age and land that it can at least be said with confidence that they know who their enemy is. They either smother the seeds of enlightenment in the bud or they so hinder its mature growth that only very belatedly does the tree of knowledge thrive and bring forth the fruit by whose wondrous power the eyes of the nations are opened to the true nature of so-called orthodoxy.[18]

The message of *Hebrew Mysteries* is that the fruit of the "tree of knowledge" is available to all who wish to taste of it. "Monkdom" can no longer oppose it. The gravest threat to enlightenment is from within, from the effort on the part of certain Freemasons to gain despotic political power through secret machinations. The implication at the heart of *Hebrew Mysteries*, although Reinhold never says it in so many words, is that the gravest threat to enlightenment is the *judaization* of Freemasonry.

The mystery at the heart of Freemasonry is the same mystery, Reinhold says, that Moses—as an initiate in the Egyptian mysteries—tried to teach all the Jews. Moses did not receive this mystery from God himself in the form of a revelation, but rather he attained to these purely rational truths after reflecting upon the Egyptian mysteries into which he had been initiated as a youth. It is important to understand Moses's motives, as Reinhold conceives them. Moses was a social revolutionary attempting to usher in an age of enlightenment. He stood opposed to the Egyptian priests and the pharaoh who sought to keep the people in blind servitude to their self-serving interests. Moses expected that he could restore freedom and dignity to the people if he revealed to them the secrets that state and ecclesiastical power had jointly turned into the instruments of mystification and tyranny. The revolution, however, failed: The people were not ready for enlightenment. "It is undeniable that contempt and hate, under whose oppression the Hebrews grew into a nation, not only resulted from but also contributed to their absence of humane feelings and their spiritless and heartless character, about which the Holy Scriptures and profane histories are in full agreement. It is to the credit of humanity that it offers but one example of such a character" (*Hebrew Mysteries* 27–28). Working with the most depraved people on earth, Moses was bound to fail.

Following the path already laid down in Mendelssohn's *Jerusalem*, Reinhold attempts in *Hebrew Mysteries* to demonstrate that the legislation Moses constructed to guide the life of the Jewish people is a "living script," what Reinhold calls "ganz Hieroglyphe [entirely a hieroglyph]," (*Hebrew Mysteries* 22). For the Jewish people themselves, the script has devolved into meaningless rituals backed by "blind faith coerced through fire and sword." Indeed, besides the oneness of God, Moses was unable to convey to the Israelites anything of value from the Egyptian mysteries.

> The character of the Israelites, a character combining in the most remarkable manner in the world the profoundest illiteracy of the uncivilized peoples who

wandered about in the region with all the depravities of the vulgar masses living in a cultivated nation such as Egypt was then, makes it superfluous to ask why any of the other treasures of the Egyptian secret teaching could not be passed on to them. How could Moses, for example, have been able to convey the doctrine of the immortality of the soul to a people to whom he said, speaking to them directly shortly before his death, "The Lord has until this day not given you a heart that can understand, eyes that can see, and ears that can hear" [Deut 29:3]? The many centuries that it took before the oneness of God could ripen into an idea of reason in the heads of the priests is the strongest proof that [for the populace] this simple teaching could never develop beyond blind faith coerced through fire and sword. Moses had either to perform daily miracles or call upon his Levites, more frequently than he might have liked, to reenact the role they played in the episode of the Golden Calf when they had to hew down 3000 Jews. Such recourse to violence, however necessary on purely political considerations, was no doubt unpleasant for Moses who would have preferred to establish his new religion on at least some measure of understanding and not entirely on the senses [Sinnen] of this people and to make the divine worship less an affair of the body than of the soul. But here his Egyptian wisdom served him well. The exoteric side of the mysteries was overladen with hieroglyphs, ceremonies and ritual laws, and this was probably the source of their later collapse. However, this was precisely the side of the mysteries for which the Israelites were more than sufficiently receptive. The very thing that would suffocate the spirit of the mysteries was not dense enough to make up for the Hebrews' lack of spirit, and thus it had to be strengthened with countless inserted clauses in order to provide sufficient matter upon which the sensibility [Sinnlichkeit] of this people could be employed. (*Hebrew Mysteries* 43–44)

Despite the over-corporealized, hyper-sensorial nature of the Hebrew mysteries, they still hold the key to deciphering the meaning of the Freemasonic rituals that also descend from the Egyptian mysteries. Once properly deciphered, they can be shown to hold a truth about the oneness and unrepresentability of God that can bring freedom from religious superstition to all humanity.

The proper interpretation of the Jewish laws requires, according to Reinhold, a historical investigation of their basis in Egyptian esoteric wisdom. As I have said, the essence of this wisdom is the oneness of God. This wisdom remained concealed from the wider Egyptian population because it directly contradicted their polytheistic idolatry. Reinhold is unclear about the origin of polytheism in *Hebrew Mysteries*, although he asserts that it is reinforced by the priestly class in order to maintain their power and privileges. In *Kant Letters*, Reinhold will explain that polytheism arises naturally from the inherent tendency on the part of human beings to represent abstract concepts through the medium of sensible intuition, as bodies existing in space and time. This is the tendency that dominates within the Jewish people. When humans sense the commanding voice of practical reason, they tend to represent it as emanating from a source with a personal will and intelligence existing within the world: "In earlier periods of the human race, when feeling spoke very loudly and reason very softly, the voice of moral reason, when it proclaimed faith in the deity, could become properly perceptible only through the medium of sensory presentations . . ." (*Kant Letters* 46). In *Hebrew Mysteries*, however, Reinhold is interested only in the *political* use of polytheism as a way of maintaining a population in blind servitude to priests who claim to be able to communicate with the gods, or rulers who portray themselves as gods on earth (as did the pharaohs), or to both groups, who collude to serve one another's power ambitions. In Egypt, the pharaoh kept the masses in ignorance ("Dummheit") by enslaving them, while the priests strengthened the bonds of slavery by nourishing their ignorance on superstitions (*Hebrew Mysteries* 75–76).

It took a prince, Moses, who had been initiated into the secrets of the Egyptian mysteries, to break free of the priestly-royal power cabal. Moses saw that he had no hope of overthrowing the power of priest and pharaoh in Egypt itself. Therefore he turned to the Jews, a population that was under order to leave Egypt because they had experienced an outbreak of leprosy (Reinhold relies on the ancient report of Manetho, recorded in Josephus's *Against Apion*). He attempts to free them from polytheistic superstition and idol worship and initiate them into the Egyptian mysteries, both the "lower" preparatory mystery rites (like circumcision) that stress moral purity and the "higher" mystery of God's unrepresentable, invisible oneness. As we have seen, the revolutionary attempt by Moses to create a society without *any* mysteries or, if one prefers, a society made up entirely of *initiates*, failed. The Israelites needed sensible objects to worship and, when finally they were freed of their tendency toward idolatry, they turned the laws themselves into "fetishes" (*Hebrew Mysteries* 86).

To displace Mendelssohn's interpretation of the Jewish people as offering a paradigm of enlightened sociality, Reinhold spends considerable time in

Hebrew Mysteries showing how the Jews failed to live up to Moses's revolutionary experiment in society-wide enlightenment. From the beginning, the people showed themselves to be unprepared for the freedom from superstition that Moses offered to them. Their moral and intellectual condition, degraded through centuries of slavery, left them incapable of accepting the purity of Moses's teaching. Moses was forced to recreate the system of laws, ceremonies, and rituals that had been the "lower" mysteries of the Egyptian religion, those that prepared the initiate morally before beginning his induction into the "higher" mystery of the oneness and unrepresentability of God. Moses's new religion was supposed to avoid the excesses of Egyptian religion by keeping all secular power in the hands of the One God: Israel would have no human ruler. But this theocratic system only led to an excess of priestly power. "Any attack against the privileges of the priests or any introduction of a foreign god were state crimes punishable by death" (*Hebrew Mysteries* 77). The judicial and administrative role of the seventy elders was based upon their initiation into Moses's highest mystery (their "vision" of God described in Exodus), but the later Sanhedrin had no such initiation and they became a "state inquisition" enforcing an orthodoxy of "blind belief" (*Hebrew Mysteries* 93). Once again, mystification surrounded the now openly declared mystery of God's oneness and unrepresentability. God was now imagined not to be invisible, but only hiding Himself behind the smoke and fire of the Temple.

The supersession of Judaism promised in *Hebrew Mysteries* through Freemasonry is given its philosophical exposition in *Kant Letters*. Kant's *Critique of Pure Reason*—a revolutionary text in the history of reason itself according to Reinhold—offers the key to promulgating enlightenment throughout an entire people, the goal that Moses (both the Moses of the Exodus and Moses Mendelssohn) failed to realize. With the *Critique of Pure Reason*, Reinhold says in *Kant Letters*, "the unholy distinction between an esoteric and an exoteric religion is . . . at last overcome" (23). In *Kant Letters*, Kant is presented as fulfilling the process that Jesus inaugurated in ancient Judea, namely, the restoration of the connection between religion and morality. In Judaism, morality had entirely been replaced by an exoteric religion whose esoteric meaning was entirely forgotten. Jesus was able to penetrate to the esoteric essence of the "Hebrew Mysteries" because he *felt* the inner compulsion of the moral principle that is reason's practical side. He felt the compulsion, in other words, of a moral demand to conform one's life to a principle beyond all selfish interests and motives, a principle that alone gives human existence its dignity and worth. Jesus did not claim to offer a new *sensible intuition* of God as did the many Greco-Roman mystery cults of his day, nor did he teach that any new *speculative* conception of God was necessary as the many philosophical schools did. His teaching was purely moral and morally pure and in conformity with every human's inner feeling for the moral law: "the principles of the moral law can be discerned in the essence of reason itself," Reinhold declares (*Kant Letters* 44). The essence of reason is universality, and the moral law raises the individual into the realm of the universal by commanding action that is not guided by self-interest. Jesus sensed that within him was a voice that asked him to treat every human as a being capable of rising to the heights of moral universality, and his sense was translated into the image of a father who wants all his children to love one another just as he loves each of them. This image of universal brotherhood restored to the exoteric ceremonialism of Judaism its inner moral core, and it gave the "cold" duty of Stoic philosophers, who also had attained to the idea of universal brotherhood, a powerful emotive basis.

> The common man now forgave his enemies "for the sake of his heavenly father, who lets his sun rise over those who are good and those who are evil," and thus fulfilled a duty whose existence many moral philosophers were not able to dream of until recently [i.e., Greco-Roman philosophers like the Stoics]. The cold thinker, in contrast, who actually had been led to the conviction of this duty by his philosophy, now discovered in his religion—which teaches him to see in his enemy "the son of the universal father of humanity"—the motivation with which he was able to counter the stubbornness of his heart. In this way Christianity formed world citizens in the truest sense, and with grand undertaking it had an advantage over philosophy in so far as it in no way let itself be limited, as philosophy was, to those classes of humanity that blind chance destined to be part of higher culture. (*Kant Letters* 30)

Reinhold thus sees Jesus as having laid the foundations of a social revolution based upon the power of his conviction that he and all humans possessed a common moral identity that made them all children of "the universal father of humanity." Moses revealed the secret of God's oneness, but he could not add anything of moral value (like the doctrine of the immortality of the soul) that would convey to the people a receptivity for the indwelling moral principle of reason. The Israelites were, as we have seen, simply too engrossed by their external senses for them to have a refined, internal moral sensibility. For this reason, Judaism from the beginning lacked a connection to morality and deteriorated into formal laws and ceremonies. Jesus heard the voice of *practical reason* as the voice of a universal, loving Father who commands a pure moral law, but he left *speculative reason* free—perhaps *too* free—to try to work out the nature of this moral God. Medieval scholasticism attempted to shackle speculative reason in the service of orthodox theology. In place of the simple teaching that represented God as loving Father (an image corresponding to his moral feeling that all humans possess a common nature that unites them beyond divisions of class or nation), a great edifice of "scholastic wisdom" sprang up. "The more this monstrosity of ignorance and pride"—i.e., scholasticism—"succeeded in suppressing the use of that faculty which elevates humanity to a moral existence"—i.e., reason itself—"the more it destroyed the fruits of that beautiful union which Christ had established between religion and morality" (*Kant Letters* 31). The Reformation and the scientific revolution of the sixteenth and seventeenth centuries, according to Reinhold, broke the stranglehold of scholasticism on speculative reason. But as a consequence, speculative reason promoted a purely abstract God and forgot that practical reason offered a direct inner sensibility of God as a Father, as commanding moral voice drawing us toward an ideal of selfless action. Speculative reason constructed an image of God that "has nothing at all to do with morality" (*Kant Letters* 48). This God is "a thing of thought" that is "a cause about which one knows nothing more than that it cannot be an effect" (48).

There seem to be only two choices, according to Reinhold, facing a philosophically and scientifically sophisticated person in the modern world in regard to religious faith. Both choices Reinhold finds to be unacceptable: Either embrace a theological dogmatism that offers blind faith as the logical consequence of skepticism about revealed faith (fideism), or accept a rationalist philosophy whose God is a "thing of thought" with no connection to one's deepest moral sensibility (rationalism). If these are the only options—and Reinhold points to the controversy between Jacobi and Mendelssohn as proof that even the best of thinkers seem ranged on one side or the other—then, Reinhold warns, "we shall return again to times of religion without morality when universal superstition ruled, or we shall come to a time of morality without religion when universal nonbelief will rule" (*Kant Letters*

49). It seems that to keep religious faith, one must either abandon one's reason in favor of dogma, or use reason to uncover the moral kernel of religion and consign God to the role of cosmic watchmaker or, possibly, do without God altogether.

Enter Kant. Kant, Reinhold declares, has brought "a gospel of pure reason that will save religion by unifying it with morality through the establishment of the only ground of cognition that leads from morality to religion by means of reason" (*Kant Letters* 49). By showing that speculative reason can never prove the existence of God nor gain apodictic knowledge of his attributes, Kant has in effect drawn the curtain open on the fundamental "mystery" of God's unrepresentability and oneness. All that can be ascertained about God using reason is that no category of the understanding can be used in reference to Him. He is "one," therefore, in the sense that there is one Idea of God that is a postulate of reason; all other concepts of God import unwarranted categories that lead to insoluble paradoxes (antinomies). Kant has shown that the postulation of an Idea of God is a "need of reason" in so far as it seeks to make intelligible to itself the moral demand of practical reason to conform to a universal principle rather than act out of self-interested motives. Reason "needs" the Idea of a being who will reward moral action, but the reward must not become the motive for the action. In conforming one's action with the highest demand of duty to the moral law, the individual hopes that the action, whatever its actual consequences, also fits within a providential scheme. Kant has prepared the ground for morality and religion to be reunited on a rational basis. Kant completes what Jesus had begun. As Reinhold formulates it, Jesus reconnected moral feeling to Judaism's God by teaching that God is the universal loving Father of all humanity, and Kant is reconnecting moral feeling to reason's God by showing that our only possible idea of God is one that conforms to our feeling that our highest duty is to a universal, rational, moral law.

Reinhold presents himself as the apostle of a new religion of reason, and Kant is the savior whom he proclaims. Judaism is the failed attempt on the part of the first great Enlightenment revolutionary, Moses, to lift a society out of superstition and show a people that God is One, invisible, and unrepresentable. The laws of Moses were meant to serve as a moral training regime to prepare the people to accept the unveiled mystery of God's unrepresentable sublimity, but the people were incapable of moving beyond the sensory externalities of the laws. After having fallen back into superstitious fear of a hidden God under the rule of a despotic priesthood, the Jewish people held onto the laws and the Temple sacrifices as mysterious ceremonies demanded of them in order to please this God. In offering this critique of Judaism, Reinhold countered Mendelssohn's picture of the Jewish people as the model of enlightened sociality. Moses, to be sure, would have wanted to create a truly enlightened society, but the people were utterly incapable of sustaining his vision. Jesus broke through the tyranny of the "Hebrew Mysteries" and recognized that his moral sensibility—his receptiveness to the universal moral law of practical reason—was the one thing connecting him to Moses's unrepresentable God. It awaited Kant to draw Moses and Jesus together, to show why God must remain unrepresentable and why morality is humanity's only secure basis for faith in God. In drawing Moses and Jesus together, Kant superseded with a single stroke both Mendelssohn's abstract metaphysical deism and Jacobi's Christian *Schwärmerei*, his over-emotional zealotry on behalf of the inner sensation of God. Because Jacobi was in fact sensing the commanding voice of practical reason, he was closer to the truth than Mendelssohn. Both the biblical Moses and Moses Mendelssohn were committed to only one side of God, the unrepresentable Oneness of God, and on behalf of their goal of freeing their people from political bondage, they imagined that they had good reason to insist that the people continue to obey ritual laws and ceremonies whose only possible value, Reinhold claimed, was to awaken and nurture the moral sensibility of the individual. For Reinhold, ceremonies of this sort might make sense if they were used as symbols within the Freemasonic initiation process, but they hardly had a role to play as a continuing tradition of an entire people. Kant had delivered a new Gospel of reason, Reinhold was its preacher, and Freemasonry would be its church. Moses and Jesus had been superseded by Kant.

Kant's Religion of Sublimity

Kant was not willing to step into the role that Reinhold assigned him, namely, the new Messiah of a post-Christian enlightened humanity. Kant was far less sanguine than Reinhold about humanity's ability to reform itself and adopt a religion of reason. Where Reinhold tells the story of the history of reason within the context of humanity's religious, social, and intellectual development, Kant emphasizes that reason—the self's noumenal identity—has no history. The inheritor of Reinhold's attempt to provide a history of reason is Hegel, not Kant. For Kant, reason does not evolve from immaturity to maturity as it makes gains in self-cognition. The obstacle to the realization of the religion of reason is not, for Kant, something that is susceptible to amelioration through the best efforts of all the enlightened leaders in the world. The obstacle is not susceptible to *any* amelioration. The obstacle is "radical evil," the condition of possibility of history itself as the struggle between reason and superstition, freedom and slavery, autonomy and heteronomy. The concept of radical evil allows Kant to separate both Judaism and historical Christianity from his own new religion of reason. The separation is itself a radical one, as sharply defined as heaven is from hell. We will see that both Judaism and historical Christianity fall on the side of hell, but that only Judaism makes hell its preferred dwelling place. Historical Christianity at least preaches that heaven should be one's goal; Judaism has no other goal than to rule within the mechanical deadness of the phenomenal world. Judaism has no sense for morally sublime transcendence. Historical Christianity does point toward the pure moral law, but has corrupted the purity of its teaching by introducing the incentive of a future, heavenly reward for obedience to the law. Kant will offer a version of realized eschatology, the doctrine that the Kingdom of God—heaven—is realized within the individual in the here and now when one fulfills the will of God. The historical realization of the Kingdom of God as a worldwide age of perfect peace is a matter of *hope*, but it should not be one's incentive for acting in accordance with the moral law.[19]

Radical evil, according to Kant, is the propensity of the human being to misjudge the proper relationship between his noumenal and sensible identities. Radical evil arises from the human propensity to subordinate the *sublime* identity of the self (the identity that cannot be measured by the finite standards of the sensible world) to the *beautiful* identity of the self. "It is very beautiful," Kant says in the *Critique of Practical Reason*, "to do good to human beings from love for them and from sympathetic benevolence, or to be just from love of order" (Kant 1996b: 206; AK5:82). Such beauty would, indeed, be the highest good a human could achieve, if humans were *only* creatures of nature.[20] But "[w]e stand under a *discipline* of reason" and we are able to act out of respect for the law which our own reason gives us.

We can act out of duty to the law which reason commands, the categorical imperative. Acting out of duty to the law, we are not motivated by anything empirical (sympathy, love). To see ourselves only as beautiful and not as sublime is to "deny from self-conceit the authority of the holy law." We "defect" from our sublimity "in spirit, even though the letter of the law is fulfilled" (1996b: 206; AK5:82). To act so as to appear beautiful is to act morally, but only "outwardly" and according to the "letter of the law." In other words, it is to be *Jewish*. However, to act in accordance with one's sublime spirit is *Christian*. Radical evil is our propensity to renounce Christianity for Judaism. Judaism—putting legalism above the law—is a propensity that is inescapable for all humans.

When I use the terms *Christianity* and *Judaism* in relation to Kant's notion of radical evil, it must be made clear that I am not speaking about the historical reality of these two faiths. Historical Christianity for Kant is in the position of what I have just called *Judaism*, that is, it has not reached the point where it recognizes that only the moral law is holy; it still remains at the level of what Kant calls the "faith in the prototype" of moral perfection "according to its appearance" (*Religion-Reason* 125; AK6:119). In other words, Christianity has not recognized that the object of its faith should be the sublimity of the moral law and not its sensible appearance in the beauty of Christ.[21] "However," Kant says in pointing the way beyond the beautiful appearance of Christ to the sublimity of the moral law, "in the appearance of the God-man, the true object of the saving faith is not what in the God-man falls to the senses, or can be cognized through experience, but the prototype lying in our reason which we put in him (since, from what can be gathered from his example, the God-man is found to conform to the prototype), and such a faith is all the same as the principle of a good life conduct" (*Religion-Reason* 125; AK6:119).

So long as historical Christianity veils the sublimity of the moral law beneath its sensible appearance, it falls prey to the propensity to radical evil. In effect, this is a *judaized* Christianity, a Christianity of the letter and not the spirit. But what, then is the nature of *historical* Judaism? Kant, I will show in a moment, grants that in its distance from the sublimity of the moral law and also from the beauty of the prototype of the moral law, Judaism has acquired a sort of *negative* sublimity.[22] If the sublimity of the moral law is *heavenly*, and the beauty of Christ is the *earthly* appearance (semblance) of the moral law, Judaism is *hellish*. Before explaining this, I need to say a few more words about the moral significance of sublimity and beauty for Kant.

It may at first seem paradoxical to say that the difference between the letter of the law and the spirit of the law is the difference between beauty and sublimity. Why should the letter of the law be *beautiful*? In the *Critique of Practical Reason*, Kant contrasts the "letter" and "spirit" of the law as two different formulations of what the New Testament takes to be central commandments of the Hebrew Bible, the command to love God and the command to love one's neighbor. Kant claims that the command to love God "above all" conforms to the sublimity of the "holy law" because "it requires respect for a law that *commands love* and does not leave it to one's discretionary choice to to make this one's principle" (1996b: 207; AK5:83). Further, the love for God "as inclination" is impossible, since God is not "an object of the senses." The love of one's neighbor, Kant says, cannot be commanded as a command to love any individual because "it is not within the power of any human being to love someone merely on command." Therefore, the love that is commanded toward one's neighbor is to be construed as a command to "practice all duties to him *gladly*." This command is sublime because no human can possibly make moral duty the object of love. If he could, there would be no need to *command* this love; it would be as "natural" to the human as is self-love, which certainly needs no command in order to be effective. To fulfill one's moral duty *gladly* can only, therefore, be "an ideal of holiness" which, although "not attainable by any creature," is nonetheless "the archetype which we should strive to approach and resemble in an uninterrupted but endless progress" (Kant 1996b: 207; AK5:83).

In contrast to the holy "law of all laws"—the command to love God and one's neighbor—there is another principle, the "principle of one's own happiness": "Love yourself above all, but God and your neighbor for your own sake" (1996b: 207n1; AK5:83). What Kant means by radical evil is the choice to follow the principle of happiness *as if it fulfilled the holy law*. That is, radical evil is not the simple evasion of the holy law and the pursuit of self-love, but rather the pursuit of self-love *under the guise of holiness*. It is the *show of goodness*. That is why radical evil can seem beautiful. Radical evil is the near-perfect semblance of morality in the world. It parades itself as the love of God, and seeks to prove its love by "useless" (i.e., anti-utilitarian) deeds, deeds that seem to have no ulterior aim beyond themselves.[23] To do good to another "out of love" rather than duty seems like an act that does not seek a reward, but if one loves the individual, then the good one does is done out of *partiality*. The sublime task is to do good to someone whom one does not love (not the enemy, but a faceless individual who could be *anyone*). The love one has for the other exists because, for some reason, the other *pleases* you. Hence, the principle at work is "love your neighbor for your own sake." Self-love is masquerading as the beautiful love of one's neighbor.

There are also beautiful semblances in which self-love masquerades as the love of God. Kant speaks of these specifically in *Religion-Reason* as "counterfeit service." Kant makes it clear that in creating semblances of the holy we are worshiping ourselves in our sensible nature. Every concept of God is a way of "making a God for ourselves," that is, a way of establishing a standard for judging ourselves. If that standard is one that can be realized in the sensible world (and is therefore not sublime), there is only *idolatry*, the worship of the beauty of the human being.

> Anthropomorphism, which is hardly to be avoided by human beings in their theoretical representation of God and his being, but is also harmless enough (provided that it does influence the concepts of duty), is highly dangerous with respect to our practical relation to his will and our very morality; for, since *we are making a God for ourselves*, we create him in the way we believe that we can most easily win him over to our advantage, and ourselves be dispensed from the arduous and uninterrupted effort of affecting the innermost part of our moral disposition . . . [S]acrifices (penances, castigations, pilgrimages, etc.) have always been regarded as more powerful, more likely to work on the favor of heaven, and more apt to remove sin, since they more forcefully serve to indicate unbounded (though not moral) subjection to the will of heaven. *The more useless such self-inflicted torments are, the less aimed at the more moral improvement of the human being, the holier they seem to be.* (Religion-Reason 165; AK6:168–69; the first set of italics are Kant's, the second mine)

In the case of religion, the semblance of holiness can take the form of useless deeds performed with no ostensible aim other than to please God. In fact, in sacrificing the first fruits of one's labor, it seems as if one is acting in direct opposition to self-love. However, this is only a "delusion of religion," Kant says. Useless expenditure of one's property, like love that seems to ask nothing in return, hides its truth: it is the worship of a God who is nothing more than our own self-love.

Despite the fact that radical evil cannot be extirpated from humanity, a rational faith in God allows us to hope for the gradual progress of humanity towards a "sublime, never fully attainable idea of an ethical community" (*Religion-Reason* 111; AK6:100). Such a community, Kant says, is only conceivable as "a people under divine commands, i.e. as a *people of God*" (*Religion-Reason* 110; AK6:99). The idea of such a people is that of "the union of all upright human beings under direct yet moral divine world-governance" (*Religion-Reason* 111; AK6:101). Kant's ethical community sounds at first much like Mendelssohn's idea of enlightened Jewish sociality raised to a universal ideal: the noncoerced acceptance of the divine command to love God and one's neighbor. Kant however makes it very clear that his ethical community can only be the fulfillment of Christianity; Judaism is the limit case of a "counterfeit" religion, one in which radical evil triumphs over the "good principle." But it is not, like historical Christianity, a religion that falls prey to radical evil through the illusion of beauty. Christianity points towards morality; Judaism points in the opposite direction. Its embrace of radical evil takes it beyond religious illusions; it is, says Kant (agreeing with Mendelssohn), not really a religion at all. It is, he says (inverting Mendelssohn's claim), pure politics masquerading as religion.

Where Christianity stands fundamentally opposed to politics by preaching universal love (despite its historical failure to do so with moral purity), Judaism is purely political because it makes universal *hatred* its fundamental principle, reserving love only for members of the Jewish people. For Kant, politics that is divorced from morality is a politics guided by the principle "there is no freedom and no moral law" and "everything that happens or can happen is instead the mere mechanism of nature." Guided by this principle, politics by itself would be "the art of making use of this mechanism for governing human beings."[24] If such a politics *pretended* to embody the sublime moral law, it would strive to bring all humanity under the power of a God who demands submission to the natural law of self-love and who promises a purely natural reward—an earthly kingdom—in return. Such a politics would have all of humanity—apart from the people who embrace it—as its enemy, since there is in every human, according to Kant, a resistance to being *merely* an object in nature.[25] In making an enemy of all humanity, this politics would *appear* to be sublime. In his *Critique of the Power of Judgment* Kant says that "separation from all society" is sublime, "if it rests on ideas that look beyond sensible interest" (Kant 1996a: 157;

AK5:275). Separation that rests upon the *hatred* of the moral law is the semblance of the sublime. A politics based upon the illusory sublimity of the *natural* rather than the *moral* law is the essence of Judaism. If Judaism were right that "there is no freedom and no moral law," humanity would be doomed. Instead of looking forward to the triumph of the moral will, humanity's future would be the triumph of the will to hate. That this is what hell means, Kant makes explicitly clear in *Religion-Reason*.[26]

Kant claims that the absence of any reference to rewards and punishments in the afterlife in the Hebrew Bible (a claim that earlier in the century William Warburton in *The Divine Legation of Moses* had used to prove the divine dispensation of the Mosaic law on the grounds that God himself would guarantee rewards and punishments in this life) shows that there was an *intentional* desire on the part of Moses "to found only a political and not an ethical community" (*Religion-Reason* 131; AK6:126). And yet Moses declared that this political community was ruled over by an invisible God. Moses thus passed off something sublime (Kant in the *Critique of the Power of Judgment* says that the prohibitions on making images of God is the most sublime law in the Hebrew Bible[27]) as the sanction for what was in truth only a worldly aspiration for power. Reinhold had argued that Moses's intentions were to enlighten an entire people; Kant sees Moses as lacking anything but a political motive, a motive that expresses the essence of radical evil.

Judaism forges a people's worldly identity around a semblance of sublimity, the No-God of a purely mechanistic nature. Far from embodying a church that strives for a universal moral ideal, Judaism embodies an infinite rejection of such striving. Judaism, says Kant, "far from establishing an age suited to the achievement of the *church universal*, let alone establishing it in its time, . . . rather excluded the whole human race from its community, a people specially chosen by Jehovah for himself, hostile to all other peoples and hence treated with hostility by all of them" (*Religion-Reason* 131; AK6:127). This is not the semblance of sublimity hiding beneath the beauty of nonutilitarian love for the other (the semblance to which historical Christianity is prone when it worships the beauty of Christ); rather it is the semblance of sublimity in a people's ultimately self-destructive *hatred* of humanity. Kant actually suggests that the loss of their political kingdom and their dispersion throughout the world may be interpreted as sublime, that is, as the representation of divine "punitive justice" on earth (*Religion-Reason* 140n1; AK6:138n1). It is possible, Kant says, to see in the dispersion of the Jewish people "the admonishing ruins of a devastated state which stands in the way of the Kingdom of Heaven to come but which a particular providence still sustains, partly to preserve in memory the old prophecy of a messiah issuing from this people, and partly to make of it an example of punitive justice, because, in its stiffneckedness, that people wanted to make a political and not a moral concept of this messiah" (*Religion-Reason* 139–40n1; AK6:138n1). Kant admits that "it is quite awkward to base edifying considerations upon this preservation of the Jewish people." The awkwardness arises from the fact that this same preservation may be taken as a sign—and is so interpreted by the Jewish people themselves—of God's "special beneficent providence which is saving this people for a future kingdom on earth" (*Religion-Reason* 140n1; AK6:138n1). Divine love and divine punishment are, so far as empirical evidence goes, indistinguishable: the continued existence of the Jewish people could be a sign of either love or punishment. It is better, therefore, to avoid the "edifying considerations" one might draw from the continued existence of the Jewish people. But Kant does not, however, shrink from describing Judaism, whether or not its continued, diasporic existence is a divine punishment, as *worthy of divine punishment*.

In discussing the truth symbolized by the Christian doctrine of heaven and hell, Kant says that the radical dichotomization of the two realms (they do not "lose themselves into one another by gradual steps" but "border on each other") is a "sublime" image which elicits horror at the "total dissimilarity by which one can be subjected to one or the other of these two realms [heaven and hell], and also the danger associated with the *illusion of a close relationship between the characteristics that qualify somebody for one or the other*" (*Religion-Reason* 79n1; AK6:60n; italics mine). One does not slowly progress from following the moral law to losing respect for the law and to allowing selfishness to govern one's actions. The very person who perfectly follows the moral law is also capable of radical evil. This can happen when following the moral law is considered to be a way of securing one's happiness, a way of entering into heaven. A person who stands on the side of heaven can flip immediately over to the side of hell by a shift in his or her perspective, by considering heaven to be a reward for obedience rather than realized in the act of obedience itself. Kant would completely agree with the adage that "the road to hell is paved with good intentions," although he would interpret it to mean that the intention to do good combined with the hope of being rewarded for one's intention is already to dwell in hell. *To step on the road to hell with one's "good intentions" is, for Kant, already to have arrived in hell*. However, one can *choose to live in hell* without the masquerade of "good intentions" if one makes self-love the maxim of one's actions *without any reference to the good*. One simply adopts as the principle of one's action the idea that one should only do what one will be rewarded for and one should never do anything simply for the intrinsic moral worth of the action, even if one hopes to be rewarded for it in the long run. One chooses to live in hell when one values each thing only as a potential source of profit. This is the principle that governs Judaism according to Kant. This is why the exilic condition of the Jews might be thought to provide an example of divine punitive justice.

The Jews are able to viewed as an example of punitive justice, Kant says, because they "wanted to make a political and not a moral concept" of the Messiah, their chosen "prototype." But the coming of Judaism's political Messiah—the prototype of radical evil's willing submission to a mechanical law and its No-God—is as little capable of historical realization as is the coming of the purely moral Messiah, Christ as the "prototype" of perfect obedience to the moral law. Kant's Christianity preaches the infinitely deferred *hope* for the historical coming of the Kingdom of God; Judaism's hope, on the contrary, is for the coming of the Antichrist, the one who would reduce morality to politics. Judaism for Kant makes the sublimity of hell its principle of existence. Judaism rejects even the semblance of heaven (doing good with the hope of a reward) and makes hell the only reality (the political realm wholly devoid of a relation to the moral). "Judaism as such, taken in its purity," says Kant, "entails absolutely no religious faith" (*Religion-Reason* 131; AK6:126). In fact, one could go so far as to say that it is the antithesis of religious faith. It was created to be an indestructible *political faith*: "Judaism was . . . *meant* to be a purely secular state, so that, were it to be dismembered through adverse accidents, it would still be left with the political faith (which pertains to it by essence) that this state would be restored to it (with the advent of the Messiah)" (*Religion-Reason* 130; AK6:126). In denying the reality of the afterlife, Judaism does not exist in some neutral space of the secular, neither heaven nor hell; Judaism is, rather, the choice of hell over heaven. In their dispersion, then, the Jews can be seen as *living in hell*. Kant says that it is "quite awkward" to make use of Jews for moral edification in this way because the Jews themselves will simply reply that they are not being punished, but rather preserved by God for their messianic reward. But however awkward it may be to point to history for confirmation of Christianity's truth, Kant has not hesitated in arguing that Judaism is Christianity's antithesis.

Judaism is so much Christianity's antithesis that it bears no real link to it at all. Christianity is "grounded on an entirely new principle" and is a "total revolution in doctrines of faith" (*Religion-Reason* 132; AK6:127). Kant says that he agrees with Mendelssohn's argument in *Jerusalem* that, so long as Christianity represents itself as fulfilling Judaism, there is no reason for a Jew to embrace Christianity. Why should the Jew remove the "yoke of external observances" only to place himself under "the yoke of the profession of faith in sacred history which, for the conscientious, is an even more onerous burden"? (*Religion-Reason* 163n1; AK6:167n1). Kant's opinion of Mendelssohn—whatever he may think of his defense of Judaism—is revealed to be quite high. Mendelssohn is too conscientious to accept the burden to his conscience that a profession of faith in Christianity as the supersession of Judaism requires. According to Kant, Mendelssohn's rejection of the Jew's need to fulfill his religious identity through conversion is really saying to the Christian: "first remove Judaism from your *religion* (though in the historical teaching of faith it may always remain as an antiquity) and we shall be able to take your proposal under advisement." (*Religion-Reason* 163n1; AK6:167n1). Kant takes Mendelssohn to be challenging Christianity to become the *religion of reason* before any Jew will rationally consider converting to it. Of course, Kant does not understand that Mendelssohn does not think that the "external observances" of Judaism are at all onerous. Kant certainly considers Mendelssohn himself to have been entirely free from the delusion of political messianism, so he can only consider his continued attachment to the law to be due to negative reasons. Specifically, Kant imagines that Mendelssohn refuses to exchange the burden of "external observances" for the burden to his conscience of affirming a belief in the divinity of Jesus, a belief that Kant himself finds incompatible with the religion of reason.

Kant's view of Judaism is far more negative than that of Reinhold. But, quite ironically, precisely because of his conception of the universal human propensity toward radical evil, Kant is almost certainly more sympathetic to Jews than was Reinhold. Although Judaism is a pure politics of radical evil, Jews themselves are no worse than all humans. All humans have a propensity to radical evil, and most—especially those who pride themselves on their respect for the laws of the state—fall prey to it. Reinhold held the Jews in "abomination," but he credited the laws of Judaism as deriving from the morally uplifting "lesser mysteries" of the Egyptian cult of Isis and Osiris. These laws allowed the rituals of Freemasonry to be properly understood, which likewise derive from Egypt. Of course, the laws are like scaffolding that must be discarded once one has attained to a rational conception of the moral source of all religion. Kant does not acknowledge the moral basis for Judaism's laws. For him, they are "a collection of merely statutory laws supporting a political state." Any moral teaching associated with these laws "does not in any way belong to Judaism as such" (*Religion-Reason* 130; AK6:125). Kant does not take the lack of morality in the laws of Judaism to reflect a particular moral failing of the Jewish people. Rather, Judaism was designed only for the sake of creating a theocratic state, but its laws are such as "even a political state can uphold and lay down as coercive laws, since they deal only with external actions" (*Religion-Reason* 131; AK6:126). Kant thus entirely rejects Mendelssohn's conception of Judaism's "revealed legislation" as being noncoercive. For Kant, no laws that concern only "external actions" can have a moral import. The noncoercive divine legislation under which the ethical community lives has a single law as its content: the categorical imperative, i.e. act in such a way that the maxim of one's action can be the maxim of all humanity. This law is "divine" because its telos or end is a world governed by no human power. This end cannot be achieved through the use of human power in the world, but nonetheless this end must guide all humanity's striving for moral progress. Kant has, in effect, rendered Mendelssohn's Judaism—the embodiment of noncoercive divine legislation—into a regulative, messianic ideal.[28]

Kant insists that no empirical, historical community can ever embody this messianic ideal. For Kant, as we have seen, Judaism is pure politics without any connection to the messianic ideal of an ethical commonwealth of sublime selves; Christianity began as a "pure religious faith" based upon this ideal, but its history displays nothing that is worthy of its origin. This history, says Kant, is only in his day changing. Only now is it possible "to expect from it [Christianity] a continuous approximation to that church, ever uniting all human beings, which constitutes the visible representation (the schema) of an invisible Kingdom of God on earth" (*Religion-Reason*

135; AK6:131–32). This invisible Kingdom of God, infinitely distant yet always drawing nearer, is the sublime horizon of human history. We have seen how Judaism for Kant represents hell on earth; it is time to understand what he imagined heaven to be.

Kant's "heaven"—the ethical commonwealth that is the invisible Kingdom of God—is populated by noumenal persons and not empirical individuals. All humans confront a choice to identify themselves as noumenal selves or empirical individuals. The predisposition to personhood, or "personality" as Kant prefers to put it, "is the susceptibility to respect for the moral law as *of itself a sufficient incentive to the power of choice*" (*Religion-Reason* 52; AK6:27). In other words, the human being rises to the level of person not merely because of his or her freedom to choose, which might only be a freedom to choose among self-interested incentives, but because this freedom to choose can find its incentive in the respect for the universal moral law that the individual's own reason commands. Human freedom is thus only real self-determination when the human rises to moral personhood as a rational being whose reason is self-commanding and whose will is self-obedient. Put more succinctly, moral personhood consists in the exercise of practical reason.

In the *Critique of Practical Reason*, Kant identifies *personality* as the sublime subjectivity of the human being. At the conclusion of a rather extraordinary paragraph that apostrophizes "Duty," which Kant calls a "sublime and mighty name that . . . requires submission," Kant asks "[W]hat origin is there worthy of you and where is to be found the root of your noble descent . . . ?" Without directly answering this question, which in *Religion-Reason* he will declare to be "inscrutable," Kant identifies Duty with personality:

> It [Duty] can be nothing less than what elevates a human being above himself (as part of the sensible world) . . . It is nothing other than *personality*, that is, freedom and independence from the mechanism of the whole of nature, regarded nevertheless as also a capacity of a being subject to special laws—namely pure practical laws given by his own reason, so that a person as belonging to the sensible world is subject to his own personality insofar as he also belongs to the intelligible world; for, it is then not to be wondered at that a human being, as belonging to both worlds, must regard his own nature in reference to his second and highest vocation only with reverence, and its laws with the highest respect. (Kant 1996b: 210; AK5:86–87)

198 Reinhold and Kant

Respect, Kant had earlier explained, is the feeling one has before a person that affects us as do, for example, "lofty mountains, the magnitude, number, and distance of the heavenly bodies, the strength and swiftness of many animals, and so forth" (1996b: 202; AK5:76). That for which we feel respect "humiliates us in our self-consciousness" (1996b: 200; AK5:74). "The idea of personality," Kant says, awakens respect "by setting before our eyes the sublimity of our nature" (1996b: 210; AK5:87). Personality, he says, is *holy*.

The choice of the self's orientation towards "the sublimity of our nature" or towards its empirical individuality is a choice between two ways of orienting oneself as a rational being whose actions have consequences within the empirical world. Does one take one's guidance from practical reason, which has no regard for the empirical consequences of action, or from prudential reasoning, which judges between the possible outcomes of actions as more or less likely to lead to "happiness," however one may define it? The propensity (Hang) of every individual is to place prudential reasoning above the maxim of one's sublime nature: how else would one orient oneself in a world where every action triggers a chain of consequences, sometimes with life-and-death import? But this subordination of our sublimity to empirical "happiness," if made into the maxim of action, is what Kant calls "radical evil." (Once again: the radical evil of those who put happiness above the categorical imperative as their maxim, a radical evil that hides under the semblance of morality; Judaism is the open and naked adoption of profit and power as the maxim of a nation's actions; Judaism reveals the Machiavellian truth behind other people's self-deluded eudaimonistic morality of happiness). Countering this propensity towards radical evil is the predisposition of every human toward moral personhood. The choice to orient oneself in accordance with practical reason may seem like choosing to "fly blind" in the world, but it is the only way to realize oneself as an autonomous being who acts in accordance with a universal moral law. To choose to blind oneself to the worldly consequences of one's actions is to orient oneself towards sublime holiness.

Perhaps an image is most helpful here. Picture a human's empirical existence in time as a line on a plane that includes other such lines and the entirety of the phenomenal world. Each human "line" begins with a point, which is temporally his or her birth, but, understood as the beginning of a being endowed with freedom, the point represents the eruption into the phenomenal world of a being with a *propensity* toward radical evil, but not a necessary compulsion to act upon that propensity. The freedom of the human to orient herself as a natural object in the phenomenal realm or as a moral being cannot be further explained. It is "inscrutable." It is not a result of the human's rational being, since reason cannot *turn against itself*. Nor is it a result of the human's empirical identity, since this identity lacks freedom *tout court*.

Every other object in the phenomenal world besides the human being has a beginning point, but causal lines lead toward it and wholly determine its existence. In the case of the human, such determining causal lines also exist, but they are not determinative of the direction of the human line. However, the propensity toward radical evil, unless a new orientation replaces it, leads to a *self-determination* to orient oneself as a being like all others on the plane of the phenomenal world. Radical evil is the choice to be like any other object in the phenomenal world. Radical evil chooses to orient the self along a line of sight that is simply the causally determined line of existence of the individual. This line of sight seems to lead in a straight line toward the horizon, but it is only the individual's perspectival vanishing point and it is not a common horizon at all. Each empirical individual has his or her own line of vision on the plane of the phenomenal world.

To understand how it possible to choose sublime *personhood* over this empirical individuality, we need to recall that the self naturally believes itself to be upright while looking along its line of sight in the phenomenal world, but the self can, if it so chooses, imagine itself to have an identity that is not entirely contained within the phenomenal plane. The self can command itself to act in accordance with a rational, unconditioned (i.e., dependent upon nothing external to the will) maxim. Taking its sense of itself from this command of unconditioned universality (the categorical imperative) rather than from any empirical, conditioned (i.e., dependent upon external contingencies) maxim of action, the self discovers that its true orientation is the reverse of the "natural" one of the phenomenal plane. Reversing its orientation, the self mirrors the sublime "prototype" of humanity that Christianity names *Christ*. The self's prior orientation on the phenomenal plane is recognized to be a false one.[29]

There is a wonderful scene in the movie *Pirates of the Caribbean: At World's End* (2007) that captures the redemptive power that comes with the reversal of one's natural up-and-down orientation. Captain Jack Sparrow of the *Black Pearl*, played by Johnny Depp, is seeking to lead his crew out of the land of the dead. He believes that the land of the living lies on the horizon where he sees the last rays of the setting sun, but he has no idea whether he can arrive at this point in the brief time remaining to him before the light is extinguished and all hope of sailing back into life is lost. Deciphering a rune on his map, he realizes that the ship is upside down, although it seems to be sailing on the surface of the water. Death and life are inversions of one another, just as the temporal and ideal realms in the Kantian image I have just sketched. But the movie adds another element that is also central to Kant's *Religion-Reason*. Captain Sparrow cannot capsize the boat without the assistance of the entire crew. Each member of the crew realizes, without Captain Sparrow having to say anything, that as the Captain runs from starboard to port he is attempting to create a swaying motion that will eventually capsize the Black Pearl. They realize, too, why Sparrow is attempting to capsize the boat. Each crewmember joins Sparrow in running back and forth across the width of the boat until the boat tips over and, just as the sun descends on the horizon, the ship is righted once again. On the horizon the sun is rising. The land of the living has been reached.

The Kantian theme that this scene from *Pirates of the Caribbean* figures is that of the "Kingdom of God on earth." Kant argues that the reorientation of the self can only be done by the self's own choice to picture itself as "upside down" in its "natural" state and only upright when it is aligned with the ideal human figure that it can discern when it chooses to reverse its orientation. However, the self not only needs to have faith that its journey in time, while orienting itself in relation to the ideal human figure, is on a straight path towards the horizon (the land of the living, so to speak), it also needs to have faith that *all of humanity* will join in walking upright toward the sublime horizon of the noumenal plane. For a horizon, to be more than a mirage, cannot be one that only appears to a single person. Even in a dream, every individual tacitly accepts that his or her horizon is the same for everyone in the dream. Even in a theater, we persuade ourselves that the horizon of the painted scenery is also our horizon, if we wish to imaginatively enter the world of the characters. Now, so long as the natural orientation determines one's line of vision, the astronomical horizon is shared but the moral horizon is never commonly shared. Each person journeying on the line of sight of the temporal plane is seeking her own happiness, the moral horizon of a private dream. At best, a group of people may be persuaded to pursue the horizon along a path laid down by a religious or political leader. But in no case, according to Kant, is the horizon defined as one that is universally valid for all humans. The only such horizon is that which is visible on condition of reorienting the self. It is the same true horizon no matter what may be one's "private" line of vision. The problem is, as I have said, that this universal moral horizon is not signposted along any line of sight in the temporal plane. However, the individual must hope that the universal moral horizon intersects with the path that humanity as a whole is traveling through time. A universal horizon that only one person can reach is self-contradictory. Put differently, humanity cannot "right itself" with only one person's reorientation, and one person cannot remain convinced of being upright without the faith that all of humanity will ultimately stand upright too. "Now, here we have a duty *sui generis*, not of human beings toward human beings, but of the human race toward itself" (*Religion-Reason* 108; AK6:97). In the movie, the ship is righted once and for all and the transition from death to life is instantaneous and permanent. For Kant, the human knows himself or herself to be always caught between two possible orientations. The progress of humanity toward its universal horizon is something that a moral being must hope for, but the evidence of this progress can be found only in the dissolution of all the limited horizons that only one part of humanity can see. "It is therefore a necessary consequence of the physical and, at the same time, the moral predisposition in us—the latter being the foundation and at the same time the interpreter of all religion—that in the end religion will gradually be freed of all empirical grounds of determination, of all statutes that rest on history and unite human beings provisionally for the promotion of the good . . ." (*Religion-Reason* 127; AK6:121).

The moral faith that Kant offers as the religion of reason is based on the faith that all humanity will join together to at least share a single horizon of hope. When it does so, humanity will no longer fall prey to the illusion generated by radical evil, the illusion that one's private line of vision is leading toward a common horizon (happiness) and is not, rather, pointing *downward*, toward a living hell on earth. "The basis for the transition to the new order of things," Kant writes, "must lie in the principle of the pure religion of reason, as a revelation (though not an empirical one) permanently taking place within all human beings . . ." (*Religion-Reason* 128; AK6:122). At the end of the *Critique of Practical Reason*, Kant offers an image to which this permanent revelation of the sublime moral law might be compared: the "starry heavens above me" that "fill the mind with ever new and increasing admiration and reverence" (Kant 1996b: 269; AK5:161). The "starry heavens above" and the "moral law within" are not "veiled in obscurity" nor are they "in the transcendent region beyond my horizon." "I see them before me," Kant says, "and connect them immediately with the consciousness of my existence." While the sublimity of the starry heavens "annihilates, as it were, my importance as an *animal creature*," Kant says that the sublimity of the moral law "infinitely raises my worth as an *intelligence* by my personality, in which the moral law reveals to me a life independent of animality and even of the whole sensible world, at least so far as this may be inferred from the purposive determination of my existence by this law, a determination not restricted to the conditions and boundaries of this life but reaching into the infinite" (1996b: 269–70; AK5:162).

There is, I think we must admit, something truly sublime about Kant's religion of reason as the ongoing revelation of the infinite horizon that resides within humanity. It takes us beyond Reinhold's rather naive faith in the Enlightenment as dawning with Kant's *Critique of Pure Reason*. As Reinhold glimpsed the religion of reason just around the corner with Kant's new work, Kant saw it receding to an infinitely distant horizon. Kant's passion for a heaven that is "infinitely removed from us" mirrors, uncannily, the Jewish messianic passion—taken by Kant to be a life in hell dedicated, despite the world's disgust with such open rejection of all morality, to the principle that only what makes a profit is good—for a seemingly infinitely deferred redemption. Everyday, earthly existence seems to be poised between heaven (the inward sublimity of personality) and hell (the reduction of the human to a mere "animal creature"). Everyday existence, one might say, is poised between Kant's Christianity of sublime hope (for the coming of the ethical commonwealth) and the Judaism of sublime despair (the rejection of hope and the embrace of the animal creatureliness of humanity).

The challenge of Kant's religion of reason is to discover a way to connect the sublime horizon of hope with this earthly existence, to discover some signposts that might shine brightly, like the sun in the daytime and the moon and stars at night, to guide humanity's diurnal path. The horizon of humanity's hope and the horizon of humanity's diurnal existence need reconciliation if we are to live in peace within the rhythm of day and night, the time of our mortal lives. If revelation takes place in the realm of the sublime, it must find a way to be incorporated into the shape of life as it is lived in the phenomenal plane.

There is a telling passage in the *Critique of the Power of Judgment* where Kant imagines what it would be like to accept the sublimity of the moral law but to deny that there is a God who judges humanity as a whole to be worthy of this sublime law. Kant pictures Spinoza to be someone like this, a "righteous man" who "does not demand any advantage for himself from his conformity to this law," but who also knows that he and other righteous men, for all their "worthiness to be happy" will nevertheless be just as subject to the natural laws as "all the other animals on earth" whose fate is to be engulfed in "one wide grave" and flung "back into the abyss of the purposeless chaos of matter from which they were drawn" (1996a: 317–18; AK5:452.) Kant can only imagine that this righteous man would either cast his lot with nature and throw off the burden of the moral law or accept "the existence of a moral author of the world" at least from "a practical point of view." This passage is telling because it shows so clearly that Kant cannot imagine any happiness *in the here and now* of daily life. This is not (or not only) a matter of personal psychology. Perhaps it is best described, using Eric Santner's neologism, as Kant's *psychotheology*. This psychotheology is based upon Kant's *judgment* that behind the appearance of the world stands the "abyss of the purposeless chaos of matter from which they [all living things] were drawn." This is the world under the dominion of the *past*. The sublime horizon of hope, the future, has no place in this world. It has no *presence* here. It is only sublime. The future as the *next moment* is only the coming-to-be of the past. And the present is, once one is conscious of it, already past.

The impossibility of finding happiness in the moment is exactly what Faust staked his immortal soul upon in Goethe's version of the legend. Kant stakes his immortal soul—his *personality*—upon the very same condition, but, unlike Faust, Kant makes the wager with himself on terms he cannot fail to win, given the critical chastening of any possible Faustian metaphysical ambition that he once had. Kant has convinced himself that there is nothing in the world worth knowing that he himself—his own cognitive power, that is—has not put there. No experience will ever surprise him or render him *ecstatic*. Kant is therefore proof against all forms of fanaticism, but he is also proof against the miracle of *ordinary life*. To assure himself that he is right, Kant makes his life conform to the rigors of the repeating cycles of the hands of a clock. There is no *holiday* for Kant, neither in his sublime religion of holy law nor in his life.

Kant shows that the relationship between sublimity and beauty (infinity and finitude) is the fundamental question for any religion of reason—for any reconciliation of philosophy and revelation—but it is Hegel, to whom I will now turn, who shows that the infinite rhythmic temporality of *life* and not the mechanical regularity of a clock makes possible the disclosure of the world's beauty in the here and now. This will be a lesson that will guide Rosenzweig's recuperation of Judaism as the living embodiment of eternal beauty. But Kant's lesson—that history is only truly oriented by a *sublime hope* inclusive of all humanity—is one that Rosenzweig also inherits.

FIVE

Beautiful Life: Mendelssohn, Hegel, and Rosenzweig

> Sehen Sie nun, was uns verloren ging, als unsre Großväter das *schöne Leben* verließen und in ein Leben sich hinausreißen ließen, wo die Schönheit eine Insel, eine isolierte (l'art pour l'art) Erscheinung, ein Götze war. Und was wir widerzugewinnen haben und wiedergewinnen werden? Ein Leben, als ganz Kunstwerk, eines das ganz *schön* ist, weil es ganz Leben, ganz *unser* Leben sein wird.
>
> (Look what we have lost when our grandfathers abandoned the *beautiful life* and let themselves be seduced by a life where beauty was an island, an isolated appearance [l'art pour l'art], an idol. And what can we win back and what will we win back? A life that is wholly an artwork, that is wholly *beautiful*, because it will be wholly life, wholly *our* life.)
>
> FRANZ ROSENZWEIG, "Anleitung zum Jüdischen Denken" ("Instruction for Jewish Thinking") (1921), (*Zweistromland* 615)

Introduction: Reading Mendelssohn through Hegel

Hegel's philosophical supersession of Judaism—perhaps the central theme of his early (pre-1800) theological writings—is the most challenging of those I will explore and the most consequential for Rosenzweig. Quite unlike Reinhold and Kant, Hegel acknowledges finite, embodied life as the heart of religion.[1] To a great extent, Hegel comes to accept the point that Jacobi had been pressing against the new Spinozism in German philosophy, namely, that reason and universality were inimical to faith in a *living* God and that freedom begins with the defiant rejection of the God of the Enlightenment, the Supreme and Necessary Being. In the discussion of Jacobi that forms the second chapter of his work *Faith and Knowledge* (1802), Hegel quotes a passage from *Jacobi to Fichte* that states that "in defiance of the will that wills nothing" he, Jacobi, would "even will to pluck the ears of wheat on the Sabbath for no other reason than that I am hungry, and because the law is made for man and not man for the law." Hegel says that these words are "beautiful and quite pure" and goes on to explain:

> Jacobi is speaking in the first person: *I am* and *I will*. But this cannot jeopardize the objectivity of the passage. The expression that the law is made for man and not man for the law—without regard to the meaning it has where Jacobi took it from—certainly acquires in this context a more universal meaning, but it also retains its true meaning. This is why we have called this passage quite pure. Ethical beauty ... must have the *vitality of the individual who refuses to obey the dead concept*. (Hegel 1977: 144; italics mine.)

Hegel finds in Jacobi's insistence upon defiant subjectivity a salutary antithesis to the abstract, *dead* universality of Enlightenment reason. But Jacobi, Hegel argues, does not offer any objective content for the subjective will. Jacobi remains fixed at the level of defiance. Hegel will argue for an embodied fusion of finite subjectivity with the objectivity of *infinite love* as the way beyond Jacobi. Such a fusion of the finite and the infinite will also allow Hegel to get past the Kantian emphasis on the ethically sublime categorical imperative. Hegel will argue in *The Spirit of Christianity and its Fate* (1799) that the fusion of finite subjectivity and infinite love is given concrete and *beautiful* form in the commensality of the Last Supper.

In this chapter I will show how Hegel's conception of the beauty of the embodied love in the Last Supper is, in fact, deeply indebted to Mendelssohn's conception of the Jewish people as the "living script" of a revelation. This is a debt that Hegel nowhere openly acknowledges. Whenever Hegel explicitly discusses Mendelssohn in his early theological writings, it is only to attack him. Like Kant, Hegel inverts Mendelssohn's claim that Judaism is the ideal configuration of a noncoercive society and he argues rather that Judaism is entirely composed of coercive laws. Hegel carries Kant's characterization of Judaism as pure politics—the embrace of a life wholly oriented by a view of the world as a lifeless mechanism—to its extreme conclusion. As I pointed out in the previous chapter, Kant thought that the apparent absence of any reference to an afterlife in the Hebrew Bible showed it to be the blueprint for a merely "political faith." Hegel went further and took the purely this-worldly rewards and punishments of the Hebrew Bible as evidence that the Jews had reduced themselves to a condition *below* the political, a condition of enslavement so profound that they "renounced the capacity to will and even the very fact of their existence" (*Spirit-Fate* 196;

254). In place of their will to survive, Hegel says, the Jews "wished only for a continuation of the possession of their land through their posterity, a continuation of an undeserving and inglorious name in a progeny of their own" (*Spirit-Fate* 196; 254). Hegel's characterization of the Jews and Judaism in *Spirit-Fate* and his other early theological writings is a direct assault upon Mendelssohn's presentation of Judaism in *Jerusalem* as an exemplarily enlightened form of sociality. Hegel's is certainly the most sustained attack on Mendelssohn written during this period and it is surpassed only by Hamann's *Golgotha and Scheblimini!* for the venom of its tone.

Rosenzweig was a very close reader of Hegel's early theological writings, as I will discuss in more detail shortly. Rosenzweig was profoundly influenced by his study of these writings. Following Hegel in his emphasis upon the *beauty* of religious existence, Rosenzweig rejects the Kantian postulation of the Kingdom of God as a *sublime* "ethical community" of noumenal selves united by the shared horizon of the moral law. In place of this sublime vision of the Kingdom of God, Hegel and Rosenzweig see the *beauty* created in the shared life of a historical community as the closest earthly approximation of the Kingdom of God. Hegel, however, is quite explicit about denying that beauty resides within the Jewish people. Their "animal existence was not compatible with the more beautiful form of human life which freedom would have given them," Hegel declares (*Spirit-Fate* 202; 258). The spiritual poverty of the Jews was such that "when they looked into their own hearts, there was nothing left there to see: they had renounced all nobility and all beauty" (*Spirit-Fate* 241; 290). Hegel offers two exceptions to this negative characterization of the Jews: the annual festivals enjoined by Moses and the communal life created by the Essenes at the time of Jesus. "The three great yearly festivals, celebrated for the most part with feasts and dances," Hegel writes, "are the most human element in Moses' polity" (*Spirit-Fate* 193; 252). The Essenes, Hegel explains, sought to create an "eternal entity" out of their commonly shared life "which would make them into a living unity without multiplicity" (203; 259).

While it is tempting to credit Hegel's remarks in *Spirit-Fate* about the "feasts and dances" of "Moses' polity" and the "living unity" of the Essenes as contributing to Rosenzweig's identification of the festal cycle of the Jewish year as enabling Jewish individuals to embody beauty within a unified and eternal peoplehood, I will argue in this chapter that Rosenzweig in fact reads *Mendelssohn* through Hegel's early theological writings and recovers

Mendelssohn's conception of Judaism's embodied eternality against Hegel's reading of it as mere "animal existence." Although Rosenzweig seems primarily indebted to Hegel, he is, as I will argue in this section, even more deeply indebted to Mendelssohn. Rosenzweig, without being fully aware of it, is recuperating *Mendelssohn's* voice as he appropriates Hegel's theory of religion as the beautiful fusion of infinite and finite life for his characterization of the choreography of eternity that constitutes the life of the Jewish people. For it was from Mendelssohn's description of the Jewish people as the embodiment of revelation in a "living script" that Hegel constructs his own portrait of the embodiment of divine revelation in the Last Supper. Before I turn to this, however, I want to say a little more about Rosenzweig's reading of Hegel's early theological writings.

Rosenzweig had worked with Hegel's *Nachlaß*, his manuscript archive in the Königliche Bibliothek in Berlin where the previously unpublished manuscripts of the early theological writings were discovered by Herman Nohl. Rosenzweig knew quite well the contents of Nohl's 1907 edition of these manuscripts, referring to it in his own publication of an early Hegel manuscript that Rosenzweig calls "The Earliest System-Program of German Idealism [Das älteste Systemprogramm des deutschen Idealismus]."[2] Rosenzweig makes significant use of Nohl's collection of early theological writings in his *Hegel und die Staat* (1920). This appropriation of Hegel's theological writings has been studied recently by Peter Eli Gordon in *Rosenzweig and Heidegger* (2003: 82–118). Gordon points out that in *Hegel und die Staat* Rosenzweig seemed "quite uninterested" in Hegel's very negative characterization of Judaism in these early works, especially in *The Spirit of Christianity and its Fate*. Gordon argues that this text, however, played a major role in shaping Rosenzweig's conception of Judaism in the *Star*. In particular, Gordon claims that Hegel's portrait of Jesus as someone completely withdrawn from history is what lies behind Rosenzweig's interpretation of the Jews as a people outside politics and history. I will discuss this at greater length below, but for the moment I want to note only how significant are the early theological works of Hegel for understanding the genesis of Rosenzweig's thought.

Although it is clear that Rosenzweig was a very close reader of Hegel's early theological works, the fact that these works are engaged in a direct assault upon Mendelssohn's *Jerusalem*, although noted by Herman Nohl in his extensive commentary on the manuscripts, has not led to a reassessment of Rosenzweig's relation to Mendelssohn. Rosenzweig, I will argue, reads Mendelssohn *through* Hegel's early theological writings. When Rosenzweig comes to adopt Hegel's emphasis on the *beauty* of religion in the *Star*, he is actually recovering *Mendelssohn's* voice through the Hegelian text. Herman Nohl, as I have said, tells us that the "traces" of Hegel's engagement with Mendelssohn's *Jerusalem* are visible throughout all the manuscripts dating from the 1790s (404). Indeed, he points to "the fine word [das schöne Wort]" coined by Mendelssohn in *Jerusalem*, which Hegel adopts in his early "Popular Religion and Christianity," namely "Buchstabenmensch [letter-man]" to refer to someone wholly lacking creativity and independence of thought.[3]

Hegel's debt to Mendelssohn goes much deeper than word choice, however. Mendelssohn, first of all, serves Hegel as the major target of his assault against Judaism. Throughout his early theological writings, Hegel is explicitly concerned to demonstrate that Mendelssohn's claim that Judaism is an embodiment of enlightened sociality is not merely wrong, but the inversion of the truth. When, therefore, Rosenzweig in turn inverts Hegel's interpretation of Judaism, he is restoring Mendelssohn's vision of Judaism's historic significance as the living witness against idolatry and despotism. I do not know if Rosenzweig was fully aware of the Mendelssohnian intertext in Hegel (although he certainly read Nohl's paragraph detailing the influence). My point here does not have so much to do with Rosenzweig's conscious intentions as it does with the inherent logic of philosophy's attempt to construct a religion of reason in the aftermath of the Spinoza Quarrel. Rosenzweig's Jewish and philosophical identity, as I have argued extensively in Chapter 3, is shaped in response to 1800. What this date signifies is the closing off of a breakthrough of revelation in history when Kant's *Critique of Pure Reason* shattered the Enlightenment's dream of replacing "superstition" with "reason," or, put differently, of replacing faith in God with knowledge of God. When Rosenzweig seeks to dismantle the idealist edifice of 1800, whether he is aware of it or not, he will be brought back to Mendelssohn. Mendelssohn's Jewish-philosophical project is also Rosenzweig's own. I have spoken of the historical configuration that joins Mendelssohn and Rosenzweig in my introduction. I opened the introduction with a quotation from Amos Funkenstein's *Perceptions of Jewish History* stating that Mendelssohn and Rosenzweig define the beginning and end of the history of German-Jewish philosophy. Funkenstein also claims that Rosenzweig "returns to the origin," to Mendelssohn in other words, because like him he refuses to translate Judaism into any of the prevailing idioms of German culture, philosophy first among them. In returning to 1800, Rosenzweig is releasing the voice of Mendelssohn as much as he is finding his own. The voice he releases is one that speaks to him through Hegel's supersession of Judaism in *The Spirit of Christianity and its Fate*. Mendelssohn's impact upon Hegel's early theological writings is both extensive and deep. One may find Mendelssohn even in Hegel's fundamental point that Christianity is an *embodied* revelation. As I have said, Hegel's *Spirit-Fate* introduces a concept of the embodied nature of religion that Rosenzweig will embrace. Mendelssohn had argued that Judaism, lacking a creed or set of revealed doctrines, is not properly called a religion. Rather, the Jewish people, living in accordance with the orally transmitted interpretation of the written ceremonial laws, are the corporate embodiment of the revealed legislation, its "living script." This emphasis upon embodied ceremonies is central in Hegel's *Spirit-Fate*. I am not arguing that it derives entirely from Mendelssohn's interpretation of Judaism. As we will see in the next section, Hegel's notion that religious beauty is discoverable in finite, embodied life is in part a development of Kantian aesthetic theory into the realm of religion. But there is reason to believe that Hegel found significant reinforcement for this move from Mendelssohn's claim that Judaism was a "living script" that fused perfectly the medium of representation with its represented content, a fusion that is the essence of the beautiful representation according to Mendelssohn's own aesthetic theory.[4] Hegel's use of Mendelssohn's claim that the Jewish people are a "living script" is most apparent in his interpretation of the Last Supper, the Jewish Passover ceremony that Jesus "fulfills" before his death. If we want to understand how Rosenzweig "reads Mendelssohn through Hegel" as I have said, it is important to attend to this critical passage in Hegel and, in particular, its description of an ideal form of writing. (I will offer a fuller description of Hegel's analysis of the Last Supper in a later section.)

Like Mendelssohn with his interpretation of Jewish ceremonial practices as a "living script" of revelation, Hegel sees the significance of the Last Supper as lying in its fusion of action and interpretation. Also, not unlike what Mendelssohn says about the Israelites' reversion to idolatry after Moses's departure from them after God's delivery of the Ten Commandments, Jesus's fusion of action and sign in the Last Supper cannot be sustained by the disciples. Although Jesus's love is the fully present meaning that the act of sharing bread and wine as his flesh and blood signifies, this loving action leaves behind itself a bodily remainder, the bread and wine in the mouths of the disciples. This bodily remainder makes the ritual of communion inherently different from the Jewish ceremonies that consist in purely "transitory" acts in which "there is nothing lasting." This transitoriness is the essential quality of the "living script" that the Jewish ceremonial law becomes in the embodied existence of the people. Hegel contrasts the bodily remainder of Jesus's love with an ideal form of writing that would disappear upon being read. This ideal writing is like Mendelssohn's "transitory" signs of the "living script" of the Jewish ceremonial law. Like Mendelssohn's "living script," Hegel's ideal writing is an antidote to idolatry, the fetishization of the sign. Here is Hegel's description of the ideal writing, preceded by his discussion of the Last Supper:

> [B]ecause they [the disciples] eat the bread and drink the wine, because his body and his blood pass over into them, Jesus is in them all, and his essence, as love, has divinely permeated them. Hence the bread and the wine are not just an object, something for the intellect. [*They are not objects of belief; Hegel is reiterating Mendelssohn's point that revelation must be lived, not affirmed as a proposition.*] The action of eating and drinking is not just a self-unification brought about through the destruction of food and drink, nor is it just the sensation of merely tasting food and drink. The spirit of Jesus, in which his disciples are one, has become a present object, a reality, for external feeling. Yet the love made objective, this subjective element become a *thing*, reverts once more to its nature, becomes subjective again in the eating. *This return may perhaps in this respect be compared with the thought which in the written word becomes a thing and which recaptures its subjectivity out of an object, out of something lifeless, when we read. The simile would be more striking if the written word were read away, if by being understood it vanished as a thing, just as in the enjoyment of bread and wine not only is a feeling for these mystical objects aroused, not only is the spirit made alive, but the objects vanish as objects. Thus the action seems purer, more appropriate to its end, in so far as it affords spirit only, feeling only, and robs the intellect of its own, i.e., destroys the matter, the soulless.* (*Spirit-Fate* 250–51; 299; italics mine)

What Hegel is describing is the failure of the Last Supper to "fulfill" the Passover ceremony. The failure is not on the part of Jesus, but on the part of the disciples. The love that ought to have united them with Jesus was still tied to the body, which they could not do without. They were like the

Israelites after Moses left them behind: "After the supper the disciples began to be sorrowful because of the impending loss of their master, but after a genuinely religious action, the whole soul is at peace" (*Spirit-Fate* 252; 301). What the Last Supper ought to have been like is a written text whose reading transforms the meaning into pure subjectivity, pure spirit, leaving no remainder behind. Hegel is working within the very same problematic that Mendelssohn explored in his treatment of writing in its relation to Jewish ceremonial law in *Jerusalem*.

The difference between the two thinkers is that Hegel is seeking a way to overcome the problem of time in a way that Mendelssohn is not. Hegel faults the Last Supper for reverting back to objectivity, for leaving a bodily remainder, an excess. He is seeking a kind of reading that would consume the text's objectivity and consummate its subjectivity in such a way that not only the text itself but the meaning of the text would be fully and finally understood. The text would be removed from temporality entirely and brought into the instantaneous fulfillment of meaning in pure spirit. Such would be the ideal writing for Hegel. For Mendelssohn, ideal writing is also one that resists fetishization. It does so by becoming a "living script" in the bodily performance enjoined by the law. The oral law that necessarily accompanies the written law is the excess, the supplement, that makes interpretation of the written law necessary and that also defines the hermeneutic horizon of the interpretive process. The oral law is never fixed, but always leads to new interpretive possibilities. The performance of the written law by their elders spurs questions in the minds of the young people who witness it. Their questions lead to new meanings being read into the written law, and new ways of fulfilling the law.

Mendelssohn denies explicitly that the ideal writing of the "living script" is ever able to be transformed into a purely spiritual fulfillment. The meaning of the script is always recreated in the living temporality of cross-generational teaching. The never-exhausted remainder of meaning that the oral interpretation and bodily enactment of the written law is designed to permit constitutes a living bond of speech across the generations.

> These laws were revealed, that is, they were made known by God, through *words* and *script*. Yet only the most essential part of them was entrusted to letters; and without the unwritten explanations, delimitations, and more precise determinations, transmitted orally and propagated through oral, living instruction, even these written laws are most incomprehensible or inevitably became so in the

course of time. For no words or written signs preserve their meaning unchanged throughout a generation. (*Jerusalem* 127–28; 2:115)

For Mendelssohn, the ideal writing is one that draws the generations together in conversation, in a bond of unending interpretation. Only by such a form of writing—and Mendelssohn admits that Israel has fallen far from the ideal—can any society avoid dissolving into a collection of "Buchstabenmenschen" who are merely walking books. Hegel's recipe for an ideal writing would transform the "letter-men" of society into pure spirits; Mendelssohn would return them to the open-ended life of embodied speakers. Throughout *Spirit-Fate*, Hegel disparages Jewish embodiment—e.g., the disciples' mourning over Jesus—with the true "religious action" in which material objectivity is perfectly unified with spiritual subjectivity.

If there remain doubts that Hegel in *Spirit-Fate* is erasing/rewriting Mendelssohn's theory of ideal writing and its tendency to fall into idolatry, we may find some further evidence for this in another passage dealing with the contrast between pagan religion and Judaism. After Hegel discusses the failure of the Last Supper to unify body and spirit without remainder, he contrasts Jesus's Jewish disciples to the Greeks whose worship before statues of Apollo and Venus allowed them to retain a "soul at peace" because of their aesthetic rapture before the beautiful forms of the marble. "In looking at the shape," Hegel says, "we are permeated with the sense of love and eternal youth." The fetishization of the material statue is overcome through its aesthetic transformation into pure form. But what happens in the Last Supper, where love permeates the disciples by means of bread and wine, is like what would happen if the statues were "ground to dust": "The dust can remind us of the devotion, but it cannot draw devotion to itself. A regret arises, and this is the sensing of this separation, this contradiction, like the sadness accompanying the idea of living forces and the incompatibility between them and the corpse" (*Spirit-Fate* 252; 301). What moves Hegel to speak about statues that are ground to dust? I believe that we may hear an echo of the grinding down to dust that is what Moses commands the Israelites to do to the Golden Calf. Also, grinding to dust is what the Christians did to the pagan statuary within the temples they rededicated as churches. Unlike Mendelssohn's God, who can forgive the Israelites' reversion to idolatry, Hegel cannot forgive the Jewish-Christian assault on pagan beauty. His revenge upon this iconoclastic impulse at the heart of Judaism and

Christianity is his creation of a portrait of the "beautiful soul," Jesus, who is the enemy of Judaism, but also of a Christianity that has never yet overcome its dependence upon the bodily remainder of Jesus in the communion meal. Jesus as the pure image of beauty, unlike the pagan statues and unlike the bread and wine in the communion, can only be consummated without remainder in the purity of spirit, in *philosophy*, in other words. Or so Hegel would have us believe. Philosophy reads Jesus without a mournful remainder, leaving behind neither dust, nor bread, nor wine. Philosophy gives Jesus back his pagan beauty. A paganly beautiful Jesus is an *uncircumcised* Jesus.

When Rosenzweig reads Mendelssohn's Judaism *through* Hegel, he is recovering from its philosophical erasure Mendelssohn's vision of the Jewish people as a living script. We might say that Rosenzweig is reading through the mournful covenantal commensality of Last Supper to the joyous commensality that Mendelssohn speaks of when he discusses the ritual of circumcision. The festive meal that concludes every circumcision ceremony is described by Mendelssohn in a footnote at the opening of the second section of *Jerusalem*. Mendelssohn mentions a hypothetical case that was raised against his argument that no religious office should require of its would-be occupant a sworn oath to a religious creed. The case involves a Jew who is hired to perform circumcisions by the Jewish community. What would happen if this Jew begins to have doubts concerning the law of circumcision? Should he be allowed to perform circumcisions? Mendelssohn replies that the circumciser should give up his ritual role if he cannot in conscience fulfill it, but that there is no need for him to swear fidelity to the "doctrine or law of circumcision." In a footnote, Mendelssohn explains that the circumciser, in fact, neither occupies an office with a "specific rank" nor is there any remuneration given to the person who performs it. "On the contrary, whoever possesses the [requisite] skill performs this meritorious act with pleasure. Indeed, the father, who, properly speaking, is obliged to perform the duty of circumcising his son, usually has to choose among several competitors who apply for it. The only reward which the circumciser can expect for his performance consists in his being seated at the head of the table at the festive meal following the circumcision, and in his saying the blessing after the meal. According to my seeming 'new and harsh' theory, all religious offices ought to be filled in like manner" (*Jerusalem* 82n1; 2:14n1). In the forging of the covenant anew, the circumciser is but a proxy for the child's father. The meaning of the act does not depend upon the mental state of the circumciser. The act renews the covenantal bond across the generations in the corporate body of the Jewish people. The foreskin is a cast-off remainder of the act, but the symbol of the covenant is not connected to this remainder as it is with the bread and wine of the Last Supper. Rather, the symbol of the covenant is inscribed in the living flesh of the corporate body of the people. The commensal meal of the circumcision feast celebrates birth into the eternal body of the people, Rosenzweig will say. Hegel's Last Supper, though Jesus meant it to celebrate the possibility of an undying new community of love, slipped into grief over the soon-to-be dead Jesus as the disciples sensed the disappearance of the wine and bread in their mouths.

Hegel says that the Jewish law was "a direct slavery, an obedience without joy, without pleasure or love" (*Spirit-Fate* 206; 262). "Religious practice," Hegel avers, "is the most holy, the most beautiful, of all things" (206; 262). But Jewish practices are "empty" of any "spirit of beauty." As we will see in the next section, Hegel believes that religious practices realize the spirit of beauty by unifying finite life with infinite life. This is exactly what circumcision means for Rosenzweig. Joining the passing generation of grandparents to the new generation, circumcision ensures "the true eternity of life, this conversion of the heart of the fathers to the children" (*Star* 354; 372). The joyous celebration of the festive meal after a circumcision ceremony is thus, for Rosenzweig as well as Mendelssohn, the very model of a *beautiful life*. Hegel, as we shall see, considers no nonpagan religious ritual—certainly no Jewish ritual and not even a Christian one—as capable of being beautiful. That is why, in 1800, Hegel imagines that a new religion is needed, one that would bring beauty back to life.

Infinite Life, Judaism, and Christian Fate

In a manuscript dated to 1800 that Herman Nohl called *Fragment of a System* (*Systemfragment von 1800*; hereafter *Fragment*) because it is missing thirty-five of its thirty-seven sheets (Hegel 1907: 343–51), Hegel develops the theory of what he calls "infinite life." Hegel relies heavily upon certain ideas that Kant developed in his *Critique of the Power of Judgment* (1790), namely, that nature, insofar as it appears as an organized manifold of parts whose identity is inseparable from the whole, can be judged as a work of art: "with regard to its [i.e. nature's] products as systems, e.g., crystal formations, various shapes of flowers, or the inner structure of plants and animals, it proceeds *technically*, i.e., as . . . an art" (Kant 1996a: 20; AK20:217–18). Although one is entitled to judge nature as a whole as art, that is, as an internally organized system rather than a mechanical aggregation of parts, Kant says that to speak of nature as alive would be to go beyond what is observed and attempt to describe the in-itself. It is fairly easy to distinguish between the sort of thing whose organization appears purposive and the sort of thing that does not, but it is an entirely different thing to *explain* purposiveness. In an "organized natural being" each part "is conceived as if it exists only *through* all the others," by which Kant means that they as a whole are capable of self-repair and self-reproduction. Kant contrasts this to the organization of a watch in which "one part is certainly present for the sake of the other but not because of it" (*Critique of the Power of Judgment*, Kant 1996a: 246; AK5:374). "An organized being is thus not a mere machine" because "it has a self-propagating formative power" (246; AK5:374). One might think that Kant would be willing to call this *life*, but what is the source of life? Kant says that it is useless to search for an explanation of how the "formative power" is related to what is meant by *life*, especially if it requires an appeal to an "alien principle" in matter called *soul*.

Hegel in the *Fragment* attempts to show how the concept of life can be used to clarify the essence of "self-propagating formative power" that is within every organized natural being. Hegel seeks to put *soul* back into nature without, however, adding it as an "alien principle." He finds a solution in what might be called a dynamic conception of life, one that sees it as an inherent tension within nature itself. Hegel declares, "the multiplicity of life has to be thought of as being divided against itself." The unified organism holds itself together against a centrifugal force that drives each part of it into a state of separation. The "formative power" is one that overcomes the tendency toward dissolution of the whole. "It is self-evident that this life, whose manifold is regarded purely as being related and whose very existence is exactly this relation, can also be regarded as being differentiated in itself, as a mere multiplicity" (*Fragment* 309; 345). We may also relate this to the distinction in Kant between the two orientations of the human. There is an orientation that places the human in relation to a universal horizon and another that regards the individual as a part (with incentives that are nothing more than "partialities") of "mere" nature. The tension between two ways of orienting ourselves (towards the universal or towards the particular) and judging the world (as artful whole or mere multiplicity) is projected by Hegel into all of nature. At every instant, nature itself is in tension between its identity as a mere multiplicity of parts and as an organized unity of forms. Humanity—consciousness—is the site where this tension is experienced by organized beings who are both participants within and spectators of nature:

> If . . . we presuppose individual lives, namely, ourselves as the spectators, then that life which is posited outside our own restricted spheres is an infinite life with an infinite variety, infinite oppositions, infinite relations; as a multiplicity, it is an infinite multiplicity of organizations or individuals, and as a unity it is one unique organized whole, divided and unified in itself—Nature. (*Fragment* 310; 346)

Nature as the tension between living unity and mechanical multiplicity appears to the human spectator/participant as the tension between the whole of nature and his own individual life. That is, the individual who sees himself as separate from nature sees himself as separated from the living whole and thus as a mere mechanical part. As a reflecting judge of nature, Hegel says, the individual sees the whole in a condition of dismemberment and he sees himself as one dismembered part among the others: the positing consciousness "is at the same time a part, i.e., something for which there is something dead and which is itself something dead for other parts" (*Fragment* 313; 348). Religion, says Hegel, is what enables the separated human to transcend his finitude and rise "to infinite life": "This partial character of the living being is transcended in religion; finite life rises to infinite life. It is only because the finite is itself life that it carries in itself the possibility of raising itself to infinite life" (*Fragment* 313; 348). Religion undoes what reflection (self-consciousness) inflicts upon the individual, namely, separation from the whole. Kant had shown that judgment must remain subjective and can never reach to an understanding of the "propagating force" in nature's organized beings and in nature as a whole. Life as animating soul remained an "alien principle." Religion for Hegel is what makes it possible to overcome reflection and discover the objective basis for the subjective judgment that nature *seems* alive by revealing the "life that it [finite life] carries in itself."

Religion overcomes alienated reflection precisely because it brings to expression the consciousness of life within the finite human after the human is aware of his diremption from the infinite whole of life. In order to see himself as alive once again the individual must sense himself as *reborn* as a participant in an infinite life that is present in every part and not just in the whole. The individual experiences infinite life as the movement from death (sensed as diremption from the wholeness of nature) back to life, and this is done through the ritual of sacrifice. In sacrifice, the individual renounces his separated, private identity (as spectator) and offers up a part of his claim upon a part of the whole of life (an animal from his flock) and restores it to the whole. The animal as separated from the whole of life is considered as if dead as it approaches the altar; slain upon the altar, it is restored to (infinite) life. The animal is removed from the sphere of the private and returned to the whole: "Only through this uselessness of destroying, through this destroying for destroying's sake, does he make good the destruction which he causes for his own particular purposes. At the same time he has consummated the objectivity of objects by a destruction unrelated to his own purposes, by that complete negation of relations which is called death" (*Fragment* 316; 350). The death of the victim is seen as the "consummation" of the separated existence of the part from the whole; since it is not done for the goals of the part but is, rather, useless destruction, it can only be done for the sake of the whole. The life of the part is returned to the whole. Death is transcended in the infinite life of the whole.

The ritual of sacrifice is not performed only once. The repetition of the sacrificial act is the way that infinite life regenerates itself. Life and death constitute a rhythmic alternation; if the infinite life of the whole did not renew itself through birth, it would simply fall asunder into mechanical multiplicity. But how is birth achieved in sacrifice? How is the animal reborn? Hegel reminds us that the individual does not always simply destroy the animal. While he may burn a part of the animal on the altar, the rest he shares with friends: "The rest he destroys to some extent by taking away as far as possible its character as private property and sharing it with his friends" (*Fragment* 316; 350). Commensality of the sacrificial meal allows the individual to feel a rebirth of the animal not merely within his own finite body, but in the constantly regenerated communal body that extends both spatially and temporally beyond his finite identity. So long as a people feels itself to be an integral part of the whole of life, the destruction of a separated part of the life of the people that is then returned to life by being consumed by the people can elevate the individuals and the people to the "infinite life" they worship during their sacrificial rituals. "The most perfect integration is possible in the case of peoples whose life is as little as possible separated and disintegrated, i.e., in the case of happy peoples." "Happy peoples" can alternate from separated spectators to reintegrated participants in infinite life through the ritual of sacrifice. The ritual of sacrifice brings to expression the rhythm of life itself as death is followed by renewed life, in this case, the renewed life of the community. Happy peoples do not feel themselves sundered from the fullness of life. Naively, they feel themselves surrounded by divine life. They live within a living cosmos.

But this naive happiness does not last. For a reason that Hegel does not go into in *Fragment*, a people eventually arises that becomes, or is perhaps forced by an exigent circumstance such as a drought (that is the explanation offered in *Spirit-Fate*), to become conscious of its separation from the whole of life around it. Nature is sensed as threatening. Such a people is "unhappy" and can no longer reintegrate itself so easily through the ritual of sacrifice. Because of its sundering from the whole of nature as infinite life, an unhappy people learns to sense the whole of nature to be "mere nature," a mere dead mechanical assemblage of parts, and its own life as threatened by imminent death. The tension within infinite life between unity and multiplicity cannot be resolved. The living unity of nature is no longer integrated within the whole, but it stands as an abstract idea opposed to nature's multiplicity. As an abstract idea, this unity is infinitely remote from the multiplicity it ought to unify. The group senses its ever-threatened life to be wholly dependent upon this remote unity, and it senses itself as at war with the rest of nature, all of whose parts are now in opposition to one another. The infinitude that sunders the group from the rest of nature (as pure object) on the one hand and from the infinite living unity (pure *soul* or subject) on the other hand, leads to a religion that "can be sublime and awful, but it cannot be beautifully humane" (*Fragment* 318; 351). For a people with such a religion, Hegel says, "their highest pride must be to cling to separation and maintain the existence of the unit [das Eine]" (*Fragment* 317; 351).

Hegel is speaking of the Jewish people. If it is not clear enough from this passage, one can easily be persuaded by comparing this description of the unhappy people with his explicit description of Judaism's founding father in *Spirit-Fate*, written at around the same time as *Fragment*: "The whole world Abraham regarded as simply his opposite; if he did not take it to be a nullity, he looked on it as sustained by the God who was alien to it. Nothing in nature was supposed to have any part in God; everything was simply under God's mastery" (*Spirit-Fate* 187; 247). In the *Fragment*, Hegel argues that the unhappy (Jewish) people sense the world to be composed of dead, mechanical nature and they project their own finite separation from the infinite whole of nature upon their God, who is represented as "infinite and beyond the heaven of heavens, exalted above all connection and all relationship," a God who "hovers all-powerful above all nature" (*Fragment* 318; 351). In *Spirit-Fate*, Hegel puts the same thought this way: "Outside the infinite unity in which nothing but they [the Jewish people], the favorites, can share, everything is matter (the Gorgon's head turned everything to stone), a stuff, loveless, with no rights, something accursed which, as soon as they have power enough, they treat as accursed and then assign to its proper place [death] if it attempts to stir" (*Spirit-Fate* 188; 248). We have seen how Kant portrays the Jewish people as embracing pure politics over morality and thereby aligning themselves with a view of nature as purely mechanistic. Hegel carries this portrait to its logical conclusion. The Jewish people in their unhappy separation from the infinite life of nature become the instruments of their infinitely separated God's annihilating hatred of life.[5]

Hegel's *Fragment* does not end with a description of a people's "unhappy" separation from infinite life. Rather, Hegel concludes by equating the condition of philosophy in Germany in 1800 with this unhappiness, or, to put it more clearly, Hegel identifies the contemporary condition of philosophy as a form of Judaism. Philosophy preserves the identical "deadening" of nature. It posits an infinitely distant God who "hovers" over nature. Contemporary philosophy only differs from Judaism because the philosopher identifies himself with God, whereas the Jew only claims to be God's favorite. This is what is happening in German philosophy, in which one places oneself "as pure Ego above the ruins of this body and the shining suns, above the countless myriads of heavenly spheres, above the ever new solar systems as numerous as ye all are, ye shining suns" (*Fragment* 318; 351). In other words, one sees oneself as a sublime, divine Ego. Kant's noumenal self, sublimely distant from nature, obeyed a sublime moral law; in Fichte, the Ego throws off the law and becomes (Judaism's) alienated, lifeless God.

Linking contemporary German philosophy and Fichte's Ego philosophy in particular with Judaism, Hegel reiterates a point that is at the center of Jacobi's *Jacobi to Fichte* (1799), namely, that Fichte should be declared King of the "Jews of speculative reason" because he brings salvation by declaring that God is not an object outside humanity before whom one's only proper attitude is servility, but rather God is Ego and his (my) one command is "I shall not have other Gods outside Me" (*Jacobi to Fichte* 524; 48). Hegel puts the equivalence of Judaism and Fichte's philosophy this way:

> When the separation is infinite, it does not matter which remains fixed, the subject or the object; but in either case the opposition persists, the opposition of the absolutely finite to the absolutely infinite . . . The opposition would not be overcome in a beautiful union; the union would be frustrated, and opposition would be a hovering of the Ego over all nature, a dependence upon, or rather a relation to, a Being beyond all nature. This religion can be sublime and awful, but it cannot be beautifully humane. And hence the blessedness enjoyed by the Ego which opposes itself to everything and has brought everything under its feet is a phenomenon of the time, *at bottom equivalent to the phenomenon of dependence on an absolutely alien being which cannot become man.* (Fragment 318–19; 35; italics mine)

If Fichte's philosophy offers nothing more than the inverse equivalent of Judaism, then the path beyond Fichte would be a philosophy that shows how the infinite life of God can "become man," that is, how infinite life and finite life can be unified. Jacobi had declared in *Jacobi to Fichte* that "God must be born in man if man is to have a *living* God and not just an idol" (*Jacobi to Fichte* 523; 43). It is clear that Hegel in *Fragment* would agree. But Hegel, unlike Jacobi, does not think that the living God who is born in man is born in each individual as a separate, finite being.[6] The entire argument of *Spirit-Fate* is that *only in a mutually loving community can the living God be born and reborn.* If "happy peoples" can reenact their participation in infinite life with sacrifice, then when a people is separated from this infinite life, God must become a man (or a man must become conscious of God within himself). But where Jacobi thought this was all that was necessary for every human to "have a living God," Hegel knows that the God-man must become an *object of sacrifice.* As with happy peoples, the sacrificed God-man must annul himself as object entirely in an act of death (as a separated being) and rebirth (in a community). Only through sacrifice can infinite life and finite life be reconciled. But it is not the particular death and resurrection of the God-man that reveals the living God; it is the community's enactment of this death and resurrection that reveals the living God, the infinity of life ever reborn in finite life. Such, at least, is what *Spirit-Fate* offers as the truth of Christianity. But the fact that Christianity is tied to the person of Christ causes its fall into objectivity, into a condition of separation from infinite life. In the end, no religion can reconcile finite and infinite life. Only philosophy can bring about the reconciliation of infinite and finite life in the "speculative Good Friday" that Hegel speaks of at the end of *Faith and Knowledge* (191). Christianity still clings to the historical Jesus who, in offering himself as a sacrifice to be consumed by his community of followers at the Last Supper, ought to have disappeared. But philosophy can dispose with this historical, bodily remainder or residue. "The offering up of the residue, controlled, prolonged and fixated, is Hegel's philosophy," writes Werner Hamacher in his insightful study of Hegel's *Spirit-Fate* in relation to his other texts on religion and the concept *life* more generally. "This philosophy," Hamacher continues, "prepares the meal of the absolute, and, sitting down with itself for company at its own table, consumes even its own subjectivity."[7]

As we will see, Rosenzweig recuperates from Hegel's interpretation of Judaism and Christianity the key to overcoming Hegel's "speculative Good Friday." For Rosenzweig, the Jewish people are the beautiful fusion of finitude and infinitude, temporality and eternity, and the Christian peoples bear the fate—not as failure but as destiny—of shaping historic temporality into the beautiful form of Christ's self-sacrificial love, a form celebrated in the communion meal. The "failure" of this communion meal is the condition of possibility of history as the unfolding of Redemption in time. Instead of inscribing eternity upon the body as in the Jewish covenant, the Christian covenant leaves the individual tethered to unredeemed history.

The Last Supper Once More

At the center of Hegel's *Spirit-Fate* is an analysis of the Last Supper. I have already looked at this analysis in relation to the theme of ideal writing and its refraction of Mendelssohn's conception of Jewish ceremonial performance as the embodiment of a "living script." I now want to return to Hegel's treatment of the Last Supper in order to show how it is, for him, an ultimately failed sacrifice, an "unhappy" sacrifice. It does not instantiate the perfect beauty that arises from the union of finite life and infinite life. For Hegel, the consummation of the union of finite and infinite life takes place only on the plane of pure Spirit, in philosophy.

At the Last Supper, Jesus shares with his disciples bread and wine. He tells them that "this is my flesh and blood," and thus identifies himself with the paschal lamb that is part of the Passover meal. If these words are taken to only be metaphorical and to point toward his death on the cross as the "true" sacrificial lamb, then, says Hegel, we have misunderstood the meaning of the Last Supper narrative. The Last Supper is not a shadow of a future event; in itself the Last Supper reveals how "finite life" can be raised into "infinite life." But the Last Supper, as a single historical act, is only meaningful when it is lifted by Jesus into a command: "Do this in memory of me." The referent of "this," however, is not tied to a single place and time (how could one repeat *the* Last Supper?), but is the sharing of bread and wine *with the consciousness that Jesus's sacrificial death is transcended in the commensal community*. And the community formed by Jesus at the Last Supper of those who hear the command "Do this in memory of me" as a command whose force extends *even beyond their own finite lives* is therefore one that sees itself as no longer a community of participants in a single meal, but in an ever-recurring meal. The Last Supper ought to, but ultimately fails to, create an eternal community across time that experiences itself as the resurrected love of Christ. In my phrase "resurrected love of Christ" there is an ambiguity that captures Hegel's claim that the Christian commensal community should not be thought of as an allegory of Christ, but as the very presence of Christ in the world. In the phrase, both senses of *of*—love for Christ and Christ's love for the community—are collapsed into one:

> A spectator ignorant of their [i.e., the disciples'] friendship and with no understanding of the words of Jesus would have seen nothing save the distribution of some bread and wine and the enjoyment of these . . . Objectively considered, then, the bread is just bread, the wine just wine; yet both are something more. This "more" is not connected with the objects (like an explanation) by a mere "just as": "just as the single pieces which you eat are from one loaf and the wine you drink is from the same cup, so are you mere particulars, though one in love, in the spirit"; "just as you all share in this bread and wine, so you all share in my

sacrifice"; or whatever other "just as" you like to find here. Yet the connection of objective and subjective, of the bread and the persons, is here not the connection of allegorized with allegory, with the parable in which the different things, the things compared, are set forth as severed, as separate, and all that is asked is a comparison, the thought of the likeness of dissimilars. On the contrary, in *this* link between bread and persons, difference disappears. (*Spirit-Fate* 249; 298)

"Difference disappears" in the commensality that Jesus celebrates with his disciples. Yet, ironically, difference disappears *too well*. That is, Jesus permeates the disciples in their consciousness of being united with his life through love. He dies as an individual and is resurrected in them. But he accomplishes this through bread and wine, which must be consumed. The objective love presented in the shared food and the subjective consciousness of love are incapable of becoming truly unified because the objective is destroyed, and love (as the unifying power of life itself) cannot be destroyed. "[T]here is a sort of confusion between object and subject rather than unification," Hegel writes (*Spirit-Fate* 251; 300). To be sure, through faith one can feel that the bread and wine are flesh and blood, but one does not eat with faith's feeling: "To faith it is the spirit which is present; to seeing and tasting, the bread and wine. There is no unification for the two" (*Spirit-Fate* 252; 300).

There is, then, a return from participatory wholeness (the elevation of finite life into infinite life) to mere spectatorship, to difference. Hegel ultimately cannot accept that the Last Supper is the ultimate revelation of the infinite wholeness of life. It does not exist except in faith; it requires a reorientation of separated spectator into participant, and this must be preceded by an act of belief that separates believer from perfect union with the object of belief. In the commensality of the Last Supper, "pure life" is revealed, but "if it comes into consciousness as a *belief* in life, it is then living in the believer and yet is to some extent posited outside him" (*Spirit-Fate* 254; 303). The moment of commensality disappears when the "flesh and blood" of Jesus enter the body of the participant and become, once again, a particular part of separated life. "After the supper the disciples began to be sorrowful because of the impending loss of their master . . . And, after enjoying the supper, Christians today feel a reverent wonder without serenity or else a melancholy serenity, because feeling's intensity was separate from the intellect and both were one-sided, because worship was incomplete, since something divine was promised *and it melted away in the mouth*" (*Spirit-Fate* 252–53; 301; italics mine). The old dichotomy of spirit and body remains. The world rushes back in. The intellect divides what had once been unified.

Christianity fails to escape its "fate," and so it falls backwards towards *Judaism*. "The spirit of the Christian communion," Hegel writes, "saw mundane realities in every relationship of self-developing and self-revealing life." Whether this *worldly* spirit depended upon food, or upon a physically resurrected body, the communion, which began with the spirit of love, ended in the realm of everyday objects. Love's "greatest enemy," he says, is "objectivity." In explicating Jesus's rejection of divorce, Hegel says that it would be an outrage to set the legal rights of one or another member of the couple against the unifying power of love, even if only one member continues to love the other. Such legal rights are, we might say, "objective," i.e., they divide persons into separated subjects who see one another as objects, whereas love is the transcendence of such objectivity. Because in the Christian communion objectivity defeats love, "the result was that it [the Christian communion] remained as poor as the Jewish spirit, though it disdained the riches for the sake of which the Jewish spirit served" (*Spirit-Fate* 288; 331). Historical Christianity, Hegel is saying, has not really superseded Judaism.[8]

Hegel's Children

What Hegel is looking for is a religious community—a perfect commensality—in which spectatorship is wholly transformed into unbroken participancy. This means that the distance between a separated part of life represented in the individual and the whole life of the community would be overcome. Hegel offers several examples of such a transformed spectatorship, and all of them lead to a spectatorship of oneself as a *child*. To see oneself as a child is to see the whole world in the light of a new dawn, a new life that is no longer overshadowed by the past, what Hegel calls "fate." It is more than this, however, because the light of the new day is nothing other than the light within oneself shining into the new world. The child does not enter an already-existing world; the child brings the world into existence. The relation between life, light, world, and child is what Hegel discovers in the exordium to the Gospel of John: "In the beginning was the

Logos; the Logos was with God, and God was the Logos; in him was life" (quoted in *Spirit-Fate* 256; 306).

Hegel argues that God and Logos are related as unity is to the multiplicity of "infinite partitioning." For Hegel, the key to John's exordium is "in him was life." The single part of the infinitely partitioned God is "something dead" when taken by itself, but it is also "a whole, a life." Each part is both dead and alive; it holds both possibilities within itself. The overcoming of this division happens through reflection, through self-consciousness. When a single life reflects upon itself as alive, it sees that "in it" is life. It then "is life and life understood (light, truth)" (*Spirit-Fate* 258; 306). The single life in its self-reflection is both life and light. This single, self-reflecting life/light is *man*, and "the world itself and all its relationships and events are entirely the work of the man who is light" (*Spirit-Fate* 258; 306). Jesus understood himself to be a part of the infinite life/light, and, since the light of reflection is itself indivisible, Jesus saw himself as one with God, his Father. Indeed, he saw that all humans were "children of God," co-creators of the world. Those who recognize themselves in Jesus "do not become other than they were, but they know God and recognize themselves as children of God, as weaker than he, yet of a like nature in so far as they have consciousness of that spiritual relation suggested by his name as the 'man' who is 'lighted by the true light.' They find their essence is no stranger, but in God" (*Spirit-Fate* 259; 306).

To see oneself as a child is to see oneself as a child of God. When the members of a community see themselves as children of God, they are bound together as a whole that is realized in every part. Hegel contrasts the mere aggregation that is the modern state with the "natural" unity of a people who identify themselves as descendents of a common forefather:

> Even in the expression "A son of the stem of Koresh," for example, which the Arabs use to denote the individual, a single member of the clan, there is the implication that this individual is not simply a part of the whole; the whole does not lie outside him; he himself is just the whole which the entire clan is. This is clear too from the sequel to the manner of waging war peculiar to such a natural, undivided people: every single individual is put to the sword in the most cruel fashion. In modern Europe, on the other hand, where each individual does not carry the whole state in himself, but where the bond is only the conceptual one of the same rights for all, war is waged not against the individual, but against the whole which lies outside him. (*Spirit-Fate* 260; 308)

Of course, Hegel does not want to return to a "natural" community like that of the Arabs he imagines: it is an unreflective unity. It is necessary to first recognize that separated individualities of the merely conceptual unity of the community are *dead*, in order to recuperate a vision of the life of the community as *children*, not of a common biological ancestor, but of God. Only as children of the spirit can a community be children of light.

Thus, ultimately, what Hegel is proposing is a community of sons of God who come to know themselves as identical with the whole, which is God. Every part reflects the whole and the whole is entirely within each part. This is what Hegel calls a "relation of spirit to spirit," a relation where there is no division between the related elements: "The relation of spirit to spirit is a feeling of harmony, is their unification; how could heterogeneity be unified?" (*Spirit-Fate* 266; 313). Jesus was the realization of this spirit-to-spirit relationship, a relationship he spoke of when he declared that "The father is in me and I in the father" (John 14:11). Commenting on this verse, Hegel writes that the Jews could not "recognize divinity in a man" because they lived in radical separation from the divine, from the whole of infinite life. Divided from the whole of life, "they felt themselves to be nothing" and therefore they could only think of an individual man as just like themselves, nothing (*Spirit-Fate* 265; 312). Separated from infinite life and separated from one another, the Jews could only understand themselves to be "sons of man," not "sons of God."

Before continuing with the theme of divine paternity and human sonship in Hegel, I want to return for a moment to Moses Mendelssohn. In Chapter 1, I had occasion to discuss Mendelssohn's claim that the divinely administered punishments associated with some of the laws of the Bible (for the infraction of the first Sabbath, for example) were expressions of God's love and were not like the punishments the state inflicts upon lawbreakers. In effect, God's punishments express His *forgiveness* toward His people. God uses punishment to draw the people back toward Him. (Hegel's lengthy discussion of punishment in *Spirit-Fate* can be read as a critique of Mendelssohn's position.) After this discussion, Mendelssohn summarizes the points he has made by quoting at length from Psalm 103, which he reads as an extended reflection upon the forgiving love of God as revealed to the Israelites after the sin of the Golden Calf (*Jerusalem* 125; 2:110–111). In Mendelssohn's rendering of the psalm, one verse reads: "Even as fathers have compassion upon their children, / So hath the Lord compassion upon them that revere Him." In a footnote attached to the translation of the psalm, Mendelssohn encourages the reader to examine the entire psalm because its contents are "altogether of the utmost importance" (*Jerusalem* 125; 2:112). The psalm is an expression of thanks, Mendelssohn says, for the "divine promise of his grace and paternal mercy" (126; 2:112). When Hegel goes to such lengths to deny to the Jewish people any capacity to recognize in Jesus's forgiving love a sign of his divine sonship, he is directly contesting Mendelssohn's reiterated claim that it was first through the Jewish people that God revealed Himself to the world as a loving and merciful Father.

Let me now return to Hegel. To come to know oneself as a son of God is to come to know oneself as one with Jesus: "The living association with Jesus is most clearly expounded in John's account of his final discourse: They in him and he in them; they together one; he the vine, they the branches; in the parts the same nature, a life like the life in the whole" (*Spirit-Fate* 268; 314). To see the face of Jesus clearly, for who he is, is to see one's own face, one's face as child of God. "Whosoever is capable of sensing in the child the child's pure life, of recognizing the holiness of the child's nature," Hegel writes in paraphrase of Jesus's speech in Matthew 18 about the need to become like children in order to enter the Kingdom of God, "has sensed my essence" (*Spirit-Fate* 269; 315). To despise "these little ones" is to despise God, "for I say unto you that in heaven their angels do always behold the face of my father in heaven" (*Spirit-Fate* 269; 315).

The angels who "behold the face of my father in heaven," Hegel explains, are representations of the "sons of God" in their fusion through beholding themselves and the whole as one living unity: "The opposition of seer and seen, i.e., of subject and object, disappears in the seeing itself" (*Spirit-Fate* 270; 316). The spirit-to-spirit relation is a relationship entirely made out of a *relation*; the individualities have disappeared, and remain only as possibilities of separation, not as realized separate beings: "Their difference is only a possibility of separation. A man wholly immersed in seeing the sun would be only a feeling of light, would be light-feeling become an entity. A man who lived entirely in beholding another would be this other entirely, would be merely possessed of the possibility of becoming different from him" (*Spirit-Fate* 270; 316). This union of all within the beholding-of-the-other is the condition of "angels," and to fall into the world, to fall into the realm of darkness *and the realm of the Jews*, is the "fate" of all the angels, as it is the fate of Jesus. "The deepest, holiest, sorrow of a beautiful soul, its most incomprehensible riddle, is that its nature has to be disrupted, its holiness sullied" (*Spirit-Fate* 269; 315).

But there is a path back to unity, to recuperation of what has been lost. It is the path of "becoming as children" once more. While faith in Jesus as the son of God is a first step on this path, it remains in the sphere of separation until the individual recognizes himself as Jesus, as God, and as the unifying spirit that brings division into wholeness:

> The culmination of faith, the return to the Godhead whence man is born, closes the circle of man's development. Everything lives in the Godhead, every living thing is its child, but the child carries the unity, the connection, the concord with the entire harmony, undisturbed though undeveloped, in itself. It begins with faith in gods outside itself, with fear, until through its actions it has [isolated and] separated itself more and more; but then it returns through associations to the original unity which now is developed, self-produced, and sensed as a unity. The child now knows God, i.e., the spirit of God is present in the child, issues from its restrictions, annuls the modification, and restores the whole. God, the Son, the Holy Spirit! (*Spirit-Fate* 217; 318)

Hegel claims in his discussion of the need to "become children again" that he is offering a philosophical interpretation of the exordium to the Gospel of John. It is important to note that this is most definitely *not* the Johannine Christianity of hope that Rosenzweig thought was opened up in 1800. In fact, Hegel's religion of infinite life, although put forward as the philosophical realization of the Gospel of John, denies that the communion of loving fellowship can sustain itself in history as a faith community. It must become philosophy in order to know itself as the union of finite and infinite life. This is very different from Hölderlin's chastened renunciation in his great poem of 1803, *Patmos*, of the quest to see the face of God and know more about Christ than is permitted to humans.[9] Hölderlin's simple poetic expression—"Denn noch lebt Christus [Since Christ still lives, l. 204]"—is an affirmation made in the *absence* of Christ's complete self-disclosure as the light of the world. Just preceding this line of the poem we read:

> Still ist sein Zeichen
> Am donnernden Himmel. Und Einer stehet darunter
> Sein Leben lang.
>
> (Quiet is his sign
> In the thundering heavens. And One stands beneath it
> His life long.)
>
> (ll. 202–4)

The poetic expression affirming that Christ lives is spoken not as the affirmation of the *fusion* of finite life with infinite life, but in the recognition of their *separation*. It is spoken as a consolation under a thundering heaven, and in the illumination not of the fullness of light, but in the "quietly-radiant power that falls from the holy scripture." Hölderlin recognizes that the less brilliant but nonetheless radiant materiality of scripture, of the "fixed letter," may yet offer hope to eyes "too shy to see the light." In contrast, Hegel finds the text's materiality to be a hindrance. He dreams of a text that would be "read up" into pure spirituality the way that the food of the communion is eaten up. Only the text's consumption would leave no remainder, as subject (reader) and object (text) become one. In the communion meal, the subject's embodied finitude is the remainder. Spiritualization as translation into light has failed. The world, as John says, did not know the light. Hegel adds: the world *cannot* know the light. Only spirit knows spirit, only light sees the light, in perfect unity. Hölderlin understood that what Hegel was seeking was not infinite life, but the infinite stasis of death. And Rosenzweig, in 1919, also understood that Hegel's philosophical supersession of Christianity in 1800 was blocking the light "in the thundering heavens" that Hölderlin glimpsed, the light of revelation and hope in the "quietly-radiant power that falls from the holy script."

Rosenzweig's Children

Rosenzweig, no less than Hegel, sees in the face of the child the image of the eternal. But where Hegel wants to see only one face, repeated in every child, the face of an eternal life that makes every child one part of a living whole, Rosenzweig wants to preserve the absolute uniqueness of each child's face. For Hegel, the ideal is to recreate the father in the child. For Rosenzweig, with every child, a new universe is created. For Hegel, birth as separation from infinite life is a sullying of the perfect, pure beauty that comes with the spiritual fusion of father and child. For Rosenzweig, birth is revelation. It is the condition of the possibility of beauty in the world.

Rosenzweig sees both Judaism and Christianity to be religions that, in different ways, join finite and infinite life together in a beautiful whole. The Jewish people gain a purchase on eternity through a covenant renewed in the flesh of its corporate body. This is an eternality achieved through natural birth; the Christian achieves eternality through *rebirth*. Circumcision in Judaism is replaced by baptism in Christianity. Rosenzweig's understanding of the difference between two kinds of eternality, one stamped upon the biological rhythm of birth and death, and the other upon the spiritual rhythm of death-in-life (pagan separated selfhoods) and rebirth-to-life (opening the selfhood to love), is very much indebted to Hegel's *Spirit-Fate*. Ultimately, both forms of eternality are representations of the idea that all humans are children of God. To be a child of God is, for the Christian, to stand within a covenantal bond that links one to every other Christian as brother or sister in the eternal simultaneity of the Church. To be a child of God is, for the Jew, to stand in a covenantal bond that makes one a link in a generational chain. The Christian never has a Christian parent or child: the Christian is reborn in Christ. His birthday is always celebrated on the same day of the year, Christmas. In every baptism, "the adoration of the divine child is renewed" and "Christianity begins again from the beginning" (*Star* 397; 416). To a large extent, Rosenzweig adopts the Hegelian interpretation of the Christian as one with Christ. But he contrasts Christian unity in a simultaneity of brotherhood with the temporality of Jewish people, in which a child enters into the eternal stream of the people's life.[10]

Rosenzweig's debt to *Spirit-Fate* is perhaps most evident in his description of Christian eternal simultaneity. "The Church," he writes, "is the mutual participation of all those who see one another" (*Star* 366; 383). Each person sees the other as Christ, as a brother in the spirit. In becoming a community in which seer and seen are one, the church is a community that transcends all separateness, whether of nations, classes, or ages. Christ is the eternal center of time, the place where spatial distance is annulled and unity of love attained. Of course, the eternal now of the church is moving through history, is "on the way" from the Cross to the Second Coming. To be on the way is to make every moment in the unfolding of history a center, a place where Christ is revealed as the face of the love of the nearest one, calling the separated individual out of his or her fated difference from all others into a rebirth, into a new childhood. "He who therefore beholds himself on the way," Rosenzweig says, using the trope of seeing that he has learned from Hegel, "is at the same point, namely, the exact central point, of time. The brotherliness is that which transposes men into this central point. Time is already laid conquered at its feet; love only still has to fly over the separating space. And so it flies over the enmity of peoples and the cruelty of race, the envy of classes and the limitations of age; and so it brings it about that all those who are enemies, cruel, envious, limited behold each other as brother, in the one same central moment of time" (*Star* 366–67; 384). We have seen how Hegel understands Christianity's "fate" to be its falling back into the spirit of division and separation that Hegel sees in the merely "conceptual" unity of the nation-state. For Rosenzweig, this reversion to temporality is the Christian's necessary return from the unity of brotherliness in Christ back into the divided condition of historical individuality, marked by separate nations, classes, ages, and races. Since the Jew's temporality is framed within the living rhythm of birth and death, he has no reversion to division so long as he remains within the unity of the Jewish people. But the Christian divides his life between "the great twofold order of State and Church" (*Star* 373; 390). The task of the Christian is to bend the temporality of the state into a shape that conforms to the temporality of the church. What this means is that the time of the world, the state, must have a center point to which it returns: it must cycle around. The year—the earth's movement about a center point—is the great image of the eternal now. The Christian lives in the order of temporality and the order of simultaneity when he "weaves the halo of eternity"—the ecclesiastical year—through the secular year with its secular holidays. The church "grows into the people and its history by going along with its memorial days with its blessing" (*Star* 391; 410). The church must never bless any historical moment as the coming of Redemption, but it may bless it as "on the way." In this way, Christianity "sows eternity into the living" (*Star* 391; 410).

But the Jewish people have sown eternity in their life by foregoing life in history. The idea that the Jewish people have overcome the "fate" of all other peoples by withdrawing from history is indebted, as Peter Eli Gordon has argued, to Hegel's portrait of Jesus in *Spirit-Fate*. "Beauty of soul," Hegel writes, "has as its negative attribute the highest freedom, i.e., the potentiality of renouncing everything in order to maintain one's self" (*Spirit-Fate* 236; 287). The beautiful soul, fully realized in Jesus, frees itself from all entanglements with an alien fate by renouncing its ties to the world. But for Hegel this withdrawal from the world is a radical severance of all ties with other humans, and Hegel speaks of this as what happens to Jesus at his baptism in the river Jordon: "In immersion there is only one feeling, there is forgetfulness of the world, a solitude which has repelled everything"

(*Spirit-Fate* 275; 319). Rosenzweig, however, describes the withdrawal of the Jewish people from history as a recovery of life in its communal fullness.

The difference between Hegel and Rosenzweig on this point consists in their different understandings of how God and humanity meet in time. For Hegel, God is immanent within the life of the individual, not his or her biological life, but the life that unifies separated beings, life as love. For Rosenzweig, love reveals God to the individual, but it also drives the individual outward towards the other, the "near one." And quite unlike Hegel, but entirely in agreement with Jacobi, Rosenzweig insists that love *particularizes* the individual, that is, love makes the individual aware of his or her uniqueness, what Rosenzweig captures with the formula "B = B," as I have explained at length in Chapter 3 (in "Language as the Site of Revelation"). This uniqueness is what Rosenzweig refers to as the "miracle of birth," the *createdness* of the individual. Nowhere is Rosenzweig more at odds with Hegel than in his rejection of the organicist model of love as mediating the disappearance of separate parts into a whole. So, revelation (love) leads to an awareness of creation, of irreducible uniqueness. What Hegel posits as the accomplishment of love, the fusion of all separated beings into a unity, is for Rosenzweig the infinitely deferred, the *sublime* goal of temporality: Redemption. Thus, Rosenzweig complicates the Hegelian model of God's relation to time by dividing the relation between finite life and infinite life, as Hegel would call the human individual and God, into three moments: Revelation, Creation, and Redemption. The Jewish people embody these three moments in the rhythm of their week and their ecclesiastical year.

The triple relation of God to time is contained within the Sabbath day, represented in the Hebrew Bible as the last day of creation, the first day of the first human pair, and the recurrent day of rest. The Sabbath shapes the life of this singular people by removing it from all "natural," that is, pagan time reckoning. The lunisolar year of the Jewish people, shared with all other peoples who also shape their lives by the movements of the moon and sun, is not commensurate with a fixed number of Sabbaths. But the triple temporal significance of the Sabbath—as singular recapitulation of Creation, Revelation, and Redemption—casts its shadow upon the Jewish lunisolar year in the form of the three pilgrimage festivals: Sukkot (Tabernacles), Pesach (Passover), Shavuot (Pentecost). Rosh Hashanah, the day celebrating God's enthronement as King, opens what was once the civil year, but the divine King does not remain withdrawn in his palatial glory, but joins history with his people, who wander in the desert of the world under his shelter (Sukkot); who experience his liberation from the oppressive powers of the world (Passover); and who receive the revealed law whose fulfillment will bring an end to their wandering (Pentecost). There is no celebration of the conquest of Canaan, for Redemption is not celebrated in the form a pagan people might perform, as a triumphal entrance of a king into his palace. The human king—the Anointed One, the Messiah—who will ultimately be enthroned as God's adopted son (so the Psalms describe him) will rule over all peoples and bring a peace that will usher in an unending Sabbath. Until that time, the Jewish people witness to the falsehood of all triumphal pretensions of every human king and kingdom. The festival of God's enthronement that opens the civil year does not mark the establishment of any earthly kingdom, but rather opens up into a cycle of holy days celebrating the round of time from the promise of Redemption (Sukkot) to the giving of the Law (Shavuot).

The Christian Sabbath day and ecclesiastical year, according to Rosenzweig, do not stamp the cycle of biological birth and death, the cycle of generations, with eternity. Rather, they stamp the cycle of historical time, the birth and death of nations, with the linear progress of the "way of the Cross" through time. The Christian ecclesiastical year transforms the historical life of nations into a spiral, not a closed circle as with the Jewish people. The difference between the Jewish and Christian Sabbaths is telling. The Jewish Sabbath is the close of the week, and it is closed upon itself as a holy day removed entirely from the six days of the week, the days which are not days of historical work but of the work of mortal humans, the "sweat of the brow." The Jewish Sabbath is a taste of redemption in time, and it culminates in an afternoon prayer (the weekday begins at sundown) focused upon redemption. But the Christian Sabbath, Rosenzweig claims, is a day that celebrates the ever-new creation of every human in Christ. "The Christian is eternal beginner; the completing is not his affair ... And therefore Sunday, with its power radiating its blessing over the daily work of the week, is the authentic image of this ever freshly, ever youthfully, ever newly shining power of Christianity upon the world" (*Star* 380–81; 399). The Christian Sabbath is a preparation of the individual to enter the world of history and carry forward its work. The holiday corresponding to the Christian Sunday is Christmas, a holiday that Rosenzweig says has become the secular world's holiday, "a sign for Christianity's outer capacity for spreading over life" (*Star* 390; 409). From out of the holidays of the re-creation of humanity, Sunday and Christmas most especially, the Christian enters into the world's procession through time, as if in a spiral dance towards Redemption: "It is again such that the idea of Redemption finds in the closed space of the church as little room as in the closed circle of the ecclesiastical year: it opens the circle into a spiral, it bursts open the locked gate, and the procession goes out into the city" (*Star* 395; 415).

Unlike Hegel, Rosenzweig does not see the "fate" of Christianity, its reversion into historical temporality, to be its failure, but rather he sees it as its very mission. Christianity renews historical time, places it on its way towards redemption. When Christians gather to celebrate the holy days of the ecclesiastical year, they are renewed for their historical task. Reading Hegel's description of the Last Supper in *Spirit-Fate* against the grain, Rosenzweig will focus on the possibility offered in the covenantal commensality at the heart of Christianity of transforming the common into the holy and the everyday into the holiday. In his *Little Book*, Rosenzweig will extend his notion of covenantal commensality in the *Star* to show that every day can be a holiday that celebrates the renewal of the covenant between God and all humanity. "The holiday will serve as the training school for the every day," Rosenzweig writes near the end of his *Little Book*. The holiday celebrates the overcoming of the past in a new creation. "Once a man's legs are accustomed to its rhythms, he will have no difficulty walking the streets of the work-a-day world. The gait is the same. If he has been well-trained here, he will not stumble later. Rather he will halt in amazement at how simple life actually is" (*Little Book* 99). In the *Star*, as in Hegel's *Spirit-Fate*, it is the sacrament of the meal that brings to life the eternal presence of revelation in the world. The communion, Rosenzweig writes, is the "sign and bearer of Revelation," of the triumph of eternal life over death, of the rebirth of the new in every instant. In Judaism, the Passover meal celebrates the birth of the people; in Christianity, the sacramental meal celebrates the rebirth of the individual. The Passover meal ends with the promise of redemption ("Next year in Jerusalem") and places the Jew back into temporality as a time of messianic expectancy. The sacramental meal in Christianity places the Christian back into historical time, into the task of overcoming the senescence of the nation by turning its course inward to spiral around the center, around Christ, and outward toward a brotherhood beyond the division of nations.

For Rosenzweig, the Christian community, the church, is charged with the task of defeating paganism, first, in the early centuries of the Common Era, through evangelism and then, after the conversion of Constantine, through war and the expansion of the Roman Empire. "All worldly history is about expansion," Rosenzweig writes, and for this reason "[p]ower [*Macht*] is the fundamental concept of history" (*Star* 427; 450). Christianity is linked to the spatial expansion that is the goal of worldly power. It gives this spatial expansion an orientation in time, reconfiguring the history of power in relation to the event of Christ. The church dissolves the pagan individuals who are only instruments of power's expansion into singularities standing in relation to Christ as Lord. It then sends them back into the world to bear the burden of the tension between worldly power and divine lordship. The Christian task is to bend space to mirror eternity, and this can only be accomplished by making spatial expansion grow from an orienting center, from Golgotha. The world's expansion becomes an ever-widening circle, all of whose points are equidistant from this center. The entire globe is the terminus of this expansion, but upon reaching this terminus the globe ceases to be a spatial reality and enters the realm of eternity, of a temporality that does not measure spatial expansion. In a sense, therefore, the Christian *saeculum* holds the world in tension between space and eternity. This tension can only be resolved by transforming space into gathering points along the way of Christian life: the gathered community of the faithful in worship, meeting at appointed times of the ecclesiastical year. What Rosenzweig calls the "round-dance" ("Reigen," *Star* 398; 418) of the ecclesiastical year imposes the shape of eternity upon space and allows the peoples of the world to acknowledge that none of them, except for the Jewish people, has reached the limit of space and entered the realm of eternity.

Judaism, for Rosenzweig, is not at all connected to history's expansive movement because the Jewish people have no homeland. They are not fixed in space, and therefore they have ceased to have any expansive power. Rather, they have rooted eternity in their very bodies. Christianity is historical in its process of growth in the world, but Judaism's growth is only that of the individual's life cycle. The people itself is eternal. To gain his purchase on eternity, the Christian has a different relation to corporeality than the Jew. The Christian eternalizes the body through *art*. The Jewish people literally embodies eternity within itself, recreating itself anew within the configuration of the annual round of the holidays of Creation, Revelation, and Redemption. The Christian, however, bodies eternity forth in art, representing the body's passion—its suffering under the burden of time and death—within a form whose content, as Rosenzweig explains in a section of the *Star* entitled "The Configuring of Suffering" (*Star* 399–400; 418–19), is always tragic. But tragic content reconfigured within the beauty of sensible form allows the soul to endure its suffering within the net of time. The problem for the Christian, however, is to find a way to endure suffering not only as a single, embodied creature, but as a member of community. For the Christian, art points toward the Cross where the remembrance of suffering is transfigured into hope. For the Jew, life itself is the art of hope, of messianic expectancy. Since this aesthetics of eternity and temporality is something that Rosenzweig inherits from Hegel's early theological writings, I will devote the concluding pages of this chapter to explicating it in more detail.[11]

Art and Hope: The Sorrows of Christian Life

The consciousness of their historical finitude is precisely what Christianity brings to the peoples of the world, according to Rosenzweig. Christianity teaches peoples that they are "on the way" to a destiny beyond their temporal limits, even as it makes them aware that history is not just the "rise and fall" of peoples without meaning or goal. The "foreign figure of the crucified man" is the sign of the failure of every mythic hero to achieve transcendence of death, for only love is as strong as death:

> There has been a dispute among the peoples of the world, since the supranational power of Christianity came among them; since a Siegfried has wrestled everywhere with this foreign figure of the crucified man, already suspected because of his appearance, one who is blond and blue-eyed, black and gracefully limbed, brown and dark-eyed like oneself, with this foreigner who opposes every approximation, attempted always again, of their own desired image. For the Jew alone there is no division between the supreme image that is placed before his soul and the people into which his life leads him. He alone possesses the mythic unity that was lost and had to be lost to the peoples of the world through Christianity; had to be—for the myth they possessed was pagan myth that led away

from God and from the neighbor by leading them into themselves. (*Star* 348–49; 365)

Christianity offers the vision of a God who dies for love of every particular human. It brings an end to the pagan myth in which divine immortal life is made impure by any proximity with death.

But Christianity does not bring an end to the pagan dream of overcoming death through the heroic deed that is monumentalized in song. The greatest heroic deed is the one that founds a city or a nation. Christianity does not put an end to the pagan violence of heroic lawgiving. The state, Rosenzweig says, insists upon forging its own version of eternity in the midst of time. It escapes from the pressure of time's inertia, the pressure of custom and tradition, by creating a new law forged in violence. Like the hero in combat, the state immortalizes itself by risking its life in war and revolution: "[W]ar and revolution are the only reality that the State knows, and in every moment where neither one nor the other would take place—and be it only in shape of thought of war or revolution—it would no longer be State" (*Star* 353; 370). Christianity does not destroy the pagan state because it needs it in order to participate in history: "With no State, then, no world history" (*Star* 354; 371). The Christian must ever go forth into world history, surrendering himself again and again to the state's "war-cry." But the Christian will always know that the only true eternity in time is the eternal now which is the rebirth of the soul in Christ, celebrated on every Sunday and every Christmas. How does the Christian live within the tension of these two eternities, one forged in putting life at risk and the other in the promise of rebirth?

The answer, for Rosenzweig, lies in art. The Christian is alone on the Way of the Cross as the spiraling procession dance towards Redemption. On the Way of the Cross, the Christian senses himself to be the center of two conflicting powers, the ever-forward thrust of time and the ever-backward pull of the beginning, of the Cross. "In the ever-returning circle of the year, for him his never-aging relationship of a child to God again and again flows into the relationship of a child to the world as he grows from youth to old-age, and back again; and each preserves and renews itself in the other" (*Star* 398; 418). Hegel had spoken of the tension between the "son of God" and "son of Man" as the tension between infinite life and finite life. Rosenzweig sees the same tension, but interprets it differently.

For him, it is the inescapable tension between ever-youthful life and the world's senescence. The world must pass away into its own youthful renewal, and this will take place on the Day of Judgment. Aging as a "child of the world" is the visible reminder of the world's senescence. The Cross promises rebirth, but it does not negate the world's death. It does not negate the war-cry of the state that struggles against the world's fall into decay. The solitary Christian on the Way of the Cross finds in art a way to overcome the tragic suffering that comes from his realization that the world must pass away, that all its beauty is transitory.

In discovering his consolation in art, the Christian rediscovers what the pagan always knew. Seeking consolation in art for the world's demise, the Christian returns to the mythic world. In the pagan world, art provided a triumph over the mortality of the individual. The epic poem memorialized the hero; the Pindaric ode to the Olympic victor captured the athlete in his eternally present moment of glory; the lyric poem captured the moment of love's rapture. In each case, an immortal god presides over and is somehow embodied within mortal life. The poem's outer form (whether epic, epinician, or lyric, for example) matched its inner form (the meter and rhythm of its lines) and both matched its content (the achievement of immortality within a mortal life). Rosenzweig sees all art as having its origin with the pagan world of myth, and in a certain sense recreating it even in the modern period: "Still today, all art remains under the law of the mythical world . . . [T]he work of art must be closed off by a crystal wall from all that it is not; a kind of breath from that 'easy life' of the Olympian gods must rest over it, even if the existence it reflects is to be made of misery and tears. In the threefold mystery of the Beautiful—outer form, inner form, content—the first of its thoughts, the miracle of outer form, the 'that which is blissful in itself,' originates in the metaphysical spirit of myth. The spirit of myth founds the realm of the Beautiful" (*Star* 46; 41). With the coming of Christianity, art is needed more than ever. Christianity brings to the pagan a heightened awareness that the world is always perishing, that the whole world is mortal.

The denouement of this growing sense of the world's mortality comes in the person of Goethe. I have spoken in Chapter 3 (in "Christianity and Paganism: 1800") about Goethe's *The Natural Daughter*, a play that deals precisely with the irrevocable loss of the one people upon the earth who managed to lead an entirely beautiful existence: the Greeks. Rosenzweig's sense of art's origin in myth and its place in Christendom as consolation for the evanescence of the beautiful life of a people comes directly out of Goethe, and also Hölderlin. It directly contests Hegel's dream in 1800 of the rebirth of Greek (pagan) beauty, of the fusion of infinite and finite Life. In Goethe's *The Natural Daughter* and Hölderlin's *Patmos* we can find an expression of the sorrowful acceptance of the transitoriness of the natural beauty of the pagan world, of the mournfulness of history, of the mortality of the world. But Rosenzweig finds in such art an opening to hope, as well. It is important Goethe declares himself at once the last pagan and the first Christian. Goethe witnesses to the mortality of all worldly things, but also to hope.

When Rosenzweig speaks about art as offering consolation for a world-consuming suffering, he does not mean that it suffuses the world once more in beauty. Rather, art holds before the soul a vision of loss: "the soul is refreshed in the enduring of the suffering" (*Star* 400; 419). Not through forgetfulness, but through "remembering of its old days" does the soul find consolation. "Not past happiness, only past sorrows are the bliss of the soul in each present. It renews itself in itself. And art forges for it this ring of life" (*Star* 400; 419). Let us recall that Rosenzweig had penned these lines not long after World War I. For many poets and writers who lived through the Great War, it seemed that there could be no consolation for the tremendous losses they suffered except in art. Speaking about the art of the postwar generation, Erich Auerbach captures nicely what Rosenzweig means by art's power to forge a "ring of life" out of the soul's suffering. Beginning his reflections on postwar art with a passage from Virginia Woolf's *To the Lighthouse*, Auerbach says that the novel "breathes an air of vague and hopeless sadness." But although suffering permeates the work, there is also an artistic transfiguration of one ordinary moment, seemingly randomly chosen from among all the moments of life, that points beyond the sadness of the world: "It is precisely the random moment which is comparatively independent of the controversial and unstable orders over which men fight and despair; it passes unaffected by them, as daily life" (Auerbach 1953: 552). Auerbach sees in this turn toward the beauty of the transitory and random moment in the midst of a suffering world a completion of the artistic turn toward the beauty of the common life of humanity that began with the New Testament. Rosenzweig also senses that art offers a consolation that seems to make the Cross no longer necessary.

Rosenzweig suggests that perhaps, if art can offer such forms of consolation for the Christian soul as it passes on its way through the world, there is no further need for the Cross: "It [art] seems really to substitute most perfectly for the Cross. Why should the soul still need it if it finds preservation and renewal in itself?" (*Star* 400; 419) The answer that Rosenzweig gives has to do with the limitation of art's consolation. The individual soul may find itself renewed in the artistic transfiguration of suffering, but the individual cannot find a connection with the rest of humanity. "The lonely soul of pagan stock," Rosenzweig writes, "for which the ultimate unity of the We does not circulate in the blood"—as it does for the Jew—"only discovers this unity facing the Cross of Golgotha. Only under this Cross does the soul know itself to be one with all souls . . . In its own heart, it now suffers along with the cycle of eternal suffering and eternal joy, which the heart that suffered for many and for it, too, on the Cross, drives on" (*Star* 400-1; 420). Artistic transfiguration of suffering consoles one soul; the vision of suffering on the Cross consoles each soul together with all souls.

Again, Erich Auerbach helps us to understand what Rosenzweig has in mind here. As I have said, Auerbach sees the consummation of Western mimesis in *To the Lighthouse* to have its starting point in the New Testament. The literary procedure of mimesis in the New Testament involves fusing classical historical seriousness with attention to "random everyday life." It is a procedure that "entails entering into the random everyday depths of popular life, as well as readiness to take seriously whatever is encountered there" (*Mimesis* 44). With Virginia Woolf, this mimetic procedure reaches its fulfillment. One could call it the sanctification of the everyday. What Rosenzweig claims can only be experienced before the Cross is given figuration in Woolf's text, namely, the experience of a shared humanity beyond all divisions of nation, class, or age: "The more numerous, varied, and simple the people are who appear as subjects of such random moments, the more effectively must what they have in common shine forth . . . Beneath the conflicts, and also through them, an economic and cultural leveling process is taking place. It is still a long way to a common life of mankind on earth, but the goal begins to be visible" (*Mimesis* 552). According to Rosenzweig, when the soul joins its private artistic "ring of life" with others before the Cross of Golgotha, "the soul on the way experiences its eternity, unconcerned that the world is not yet at the goal" (*Star* 401; 420). In other words, the soul that sees the Cross through the transfigured "random moment" of everyday life perceives the "eternal suffering and eternal joy" that joins it with all humanity, regardless of the fact that, as Auerbach says, "it is still a long way to a common life of mankind on earth."

In Chapter 3 I spoke about the significance of Goethe for Rosenzweig. Goethe figures as the "first of the Fathers" of a new church (*Star* 303; 318), what Rosenzweig calls the "Johannine Completion" in which hope rather than faith and love provides the guiding theme. Hope guides the Johannine completion of Christianity because it binds the individual as a living being of flesh, blood, and spirit to the whole of history. The hope it expresses is that *one life*, one's own life, may become a part of a whole that is neither state nor church, but the eternal life of the world. It is a democratic hope that every individual may be "world-historical," not just a Caesar or a Napoleon. It is not by accident, then, that Rosenzweig connects Johannine Christianity with the revolution that closes the eighteenth century in Europe and ushers in the age of "liberty, fraternity, equality." I think we may say that Rosenzweig's Johannine Christianity is very close to what Auerbach is speaking about when he places Woolf's attention to the random everyday moment at the end of a transformation of our perception of the world that begins with the New Testament. It is a Christianity that offers hope in the midst of suffering by revealing the holiness in the mundane, random moment of life. There is both sublimity and beauty in this Christian hopefulness.

And, finally, the holiness of the everyday life of humanity is made visible in the corporate existence of the Jewish people. The Jewish people live within the beauty of the sanctified, random moment. They draw all the moments of their life into a circle that renews itself outside of what Auerbach calls the "the controversial and unstable orders over which men fight and despair," what Rosenzweig simply calls "the State." In the Jewish people, all the peoples of the world, insofar as they see themselves on the way toward Redemption, see what they are hoping for: a wholly beautiful life. "This great circle of Redemption," Rosenzweig writes, "closes in the year of the eternal people. On it, that always unknown bearer of that prophecy to the peoples which they had to believe as already fulfilled in the vicarious suffering of the individual for individuals"—one soul at a time, in other words—"they live to see the enclosed eternity toward which they themselves helplessly extend" (*Star* 401; 421). When the peoples gaze upon the

Cross, they see the beginning of their Way; when they gaze upon the Jewish people, they see where the Way leads. Both groups live in hope: the Christians hope for the "great renewal of all things" when the tears will be wiped from every face; the Jews hope for the Messiah when every knee will bend before the Lord. But in the Jew's face there are no tears, for he does not suffer, as the Christian does, the tension between history and Redemption.

Rosenzweig knows that the state stands opposed to the eternality of the love-linked souls of the Christians on the Way toward a common life of humankind on earth as well to the eternality of the Jewish people. The state seeks its own form of eternality in revolution and war. The *Star* is Rosenzweig's song of peace. He asks all those who would be faithful to the revelation of eternity in time to join with him in offering this song to God. This song is the world's bridge between the tragic silence of the pagan self and the noisy, triumphal pageants of the pagan state.

How does this vision of the Jewish people connect with Mendelssohn's notion that the Jews are the "living script" of revelation? Mendelssohn would certainly agree that the Jewish people's life is beautiful insofar as it brings to expression God's benevolence as the entirely noncoercive bond joining one person to another. But Mendelssohn did not consider that this beauty or the principle upon which it was based had no relation to history and the life of the state. If we are to "close the circle" and join Mendelssohn to Rosenzweig, we must find a way to bring Rosenzweig's Jewish people back into relation with the life of the "other" peoples. This is the task of the next two chapters.

SIX

Mendelssohn, Rosenzweig, and Political Theology: Beyond Sovereign Violence

Overview

In the previous chapters I have attempted to show how Rosenzweig frees Mendelssohn's vision of Jewish existence as embodied revelation from its repression beneath the edifice of idealist philosophy, an edifice constructed in the aftermath of the Spinoza Quarrel. Breaking through the systematizing philosophy of 1800, Rosenzweig opens a path toward a Judaism lived as a continuing conversation between the generations, a dogma-free sociality that is, for Mendelssohn, the model of enlightened, democratic sociality more generally. But Rosenzweig's conception of Jewish life as lived outside of politics and history is very far indeed from Mendelssohn's hope that Jewish corporate existence might provide a model for an enlightened civic polity. This chapter and the next seek to draw Rosenzweig closer to Mendelssohn. I will argue that what stands in the way of a rapprochement between Rosenzweig and Mendelssohn on the plane of politics is Rosenzweig's conception of the state as created and sustained by violence, a view that runs counter to Mendelssohn's conception of the state as, ideally, the institutional framework created and sustained by the will to perfect the world through benevolence. For Rosenzweig, the state by its very nature seeks to usurp the place of God in the world; for Mendelssohn, it can become the expressive medium of God's will. With these two very different conceptions of the state, Rosenzweig's and Mendelssohn's political theologies are bound to diverge.

I will argue in this chapter that we can take a first step towards a rapprochement between Mendelssohn and Rosenzweig by unpacking the political implications present in Rosenzweig's concept of creation as "constantly brimming-over newness . . ., the 'beginning' from where the constantly new births of the plenitude spring up" (*Star* 145; 148). To see how this concept of creation can be made the basis of a political philosophy, I will turn to Hannah Arendt and her discussion of how the power of "beginning"—the "absolute of temporality" as she also calls it—is the founding principle of the democratic state. Bonnie Honig has recently proposed an approach to Rosenzweig's and Arendt's concept of the miracle—and miracle is but another name for the unprecedented singularity of "beginning"—that is very close to what I am arguing for in this chapter. Like Honig, I read Arendt's effort at describing the *democratic* power of the miracle of natality to be "a deliberate effort to counter Schmitt" (Honig 2007: 82). Arendt's miracle, Honig explains, is "a metaphor for action in concert rather than the identity-forming division of friend-enemy" (82). Thus, the Arendtian miracle stands opposed to the violent irruption of the sovereign decision in a time of exception whose power Schmitt likens to a miracle. While I entirely agree with Honig that Rosenzweig's concept of the miracle (and creation) is directly related to Arendt's and, like hers, stands in complete contrast to Schmitt, I do not think Rosenzweig himself imagined that it could be used to articulate a democratic, redemptive political praxis against the sovereign decisionism of Schmitt. In this chapter I will show how, in fact, Rosenzweig and Schmitt are in fundamental agreement about the nature of sovereignty as revealed in the irruptive violence of a decision to risk the state's very existence in war. I think that Honig would agree that Rosenzweig's discussion of the state in the *Star* has too quickly abandoned the space of the political to the inevitable violence of war. In order to recuperate a redemptive, democratic politics from Rosenzweig's concept of creation, I will, like

Honig, draw upon Arendt, but I will also situate Arendt in relation to the political theologies of Mendelssohn and Spinoza. Then, in the next chapter, I will unpack, with the help of Stanley Cavell, the political implications of Rosenzweig's concept of language as the site of revelation. Aided by the political philosophies of Arendt and Cavell, I seek to establish a rapprochement between Mendelssohn and Rosenzweig on the plane of the political.

Hannah Arendt and Stanley Cavell share Rosenzweig's fundamental concern to restore philosophy's faith in ordinary language and the human world that language helps to sustain. It is not at all accidental that Arendt and Cavell foreground the promise of democracy in America in their reflections about philosophy and its future. For both thinkers, philosophy's task is to awaken us to the responsibilities we bear simply by virtue of inheriting a common language. America for Arendt and Cavell names the site—not necessarily limited to the geographic region called the "United States of America"—where the moral burden and redemptive promise of our common words might be fulfilled. In this respect at least, Arendt and Cavell are heirs of the Enlightenment's hope for a sociality based upon the acceptance of mutual pledges of fidelity rather than upon an awed reverence for supernatural or human power. As heirs of this Enlightenment hope, they are Mendelssohn's kin. Mendelssohn's *Jerusalem* is devoted to demonstrating that the ideal polity is built upon freedom rather than coercion, benevolence rather than violence. By drawing Rosenzweig into relation with Arendt and Cavell, I hope to be able to bring him closer to Mendelssohn.

Arendt and Cavell are not alone in believing that the fates of philosophy and democracy are interlocked. Jacques Derrida, especially in his later work and most particularly in *The Politics of Friendship* (1997) and *Rogues* (2005), has no less insistently called upon philosophy to become a responsible partner in the formation of a "democracy to come." Derrida's relationship to Rosenzweig has been explored before, and Derrida himself has acknowledged his philosophical kinship with Rosenzweig.[1] The contribution I wish to make in this chapter and the next is to place Rosenzweig in relation to his younger American—whether *naturalized* like Arendt or *native-born* like Cavell (terms whose ever-contested meanings are constitutive of America)—philosophical "cousins." Stanley Cavell has frequently spoken of the importance of "migrancy" in the constitution of America,[2] and so one might say that I am interested here in imagining an "immigrant Rosenzweig." In particular, I am interested in bringing Rosenzweig into relation with the dream of America, a dream of democratic civility born in the Enlightenment and given one of its profoundest expressions in Mendelssohn's *Jerusalem*. At the heart of this Enlightenment dream of democratic civility is the idea that conversation enacts and sustains citizenship.

In the final line of her book, *Citizen-Saints: Shakespeare and Political Theology*, Julia Reinhard Lupton beautifully captures the hope and risk of civic, democratic conversation. Lupton's book broaches many themes that are related to my concerns in these chapters, and I will return to it at the end of the following chapter. For now I want only to attend to her book's concluding words. Let me briefly set the context. A few pages earlier, at the opening of the epilogue, entitled "The Literature of Citizenship: A Humanifesto," Lupton had invoked Pedro Almodóvar's film *Talk to Her* (*Hable con Ella*, 2002). One of the film's central characters is a nurse who carries on loving talk (and talk of love) with (to) one of his comatose patients, a woman with whom he had earlier fallen in love but had always lacked the courage to approach. Through his love, though only indirectly, he awakens her from her coma. Tragically, her reawakening does not bring her closer to him. While she had been comatose, the nurse, impelled by his need to make contact with her, had intercourse with her—raped her, in other words—and made her pregnant. The delivery of the child brings her unexpectedly back to consciousness, but she never meets the father of her child. Not long before the delivery of the child, while awaiting trial for the rape, the nurse commits suicide. Lupton closes her book with a reference to the film and to the necessary risks—freedom cannot be programmed for happiness—of democratic conversation: "Talk to her, *talk to them*: who knows what forms, moods, and shapes of consent might awaken in response?" (Lupton 2005: 216). These final words, with their invocation of talk as both the basis of consensual politics and as risk-taking, as even a risk-taking with life and death stakes, resonate powerfully with the final two words of her book's subtitle, "political theology."

Political theology is exactly what Mendelssohn sought to redefine in *Jerusalem* in the terms of an enlightened ethos of conversation—Rachel Varnhagen's salon is perhaps one of the few sites where it flourished in Berlin in the period immediately following Mendelssohn's death[3]—that would allow the Jews to enter into civic conversation with their neighbors. It is in the spirit of this kind of political theology that Lupton writes her defense of the "literature of citizenship," a literature that she says breaks with myth and tribalism, what Rosenzweig would call "paganism." Certainly, Mendelssohn's *Jerusalem* may be counted as a signal example of the literature of citizenship, though perhaps it is also its least well-known example. By using the phrase "political theology," Lupton, however, does not mean to invoke Mendelssohn's *Jerusalem* or Spinoza's defense of democracy in the *Theological-Political Treatise*. Rather, Lupton has chosen the phrase "political theology" largely in order to contest the profoundly anti-democratic cast that it was given by the twentieth-century's foremost opponent of a Mendelssohnian—democratic and consensual—political theology: Carl Schmitt.[4] In pursuing a democratic political theology, I will, like Lupton and in part following her lead, also have to grapple with Carl Schmitt.

That talk and conversation alone can sustain democratic citizenship is a point that Lupton finds to be a source of risk, but also of hope. But the "endless conversation" of democracy is precisely what Carl Schmitt saw as democracy's greatest weakness.[5] As I will show in what follows, the passage across the Atlantic that my "immigrant Rosenzweig" will take is a passage away from the view—Schmitt was its clearest exponent in his *Political Theology* (1922) and *Concept of the Political* (1927)—that the modern state gives birth to itself and renews itself in violence, a violence that puts an end to conversation in the single-voiced shout that acclaims "The State has died—Long live the State!" Rosenzweig's concept of the political is, like Schmitt's, at odds with the liberal democratic state whose birth, though it may of course involve violence, is legitimized through consent realized in promises of fidelity and acts of covenant-making.

In a perceptive discussion of Rosenzweig's concept of the birth of the sovereign state in violence, Eric Santner has shown how its conceptuality also informs Walter Benjamin's 1921 essay, "Zur Kritik der Gewalt [Toward the Critique of Violence]."[6] This essay, Giorgio Agamben has argued persuasively, was almost certainly read by Carl Schmitt.[7] Agamben claims that Benjamin's essay informs Schmitt's argument in his 1922 work *Politische Theologie* (*Political Theology*) that an extralegal exercise of power is necessary both to bring into being and to preserve the sovereign state. Certainly, Benjamin and Schmitt were dealing with very similar juridico-philosophical themes in the 1920s and the lines of influence run in both directions. But I will argue that Rosenzweig, and quite possibly Benjamin as well, was indebted to Carl Schmitt's early work, *Der Wert des Staates und die Bedeutung des Einzelnen* (*The Value of the State and the Meaning of the*

Individual) (1917). This early work addresses the question of the relationship between right (Recht) and sovereign power/violence (Macht/Gewalt). Schmitt develops an anti-positivistic juridical philosophy in which the highest instance of violence-wielding power in the state is legitimated by a theoretically prior right rather than by the merely empirical fact that it is able to wield such violence. This may seem to run counter to Schmitt's later view that sovereign power is legitimated not in virtue of its conformity to a legal norm but by the ability of the power to decide in those cases where legal norms fail to apply (the "state of exception"). But the discrepancy is only apparent. The right that legitimates violence-wielding power has no positive content. It realizes itself precisely through the founding act by which the legal state (Rechtstaat) comes into being. Right is actualized, according to *Der Wert des Staates*, through an extralegal foundational violence that inaugurates the law.

Rosenzweig, as a scholar of the Hegelian philosophy of the state, would almost certainly have been familiar with Schmitt's treatment of the state in the *Der Wert des Staates*. Schmitt's anti-positivistic juridical theory in this book is heavily indebted to Hegel. It should not be surprising, then, if we find that there are very close parallels between Schmitt's work and Rosenzweig's discussion of the state in the *Star*.[8] Rosenzweig does not agree with Schmitt's assessment that the individual only acquires meaningful existence through the state, but he does not contest Schmitt's view that the state is created and sustained by violence (Gewalt) and that it seeks to unify the empirical heterogeneity of its members within itself. In later works, Schmitt will draw closer to Rosenzweig as he comes to underscore the need for a "natural" homogeneity of *Volk* in order to create a unified state.[9] Upon such premises, there is no hope for formulating a political theology of democratic citizenship. It is therefore necessary to disentangle Rosenzweig from the Schmittian vision of the political.

In this chapter I will begin, and in the next I will complete, my portrait of an "immigrant Rosenzweig." I will first of all place into the clearest possible light the lineaments of Rosenzweig's Hegelian notion of the state, one he shares with Carl Schmitt. I will show that Rosenzweig's concept of the political depends upon the view, adumbrated in Schmitt's *Der Wert des Staates*, that the state is created and sustained by violence. This violent self-creation is precisely opposed to the "constantly brimming-over newness" that marks the world's creation. The states that arose in the early modern period as successors to Charlemagne's empire are "rebels against the unity of the law of a world created by the one creative power, which was under the emperor's guardianship" (*Star* 373; 391). The state is, for Rosenzweig, a sort of "anti-world," a false totality that would stand on its own against the creative power that moves the world towards the future and towards redemption. It seeks to transform the creative birth of the new into the fixity of the "natural nation [*natürliche Nation*]" (*Star* 371; 391), as Rosenzweig says, playing on the Latin root (*natus* from the verb *nasci*) of both *nature* and *nation*, which means *born*. That the state seeks to create a self-enclosed world that gives expression to a "natural nation's" striving for permanence is a Hegelian position that is embraced not only by Rosenzweig, but also by Carl Schmitt. After discussing Rosenzweig's political theology in the *Star* and its connection with both Hegel and Schmitt in the next section, I will turn to Arendt's critique of Schmitt's view of the state as born in violence. Arendt, as I have previously said, sees the democratic state—the state founded in the American Revolution is her prime example—as created not through violence, but through the power of "beginning," the act that binds a human plurality together through mutual promises to nurture and preserve the very power of beginning—freedom, in other words—as the highest principle of the state. After showing how Arendt's concept of beginning gives political meaning to Rosenzweig's concept of creation, I will turn in the final section of this chapter to a description of the political theology of Mendelssohn in *Jerusalem*. I will show how it both inherits and criticizes the work of Spinoza in his *Theological-Political Treatise*. Most importantly, Mendelssohn offers a conception of the political that is not structured by a notion of sovereignty as a unified, decisive will as with Hobbes. Nor does Mendelssohn offer a picture of the unity of the state as grounded in the commonality of birth. I will show how Mendelssohn's political theory draws its inspiration from Spinoza's conception of the democratic state as the site where the conjoined power of the multitude (Arendt speaks of this as the "plurality") gives expression to the self-causing power of God. In other words, democracy, according to Spinoza, is the form in which divine creation expresses itself humanly. My contention is that this conception of democracy not only inspires Mendelssohn's political theology in *Jerusalem*, but also connects with Arendt's view that the democratic state nurtures and sustains the power of "beginning." By drawing Mendelssohn and Arendt into connection with Spinoza's theory of the democratic state, I will have prepared the ground for a reconstruction of Rosenzweig's political theology that envisions the possibility of a democratic redemptive politics. Rosenzweig, just like Spinoza, Mendelssohn, and Arendt, wants to show how the creative power that sustains the world can acquire a human face. But the state can never be the face of this creative power so long as it is only viewed as an "anti-world." Arendt, working within the tradition of Spinoza and Mendelssohn, shows how the democratic state can be a human world where the principle and miracle of "beginning"—Rosenzweig's "Creation"—is nurtured. This Arendtian translation of Rosenzweig's concept of creation is offered as a first step towards imagining an "immigrant Rosenzweig" who has shed his Schmittian-Hegelian belief in violence as the inevitable heart of the nation-state. In this chapter, then, I will begin by drawing as starkly as possible the contrast between Mendelssohn's and Rosenzweig's concepts of the state, but I will also point towards their rapprochement through a rethinking of the political implications of Rosenzweig's concept of creation. In the next chapter I will complete my portrait of an "immigrant Rosenzweig" by drawing on Cavell to develop the political implications of Rosenzweig's theory of language as the site of revelation.

Rosenzweig and Schmitt on the Political

Rosenzweig's attitude towards the modern nation-state is largely shaped by his experience of World War I. As I explained in the introduction, Rosenzweig published two works shortly after the war, *Hegel und der Staat* (1920) and the *Star* (1921). Both books share a critique of what Rosenzweig identifies as the epochal year 1800, the year when "paganism" reemerges on the world scene in two interlocked forms: the nation-state and idealist philosophy. The nation-state is born after the final collapse (in 1803 to be precise) of the thousand-year Holy Roman Empire, when "the crown was removed from the head of the Roman emperor, and the neo-Frankish national emperor"—i.e., Napoleon—"put it on himself" (*Star* 373; 391). Napoleon is the emperor of a new kind of state, a state founded upon the sovereignty of the people: the nation-state. "[T]he will to be the empire [Wille zum Reich]," Rosenzweig explains, "now seemed to have passed over to the peoples" (*Star* 373; 391). The nation-state becomes the vehicle of each people's "will to empire." Rosenzweig hopes that this "world-oriented will" will assume a "new configuration" that takes it "beyond the national," but he is certainly aware that its first flowering is *imperialism*. The nation-state is a new form of paganism because it seeks to extend itself to encompass the world, to create a permanent presence upon the earth that does not acknowledge any reality—neither a transcendent God nor a future Redemption—beyond its borders.

Idealist philosophy, according to Rosenzweig, is the other face of the resurgent paganism of the post-1800 epoch. The nation-state's universalizing "will to be the empire" is mirrored in idealist philosophy's attempt at "cognition of the All [Erkennen des All]" (*Star* 11; 5). Both the nation-state and idealist philosophy are illusory attempts to deny the reality of death: in the first case, the inevitable death of a people; in the second, the inevitable death of the individual. In Hegel, idealist philosophy and the nation-state join together, according to Rosenzweig. The universalizing drive of the nation-state as the culmination of history and idealist philosophy's universalizing drive to cognize the All find their single expression in Hegel's philosophy of the state. This is the basic argument of *Hegel and the State*. In the *Star*, Rosenzweig attempts to unveil the illusions upon which both the universalizing drive of the nation-state and that of idealist philosophy are constructed. In Chapter 3 I discussed Rosenzweig's critique of idealist philosophy's pretension to cognition of the All. In regard to the nation-state, Rosenzweig's critique is both simple and succinct, the fruit of his and his entire generation's experience of war: The nation-state is no less mortal than is the individual, no less doomed to extinction. History will ultimately consign every people, except for the eternal Jewish people who have renounced their ties to the state (through territory and national language), to death. Unlike the death of the individual, however, the death of the nation-state is never natural, never the end result of a gradual decay. Rather, every nation-state lives and dies through war. The "Wille zum Reich [the will to be the empire]" can only lead to war. The modern epoch, the epoch after 1800, is the epoch of war. The hope for redemption, the hope that guides the third and final Johannine church, is the hope for world peace, for the coming of the Kingdom of God. "Precisely because they are not real peoples of God, but only on the way to becoming so," Rosenzweig says of the world's many nation-states, "they cannot draw those distinct borders [between political wars and religious wars waged on behalf of Kingdom of God]; they cannot at all know how far God's will is realized in the warlike destinies of their states. Somehow—the how remains puzzling; the people must become accustomed to the idea of a possible destruction; whether as a people it will be used as a stone in the edifice of the Kingdom—the consciousness of the individual decides nothing concerning this; the war alone decides, which rages on above the consciousness of the individual" (*Star* 350–51; 367–68). The hope for world peace cannot be actualized in politics because all politics in the modern epoch is the politics of war. And any war in which nation-states engage is always seen by them as a holy war, a war between Christ and Antichrist. Rosenzweig does not, to be sure, endorse this apocalyptic view of war. Secular history is not the "history of the Kingdom of God" because, Rosenzweig says, "that which is eternal has no history" (*Star* 374; 392). Yet this does not make modern war any less global, or any less pitiless, than apocalyptic war. And what is apocalyptic war if it is not the "war to end all wars"?

Rosenzweig's rejection of the redemptive potential of politics on the grounds that the political is *war under the false banner of the apocalypse* is shared with many others of his generation who were disillusioned with the catastrophic slaughter of World War I. When Rosenzweig calls for a new Johannine Christianity of hope, he is, like Karl Barth and others involved in the Patmos circle and the journals *Zwischen den Zeiten* or *Die Kreatur*, calling for a radical depoliticization of theology. Such depoliticization was seen as a restoration of the purity of messianic expectancy concentrated in "today" and "tomorrow" rather than what Rosenzweig called "the day after tomorrow" of the state's historical time. Although drawing a very different conclusion about the demands of political life in postwar Weimar, Rosenzweig and Barth and others like them would agree with the words of Max Weber, the most realistic analyst of the dilemma facing the generation of 1918. In a speech delivered to university students that year, published in 1921 as "The Vocation of Politics," Weber put the issue succinctly: "He who seeks the salvation of his soul, of his own and of others, should not seek it along the avenue of politics, for the quite different tasks of politics can only be solved by violence" (Weber 1958: 126).

Mark Lilla in *The Stillborn God* (2007) characterized Rosenzweig and Barth as key figures in the emergence of a new messianic political theology in Weimar Germany. Lilla believes that Barth and Rosenzweig, by calling for a Christian and Jewish rededication to a *depoliticized* messianic expectancy "today," opened the floodgates for the *hyperpoliticized* messianism that emerged in Nazism, "the foulest of modern ideologies" (Lilla 2007: 260). Although (somewhat surprisingly) he is mentioned only once in passing in Lilla's book, Max Weber's realistic assessment of the dangers of linking politics and theology is one with which Lilla would certainly agree. But it is hardly fair to place Rosenzweig and Barth in the same camp as one of Weber's foremost critics, Carl Schmitt. Schmitt, an unnamed but overarching presence in Lilla's book, desired precisely to reintroduce the theological dimension of apocalyptic war into current politics. Jacob Taubes made this point when he spoke of Schmitt as "apocalypticist of the counter-revolution" (Taubes 1993: 96). Taubes, like Lilla, draws Schmitt and Barth into one ambit (Taubes 1993: 86–97), but he rightly focuses on Schmitt as the theorist of apocalyptic politics. Schmitt did not rely upon Rosenzweig or Barth in articulating his vision of an apocalyptic politics. Schmitt certainly did not follow the lead of Rosenzweig or Barth when he found his way to supporting "the foulest of modern ideologies" after Hitler came to power in 1933. When I mention Rosenzweig and Schmitt in the same breath, it is not to accuse Rosenzweig of complicity in the rise of a "foul" political theology. My aim, unlike Lilla's (and more like Taubes's), is to reenliven the hopes and aspirations of Rosenzweig's political theology by separating it from its Hegelian conception of the state as legitimized through violence. The really dangerous political theology—that of Carl Schmitt, for example—is one that *divinizes violence*. The divinization of violence is also possible within the political tradition that Lilla identifies positively as responsible for what he calls the "Great Separation" of church and state introduced by Thomas Hobbes. The divinization of violence, although it is quite at odds with Hobbes's own political and philosophical intentions, is dangerously implicit within the characterization of the Leviathan state as a "mortal god."

Where Lilla vilifies Rosenzweig's political theology as a precursor to Nazism, Leora Batnitzky offers the completely opposite view in *Idolatry and Representation*. Batnitzky argues that Rosenzweig's turn away from the political was an embrace of a "messianic politics" that sought to stand up against the modern state's "fanatical nationalism" fueled by the illusion that it is the vehicle of redemption in the world (Batnitzky 2000: 180–81). Batnitzky speaks sympathetically of Rosenzweig's view that the Jewish people have renounced the state and politics in order to witness to—and possibly become martyrs to—the futility of the state's aspiration to achieve a worldly, secular permanence. She says that "[t]his act of witnessing is an act fraught with risk" (2000: 181). The Jewish people's stateless eternity holds a mirror to the idol of the state.

Batnitzky is right when she says that, for Rosenzweig, the Jewish people challenge the "pagan" idolatry of the state, but so also does the Johannine church, and in a far more direct way. Rosenzweig in fact does seek to draw revelation's power into history, and this is where it is perhaps more apt to speak of his "messianic politics." The Jewish people have, to be sure, an indirect impact upon the historical peoples of the world, but the Jewish people renounced any direct engagement in history, even to be concerned whether it is moving closer to redemption or not. Perhaps, even in regard to his description of Johannine church and its hope for world peace, it is more apt to describe Rosenzweig as an advocate of "messianic *apolitcs*."

Rosenzweig's rejection of the redemptive potential of politics, differently judged by Lilla and Batnitzky as complicitous with or risking everything to oppose the "foulest ideology" of "fanatical nationalism," has been perhaps more realistically assessed by Peter Eli Gordon as "the eclipse of the political" (Gordon 2003: 110). This eclipse of the political is, Gordon argues, part of Rosenzweig's wrestling with the implications of Hegel's *Spirit of Christianity and Its Fate*, a text which Rosenzweig in *Hegel and the State* saw as critical for the development of Hegel's political philosophy. I have spoken in the previous chapter of Rosenzweig's reinterpretation of Hegel's argument in *Spirit-Fate* that Christianity failed to overcome its "fate" because it failed to overcome its mourning over the death of Jesus. I claimed that Rosenzweig saw in this "failure" the possibility of a Johannine Christianity of hope that grows out of but does not deny mourning. This is the Johannine Christianity that is announced in Hölderlin's poem *Patmos*, written in 1803 immediately after the dismemberment of the Holy Roman Empire. The Great War, Rosenzweig said in a diary entry I quoted in Chapter 3 (in "Christianity and Paganism: 1800"), has finally made the emergence of Johannine Christianity possible, closing a chapter on Christian triumphalism within the *saeculum*, but also ending the Hegelian dream of consummating Christianity through the *political communion* of the state. Peter Eli Gordon rightly points out that Rosenzweig had come to lose faith in such dreams of a *secular* sublation of the individual within a wider, all-embracing totality. Gordon writes that

> the state had come to be associated for Rosenzweig with the eclipse of the individual. As we have seen, the fate of Jesus is for Hegel a model for the predicament of finitude in general; the struggle between Jesus and his society showed that any engagement in the political world demanded surrender in the face of irresistible authority. From this story, Rosenzweig appears to have concluded that finite subjectivity and the state are necessarily opposed. Since the full realization of the state's purposes on earth demands the eclipse of the individual, Rosenzweig came to believe that the preservation of finitude required a life *elsewhere than politics*.
> (Gordon 2003: 111)

Peter Eli Gordon rightly places Rosenzweig's rejection of the redemptive potential of the political within the context of his engagement with Hegel, and I have suggested how this engagement is also part of a response, shared by many others who read Hölderlin's *Patmos* as a prophetic message seemingly addressed to them, to the horrifying collapse of the European order of states in the Great War and the failure in Germany after the war to forge a framework for a politically viable solution to the social and economic ruin that the war and the ensuing defeat caused. But, unlike Benjamin, for whom messianism possessed a revolutionary "force" that could be turned against the state, Rosenzweig's depoliticized messianism does not so much contest the Hegelian notion of the state, as concede to it the entire territory of the political. This is a point that is somewhat obscured by Gordon's description of Rosenzweig's theory of the state as the "eclipse of the political." Rosenzweig's rejection of any form of redemptive politics is not really an "eclipse" of the political, but rather the abandonment of the political to stand naked beneath the harshest possible light: the light of exploding bombs of war.

Leora Batnitzky acutely sums up the issue that for me is central to understanding Rosenzweig when she writes that "Rosenzweig agreed with Hegel" that "the time of the nations . . . is the time of war" (Batnitzky 2000: 180). Rather than rejecting a Hegelian concept of the state, Rosenzweig accepts in large measure the interpretation of the state propounded by the foremost Hegelian jurist and legal thinker of the day, Carl Schmitt, whose *Der Wert des Staates* argues that, as Gordon puts it in regard to Hegel, "the full realization of the state's purposes on earth demands the eclipse of the individual" (111). Rosenzweig, accepting this claim, turns to a depoliticized revelation, differently brought to concrete life in Johannine Christianity and Judaism, in order to counter the totalizing claim of the state upon the individual.

In order to connect Rosenzweig with a democratic and redemptive view of the political, it is necessary to confront Rosenzweig's Hegelian-Schmittian conception of the state head on. Only then can we find our way back to Mendelssohn and the problem articulated in the very first sentence of *Jerusalem*: "State and religion—civil and ecclesiastical—secular and churchly authority—how to oppose these pillars of social life to one another so that they are in balance and do not, instead, become burdens on social life, or weigh down its foundations more than they help to uphold it—that is one of the most difficult tasks of politics" (*Jerusalem* 33). In an article entitled "Mendelssohn and the State," Willi Goetschel argues that Mendelssohn provides a much-needed "critical alternative to the sovereign-based theory of the state" that focuses upon the "in-between space of critical exchange" in which "conflicting claims between different kinds of rights can reach a just adjudication" (Goetschel 2007: 476). According to Goetschel, Mendelssohn's theologico-political theory in *Jerusalem* develops a concept of power derived from Spinoza, a concept that was developed in direct contestation with Hobbes. This concept conceives of power as different from "might" or "violence." Rather, power is, as Goetschel puts it, a "composite phenomenon, which is why it is impossible to reduce the complexity of political life to a mere calculus" (475).

As Goetschel points out, the Spinozist-Mendelssohnian concept of power underlies a democratic version of the political and contrasts with the "sovereign-based theory of the state" which grows out of seventeenth-century absolutism. One of the foremost exponents of this "sovereign-based" theory in the seventeenth century was Thomas Hobbes, and in Weimar Germany its primary theoretician was the same Carl Schmitt who also argued for a Hegelian conception of the state. Schmitt's political philosophy can be described as a fusion of Hobbes and Hegel. In his *Der Wert des Staates*, Schmitt articulates a theory of the state that joins Hegel's idea of the *Rechtstaat* to Hobbes's Leviathan, the mortal god who is the superperson transcending the atomized, empirical selves engaged in a "war of all against all." Schmitt sees right as logically prior to the state, and the state as logically prior the individual. This is Schmitt's Hegelian reversal of Hobbes's chronological development of right out of the state which in turn emerges from individuals. Despite his Hegelian reversal of Hobbes, Schmitt preserves Hobbes's emphasis on the *decisive will* as the quintessential property of the sovereign superperson, i.e., the state. Right is logically primary because the sovereign decision is not merely arbitrary or self-serving (otherwise it would not be qualitatively different than the will of the empirical individual in the prepolitical state of nature). Right as the object of sovereign decision making cannot be deduced from the interests of the individual members of the state, which would turn right into the result of a calculus of "interest collisions" (*Der Wert des Staates* 28). Right cannot be deduced at all; it is constitutive of the state. But how can the state be constituted by right if right is itself produced through sovereign (state) decision? This is the problem of the legitimacy of constitutional law to which Schmitt recurs throughout the decade of the 1920s. It is a problem that has its origin in Edmond Sieyès's discussion of the legitimacy of the French Revolutionary Constituent Assembly as arising from the sovereign power of the people. It is a problem that was also dealt with during the early years of the American Revolution as the various colonial states sought to redefine themselves as a sovereign nation.[10]

In his 1917 book, Schmitt is very close to his later definition in *Concept of the Political* of the sovereign as "the one who decides in a state of emergency." In *Der Wert des Staates*, Schmitt does not specifically invoke the state of emergency, but he does speak about the moment when a new "norm" is established through a new valuation ("Bewertung"). As I have mentioned, Schmitt's juridical philosophy is anti-positivistic, and his concept of valuation is part and parcel of his attack on the notion that the law reflects norms derivable from economic or social conditions. Schmitt's concept of valuation as norm creating is perhaps most clearly articulated in another anti-positivistic theory of the norm, namely, the physiological theory of health developed by Georges Canguilhem in *The Normal and the Pathological* (1943). Although written some time after Schmitt and with no apparent connection to Schmitt's work, Canguilhem, exactly like Schmitt, is engaged in a critique of positivism. Canguilhem's discussion of the norm in physiology and biology offers an accessible point of entry to the more abstract reflections of Schmitt.[11]

Canguilhem is interested in what entitles a scientist to declare, for example, "98.6 degrees Fahrenheit is the adult human body's healthy temperature; body heat above or below this temperature is symptomatic of disease." Canguilhem insists that this judgment cannot be legitimated by calculating average body temperatures, as the positivist model of physiology suggests.

Why should the average be normative? It is quite possible that the average body temperature of a given population reflects a diseased physiology. If the medical norm is not to be merely the average temperature of most human bodies, it must reflect the body's successful achievement of a balance of biological forces in battle with each other. The normative temperature is a sign of the body's own norm-creating power. The healthy temperature of the body is what the body ought to display—it is a norm—because it is at that temperature that the body is able to maintain itself in readiness to meet internal and external environmental challenges or threats. In other words, the physiological norm is what allows the body to create new norms when it is under pressure to change. "The physiological state is the healthy state, much more than the normal state. *It is the state which allows transitions to new norms.* Man is healthy insofar as he is normative relative to the fluctuations of his environment" (Canguilhem 1991: 228; italics mine).

The legal norm that creates the state is, according to Schmitt, the state's coming into sovereign power as a norm-creating entity. There is no "objective" norm that defines what is right; right is defined by the fact of its being established as right: "das Recht ist etwas, das mit Recht verwirklicht werden soll [Right is that which ought by right to be realized]" (*Der Wert des Staates* 34). Schmitt shows his debt to Hegel when he declares that right "als reine, wertende, aus Tatsachen nicht zu rechtfertigende Norm [as pure, value-positing norm that is not justified by facts]" is logically ("logisch") the first of the triad "Right, State, and Individual," despite its apparent chronological belatedness in relation to the other terms. Schmitt shows his debt to Hobbes when he says that the state as a sovereign superperson ("überindividuelle, nicht interindividuelle Instanz") is the only "subject" of the "Rechtsethos [the ethos of right]," a subject whose existence consists precisely in enacting itself as the sole law-establishing "instance," the "highest power." Just as Canguilhem defines the normative state as the one that "allows transitions to new norms," so Schmitt asserts that right is what establishes the condition for the perpetuation of right. The state is the medium of the self-reproduction of right. The state, then, acquires its identity through time by serving as the medium in which right recreates itself over and over again as it meets internal and external challenges to its legitimacy. Violence is the means by which right recreates itself over time and acquires continuity ("Kontinuität"). Apart from right, violence is blind power erupting in discontinuous moments:

A simply factual violence [Die lediglich faktische Gewalt] can never elevate itself to any point of justification whatsoever without presupposing a norm upon which its justification is legitimized. In relation to merely factual violence there are only concrete, specific cases, never an organizing will that binds them together into a rational unity; there are only punctual expressions of a blind power, not a continuity. (*Der Wert des Staates* 48)

Schmitt thus can speak of right as constitutive of the state because it legitimizes the state's constitution as such, as an enactment of supraindividual decision. Right arises chronologically *after* the state founds itself upon a constitution as the executive seat of decision making, but the state cannot in theory make law prior to its constitution (taken in both senses of the word, as founding and as founding law). Schmitt's Hegelian solution to this paradox is to assert that right precedes the state and is also the state's first decision, its decision to exist as *Rechtstaat*.[12] Sovereignty gives birth to itself by constituting its own precedent: It can declare the law because it already has done so.

This is the interpretation of the state that Rosenzweig offers in the *Star* where he discusses at the end of book 1 of part 3 the difference between the "true" eternality of the Jewish people and the "illusory" eternality of the state (*Star* 348–55; 364–72). "The Jewish people is in itself already at the goal toward which the people of the world are just setting out," Rosenzweig writes (*Star* 351; 368). The Jewish people have attained their eternality by shaping their lives in conformity with the cycle of creation, revelation, and redemption that flows through the annual holidays and is repeated every week within the space of the one day, the Sabbath. They have no need to actively shape the world's temporality in accordance with this cycle, as do the other peoples of the world. The "matter" which serves the Jewish people as the medium of their artistic recreation of life in the image of the eternal is their biological life, their mortal bodies (their "blood" as Rosenzweig would say). Jewish law is, as I have explained in greater detail earlier in the book, the choreography of the eternal life of the Jewish people.

The other peoples of the world, however, must first shape themselves into states in order to attain some permanent hold on time. The law of the state is not like the law of the Jewish people. Rather than forming the choreography of eternality in life, the law of the state is a violent incision into the flow of life. "Against the hours of eternity, which the State in the time of world history carves with a sharp sword into the bark of the growing tree of time, the eternal people every year places untroubled and intact ring upon ring round the trunk of its eternal life" (*Star* 354; 371–72). The law of the state creates an "illusory eternity [Scheinewigkeit]" in time because it must create itself *ex nihilo*, unlike the law of the Jewish people, which is commanded by God. Now Rosenzweig certainly understands that in antiquity the laws were thought to be God given. But Rosenzweig is speaking about the modern nation-state. Modern states, in the Schmittian-Rosenzweigian concept of the sovereignty, legitimize their law in an act that both creates and enacts the "will of the people." In the modern state in which the people find their sovereign identity, the law achieves its permanence by enacting the birth of the sovereign people. Every law of the state is a reaffirmation of the first law that creates the sovereign body of the people.

> Violence gets life brought to its law against the law. Since the state is violent and not merely lawful, it remains at life's heels. This is the meaning of all violence, that it founds new law. [*This statement is exactly what Schmitt says about violence and the law in the quotation just above.*] It is not a disavowal of the law, as one probably thinks, fascinated by its revolutionary conduct, but on the contrary its foundation. But a contradiction is hidden in the idea of a new law. Law is as regards its essence old law. In the violent act law continuously turns into new law. And the State is therefore equally as much lawful as violent, refuge of the old law and source of the new; and in this double shape as refuge of law and source of law the State places itself above the mere flowing off of the life of the people in which custom unceasingly and non-violently multiplies and law changes. To this natural allowing of the living moment to elapse . . . the State opposes its violent asserting of the moment. (*Star* 353; 370)

A state that lacks the strength to reaffirm itself by enacting new law is a state that has been defeated by time. The sovereign state has died when it cannot affirm itself as one sovereign will. When this happens, the people itself is threatened with dissolution. The people in the modern nation have been so identified with the sovereign state that the destruction of the sovereign state spells their end. And in the Christian era, the state's wars of defense become "holy wars" in which it is decided who is and who is not to remain a "people of God" for the next stretch of world history. Every people, except the Jewish people, who have renounced sovereign statehood as their lifeblood (the Zionist dream, according to Rosenzweig, should not be to reduce the Jewish people to a territorial people), "must become accustomed to the idea of a possible destruction; whether as a people it will be used as a stone in the edifice of the Kingdom—the consciousness of the individual decides nothing concerning this; the war alone decides, which rages on above the consciousness of the individual" (*Star* 351; 367). As I have said, this view of the state consigns secular history to a recurrence of pseudoapocalyptic wars adding up to one long war "which rages on above the consciousness of the individual" until the end of time. Carl Schmitt will ultimately come to the same position as Rosenzweig, but, unlike Rosenzweig, he believes that the Kingdom of God *has a history*. He will see it as the task of the true leader to recognize more clearly than Rosenzweig thought was possible how his people "will be used as a stone in the edifice of the Kingdom." Let me be very clear: Rosenzweig's political theology is at the opposite extreme from Schmitt's horrifying call for a leader ("Führer") to take on the mantle of apocalyptic warrior, a figure Schmitt will call, employing a phrase from the Second Epistle to the Thessalonians (2:7), "the Restrainer" (of the Antichrist).[13] But precisely because Rosenzweig has so radically detheologized the political, he is defenseless against Schmitt's reclaiming of the political in the name of what he understands to be the theological necessity of apocalyptic war. Rosenzweig is clear that redemption will not be achieved through war, but Schmitt insists that only war can defend the hope of redemption against the hubristic drive of a sinful, atheistic humanity that seems intent on bending the knee before the seductive banner of "world peace under one world government." Schmitt calls for holy war against the dream of humanity's self-pacification.

For Rosenzweig, the Jews have foresworn holy war and therefore have attained to eternality. They have foresworn the state, history, and politics. Christians *qua* Christians seek to bend the violent temporality of the state—its self-renewal through "war and revolution"—towards the path of redemption by imposing upon it another temporality, the temporality of the holidays of the ecclesiastical year. The problem with this is that the two temporalities do not really intersect. The holidays do not help to renew the bonds of the state. They bear no essential relation to the law of the state, at least in so far as the law is the enactment of sovereignty's violent self-recreation. This is precisely the point where Mendelssohn's political theology can help us. We need a conception of the political that does not rest upon violence, but upon love, or, to put it in Stanley Cavell's terms, upon the acceptance of the terms that love imposes upon us: acknowledgment of our mortal finitude and the limits of our power. As I will show, love and the space of the political both grow out of a revisioning of oneself in relation to the world, a revisioning that reorients us toward the promise of the future. Hannah Arendt and Stanley Cavell make this revisioning the center of their thinking. Since Arendt is the one who directly confronts the Schmittian concept of the political, I will in the next section offer a brief description of her critique of the Schmittian notion that sovereign violence founds the state. I will show how her concept of natality or "beginning" directly opposes the Schmittian notion that the political is realized in violent, sovereign decision.[14] I believe that Arendt's concept of beginning unlocks the political implications of Rosenzweig's concept of creation, implications he was unable to see because of his Hegelian-Schmittian theory of the state. Once I have presented Arendt's theory of beginning as a critique of the notion that the state is always founded in and sustained by violence, I will turn back to Mendelssohn. Mendelssohn, I will argue, stands in a line of political thought questioning the sovereign state's violence that extends from Spinoza to Arendt.

Arendt contra Schmitt: Natality vs. Violence

Hannah Arendt's reflections on the American Revolution can serve as the starting point for a treatment of her anti-Schmittian political theology.[15] According to Arendt, the American revolution succeeded in solving the dilemma posed by the severance of a state's constituting power (Arendt, following Edmond Sieyès, calls it *"pouvoir constitutant"*) and its legitimately constituted power (*"pouvoir constitutué"*). Schmitt had identified the relationship between these two moments of power within the state as the central problem for the theory of the state. It is the dilemma of how a state can constitute a law without the authority of a constitution. Schmitt, as I have explained above, argues in *Der Wert des Staates* that right logically precedes and is embodied within the law by which a state constitutes itself. In every law the state thereafter enacts, this right is re-asserted. There is no objective right by which to judge the state; only its continuing power to recreate itself in law legitimizes the law.

Hannah Arendt in *On Revolution* (1990) argues that the men of the American Revolution solved the problem of the state differently. Rather than work within the framework of the state as the expression of a unitary sovereign will, they dismantled the twin pillars of sovereignty itself, power and authority, and refashioned the nature of the political.[16] Although the men of the French Revolution failed to to translate the revolutionary *pouvoir constitutant* into the legal structures of the *pouvoir constitutué*, the American Revolution succeeded.

> The great and fateful misfortune of the French Revolution was that none of the constituent assemblies could command enough authority to lay down the law of the land; the reproach rightly leveled against them was always the same: they lacked the power to constitute by definition; they themselves were unconstitutional. Theoretically, the fateful blunder of the men of the French Revolution consisted in their almost automatic, uncritical belief that power and law spring from the selfsame source. Conversely, the great good fortune of the American Revolution was that the people of the colonies, prior to their conflict with England, were organized in self-governing bodies, that the revolution—to speak the language of the eighteenth century—did not throw them into a state of nature, that there never was any serious questioning of the *pouvoir constituant* of those who framed the state constitutions and, eventually, the Constitution of the United States. (*On Revolution* 165)

During the American Revolution, the power to constitute the laws of the republic was not severed from the constituted institutions which that power was supposed to create.

Power, Arendt suggests, is always constituted within the realm of the political and is never found in a prepolitical "state of nature." Power emerges simultaneously with the mutual promising that constitutes the realm of the political. Arendt traces the power that was unleashed in the Revolution to the Pilgrims of the Mayflower Compact and the "confidence they had in their own power, granted and confirmed by no one and as yet unsupported by any means of violence, to combine themselves together into a 'civil Body Politick' which, held together solely by the strength of mutual promise 'in the Presence of God and one another', supposedly was powerful enough to 'enact, constitute, and frame' all necessary laws and instruments of government" (*On Revolution* 167). Arendt's emphasis here is upon the "mutual promise" that, she will argue, brings power into being: "binding and promising, combining and covenanting are the means by which power is kept in existence" (*On Revolution* 175). The private motives of the individuals who come together and form the covenant are not important, only that they understand themselves to be incapable of surviving apart from the mutual pact they enter into. "Homogeneity of past and origin," Arendt concludes, "the decisive principle of the nation-state, is not required" (*On Revolution* 174). What was discovered, and proved, in America was that "the making and keeping of promises . . . in the realm of politics may well be the highest human faculty" (175). A state of nature does not precede the mutual promising of covenant making; rather, mutual promising is preceded by an act of severance from a prior compact. We can say, in other words, that political power is always a kind of remarriage after prior divorce.

The problem of political promises that are "world-building," Arendt points out, is that they bind not only those who make them, but also their posterity. By what authority does a promise have the power to bind the future? The authority of the promise and its power do not rest in the same source. If the authority is thought to rest in some transcendent popular will that underwrites the legal constitution, we have lost the power of promise. The power of the promise resides in the mutual pledging of a plurality of humans, not in any single will, even if it is imagined to be somehow indivisible. The belief that power resides in the unanimity of the popular will and that this will authorizes the law was, according to Arendt, the source of the error that led to the failure of the French Revolution to produce a lasting constitution. And we can also see how the homogeneity of the social will stands opposed to the conversational heterogeneity required for the pursuit of happiness in marriage, or in a democratic sociality that is exemplified as (re)marriage, as it is for Cavell.

What authority, then, stands behind the mutual pledges by which the Founding Fathers bound themselves when they joined together to sign the Declaration of Independence and, later, the Constitution? Arendt points out that there is evidence to think that the authority was what was announced in the preamble to the Declaration of Independence, namely, "the laws of nature and nature's God." If this was in reality the source of authority invoked by the founders, it would be, for Arendt who believes in neither natural law nor in a legislating God, an illusory authority. She is willing to admit the possibility that only such an illusion can supply adequate authority to maintain in perpetuity the institutions created through mutual pledging. But Arendt argues that, almost without the notice of the founders, a new kind of authority was discovered. Arendt believes that the American Revolution "made a new beginning in the very midst of the history of Western mankind" (*On Revolution* 194). Cavell finds this same thought to lie behind Emerson's words in the essay "Experience," "I am ready to die out of nature and be born again into this new yet unapproachable America I have found in the West." Cavell makes much of the expression "I have found." He connects these words to the idea of political founding, and thus suggests that Emerson's writing, far from being seen as, like many other Romanticisms, purely concerned with the individual, is truly political: "The endlessly repeated idea that Emerson was only interested in finding the individual should give way to or make way for the idea that this quest was his way of founding a nation, writing its constitution, constituting its citizens" (Cavell 1989: 93). For Cavell, Emerson's authorship is the reenactment of the nation's founding. And this is exactly what Arendt declares to be the nature of America's self-authorship, its authority. The act of foundation, says Arendt, creates the authority upon which to build the Union in perpetuity. And it calls for a renewal of the founding self-authorship in each generation. The literary voices calling for renewal, like those of Emerson and Thoreau, are both authorized by the Constitution and reconstitute its authority.[17]

The authority of the act of founding is, according to Arendt, born with the act itself. It comes from the newness of the act, the fact of a beginning having been made. The act of founding has no transcendent authority; it is its own "absolute." Arendt argues that

> this "absolute" lies in the very act of beginning itself. In a way, this has always been known, though it was never fully articulated in conceptual thought for the simple reason that the beginning itself, prior to the era of revolution, has always been shrouded in mystery and remained an object of speculation. The foundation which now, for the first time, had occurred in broad daylight to be witnessed by all who were present had been, for thousands of years, the object of foundation legends in which imagination tried to reach out into a past and to an event which memory could not reach. Whatever we may find out about the factual truth of such legends, their historical significance lies in how the human mind attempted to solve the problem of the beginning, of an unconnected, new event breaking into the continuous sequence of historical time. (*On Revolution* 204)

Arendt elsewhere uses the term "natality" to refer to the "absolute" of the "new event breaking into the continuous sequence of historical time" (*On

Revolution 205). The "new event" is most aptly symbolized as a new birth, as Arendt explains, whether it be the birth of a new ruler announced in Vergil's fourth Eclogue or the birth of the Christ child in the narrative found in the Gospels (see *On Revolution* 210–11). Discussing Vergil's fourth Eclogue, Arendt writes that the poem contains "the affirmation of the divinity of birth as such, that the world's potential salvation lies in the very fact that the human species regenerates itself constantly and forever" (*On Revolution* 211). If we return to the quotation of Emerson, "I am ready to die out of nature and be born again into this new yet unapproachable America I have found in the West," we see the same linkage between messianic birth ("born again" is a Pauline metaphor for becoming a "new man" in Christ) and founding that Arendt argues for. What is more, Emerson, like Arendt, sees this natality as a radical rupture with the prepolitical "state of nature." The new beginning of a founding birth cannot be grounded in or explained by the past. Its radical newness and singleness is what Rosenzweig speaks about in his discussion of the *B* term as coming into being as a radical singularity. Arendt's natality is what Rosenzweig refers to as the revelation of creation.[18]

The political philosopher Miguel Vatter has recently offered an interpretation of Arendt's concept of natality that places it squarely within the same conceptual horizon that Rosenzweig is working with in the *Star*. Vatter's treatment of Arendt makes no mention of Rosenzweig, but this does not at all diminish the remarkable convergence one may hear in his analysis between Rosenzweig and Arendt. Stressing Arendt's frequently reiterated quotation of Augustine's dictum "that there be a beginning, man was created" (*On Revolution* 211, for example), Vatter provides an interpretation of human natality or beginning that makes it the middle term between divine creation and redemption:

> The reference to divine creation in Arendt's concept of natality indicates that origin toward which natality tears life out of life (*zoe*) in order to throw it into the world, but not before having singularized it [*rendered it unique, the $B = B$ moment of singularity in Rosenzweig before the individual is subsumed as a mere member of a species*]. Natality is the caesura of life that turns men into creatures, linking the "fallenness" of nature directly to creation and redemption. [*Rosenzweig will speak of the human as responsible for the redemption of creation.*] In the awareness of being creatures, individuals not only understand that they are ultimately strangers in the world, that is to say, that no national or ethnic identity

(*nascio-*) can ever cor-respond to their natality, but also that they exist only as the subjectivity of life itself. Natality, by giving birth to singulars, is the freedom of biological life. (Vatter 2006: 157)

Vatter's reading of Arendt shows how close natality is to Rosenzweig's notion of creation. But in what follows, Vatter reveals the distance between Arendt and Rosenzweig. Arendt takes natality as the condition of freedom and political action. Vatter continues:

Political action, in so far as it intensifies the condition of natality, is to be understood exclusively in terms of the freeing of life, and in opposition to the totalitarian attempt to dominate biological life by dehumanizing it, that is, by eliminating singularity. This is what Arendt means when she pointedly refers to action as "the redemption of life." (Vatter 2006: 157)

In this passage we can read how political action is the "intensification of natality," how the particular "beginning" that makes its appearance in the world with the American Revolution promises to nurture and sustain within its constitutional institutions the future of democratic existence, of freedom, and of humanity itself. And we may also appreciate what drives Arendt to this politicization of creation. It is her wrestling with the challenge of totalitarianism. Rosenzweig drew his political theology from out the trenches of World War I; Arendt drew hers from the out of the fires of World War II.

Unlike Rosenzweig, to summarize, Arendt sees the birth of radical singularity as holding the promise of freedom within a democratic polity. Natality as the eruption of the new links divine creation to time. The authority upon which a democratic constitution is founded is precisely the authority of creation itself, the authority of the unpredictable eruption of freedom in the world. Upon this authority, individuals promise to one another to be faithful inheritors of freedom. This means that they will not allow the law to become a collection of mechanical rules, or their lives together to become a mere matter of convenience and routine. If we can draw Rosenzweig's category of Creation into relation with Arendt's notion of natality, we can find a new foundation for his political theology.[19] In the next chapter, I will turn to Cavell in order to translate Rosenzweig's categories of Revelation and Redemption into the idiom of a redemptive political theology, but I will devote the remainder of this chapter to Mendelssohn's political theology. It is for the purpose of reconnecting Rosenzweig and Mendelssohn on the plane of the political that I am invoking the aid of Arendt and Cavell, so it is appropriate that I spend some time making clear just what Mendelssohn's political theology entails.[20]

Mendelssohn's Political Theology

In the previous section I argued that Arendt offers us a concept of the political that challenges the Rosenzweigian-Schmittian sovereignty-based concept of the political. I quoted earlier in this chapter from Willi Goetschel's essay "Mendelssohn and the State." Willi Goetschel had claimed that Mendelssohn provides a much-needed "critical alternative to the sovereign-based theory of the state." Mendelssohn, according to Goetschel, focuses upon the "in-between space of critical exchange" in which "conflicting claims between different kinds of rights can reach a just adjudication" (Goetschel 2007: 476). According to Goetschel, Mendelssohn's theologico-political theory in *Jerusalem* develops a concept of power derived from Spinoza. Spinoza's concept of power stands in direct contestation with that of Hobbes. Spinoza conceives of power as different from "might" or "violence." Rather, power is, as Goetschel puts it, a "composite phenomenon, which is why it is impossible to reduce the complexity of political life to a mere calculus" (475). For Spinoza, power is the expression of a finite being's *conatus* or drive for self-preservation. This power is not the simple equivalent of the finite being's strength or might, but is rather the capacity of a being to act in accordance with its nature. For a human, as for every finite being, acting in accordance with nature means acting in consort with other beings. It means overcoming, to the extent it is possible, one's separateness and linking one's power with the power of others.

Although Goetschel would perhaps not want to place Arendt alongside Mendelssohn, I would claim that Arendt also stands within the Spinozist tradition of political philosophy. The contrast between Hobbes's concept of power as finite strength and Spinoza's concept of power as growing in intensity through the conjoining of separate finite beings into larger unities is at the heart of Hannah Arendt's political philosophy. The Spinozist concept of political power underlies both Mendelssohn's and Arendt's political philosophy because, like Spinoza, they view the democratic state as, ideally, the site of the mutual perfecting of the human capacity to create ever more expansive forms of life. In the previous section I discussed Arendt's concept of power, and now, as a way of approaching Mendelssohn, I want to spend some time explaining the Spinozist background of his (and, I am claiming, Arendt's) thinking about the constitution of the political. If in the previous section I explored the kinship between Rosenzweig's Creation and Arendt's natality, in this section I wish to join Arendt to Mendelssohn via Spinoza, and more specifically Spinoza's concept of God as *self-creating*. In this way, I hope to construct a bridge built upon the thematics of creation-natality-beginning that will join Mendelssohn and Rosenzweig.[21]

Spinoza draws the contrast between Hobbesian might and true power on the basis of a contrast between two ways that humans project goals for themselves: through a "confused" or "inadequate" self-representation (passion) or through a "clear" or "adequate" self-representation. Of course, Spinoza considers all projected goals to be the representation of a course of action that is already determined by prior causes, but this does not mean that the nature of these representations is irrelevant to the self-regulation of the individual. How one sees oneself—how one represents oneself—is crucial to how one's being comes to expression in the world. When passions (confused ideas) set the goals of action, the individual's goals are limited to the immediate satisfaction of "partialities" (inclinations and desires justified on the basis of taste or preference). The individual's self-representation is formed on the basis of the momentarily predominant partiality, and the individual thereby exists as a limited part of the causal nexus of nature and lacks any true power. When reason sets the ends of action, however, the individual's sights extend beyond the moment and its partialities to a future that extends beyond the limits of his or her limited mortal existence. The goal of rational action is set within ever-widening circles of human fellowship and beyond, into the embracing whole of nature. Representing oneself within an indefinite futurity and expansive community, one gains a truer representation of one's nature (as a being able to contribute to the "common weal" of the human community) and thereby one expresses one's true power. This is not to say that a representation *causes* action, only that it sets the context for the expression of such power as a finite being may possess. Power is expressed (actualized) more or less perfectly in direct proportion to the truth of one's self-representation. Put differently, true power *is* true self-representation.

For Spinoza, the goal of rational action—action based upon true self-representation—is to attain to as great a measure of *permanence* for oneself as is possible. Directed towards permanence, rational action actualizes the power of the finite human being to act in conformity with goals that draw the human closer to the only truly permanent being, God. The state, according to Spinoza, is the potential site of such permanence as humans are capable of. The state that is most able to foster rational action is the state that can attain the greatest share of permanence. For Spinoza, this is the democratic state, the state where the people are sovereign and their overriding goal is the preservation of their power to act, in other words, their freedom. Arendt agrees with Spinoza that the actualization of human power can only occur through rational action, taken in concert with others, and that the goal of rational action is permanence. Arendt, as we saw in the previous section, sees permanence as the achievement of what for her is the rational action *par excellence*, the act of founding the state. Foundation takes place only through the concerted action of individuals committed to achieving permanence *together*.

For Arendt, the permanence of finite beings is not grounded in the infinite power of God as it is for Spinoza, but rather in the inexhaustible source of all coming-into-appearance that, as we have seen, Arendt calls "beginning" or "natality." Arendt's natality is, like Spinoza's power, the self-expression of being. Indeed, in her discussion of "beginning," Arendt may be heard to paraphrase Spinoza's definition of God as a *causa sui*.[22] The "beginner," according to Arendt, is the creator of something new, but this something is not different from the creator. Rather, it brings to expression the creator *qua* creator in the form of a new principle of action, a new law. The creation of the creator is the creation of the principle by which to guide further action. But the principle that guides action, if it is to be true to its origin, is only: Begin again! The revolutionary beginning must ever repeat itself in order to be faithful to the spirit of the revolution. "What saves the act of beginning from its own arbitrariness," Arendt writes, "is that it carries its own principle within itself, or, to be more precise, that beginning and principle, *principium* and principle, are not only related to each other, but coeval." Arendt continues: "The absolute from which the beginning is to derive its own validity and which must save it, as it were, from its inherent arbitrariness is the principle which, together with it, makes its appearance in the world. The way the beginner starts whatever he intends to do lays down the law of action for those who have joined him in order to partake in the enterprise and to bring about its accomplishment" (*On Revolution*

212). Those who "partake in the enterprise" with the beginner do so by committing themselves to freedom, the freedom that founds and comes to expression in the enterprise of beginning. The claim that absolute, free beginning "makes its appearance in the world" when humans partake (they part-take) in the enterprise of freedom called "democracy" can describe Spinoza's as well as Arendt's political philosophy.

For Spinoza, the state whose founding was the perfect expression of rational action was the "Hebrew state" created when the Israelites left their bondage in Egypt and declared themselves subject to no mortal being, but only to God. They heard the voice of God proclaiming the Ten Commandments and accepted these laws voluntarily, entering in a covenant with God. Spinoza, who does not believe in miracles, would say that the people were unified in their commitment to rational action guided by the most inclusive possible representation of themselves as self-determining beings, that is, as beings only determined by God. The people saw themselves as conforming, as far as is humanly possible, to a timeless law appearing in their consciences and actualized in speech. Their covenant with God was their commitment to ground themselves in the source of permanence. Spinoza explains the collapse of this state as brought on by the separation of the law-giving and law-interpreting class—the Levitical tribe—from the rest of the people. When a priestly elite imposes its limited self-representation upon the community, democratic self-representation is destroyed. The establishment of a priestly elite in Israel, according to Spinoza, was a punishment for the sin of idolatry. After the people built the Golden Calf, God diminished their power of self-representation and installed the Levites over them. Again, to translate this into Spinoza's ontology, idolatry itself is the diminishment of the truth of self-representation. Idolatry is the fabrication of passion rather than reason. Idolatry is the sign of the dominion of partiality over universality, and the separation of a priestly elite from the whole of the people is simply the expression of idolatry in different form. The sin and the punishment of the sin are one. The fall from the ideal polity of the Hebrew state is the fall of the Israelites into paganism, the reduction of their power as creatures of God to imitate the divine through freedom and their self-enslavement to a representation of themselves as mere *things*. For Spinoza, as for Arendt, this dehumanization is the very perversion of the political into the merely natural. It turns the human with a capacity to give (finite) expression to God as *natura naturans* into a merely mechanical part of God as *natura naturata*.

Like that of Mendelssohn and Spinoza, Arendt's concept of power directly contests the idea that the law is the expression of the sovereign will and that the law's power is only as great as the coercive force of the sovereign will. Arendt appeals to a notion of power as emerging from covenant-making promises, and her ontological grounding for this power lies in her notion of natality. Mendelssohn justifies his notion of power within the context of his Leibnizian-Wolffian metaphysics, a metaphysics that he sees as derived from but also correcting Spinoza. The problem that the Spinoza-Leibniz-Wolff metaphysics seeks to solve is how to explain the relationship between God's infinite power and the power of finite beings. All of them solve this problem on the basis of what might be called *distributive immanence*. God acts within and through finite beings. Every finite being attains reality by expressing divine power. Mendelssohn thought that this power had a goal, namely, the raising of the extensive infinity of finite beings—imagine it as the sheer infinity of finite beings distributed throughout space and time—towards the intensive infinity of the divine, the one infinite power sustaining the whole without diminution or division in any part of the whole. What this means is that one kind of infinity—atomized, one could say—is being driven to realize another kind of infinity (the intensive infinity of God's power). Spinoza, as Mendelssohn understood him, had erred in simply equating the infinite power of God with the *additive sum* of the power distributed among the infinite number of finite beings.

If God's infinite power is not reducible to the sum of infinitely many finite powers, then it must stand in some other relation to these infinitely many powers. For Mendelssohn, this relation is that of the will towards a chosen goal. Finite beings are the means by which God realizes His will. His will is identical in every one of them: to create a unity out of their multiplicity. Finite beings realize God's power by forming new unities with other finite beings. Working with Leibniz's view that each finite being—the monad—is the site of a representation of the whole from a single point of view, Mendelssohn thought that finite beings formed unities with other finite beings—thereby gaining in perfection, being, and power—by representing themselves in the widest possible relationships with other finite beings. In other words, the will of God was realized in finite beings when finite beings' self-representations corresponded as closely as possible with the viewpoint of God. God's will and the representation guiding God's will (the most perfect arrangement of all finite beings) are brought into greater harmony. From the perspective of finite beings, the realization of God's will is only possible in the infinite future.

Today we may find Mendelssohn's Leibnizian conception of all finite beings as capable of (indeed defined as the site of) representations (mirrorings) to be hard to accept, but we may at least countenance such an idea in relation to human beings. Finite humans grow from atomized selves toward perfection by reconceiving themselves as participants (part-takers) within a wider unifying whole. They cannot be coerced by an outside force to choose this as their self-representation since no true unity can be imposed upon parts from without. Every unity among finite beings is achieved only by each expressing God's will for perfection. The space of the political, according to Mendelssohn, is the space within which humans are able to perfect themselves. It is also possible to use this space to attempt to impose the order of a single finite will upon other wills, whether through threats of violence or through the forceful suppression of the power of self-representation, the power of each individual to shape his own representation of the world. But Mendelssohn, like Spinoza, sees this attempt as ultimately self-defeating. In Chapter 1 (in "Writing and Mendelssohn's Dialectic of Enlightenment"), I spoke of Mendelssohn's theory of the "dialectic of enlightenment" in which human history is seen as the slow spiral of illusion and disillusion, of representational fixity and representational growth. Remember that for Mendelssohn the will of God can only be realized by slowly approximating throughout all finite representations the single representation of the whole that guides God's will. But no single finite representation, however expansive and widely drawn, can possibly be identical with God's representation of the whole. Therefore, enlightenment—the dismantling of one regnant representational schema in favor of another—is an infinite and infinitely repeated task.

Mendelssohn recognizes that democracy alone allows for the divinely appointed task of humans to perfect of the world together. In this regard, he is a more astute political thinker than, for example, many of his contemporaries in the newly constituted states of America. He understands that Locke's separation of the church as concerned with the postmortem fate of the (private) soul and the state as concerned with the this-worldly felicity of the (public) citizen can open the door for unwanted collusions between church and state. But most significantly, and this is a point that Willi Goetschel has underscored in his readings of Mendelssohn, religion cannot be privatized and detemporalized without impoverishing the human being, deforming the human being into a Hobbesian self whose obligations to others have but one dimension, the satisfaction of what Mendelssohn calls "appetitive urges" (*Jerusalem* 62). The deformation of the human is a form of *ugliness*. The beauty of human existence requires us to see ourselves—to orient ourselves—in relation to our place in creation as participants in what Arendt calls "the redemption of life." This reorientation is an ongoing process, and it can only take place when one is awakened to one's relation to the world not just as a part playing a predetermined role, but as a person standing as an inheritor of a world in need of further beautification. But to reorient oneself in this way, one must already see the world as a work of beauty, as *art*. This awakening to the world as art is, for Rosenzweig, part of what revelation means. That is, the world as a *creation* (the site of "natality") is part of what revelation opens before the soul. That this world calls forth a response to renew creation in love is something that both Mendelssohn and Rosenzweig agree upon. It is only Mendelssohn, however, who situates the loving act of recreation within the space of the political. In this chapter I have argued that Arendt points the way toward a rapprochement between Mendelssohn and Rosenzweig by showing, with her interrelated concepts of natality and beginning, how we might unpack the implications of Rosenzweig's concept of creation for a redemptive, democratic politics. In the next chapter I will show how the work of Stanley Cavell can provide the basis for completing the rapprochement between Rosenzweig and Mendelssohn by unpacking the political implications of Rosenzweig's concepts of revelation and redemption.

SEVEN

Beyond 1800: An Immigrant Rosenzweig

Introduction

In this chapter I imagine an "immigrant Rosenzweig." I will offer an alternative, democratic vision of political theology, one that draws from both Hannah Arendt and Stanley Cavell in order to illuminate aspects of Rosenzweig's thought that he himself did not foreground in his discussion of the nature of the state. I explained in the previous chapter that Arendt's concept of "natality," perhaps the key to her philosophical anthropology, is central to her understanding of how political action can be the realization of human freedom. Rosenzweig's discussion of creation as the eruption of an unforeseen and unique singularity—he speaks of it as the birth of the new—is, I argued, quite close to Arendt's concept of natality. Rosenzweig's notion of creation can serve, as natality serves in Arendt, to describe the *nonviolent* source of the revolutionary power by which democratic societies are founded and through which they are sustained. Natality plays a far less central role for Stanley Cavell than it does for Arendt, but he does use the term in connection with the inability to *count* humans in a serial order without remainder (a *totalizing* order, in other words) in his essay "Being Odd, Getting Even" (in Cavell 1988). Natality there names the inescapability of "the oddity of being born," the uncanniness of human existence (captured for Cavell in certain texts of Edgar Allan Poe) but also its promise of a new form of human "counting," one that precisely acknowledges the other in his or her singularity. Cavell calls such counting one that forgoes the violence of "getting even."

Although Cavell has interesting things to say about natality and violence, it is Arendt's notion of natality, I believe, that best allows us to connect Rosenzweig's concept of creation to a nonviolent, democratic politics. Having discussed Arendt in the previous chapter, I will in this chapter build upon this foundation and offer a translation of Rosenzweig's categories of revelation and redemption into the idiom of a redemptive democratic politics. I will rely upon Cavell's notion of democratic sociality as a form of "festive existence" brought to life in the ongoing conversation that is modeled in a genre of American films he calls "comedies of remarriage." Cavell argues that in the films he studies, marriage is undertaken without any epistemic or legal guarantees but only on the risky territory of what he calls *acknowledgment*. Acknowledgment forms the foundation of democratic sociality because it expresses the individual's *consent* to bear the burden of responsibility that comes with a commitment to conversation rather than monologue, the latter alternative, according to Cavell, being modeled in the film genre he calls "melodramas of the unknown women."

Cavell describes how acknowledgment within the comedies of remarriage is represented as the *creation and discovery of the woman*, of a human partner who can, though the give-and-take repartee of speech, bring the solitary Adamic self—Rosenzweig would call it the "defiant" self—out of his self-enrapture. Cavell's reading of the comedies of remarriage as the creation and discovery of the woman has much in common with Rosenzweig's description of revelation as it takes place between God as lover and the soul as beloved. When Rosenzweig declares that the love of the lover "in its essence ... is unfaithful, for its essence is in the moment; and so, in order to be faithful, it must renew itself every moment" (*Star* 176; 181), he could be said to summarize the moral of Cavell's comedies of *re*marriage. What is more, Cavell, like Rosenzweig, takes acknowledgment within the framework of remarriage comedies to be intimately connected to the giving and receiving of names. As Cavell points out, before Adam is able to recognize Eve as his "helpmeet" and give her a name, he must first discover language itself. Cavell says that "in order that something be a helpmeet, namely stand in that relation of other to a human being, that being must have equally the capacity to name, and the man must name her, know her, as his, as his to know, and to be known by" (1996: 28). Rosenzweig describes God's "call by the proper name" to the beloved soul to be the introduction of the speech of God as lover to the beloved: "Love me!" For Rosenzweig this command to love is the first and perhaps only commandment ("Gebot"). It is unlike what Rosenzweig calls "law" ("Gesetz") because it makes no provision for the future, it "knows only the moment" (*Star* 191; 197). It does not compel obedience but rather awaits the response of the beloved as an attestation of its reality, and the beloved, says Rosenzweig, begins in defiance and moves into a posture of trust in the love of the lover. Cavell, very much like Rosenzweig, sees the naming of the woman in the comedies of remarriage as a prelude to a proposal of marriage that is couched as a challenge and a plea: "Marry me," which can be unpacked as "Marry me at last; give up your defiance; trust me now, I will not let you down." "Naming the woman," Cavell writes in describing the remarriage comedies, "is characterized . . . as the man's generic requirement to claim her" (1996: 29). Once the woman accepts her name and relinquishes her defiant stance against the plea "Marry me," the conversation of marriage can begin. But, as Rosenzweig and Cavell both insist, the conversation between lover and beloved is one that must always be reinitiated.

As I have said, Cavell takes the conversation of remarriage comedies to be a model of how democratic sociality is formed from the consent of the citizens to assume the burdens of ongoing conversation. In melodramas like *Gaslight* and *Now, Voyager* the woman's voice is silenced, and this for Cavell is the condition of a sociality in which each individual remains within his or her mute separation. (Arendt calls this condition "loneliness" and describes it as the quintessential sociality of totalitarianism.) By bringing Rosenzweig's conception of revelation into relation with Cavell's discussion of (re)marriage, I will show how Rosenzweig's interpretation of the commandment to love can inform a democratic vision of the law of the state. Rosenzweig says about love that "each day it learns that it has never loved as much as today the part of life which it loves; every day love loves a little more that which it loves" (*Star* 176; 181). Democratic law grows as love grows and it attains its permanence as Rosenzweig says love does: "It increases because it does not want to cease being new; it wants always to be new in order to be permanent; it can only be permanent by living in the non-permanent, in the moment" (*Star* 176; 182). Democratic law opens ever-new horizons of conversation.

If Arendt's concept of natality can be brought into relation with Rosenzweig's concept of creation, and Cavell's notion of marriage with Rosenzweig's notion of revelation, what can we say about Rosenzweig's thought of redemption? Certainly, neither Arendt nor Cavell has much patience for a messianic redemption in the distant future, but then this is hardly the heart Rosenzweig's notion of redemption either. It is precisely in order to afford a connection between the lived here and now and the time of redemption that Rosenzweig places so much emphasis upon the annual round of the Jewish and Christian holidays. In fact, it is only truly in the Jewish round of holidays that eternity is mirrored and redemption is achieved, at least to the extent that it is possible to do so within time. The Christian year is really an open spiral, always opening up into the unredeemed history of the state and its life of "war and revolution." Can Arendt and Cavell offer an alternative to Rosenzweig's version of redemption as only lived in the holidays of the Jewish (and, to a lesser extent, Christian) year?

To answer this question, it is necessary first to recall that all three—Rosenzweig, Arendt, and Cavell—share a desire to join sociality and beauty. Arendt and Cavell both invoke Kant's *Critique of the Power of Judgment* and its concept of the *communicability* of the judgment of beauty without need of concepts or rules in order to explain how language can build a social world in the absence of epistemological guarantees. Rosenzweig views art in the Christian era as preparing the soul to step outside its absorption in God's love and enter into the communing fellowship of the church. For Rosenzweig, the goal of art is to incite us to seek to transfigure our lives into art works, into beautiful dances choreographed by the Jewish and Christian sacred years. But Arendt and Cavell put art and the realm of the beautiful more generally into relation with democratic sociality. I will argue that it is possible to draw Rosenzweig's notion of redemption into relation with democratic sociality if we conceive of democratic sociality as offering the chance to participate in *unchoreographed beauty*. I will, quite specifically, claim that Cavell's discussion of Fred Astaire in his essay "Fred Astaire Asserts the Right to Praise" (2005: 61–82) offers a way of understanding how Rosenzweigian redemption—embodied, as he claims, within a gathered community's offering of thanksgiving and praise—can be found even within the "secular" life of democracy. Cavell in that essay says that when Astaire appropriates African American tap routines as he dances with a shoeshine man in the film *The Band Wagon* (Vincente Minnelli, 1953), the question whether this dance calls upon us to offer praise rather than rebuke it as racist is "a religious matter, a redemptive matter" (79). I take it that Cavell is attempting, as Rosenzweig before him, to describe the conditions in which we may create lives of beauty together by acknowledging the claims of thanksgiving and praise that the world's manifold beauty makes upon us.

Rosenzweig and Cavell on Revelation

Over the past forty years, Stanley Cavell has engaged himself with artistic and philosophic works as diverse as *King Lear* and *Bringing Up Baby*, Plato's *Republic* and Thoreau's *Walden*, all with the aim of getting philosophy to speak the language of everyday sociality. Cavell wants philosophy to engage with our common humanness, to acknowledge the fragile conditions of our togetherness. Cavell draws upon Wittgenstein for the theoretical foundation of his understanding of how meaning in language depends upon accepted conventions and the open-ended improvisation they make possible. He goes beyond Wittgenstein by arguing that our moral life is also dependent upon these conventions, and upon the acknowledgment of our responsibility for recreating a shared human world by means of them. Cavell is no less concerned than is Arendt with the political dimension of our consent to the conventions that we inherit, and, also like Arendt, Cavell seeks to redeem us from the clichés that conceal the "quiet desperation" of our compromises with the world.

Cavell sees in philosophy's penchant for skeptical doubt concerning the existence of the external world and other minds a sign of our disappointment with the fragile and limited conditions upon which our moral lifeworld is built. Cavell shows in his readings of Shakespearean tragedies like *King Lear* and *Coriolanus* that this skepticism can lead to a pathological quest to secure oneself against the disappointments of our faith in the sincerity of others. In philosophy, skepticism can lead to ultimately futile efforts to provide faith with secure epistemological and metaphysical foundations, to replace the moral burdens of *acknowledgment* with the sure signs of demonstrable *knowledge*. Philosophy's task, according to Cavell, is to free us from our futile quest for certainty, a quest that is at the heart of the history of philosophy after Descartes. Philosophy for Cavell is a therapy for the malaise of philosophy.

We may immediately note the deep connection between Rosenzweig's and Cavell's conception of philosophy. Perhaps this connection is nowhere better attested than by comparing Rosenzweig's *Büchlein vom gesunden und kranken Menschenverstand* (*Little Book concerning the Healthy and Sick Common Sense*) with any one of a number of Cavell's essays.[1] Here is the opening of Rosenzweig's *Little Book*:

> Common sense is in disrepute with philosophers. Its usefulness is restricted to the buying of butter, the courtship of a lady, or it may even be of help in determining the guilt of a man accused of stealing. However, to decide what butter and woman and crime "essentially" [*eigentlich*] are, is beyond its scope.
>
> This is where the philosopher must enter and assume "the burden of proof." Such problems are beyond the reach of common sense. These are the "highest" problems, the "ultimate" questions. To be misunderstood by common sense is the privilege, even the duty of philosophy. What need would there be for philosophy if common sense could answer these questions by itself? Is common sense even capable of asking the questions? Where common proceeds in reckless haste, philosophy pauses and wonders. (*Little Book* 39)

Rosenzweig is both praising and cursing philosophy in this passage. Philosophy "pauses and wonders," yet its wonder is transformed into questions about "essences," questions that it claims are "beyond the reach of common sense." Rosenzweig's tone in describing philosophy's claim to transcend common sense is certainly one of sarcasm. If philosophy could transcend common sense it would manage to transcend the human condition. As Rosenzweig goes on to say: "The philosopher cannot wait. His kind of wonder does not differ from the wonder of others. However, he is unwilling to accept the process of life and the passing of the numbness wonder has brought. Such relief comes too slowly. He insists on a solution immediately—at the very instant of his being overcome—and at the very place wonder stuck him. He stands quiet, motionless. He separates his experience of wonder from the continuous stream of life, isolating it" (*Little Book* 40).

That philosophy begins in wonder is a claim as old as Plato. That philosophy can only find answers to its questions by returning to common sense in order to recuperate its sense of wonder is a view of a much later vintage. It is not the same as the one that David Hume offers after having demonstrated (to his satisfaction, at least) that common sense was built upon a tissue of unfounded inferences. Hume accepted the isolation of the philosophical perspective from that of everyday life, but he returned to life within the perspective of common sense out of necessity; to live out skepticism's rejection of causality and the continuity of selfhood would be madness. Rosenzweig will call such a necessary settlement with common sense "philistinism." Hume did not think that philosophy had somehow taken a false turn when it went from wonder to skepticism, or that wonder was somehow worth recovering. But this is exactly what Rosenzweig thinks: skepticism is a symptom of philosophy's false turn; philosophy's task is to recover from skepticism by recovering a sense of wonder.

In all of his writing, Cavell insists that philosophy begins with wonder and takes a false turn when wonder becomes a provocation to self-isolating skepticism. Here is one exemplary passage in which Cavell speaks of "a perception of the weirdness . . . of the usual," what Rosenzweig calls "wonder," as the beginning of philosophy and also the provocation to philosophy's misstep into skepticism.

> In writing about Samuel Beckett's *Endgame* I express this perception of the everyday as of "the extraordinary of the ordinary," a perception of the weirdness, or surrealism, of what we call, accept, adapt to, as the usual, the real; a vision captured in the opening pages of *Walden* when its writer speaks of his townsmen as appearing to be absorbed in fantastic rituals of penance, a perception of the arbitrariness in what they call necessities . . . The ordinary is ordinary because, after all, it is our habit, or habitat; but since that very inhabitation is from time to time perceptive to us—we who have constructed it—as extraordinary, we conceive that some place elsewhere, or this place otherwise constructed, must be what is ordinary to us . . . (Cavell 1988: 9)

Philosophy loses its way because it becomes entrapped in questions that deny the common sense perspective and thereby the very source of its wonder. Philosophy seeks a different world in which to live. The passage also reveals another point of similarity between Rosenzweig and Cavell. Cavell philosophizes in conversation with writers—Beckett and Thoreau, for example—who are not "professional" philosophers. Cavell's deliberate provocation against academic philosophy is exactly the one intended by

Rosenzweig's *Little Book*. Rosenzweig begins the *Little Book* with a warning "to the *expert*" that his work, despite its appearance of being merely "for the masses," is also meant for the expert.

Both Rosenzweig and Cavell take the ordinariness of the world to be an illusion, a "construction," of our habits, our "rituals," that let us live in the midst of the "weirdness," the wonder, of the world. When wonder shatters the illusion, it should not propel us to seek another world. Rather, wonder—if philosophy does not supervene upon it and turn it into an occasion to ask after a "higher reality" than common sense offers—places us *deeper* in the everyday, or differently connected to it. The ordinary world is not an illusion, but its *mere* ordinariness is. What is at stake for us in escaping from philosophy's temptation to call the common world we inhabit an illusion? According to both Rosenzweig and Cavell, what is at stake is, first of all, whatever chance for happiness in the world we may have. But more than our individual happiness is at stake. The world itself as a *common*, that is, as a *shared*, inhabitation depends upon our willingness to forgo our dream of dwelling "some place elsewhere" than this, imperfect world.

In focusing upon the temptation to turn wonder into skepticism and skepticism into a provocation to search for a "higher reality," Rosenzweig and Cavell locate the moment of Cartesian doubt as critical for the formation of modern philosophy. Both thinkers reject the effort to overcome Cartesian doubt through some privileged form of knowledge that would secure a foundation for philosophy. They do not seek to overcome skepticism, but to make it the starting point for the recovery of a connection to the world other than through knowledge. Cavell calls this connection *acknowledgment*; Rosenzweig speaks of it as *revelation*. For both thinkers, the postskeptical connection to the world begins as a form of passivity, a letting-be of what the world offers to us rather than a demand upon the world for a more trustworthy or secure set of *bona fides*. After this initial passivity, a passion for the world, a passion for sustaining it and bequeathing it, may be born.

Both Rosenzweig and Cavell view the world's sustenance and bequeathal to depend upon language, that is, upon our taking responsibility for language by becoming what Cavell calls "passionate" speakers. Passionate speech is "a mode of speech in or through which, by acknowledging my desire in confronting you, I declare my standing with you and single you out, demanding a response in kind from you, and a response now, so making myself vulnerable to your rebuke, thus staking our future" (*Philosophy the Day After Tomorrow* 185; hereafter *Philosophy Tomorrow*). Cavell goes on to suggest, in a discussion of Jane Austen's novels, that such passionate speech is like what Austen calls "making love," speech as prolegomenon to marriage. Rosenzweig also describes such loving speech in his analysis of the Song of Songs in the *Star*. The speech of the lovers must make its way, he says, into "the bright light of the streets" (*Star* 219; 228). It must be "fully true in the eyes of the multitude" (*Star* 219; 228). This is the coming-to-be of marriage, says Rosenzweig. "Marriage is infinitely more than love; marriage is the fulfillment on the outside" (*Star* 219; 228). For both Rosenzweig and Cavell, marriage symbolizes the fulfillment of passionate speech within a world that can sustain and bequeath the chance for the rebirth of passion.

If marriage emblematizes for both Rosenzweig and Cavell the world-building of passionate speech, the solitude of the tragic hero for both thinkers is the dramatic figuration of the failure of such speech, or, better put, the hero's loss of faith in it. Rosenzweig describes the soul before its acceptance of God's passionate speech in the command "Love me!" as being like the tragic self in classical and modern theater. God's call is a moment of revelation when the soul is taken out of its defiant self-armoring. Somewhat like Cavell, Rosenzweig also likens this defiant stance to the muteness of the tragic hero in classical drama whose silence is the last protest against the decree of fate. In modern tragedy, according to Rosenzweig, the hero's defiance ceases to be mute and takes on the lineaments of one consciousness in dialogue with others on stage. But the modern tragic consciousness, like that of Hamlet for example, is no less stubbornly defiant than that of the ancient tragic hero. Rosenzweig says that modern tragic figures are like modern philosophers, seeking to overcome the imperfection of their limited consciousness and find an absolute vantage point from which to know the world. The modern tragic hero, says Rosenzweig, "would basically have to have a perfect consciousness of himself and of the world" (*Star* 226; 234). Cavell reads Shakespeare's tragedies in exactly the same way, as the figuration of Cartesian skepticism's withdrawal from world in order to find an Archimedean point from which to create the world anew, on more perfect foundations than faith alone can provide. For both Rosenzweig and Cavell, modern philosophy and modern tragedy have a common origin: the loss of faith in the power of words to bear the weight of revelation, to give speech to wonder.

Rosenzweig and Cavell part ways when it comes to understanding how revelation and wonder may be recuperated and made once again part of a common world. It is not so much that Rosenzweig believes that God must be offered a habitation in this world and Cavell seems content to leave God out of the picture. If it were only a matter of "God-talk," Cavell would have no more difficulty finding common ground with Rosenzweig than he does with Levinas. In the following passage about Levinas we may hear, with only some slight transpositions, Cavell's response to Rosenzweig's notion that God calls the soul out from its tragic posture of defiance:

> Levinas's idea is that my openness to the other—to a region "beyond" my narcissism—requires a violence associated with the infinite having been put into me: he speaks of this intervention or aggression in images of trauma, breakup, monstrosity, devastation. [*Rosenzweig does not emphasize this moment of trauma, but he does seem to speak of it briefly when he describes how heroic defiance arouses in the* spectators *of tragedy "shudders of terror" which are like the soul's "tremors of respectful fear" at the moment that it hears God's call* (*Star* 182; 188).] This event creates as it were an outside to my existence, hence an isolated, singular inside. Now when I say, in response to Descartes's Third Meditation proof, that in Shakespearean tragedy (immediately in connection with *Othello*) this traumatic effect of the recognition of the existence of God is replaced by the idea of a finite other, violence and some sense of an infinite nevertheless remain. But in originating now in the face of a finite other, violence and infinitude cannot be thought to arise from a comparison of myself with the other but from a recognition that this particular other, this creature among all the creatures of the earth similar to me, is also, or rather is therefore, absolutely different, separate from me, I would say wholly other, the one I single out and before whom I am I, eternally singled out. It is the unbearable certainty of this separation to which the torture of skepticism over Desdemona's faithfulness is preferable. (*Philosophy Tomorrow* 145–46)

Cavell could thus reread Rosenzweig's description of God's revelatory command "Love me!" to which "there must be a response" (*Star* 193; 198–99) as not originating from an infinite Other, but from a finite other.

In fact, in the remarriage comedies Cavell discusses in his *Pursuits of Happiness* and elsewhere, he explicitly identifies the role of God in Genesis with that of man who must find a way to reawaken love in the woman from whom he has been divorced. The woman is like Eve, and the man like Adam. When God creates Adam, it is not at all clear that Adam knows who he is or what he is. He is alone, but only God knows this, whatever Adam may feel ("It is not good that the man should be alone," God declares in Genesis 2:18; KJV translation). Adam is thus not yet fully human, not yet fully in possession of the knowledge of what it means to be human. Only after God creates woman from his "rib" (or "side") and brings her before Adam does Adam recognize his humanity. It is God's doing to bring the two together, but it is Adam's responsibility to recognize (Cavell would say *acknowledge*) that another, separate being like himself stands before him. She is of him ("bone of my bones, and flesh of my flesh," he says of her; Gen 2:23); she shares one humanity with him, but she is not a replication of him, or able to be reincorporated by him. Adam must come to accept "the unbearable certainty of this separation" in order to discover a way to repair the separation, to "cleave" to the woman and, if only for a moment, to become "one flesh." For Cavell, this story is the Ur-text against which the remarriage comedies must be viewed. They represent the need within every relation between man and woman (I will at the end of this chapter have something to say about same-sex relations) to reexperience the pain of separateness and achieve humanity once more by betrothing oneself to the other, that is, by cleaving to the other in trust across the chasm that cleaves one from the other.

It may seem as if only Adam is active and Eve is a mere instrument of his gaining the full stature of his humanity. But Cavell reminds us that Adam's words of recognition upon seeing the woman ("bone of my bones, and flesh of my flesh") are not the end of the story. If there is a form of marriage enacted at this first encounter ("therefore a man shall leave his father and his mother, and shall cleave unto his wife; and they shall be one flesh," Gen 2:24), there is a need for the woman to participate in this enactment, and push its stakes even further. Thus Cavell explains why the next act in the drama is that of the woman acquiring knowledge that the man does not yet possess.

> "And when the woman saw that the tree was good for food, and that it was pleasant to the eyes, and a tree to be desired to make one wise, she took of the fruit thereof, and did eat, and gave also unto her husband with her; and he did eat." Evidently the woman eats first and, as the serpent had predicted, does not die; though perhaps something in her has died, her innocence, her blindness to her existence. But what is the promised connection with knowledge? Is it her knowledge that she and the man are separate, since she can disobey? ... The tale is careful to account for her taking the fruit from the tree—she had been told of

its powers, reassured about them, and saw for herself that the tree was pleasant and good for food. What does she know of the man and see in him? One can readily enough impose a speech for her here, insert a temptation, say a test, leading to a question: I know a taste you do not know. Will you continue with God's prohibition of this taste, or will you accept his promise to make a helpmeet for you and therefore know what I know? (*Contesting Tears* 2)

With her new knowledge, the woman sees the man as more innocent and as more naive than she is. Preston Sturges's remarriage comedy *The Lady Eve* begins at precisely this point in the Adam and Eve story. The man, Hopsy Pike (Henry Fonda), meets Eve (Barbara Stanwyck) after he has been on a year-long expedition to find a new species of snake in the Amazon River basin. The man is still a companion to snakes; the woman, a duplicitous gambler and card shark, has a preternatural (call it postlapsarian) hatred of snakes. The movie traces the man's acceptance of Eve's duplicity, his willingness to accept a form of knowledge—a knowingness—that is totally unlike what science can offer. The question that arises after Eve's tasting the fruit of knowledge (knowingness) is, will the man accept her in her new strangeness from him? It was one thing to see that the woman was like him when he compared her to all the other creatures of the earth that God brought before him ("this time, bone of my bones"). It is quite another to acknowledge that the woman is now different from him (divorced from him, as Cavell would say), and to join her upon her terms of betrothal. Adam will eat the fruit, but it does not "close some gap or fill some want of knowledge," as Cavell says, but rather it makes the chasm separating him from Eve now fully known to him. The knowledge which can close the cleavage between them (recall that *to know* can mean *to have sex* in biblical Hebrew) is also the knowledge that each of them, separately, bears responsibility for good and evil. Adam may try to blame Eve and Eve may try to blame the serpent, but they know that they are guilty because they already feel the burden of their punishment: Their desire for one another cannot ever be fully satisfied. They have become strangers to one another, and each feels the need to cover a nakedness that before was innocently and un-self-consciously revealed.

Now, after both have tasted the apple, marriage—cleaving to the other—cannot be the restoration of an original unity, but the declaration that two can love even in their separateness, in their strangeness to one another.

From now on, the knowledge of love cannot be separated from one human's inability to know the other. "Then what is wanting—if marriage is to be reconceived, or let's say human attraction—is for the other to see our separate existence, to acknowledge its separateness, a reasonable condition for a ceremony of union" (Cavell 1996: 22). But philosophy, as the love of knowledge, remains tempted by another kind of union with the other, one that can only lead to tragedy. Cavell finds philosophy's quest for a prelapsarian knowledge to be figured in what he calls "melodramas of the unknown woman." Rosenzweig speaks of something perhaps a bit more comic when he talks in the *Little Book* about someone who breaks off an engagement because, over the course of the months after his proposal, he has come to feel that his fiancée's "essence" remains unknown to him and he is no longer certain, despite whatever she may say, that she is the same person she was when he proposed.

There are so many points of convergence between Rosenzweig and Cavell that, as I have said, it would be easy to gloss over the differences, the presence of God in Rosenzweig and His absence in Cavell. Cavell himself imagines someone saying about the convergences between his thought and that of Levinas that when he, Cavell, says that overcoming our temptation to *know* the other rather than *acknowledge* the other's separateness requires an "investment of a certain kind in a particular finite other," this investment is "equivalent to the idea of God" (*Philosophy Tomorrow* 151). Cavell is willing to accept that this may be true, but he is not willing to declare himself, therefore, a "religious" thinker. I am also not interested in drawing Rosenzweig and Cavell together to this extent. What I do want to stress, whatever we may say about the religiosity of Cavell's thought, is that he is altogether different from Rosenzweig when it comes the question of the nature of the political. For Cavell, (re)marriage that begins with acknowledging the separateness of the other is the emblem of democratic sociality. Marriage, Cavell likes to say, is like Kant's notion of the beautiful: there is no rule or concept by which to judge in advance whether two humans "fit." Marriage is the "union" that permits humans to live with one another without, as Rosenzweig would say, sharing an "essence," or, as Cavell puts it, by virtue of participating in one "universal" or "concept" (see his discussion of collecting and classifying in *Philosophy Tomorrow* 238ff.). For Cavell, the conditions of the possibility of marriage are the conditions of the possibility of democratic sociality. Democratic sociality is not based on an "essence" that "naturalizes" the citizen for membership in the nation. Rather, "naturalization" means divesting oneself of one's "given" identity and freely assuming responsibility for participating in the social contract.

Rosenzweig does not make the move from marriage to democratic sociality. The reason for this, as I have explained in the previous chapter, lies in the fact that he does not believe that consent is the basis of the state's constitution. The state is the realm of violence, and therefore love—even the fraternal love of the next one that, exactly as Cavell insists, acknowledges the separateness and singularity of the other—can only stand in opposition to the state. Rosenzweig describes marriage as "love's fulfillment on the outside," the "miracle made public" (*Star* 219; 228), and so far seems to agree with Cavell. But the next step into the place where love is made public is not a recommitment to the democratic union, but the soul's entrance into the Jewish and Christian choreographies of eternal life. The Christian choreography, unlike the Jewish, remains a part of the unfolding of world history as it attempts to weave the love of the next one into the violent fabric of the life of the state. But, as I have argued above, the attempt to relate to the next one as a "brother" and fellow child of God lifts the other into an ecclesial communion that is supranational and apolitical. Cavell, however, sees what he calls acknowledgment not as the recognition of an apolitical fraternity, but as a renewal of a *contract*. The possibility of divorce that is inherent in the marriage contract is precisely parallel to the possibility of the ordinary world becoming *merely* ordinary. A contract whose validity rests only upon habit is a contract that has lost its force as a *passionate utterance*, that is, as an expression of the immediacy of love.

But we can imagine another path for Rosenzweig to follow, one that takes the "defiant" soul out of its tragic isolation into the conversation of democratic sociality. In his *Little Book*, Rosenzweig makes no mention of Judaism or Christianity. His proffered "cure" for the individual who has lost faith in ordinary language to convey "essences" is to show how the quest for essences ends in nothingness, the vacuum left when the world is lost because thought has lost itself in a quest for knowledge and certainty. To return the individual to a faith in names as capable of bearing the weight of our tread in the world, Rosenzweig must show how to give them traction again. What Rosenzweig does in the *Little Book* is lead the reader who is suffering from "*apoplexia philosophica*" through a brief history of the effort to "define" God, Man, and the World. In every case, the definition ends by defining nothingness. When each term is taken separately, there is no "there there." God, Man, and World come into being together, and this being is not accessible otherwise than through language. Put differently, language is where God, Man, and World are present to and before one another.[2]

Of course, we must not personify language, as if it were itself a speaking subject. But language has a certain logic, according to Rosenzweig, in virtue of being, as he claims, a transaction between all of humanity and all of the world. Human language does not merely exist as a collection of disparate languages without any unity. If this were the case, each language would not be able to be called *human* language. But if there is no essence of man, what enables us to speak about "human" language? For Rosenzweig, all languages are human because they are able to be translated. There is no Ur-language, only many languages, but within each there is a potential for translation. This potential is present because humans share a world of things together, and the many names for the same thing in the many languages allow us to find a way to communicate, to translate, one name into another. Never perfectly, never with absolute precision, never without remainder or loss of meaning, but well enough to get along for the present. The future may bring us unexpected surprises, and teach us that our translations were faulty. And so we try again, seek to clarify our assumptions, seek to learn from our mistakes. The task is endless, but it is not worthless, or doomed. The task is endless not only because languages are not merely phonic transformations of one another, sharing identical "meanings." The task is endless because within each language we are ever engaged in a kind of internal translation, extending words into new contexts, inventing new words. Call this the poetic dimension of a language. So long as the world remains unredeemed, the task of translation continues. "Nothing teaches more clearly that the world is not yet redeemed," Rosenzweig says in the *Star*, "than the multiplicity of languages" (313; 328). Redemption, then, is the redemption of language. As we will see, this is precisely Cavell's conception of redemption as well.

As Hilary Putnam has observed in his introduction to the new English edition of the *Little Book*, the picture that Rosenzweig offers of what makes language human—its inbuilt translatability, that is, capacity for the recontextualization of its words—is very close to Wittgenstein's notion of language. What Rosenzweig foregrounds is how this recontextualization potential can be seen as a glimpse of the oneness of humanity in the presence of a common world. The translatability of language bears a moral imperative to let words flow and not attempt to fix them with one, orthodox, meaning. But can we not perhaps evade this imperative? Might we not dictate correct usage? Might we not legislate against poetry? (Plato thought it ought to be done.) Here is where Cavell and Rosenzweig will part ways, as we have already seen. Rosenzweig believes that the only surety humanity has against the threat of linguistic dictatorship and the silencing of the flow of words is the unmasterable Word of God as it is lived in the world by Jews and Christians. Cavell, on the other hand, sees democracy as the sheltering structure for the demands and joys of our mutual translations of one another, our passionate conversations.

But I imagine Rosenzweig in conversation with Cavell. I imagine an "immigrant" Rosenzweig who has found himself on American shores and has, like Cavell, read Emerson and Thoreau. He has watched the remarriage comedies, and he has glimpsed the promise of a democratic use of film by such directors as Frank Capra and Howard Hawks and Preston Sturges. I imagine Rosenzweig, perhaps, granting that the Word of God, as Cavell suggests in his reading of remarriage comedies as rewriting Genesis, may even be translated into the idiom of such art as sustains the dreams of this nation. He may even, like Cavell, find some glimpse of redemption in this common life.

Festive Existence: Rosenzweig and Cavell on Redemption

Cavell speaks about marriage as not only the acceptance of the separateness of the other (and therefore a renunciation of what he calls the temptation of a prelapsarian "incestuous knowledge"), but also of the need to repeat this acceptance every day, to awaken each day to this as one's task. "The transformation of incestuous knowledge into erotic exchange is a function I call the achievement of the daily, of the diurnal, the putting together of night and day (as classical comedy puts together the seasons of the year), a process of willing repetition whose concept is the domestic, or marriage" (1996: 82). I believe it is in his *Pursuits of Happiness* that Cavell introduces the theme, pervasive in all his later writing, of the "achievement of the daily." The theme comes up for its lengthiest treatment in Cavell's discussion, in the book's final chapter, of the film *The Awful Truth* (Leo McCarey, 1937). In discussing this remarriage comedy, Cavell wonders about the very source of comedy and he argues that it is not events that are comedic but rather our "attitude toward events" (*Pursuits* 238). Cavell points to the fact that the conclusion of remarriage comedies is not marked by a ceremony of marriage with an accompanying festival that closes the movie, as in Shakespeare's comedies, but rather the conclusion points forwards to a life lived in the manner that the couple in the movie have been seen to live it, as one continuous festival. The events in the movie are comedic because they are part of "a run of laughs, within life" (*Pursuits* 239). They are part of the "conversation of marriage," and this ongoing conversation embodies what Cavell calls "festive existence" (*Pursuits* 239).

What remarriage comedies reveal to us, Cavell argues, is how to lead life in the absence of sacred festivals authorized by religious tradition. They teach us to lead life as the continual reinvention of festival out of the dailiness of the everyday. They show us what it means to turn what in Yiddish is termed *vochedik* into what is *yontovdik*, the secular day into the holy day. I invoke the Yiddish terms because of their root meanings: *weekly* and *good day*. The Yiddish terms are informed by a distinction between the secular and the holy as a distinction between the six weekdays of creation and the Sabbath as the conclusion of the week, the day that parallels the final blessing of God over all creation, that it is "very good." The modern German *wöchentlich* that is cognate with the Yiddish *vochedik* means only "weekly" in the sense of what recurs every seven days and has no similar contrastive pairing with a term referring to sacred or festive time. The holy day, the *yontov* or the holiday, is a day on which one says of existence that it is good. It is a day of *praise*. I will later draw Cavell's discussion of festive existence into relation with his discussion of praise, but for now I would say that the festive existence which Cavell is speaking about is one that depends upon our willingness to call life "good"—to judge it to be beautiful—not on the basis of pre-established norms or concepts of what constitutes goodness or beauty, but rather because of what is unexpected, out of the ordinary. That the Sabbath should supervene upon the six work days is surprising. God's work is finished in six days and creation seems finished, too. But one more thing, a day, supervenes upon the work week, a day that does no work, but is only there as, one might say, a perpetual surprise: There is more to this creation than could be predicted in advance. But this surprising day is not altogether separate from creation. It repeats itself in the midst of the days of creation; it is the day on which humans are called upon to rededicate themselves to creation. Such rededication is what Cavell speaks about when he says that the conclusion of the remarriage comedy is not a wholly different existence from what the movie has shown us of the lives of the couple beforehand, but rather the achievement of a new attitude towards that life, as a life that is, in its repetitions and dailiness, worth rededicating oneself to, worth one's devotion.

> As the technical, or artistic, problem of the conclusion of the members of the genre of remarriage is that of providing them with epitomizing density [I would say, providing them with their Sabbath, their *yontov*], the artistic problem of the beginning of *The Awful Truth* is to preserve its diurnal surface, to present comic events whose dailiness is not interrupted by comic outbreaks but whose drift is towards a massive breakthrough to the comic itself as *the redemption of dailiness, a day's creation beyond itself.* (*Pursuits* 242; italics mine)

When Cavell speaks about the conclusion of remarriage comedies as offering "the redemption of dailiness" and "a day's creation beyond itself," I hear him to be directly transcribing the movement in the Bible's creation story from six work days to a "day beyond itself," a day beyond the other days, a day that redeems the other days: the Sabbath.

What Cavell is then saying is that, because we today no longer can secure our festivals and sacraments—our very redemption—on the basis of the authority of religious tradition, we must secure them on the basis of our ability to become revelations to one another. Thus he writes in the chapter on *The Awful Truth*:

> Kierkegaard wrote a book about our having lost the authority, hence so much as the possibility, of claiming to have received a revelation. If this means, as Kierkegaard sometimes seems to take it to mean, the end of Christianity, then if what is to succeed Christianity is a redemptive politics or a redemptive psychology, these will require a new burden of faith in the authority of one's everyday experience, one's experience of the everyday, of earth not of heaven (if you get the distinction). (*Pursuits* 240)

One's faith in one's experience of the everyday, according to Cavell, is called into question—in the register of philosophy—by skepticism, and in the register of remarriage comedies, it is called into question by the seeming faithlessness of each member of the marriage to that which initially brought them together. Their lives together are shown to have become mired in dullness, routine, "dailiness." Their lives have become entirely *vochedik*. The words they use with one another, even their very names for another, have slipped into mere repetitiveness, into mere clichés. But there is no other language in which to discover redemption than the one that has become deadened into mere ordinariness. The task is not to escape into some new language, but to reenliven the language we already share. I have previously spoken about Rosenzweig's belief that humanity's oneness is revealed in the promise of translation across languages, the possibility of communicating across the differences of language. I have said that this task, for Rosenzweig, is not different from the task of communicating within one language. It is always a matter of translation, of finding new ways of saying things. This is what Cavell means, I claim, when he speaks about the need to "redeem language" from its fall into clichés.[3]

Cavell speaks about the redemption of language as emblematized in the remarriage comedies when the man or the woman break into song. Song symbolizes the transformation of words repeated in dullness into words shared as an expression of praise, of saying together "this is good." As Cavell says about the song "The Man on the Flying Trapeze" that figures significantly in Frank Capra's remarriage comedy *It Happened One Night*: "Its folk song alternation of verse and refrain allows Capra to get from it not only a general occasion for an expression of social solidarity, but a specification of this solidarity as one in which individual (taking the verse) and society (giving the refrain) exchange celebratory words with one another in harmony and with pleasure" (*Pursuits* 249). For Cavell, the act of rededicating oneself to one's marriage vows, of undertaking them in order to turn ordinary life into a festival, the *vochedik* into the *yontovdik*, can symbolize the refoundation of democratic sociality. It can lead to the society raising its voice in song. This is, as I will presently show in more detail, the translation of the religious festival into the festival of democracy, celebrated in praise of an achievement of "high-flying" beauty and grace.

Cavell is unmistakably gesturing towards a reading of remarriage comedies as allegories of redemption outside ecclesiastical structures and liturgies, of finding new ways of joining together in songs of praise and celebration, of observing the holy days without the mediation of clergy. We have seen that Cavell insists upon the need to rededicate ourselves on a daily basis to such forms of redemption as our sociality may provide, with marriage being emblematic of all those that are based upon no form of coercion and upon no other authority but that of one's willingness and capacity to praise the goodness of the world. But here arises the crux of the problem for Cavell that Rosenzweig's appeal to the sacred holidays of Judaism and Christianity avoids: in an unredeemed world, how dare one praise goodness? For Rosenzweig, the holy days are days during which redemption is experienced precisely outside of history. For Cavell, redemption is a matter of the transfiguration of the everyday, within history.

But how can we praise the everyday when there are so many who are excluded by one form of injustice or another from its joys, its "grand laughs"? Speaking about the scene in *It Happened One Night* when a down-and-out group of bus riders join together in "The Man on the Flying Trapeze" until it is noticed that one member of the "chorus," a nursing mother, has fainted from hunger, Cavell puts the question:

> Is the idea that society has skidded *because* it, or its leadership, was blindly drawn away from attending to its business? . . . Or is it that the solidarity is compromised by those who are left outside the song of society—ones too poor to sing, whom private good will must pause to succor . . . ? (*Pursuits* 249)

To some extent, the song of praise for the achievement of the "man on the flying trapeze" is compromised by the fact that there are those who, for no good reason, are denied the hope of attaining such heights. A truly democratic society is not one where everyone's attainments are identical, but rather where everyone's aspirations can equally flourish and where nobody's "pursuit of happiness" is predetermined to failure. To sing together must not be a way of turning one's back on the next one who is excluded, but rather it must heighten the sense that the song is not yet finished. The song holds the promise of what may yet be achieved.

Cavell makes the point that every act of communal praise must also hold a rebuke against injustice in his discussion of Fred Astaire's dance number in *The Band Wagon*. In this number, Astaire plays a "has-been" movie dancer. On a trip to New York to discuss a possible comeback in a Broadway musical, Astaire enters a Forty-second Street arcade filled with such things as a booth with a large question mark on its side, another booth for taking self-portrait photographs, a shoeshine stand where a black man works, and other such commonplaces of somewhat degraded popular festivity. Cavell points out that Astaire breaks into his dance number after distractedly recalling a tune with a series of *da-da-da*s sung to himself. The scene and the "proto-song," according to Cavell, are a way of setting up the audience's vision of a merely humdrum, ordinary world, where all the fun seems forced and the one person who works in the arcade—the shoeshine man—is marked as being excluded from sharing even those degraded pleasures that his fellow citizens (all white) pursue as they stroll in self-absorbed distractedness, like Astaire when we first see him, through the arcade. Astaire trips over the outstretched legs of the shoeshine man and is then invited by him to join in a dance that becomes a pas de deux. After the pas de deux, Astaire, in Cavell's words, "moves into a trance-like solo, quasi-dancing, quasi-singing" (*Philosophy Tomorrow* 24). This entranced dancing in the movie is meant to be seen as heralding Astaire's comeback. But for Cavell it also emblematizes what dancing means, that is, dance as the transfiguration of the merely everyday body into a sort of divinized body, a body held in possession by a god. In this dance, Cavell says, we see Astaire's "having found his feet again, or having re-found his body" (24). Thus, in this ecstasy of dancing Astaire redeems his earlier degraded "out of body" existence, his failure to have joined mind and body in the joyous twirlings of his dance.[4]

But what about the black shoeshine man and his dance? Is he only a prop to prepare for Astaire's redemption?[5] If this were the case, then any redemptive politics that Cavell may hope to build upon the power of a society's shared ecstatic transfiguration of the everyday into a festival would be horribly blighted by its blindness to the injustice in its midst. Who could dance when another human is chained to the base of his stage? Cavell answers that Astaire's dance does not turn the black shoeshine man into a prop, but rather that Astaire's ecstatic rediscovery of his body begins when he joins the black man in a pas de deux, and that this rediscovery calls the movie viewers' eyes away from the gaudy machines of fun in the arcade to the dance of the white man and the black man. The spectators of the movie glimpse an "everyday miracle": "One bio-ethnological form of life has reciprocally interpenetrated another, producing an everyday miracle, namely one human being's recognition of and by another, a defeat of self-absorption, the creation of a small 'we'" (Cavell 2006: 306). The "small 'we'" created on screen for us is a vision of a more capacious "We, the people," a democratic people reborn with each "everyday miracle" that defeats the individual's "self-absorption."

When Astaire at the end of his number exits the arcade, the shoeshine man is left behind as he and Astaire "enter into a perfectly recognizable, and perfectly executed, end of a dance, a walk off" (*Philosophy Tomorrow* 76). Cavell argues that this walk off, although it leaves the shoeshine man on his knees after a final brushing of Astaire's suit, is not, or does not have to be read as, an endorsement of racial discrimination or the appropriation of black dancing by white artists like Astaire. The shot in which this exit is captured also captures the movie marquee title *The Proud Land* above Astaire's head. Cavell uses this as evidence that the dance scene is an allegory of democratic sociality:

> I take the placement above the center of the entrance/exit to suggest that the Arcade itself is a portrait or allegory of the proud land, call it America, containing not only amusements and occupations and false promises for those with nothing better to do, but a territory of magic or exemption in which such things as that walk-off can form themselves. I have called it perfect in recognition and execution. I mean that it demonstrates that these two can dance together—for a while—on an equal basis, equally choreographed, equally standing, equally kneeling, equally happy with the knowledge of their achievement in their joint work, a momentary achievement of the Kingdom of Ends, a traumatic glimpse of Utopia. But it demonstrates at the same time that they cannot leave the scene of entertainment together, and cannot for no good reason. This is against reason, against the scene of mutuality (of mutual legislation you might say) that we have witnessed. (*Philosophy Tomorrow* 78)

What is at stake for Cavell in this scene is the right to praise the beauty of the dance. Cavell argues that if we deny ourselves this right because the dance takes place in an unredeemed world, we forgo whatever chance we may have to know redemption in this world or to know what redemptive politics strives for.

To praise Astaire's dance is to see in the brilliant light of its beauty the terrible conditions of injustice that make it possible. Cavell argues that Astaire himself wished to praise the art of black dancing to which he knew his own artistic achievement was indebted. We cannot praise Astaire without a sense that in doing so we are complicitous with the evil of racial injustice. But if we therefore judge the world to hold nothing good within it that we can praise, have we not thereby declared that the movement from this world to a redeemed world demands nothing less than the destruction of this world? I take it that Cavell is speaking against apocalyptic politics when he invokes his conception of the holiday and festive life as part of a "redemptive politics."

The first step on the path of this redemptive politics must be a revisioning of *this world*, a reimagination of our world as already containing within it the promise of redemption. Indeed, the praise of what this world reveals when it is seen as a "territory of magic" can be a political act in so far as it forms a new community out of those willing to acknowledge their guilty complicity in the exclusions of this world and then assume responsibility for taking the first step in healing these exclusions by becoming a community of praise. For Cavell, this community of praise is a vanguard community, a community of the future, a community living beyond the present insofar as the present is merely what slips inexorably into the past. A community of praise draws the future into the present, making it alive (and to that extent effective) in the here and now. Cavell agrees with Emerson and Nietzsche who, he says, "understand the future as a discontinuous, unprecedented transfiguration of, and from, the present" (*Philosophy Tomorrow* 80). This is a decidedly anti-apocalyptic vision of the relation between present and future, and it is one that Rosenzweig shares. The difference between Cavell and Rosenzweig is that Cavell does not think that those whose lives are shaped by the diurnal cycle of the everyday and the holiday must forgo participation in the life of the state. Indeed, only those who form ever-renewed communities of praise can claim to keep alive the consensual basis of the democratic state.

Together, the community praises the world it sees as "good," but at the same time, as we have seen, there is a rebuke against the world as it stands as still imperfect, a world of exclusions that remain to be overcome. This rebuke is an admission of guilt, a confession of complicity, however unintended. If this confessional rebuke is not heard, then the festival becomes idolatrous. Rosenzweig's description of the Jewish holy days of redemption—the ten Days of Awe between Rosh Hashanah and the Day of Atonement—emphasizes, as Cavell does, that the individual can form a member of a community of praise only if he or she is first willing to become a member of a community of self-rebuke. The community moves from the Day of Atonement towards the Festival of Booths, the holiday of redemption celebrated within unredeemed time. Before it can celebrate this "holiday of Redemption upon the soil of unredeemed time," as Rosenzweig calls it (*Star* 347; 364), the people must pass through the communal acknowledgment of guilt on the Day of Atonement. Rosenzweig declares that it can only be God who forgives the community because the community cannot forgive itself. For Rosenzweig, to confess one's sin on the Day of Atonement is to stand together before God with all of humanity, although each Jew remains single and solitary in his or her guilt. In the communal confession, each Jew is like "a dead man in the midst of life," someone who knows no future, only the burden of the past. "Everything is behind him," Rosenzweig says (*Star* 347; 363). The confessing individual joins with others to ask forgiveness in order to have a future, in order to not remain dead in the midst of life. To have a future is to be resurrected from the deadness of a life burdened by the weight of the past.

The Jewish married male, Rosenzweig reminds us, traditionally wears on the Day of Atonement the white overgarment (the *kittel*) in which he was married and in which he will be buried. On the Day of Atonement, the *kittel* does not look backward to the wedding day, but forward to one's death. The *kittel* reminds the wearer that he is mortal. In his *Little Book*, Rosenzweig explains that the human has a tendency to want "to step outside the current" of life in order to "elude death" (102). "If living means dying," Rosenzweig writes, "he prefers not to live" (102). The individual *haunts* his body, and this, says Rosenzweig, is the beginning of philosophy's illusion that the *essence* of Man is an immortal soul that cannot die, the so-called ghost in the machine. The Day of Atonement draws the individual out of his or her "artificial life" as it calls upon the community to acknowledge that, to one extent or another, each individual during the past year has merely *haunted* his or her life. The pain that this haunting causes others results from the deadening of the moral sensitivity to the flesh-and-blood existence of the other. On the afternoon before the Day of Atonement it is customary to ask forgiveness of one's neighbors and loved ones for the pain one has inflicted upon them. But on the Day of Atonement, the Jew asks forgiveness of God for having severed the living connection of soul and body. Donning the *kittel*, one acknowledges one's mortality. Only in this way can the judgment of death be averted. Passing through the crisis of judgment, the people can then enjoy the holiday of Redemption in unredeemed time, the Festival of Booths five days later.

The Festival of Booths is a festival of hope in the midst of wandering, as Rosenzweig says: "Redemption is not present in this holiday of Redemption; it is only hoped for, it is awaited in the wandering" (*Star* 340; 356). Significantly, the Festival of Booths is a festival that celebrates the fragile home that is the site of the ongoing "marriage" between God and the people that was entered into at Mt. Sinai. The Jewish people "may not linger under the protective shadow of Sinai" but must "go into the world" (*Star* 339; 355). Much as Cavell describes the need to continually recapture life's diurnality through assuming the risk of remarriage, Rosenzweig says that the people, while dwelling under the "lightly built roof" of the sukkah, "remember that also the house of today's day at any given time, may it be ever so alluring for rest and as a secure dwelling, yet is only a tent that permits temporary rest" (*Star* 339; 355). The Festival of Booths does not follow immediately upon the holidays of revelation, Passover and Shavuot, but comes shortly after the Day of Atonement, the day on which the community acknowledges its guilt before God of having allowed life to become "artificial life," the merest haunting of the world. Haunting must give way to festive wandering, the communal embrace of the gift of the day, of diurnal transience.

Cavell, no less than Rosenzweig, understands that if humans are to awaken to life's diurnal festivity they must acknowledge their mortality. The festive existence of the day is conditioned upon the remembrance of what the day may bring, and that every day must disappear for a new day to appear. Near the conclusion of *The Senses of Walden*, Cavell invokes the New Testament book of Revelation and its prophecy of the ultimate Judgment Day in order to explain Thoreau's call for what Cavell describes as a "repeopling" of heaven and earth.

> In Revelation the Son said that he will come as the bright and morning star, and that to him that overcometh he will give the morning star. The morning star is also . . . Lucifer. The identity of Christ and Lucifer either is a curse, or else it will eventually preside over our transformation. We dead will awaken not upon judgment, but because the day of judgment will be foregone, in favor of dawning. (*Senses of Walden* 115–16)

If Thoreau's readers hear the call for "transformation" and awaken to a new day as a new people, they will be prepared to rebuild their homes and repeople this American continent, but with a full knowledge that "America exists only in its discovery" and therefore can never be *settled*. At best, this new people can build fragile structures open to the stars. One might aptly call Thoreau's experiment at Walden precisely the construction of a sukkah and the call for his "neighbors" to join him, to share this festive existence with him. Cavell traces many biblical metaphors and themes in his reading of *Walden*, but this is one that he missed.

Thoreau's *Walden* in Cavell's interpretation of it places its readers in the position of the confessing community of the Jewish people on the Day of Atonement. It calls upon its readers to acknowledge the "one sin of the ever same human heart," as Rosenzweig puts it (*Star* 344; 361), the sin of eluding the responsibility that attends our shared mortality, the sin of turning life into a living death. Commenting on the sentence in *Walden* (chap. 2, par. 22) in which Thoreau says that "Be it life or death, we crave only reality," Cavell writes of the sin of merely haunting our lives and the possibility of "reversing our direction" (he might have said *repentance*, from the Hebrew *t'shuva* for *returning*) by choosing life rather than death as our reality:

> We crave only reality; but since "We cannot know where we are" (xviii, 16) and only "esteem truth remote" (ii, 21)—that is, we cannot believe that it is under our feet [*immediately preceding the verse in Deuteronomy where Moses says that God has given the Israelites the choice between life and death, he says that God's commandment is neither in the heavens nor across the sea, but it is "very close to you, in your mouth and in your heart" (Dt 30:14)*]—we despair of ourselves and let our despair dictate what we call reality. . . . It follows that this life has been chosen; that since we are living and pursuing it, we are choosing it. (*Senses of Walden* 72)

But our choice of life, so long as it is made without reflection and is not preceded by a reversal of our direction, by our reorientation, as Rosenzweig would call it, is a choice that only confirms our "artifical" life, as Rosenzweig puts it.

I have argued in this section that it is possible to translate Rosenzweig's choreography of the Jewish holidays into the festival existence of democratic sociality as Cavell describes it. But there remains, perhaps, a question about how the vision of redemption granted, for example, in Astaire's dance might be translated back into democratic action. In the next section I gesture towards an answer.

Conclusion

Cavell's discussion of dance as an emblem of ecstatic existence, the transfiguration of the ordinary into the festive, reveals perhaps the most remarkable point of convergence between his thought and Rosenzweig's: the association of the art of dance with redemption. I have spoken in Chapter 3 about Rosenzweig's notion that redemption is prefigured in the "round-dance" of the sacred festivals of Judaism and Christianity. I pointed out that whereas Judaism's dance circles through holidays of Creation, Revelation, and Redemption, Christianity's dance is a spiral that opens back up into secular time. Rosenzweig says that it is only Christmas that could be called a holiday of redemption, although it is more properly only the beginning of the path leading toward redemption. Unlike the Jewish year, which ends with the Day of Atonement and Sukkot as the holidays of redemption, the Christian sacred year, according to Rosenzweig, lacks a special festival of redemption. Redemption as such cannot be celebrated in the Christian sacred year because it is the task of the Christian to realize the meaning of Bethlehem—and, of course, Golgotha as well—in the world. "The coming of the Kingdom becomes a concern of the world and church history" (*Star* 390; 409). Although Rosenzweig seems to reject the possibility that redemption can ever be celebrated in the historic time of the unredeemed world, he does offer one exception: the performance of dance. If we put Rosenzweig's and Cavell's praise of dance together, we can find a way to articulate how the transfiguration of *vochedik* time into *yontovdik* holiday can be the occasion of reconsecrating the bonds of a community's democratic life.

Cavell and Rosenzweig are united in finding dance to be the art form that gestures toward a redeemed sociality, a sociality in which words are no longer needed to be translated but gesture itself becomes the medium of communication. Rosenzweig says that dance is as purely communicative as are the eyes when their glance speaks of the fullness of love to another. After speaking about communal dances at "Cologne on the Monday before Lent" and other places of "the round-dance of very many dancers," Rosenzweig writes:

> The dance of the individual remains however the first gesture and even in the dance itself the simplest one, the glance. For already in it there lies the power, which remained inaccessible to the action that loosens all rigidity, and for which the word sacrificed itself in order however to conquer it, even at this price, at most for the short span of time that elapsed until the answer. The power of the glance however does not fade away with the moment. A word is forgotten and should be forgotten, it wants to fade away in the answer. But a glance does not cease to exist. An eye that has glanced at us once beholds us as long as we live. When Aphrodite danced before the blissful gods at Amor and Psyche's wedding, finally she was dancing only still with her eyes. (*Star* 395; 414–15)

The dance of the individual becomes a conjuration of love itself in the gaze, a testimony of love that brings the present moment to perfection, a perfection that cannot be forgotten as long as beauty itself or love is not forgotten. Rosenzweig ends his description with a dance of love before "blissful gods" to celebrate a wedding in which the soul (Psyche) awakens to love (Amor), where, in other words, the private (the wedding) and the public (its celebration) intersect.

If we imagine ourselves to be among those "blissful gods" gazing at a dance that awakens love, we have a fair idea of how Cavell understands the experience of the audience of a remarriage comedy. Indeed, the unforgettable gaze that Rosenzweig describes is precisely the achievement of the gaze of the movie camera. Well before his analysis of the dance number between Astaire and the shoeshine man in *The Band Wagon*, Cavell showed an interest in the special power of dance in his description of the scene in *The Awful Truth* where Cary Grant (Jerry) watches Irene Dunne (the woman from whom he is separated, awaiting the finalization of the divorce decree) dance with the man she is newly engaged to marry. It is not the dance we recall, but Grant's loving gaze, which the camera's shifting perspective—first showing the dance, then Grant watching it, then the dance again—transforms into the gaze of the audience. Jerry (Grant) becomes aware of "the awful truth," that is, the simple truth that he still deeply loves his wife and does not want to lose her. (He precipitated the divorce because of his suspicions about her fidelity, suspicions—skeptical doubts—that Irene Dunne either cannot or will not disprove, at least to Grant's satisfaction. Such is the "awfulness" of the simple truth of love, that it is always open to doubt.) Identifying its gaze with his gaze, the audience joins the stars on screen and becomes an audience of "blissful gods" for this moment. Cavell calls this transfiguring gaze of love one that offers a "a hieratic image of the human":

> Jerry pulls up a chair to the edge of the dance floor, sits legs crossed, his arms draped before him carelessly, perfectly, fronting the dancers and the camera, looking directly at the world with as handsome a smile as Cary Grant has it in him to give, in as full an emblem of the viewer-viewed, the film turned explicitly to its audience, to ask who is scrutinizing whom, as I know in film. I think of it, as a hieratic image of the human, the human transfigured on film. This man, in words of Emerson's, carries the holiday in his eye; he is fit to stand the gaze of millions. (*Pursuits* 235)

Rosenzweig would say that to carry a holiday in one's eye is to see the world through God's eyes, to bless the world. For Cavell, the holiday in the eye is the perspective on the world that is awakened in love—what Rosenzweig calls revelation—and that breaks forth into a "song and dance" in which audience and performer share a transfiguring vision of a redeemed world.

What does this transfigured vision have to do with democratic sociality? I would like to return to the movie *The Band Wagon* in order to answer this question and draw this chapter to its conclusion. Cavell, as we have seen, interprets Astaire's dance in the opening of this movie to be an allegory of a transfigured life that joins Astaire and the shoeshine man in a "traumatic glimpse of Utopia." It happens that the African American performer was indeed a shoeshine man on Forty-second Street in New York whom the director Vincente Minnelli met while scouting locations for the movie. His name was Leroy Daniels. So impressed was Minnelli by the exuberant street performance that Daniels's shoeshining involved (pirouetting, clacking of brushes, sweeping gestures with the cloth, everything that is captured in the film), that he decided to build the opening of his film around it. Cavell claims that the number offers Astaire's homage to the tradition of black dance, but it is far more than this. Minnelli conceived the number as an homage to an otherwise unknown African American who had transfigured his work into a dance not only worthy of being joined to that of Astaire's, but of providing the focal point for a sequence about Astaire's "comeback."

Astaire's comeback in the movie will ultimately wed him to another kind of dancer, the ballet dancer played by Cyd Charisse. The wedding of the dance style of the American movie "hoofer" and the European dance tradition is allegorized in the love story between Astaire and Charisse. What we see at the opening of the movie can be read as another wedding dance, the wedding dance of Leroy Daniels and Fred Astaire.[6] The joy of their dance breaks down barriers of gender, race, and class in just the same way that the dancing of Astaire and Charisse breaks down barriers of age and culture. Not only do Astaire and Charisse offer the audience a vision of marriage as transfiguring dance, but so also do Astaire and Daniels. Indeed, Daniels circles Astaire as does a bride in a Jewish wedding. Cavell writes that "the shoeshine man moves in some enhanced shuffle completely around the stand, that is to say, he completely traces a circle around Astaire, who turns with him and studies his every move (anything but dominating him)" (*Philosophy Tomorrow* 75). Cavell acknowledges that Daniels plays the role of a bride to Astaire when he writes that "[n]o one can predict (any more than it was at once predictable when God found that it is not good that the first man be alone) who or what will be apt for him," adding that in the opening number of *The Band Wagon*, it turns out that Daniels is "apt" for Astaire (Cavell 2006: 305).

Cavell is right to underscore the poignancy of the exiting dance that takes Astaire away from Daniels and leads him out into the crowd on Forty-second Street. Cavell goes so far as to says that it is "traumatically" poignant (*Philosophy Tomorrow* 77) and "tragic" (Cavell 2006: 303). In the exit, Daniels seems to both bid Astaire farewell and, remaining upon one knee as he extends his hand in his direction, he also seems to beseech Astaire to stay. Daniels, to be sure, is smiling broadly as he watches Astaire depart the arcade, but the passing of this ecstatic moment leaves its mark of sadness upon the lives, both fictional and real, of these two men. Their barrier-breaking dance is a prelude to the dancing of Astaire and Charisse, but it also casts a shadow upon all that follows. After the ecstatic performance in the arcade, the movie's "happy ending" is called into question. We at least wonder what sort of "ending" is in store for Daniels.

The dance in the arcade includes a moment that I should like to call messianic. Astaire approaches a large box-like structure with a large question mark painted on its sides. It holds within it a miniature version of the fireworks that are typical on the Fourth of July. Astaire kicks the box—he had previously turned its handles without producing any effect—and this transforms the machine into a multicolored, brightly lit, exploding musical instrument, something like a pipe organ. It plays a Sousa marching-band number in honor of the American Revolution. If we take this as somehow a celebration of an accomplished reality, as if the Revolution had fulfilled the promise of freedom, it is, as Cavell says, merely "mechanical self-praise." But if we take it as a response to the "attack" upon the question from the surprising and unexpected angle of Astaire's glancing foot as he dances around it, then perhaps we may say that the question posed by the box is answered by Astaire himself. The answer is the *dance*. The music and the fireworks are not, on the interpretation I am here offering, mechanical self-praise, but the jubilation over the moment of freedom that this dance embodies. It is a dance of redemption, a dance that declares, like the dance of Miriam at the Red Sea, that the enslavement of and to the past has been, for this moment, overcome. The pipe organ and the fireworks will retreat behind the question mark once again, but we can always hope that another dance will awaken us to the festive celebration of the redemption coiled like a taut spring within the world's debased arcades.[7]

Rosenzweig says that the Jewish people, always cycling through the holidays of Creation, Revelation, and Redemption, "lives in its own redemption," but the "peoples of the world" will only know redemption at the close of history. But this is not true of a democratic people. A democratic people lives moments of redemption when it celebrates the vision of a dance that transcends the barriers that separate one human from another. A democratic people are like the Jewish people in that its members "forget the growth of the world," that is, they forgo the violence by which a people cuts into the flow of time with its wars and revolutions. A democratic people is always "migrant," always discovering itself on the frontier of a land it cannot enter once and for all. The greatest temptation of a democratic people is to "settle" into its life, to erect walls in order to defend its borders or to lay down laws based upon some unchangeable "essence" that defines who may join the conversation of its contracted life together. Indeed, one of the greatest temptations of a democratic people is to find a false eternality in the image of a regained Eden where it would know in advance who is Adam and who is Eve. A democratic people can celebrate the public declaration of love made in the vows of marriage, but it cannot stipulate the "essence" of marriage (define it, in other words) without betraying that love. Such a stipulative definition betrays love because it cannot be predicted in advance who the partners in the dance of love will be. For all we know, the dance between two men who find each other to be ecstatically beautiful may inspire, one day, a love story no more and no less surprising than one between an American hoofer and a ballerina.

At the beginning of the previous chapter I claimed that the concluding words of Julia Reinhard Lupton's book *Citizen-Saints: Shakespeare and Political Theology* could serve as a fitting synopsis of the risk and promise of a democratic sociality that would forgo sovereign power in favor of ever-renewed mutual commitments to noncoercive, open-ended conversation. Those concluding words, as I explained, quoted the title of a Pedro Almodóvar film, *Talk to Her*. Lupton concludes her book with these words: "Talk to her, *talk to them*: who knows what forms, moods, and shapes of consent might awaken in response?" (Lupton 2005: 216). What Lupton is proposing in these words is nothing less than to reimagine the space of the political as the space of *matrimony*, and throughout her book—as throughout this chapter—marriage serves as both metaphor and emblem of a nonsovereign relationship among humans inventing and negotiating life without fixed rules, life without a concept as Cavell would say, in short, a *beautiful* life. I have suggested that in a democracy even matrimony itself, beyond its identity as a pas de deux, must be open to reinvention. In her discussion of Shakespeare's *Measure for Measure*, Lupton captures the point I have been pressing. Her discussion pivots around the speech of Claudio in defense of the "true contract" of marriage he has entered into with Julietta, despite the fact that it has not yet been given the legitimate approval ("the denunciation") of "outward order" (*Measure for Measure* 2.142–52).

> Thus stands it with me: upon a true contact
> I got possession of Julietta's bed.
> You know the lady; she is fast my wife,
> Save that we do the denunciation lack
> Of outward order. This we came not to,
> Only for propagation of dower
> Remaining in the coffers of her friends,
> From whom we thought it meet to hide our love
> Till time had made them for us. But it chances
> The stealth of our most mutual entertainment
> With character too gross is writ on Juliet.

The "true contract" of Claudio and Julietta, according to Lupton, "firmly installs this marriage in the civil rather than the sovereign sphere, eluding regulation by church and state and withdrawing the semiotic energy of the marriage metaphor from the symbolic operations of sovereignty" (2005: 148). "By choosing this path to marriage," Lupton adds, "Claudio and Julietta not only separate their union from direct supervision by the state and its church, but they also instantiate, in the equality and mutuality of their bond, an image of civil relation distinct from the one that authorizes absolute sovereignty" (146). The union of Claudio and Julietta places the husband-wife relation within a "horizontality" of equality and mutual respect, removing it from the "vertical" sovereign relation of master and subject. The union "threatens to establish horizontality itself as a norm, indeed as the norm of norms, as a measure for measures, a principle of social equivalence with the potential to realign the civil and civic fields in their interlinked entireties" (147–48). I would add, and Lupton also insists upon this point, that the horizontal realignment of civil and civic fields involves also a fundamental realignment of the civil and religious fields. To the extent that the law of matrimony is based upon free and loving consent rather than outward order, it is, Mendelssohn would say, the expression of divine benevolence. Indeed, the "true contract" that binds Claudio and Julietta is what lies at the heart of Mendelssohn's vision of the state, as I argued in the previous chapter. Although Rosenzweig does not share this vision of the state (he is too enmeshed in a Hegelian perspective on state sovereignty), I have tried in this chapter to imagine a conversation between Rosenzweig and Cavell that would draw Rosenzweig beyond 1800 and also *beyond sovereignty*. I have tried to imagine an immigrant Rosenzweig who would be willing to acknowledge the transformative power of a redemptive democratic politics.

EPILOGUE

Pirates of the Caribbean Once More

I would like to return to the topic of radical evil, the centerpiece of what I dubbed Kant's "sublime" religion of reason. In the previous chapter I suggested, following the lead of Stanley Cavell, that the beauty of a dance number between Fred Astaire and an African American shoeshine man offers a glimpse of redemption in everyday time that rebukes the injustice of this yet-unredeemed world. I argued that the spectators of redemptive beauty can become the agents of a democratic redemptive politics. It might seem that radical evil and the sublime horizon of hope offered in Kant's religion of reason simply have no place in a redemptive politics built upon the beauty of the everyday and common world we inhabit. To do justice to Rosenzweig's Kantian inheritance, I want to show how the sublime horizon of hope remains pertinent for any redemptive politics. After having argued in Chapter 3 that Rosenzweig's philosophy of revelation allows us to imagine a reconciliation between Mendelssohn and Jacobi, I now want to propose that Rosenzweig points to a reconciliation between Mendelssohn and Kant, between a philosophy of the beautiful and a philosophy of the sublime.

I will begin by returning to my example of how, according to Kant, radical evil is overcome by a radical change of orientation, a new perception of the temporal horizon. I took as my example of how this reorientation works the scene from *Pirates of the Caribbean* in which Captain Jack Sparrow (Johnny Depp) recognizes that his ship cannot escape the land of the dead without turning upside down. Depp, without saying why he is doing it, begins to run from one side of the ship to the other. His shipmates slowly, one by one, realize that he is trying to overturn the ship in order to gain access to another horizon, the horizon of the living. They join him in running back and forth and together succeed in overturning the ship. They rejoin the land of the living just as the sun sets in the land of the dead. Witnessing a green flash as the boat turns upside down, they find themselves gazing on the sunrise after the ship rights itself once again.

I spoke about this scene in relation to Kant's religion of reason. I emphasized how Kant's religion of reason seeks to reorient humans in relation to another horizon, a horizon of hope, which is infinitely distant from the everyday world, the phenomenal world, in which, according to Kant, cause and effect rule and freedom is impossible. The "settlement" most humans make with this everyday world as the horizon of their expectations—the horizon of their personal happiness—is, according to Kant, the very essence of radical evil. In choosing to orient themselves in accordance with this world's horizon of happiness, and to either forgo or forget the horizon of hope that entails the risky overturn of their "ship of life," humans forgo their freedom. They also forgo any hope they may have of winning for themselves something more than happiness, namely, their dignity as autonomous beings. They forgo what Kant calls *respect* for their sublime selfhood.

Kant's emphasis upon the sublime realm of morality distinguishes him sharply from Mendelssohn. Mendelssohn saw morality and the human capacity for the perception and creation of beauty to be interconnected. For Mendelssohn, to act morally is to perfect the world, to make it more beautiful. "Since each free being," Mendelssohn writes in his essay "On Evidence in the Metaphysical Sciences," "'is ethically compelled to determine himself in his choice according to the most trenchant motives, then he is also obligated to orient his choice to the rule of perfection, beauty, and order, or, what is the same, the free being is obligated to bring about as much perfection, beauty, and order in the world as is possible to him" (1997: 297). The difference between their views reflects a difference in their metaphysics and may therefore seem part of Kant's "supersession" of Mendelssohn. From as early as Reinhold's *Letters on the Kantian Philosophy*, Kant has been seen as making Mendelssohn's philosophy obsolete. But this ignores the fact that Mendelssohn wrote his last metaphysical work, his *Morning Hours*, some four years after the *Critique of Pure Reason*. It was Mendelssohn in the preface to this work who gave Kant his most famous moniker, the "all-crushing [alles zermalmenden]." Mendelssohn's goal in *Morning Hours* was to counter the rising empiricism and materialism that rejected the overblown idealism of the earlier philosophical generation, the generation of Mendelssohn but also of Kant. This rising materialism lent support to a new skepticism about the existence of the world and of God. Answering this skepticism required going beyond the older "school metaphysics." Mendelssohn's goal in *Morning Hours* is not different from Kant's in his *Critique of Pure Reason*, namely, to respond to the new skepticism and to find space for a rational faith in God. Their methods are different, however. Mendelssohn still believes that the common-sense world can offer the best access to a rational faith; Kant believes that the common-sense world must be abandoned. Mendelssohn, in fact, is not holding on to an outmoded school metaphysics that Kant realizes is defunct. Rather, Mendelssohn is attempting a recuperation of the common world and common sense that Kant also will later attempt in his *Critique of the Power of Judgment* (1790), the work in which Kant seeks to legitimize both the human capacity for the aesthetic judgments of beauty and sublimity and the so-called teleological judgment that the world expresses a divine purposiveness. Kant, it seems, came to share Mendelssohn's sense that the common world was more than the site of causally determined objects on the grid of space and time. Mendelssohn's *Morning Hours* should not be dismissed as having been made obsolete by Kant. Rather, Mendelssohn and Kant can be viewed as complementing one another. In Rosenzweig, I will suggest, they find their reconciliation.

Kant in the *Critique of Pure Reason* countered the skepticism of Humean empiricism by reverting to a sublime world, the noumenal world, as the refuge of Idealism's confidence in Reason. Mendelssohn thought that Kant had won back the world from empiricism at too high a price. The empiricists, claiming that all knowledge must begin with sense perception, had been led to call into question the reality of what did not present itself through the senses. Since we do not perceive the relation of cause and effect and since we do not even perceive the independent existence of objects when they are not perceived, empiricists were led to a radical skepticism about the common world that humans believe they live in, a world of causes and effects and objects that persist when they are not perceived. Kant countered this skepticism by showing that the common world humans live in is the *construction* of the human mind, a mind that imposes order upon sensory impressions and thereby makes it possible to talk about perceptions—associate them in virtue of their similarity, the basis of all knowledge according to the skeptics—in the first place. But the price for recovering this common world from the skepticism of the empiricists was to make it so tightly constructed by the mind as to leave no room for freedom, for an event that was not determined by the nexus of causality in which the mind constrained all possible objects to find their temporal place. But in the realm of the "thing in itself"—the realm of the mind in itself and whatever might be responsible for the impressions that were shaped into meaningful perceptions—there was a place for freedom. This was the sublime realm of the Ideas of Reason: God, Freedom, and the Immortal Soul.

Mendelssohn thought that Kant had not, in fact, won back the humanly inhabited common world from the empiricists, and he did not believe that God and Freedom and the Immortal Soul had no place in the common human world. Again and again throughout *Morning Hours*, Mendelssohn insists that Reason *is* common sense (see 3:33, 6:54–55), a slowed-down common sense, measuring its steps more cautiously but taking the same steps nonetheless. Mendelssohn started with the empiricists' skepticism about the existence of the external world and took their evidence in exactly the opposite direction. The skeptics took the fact that every perception offers only one point of view on any object and that no perception can take in the object itself as evidence that we have no ground to believe that any object actually exists. Mendelssohn took the perspectival nature of perception as evidence that objects only exist in a *common* world, a world constructed by finite minds working together to separate private illusions from public and provisional truths. Public truths are always provisional because objects do not force their common properties upon perceivers, but rather these common properties are what humans consent to at any time, what common sense declares them to be. Reason's task is to call the consensus of common sense into question, to seek to refine the consensus by applying standards of consistency and by checking it against the evidentiary basis it appeals to. Discussing how the common world of common sense is built up, Mendelssohn writes:

> What we know only on the basis of one sensation, has in itself merely the presumption of reality, which is grounded on the customary association of similar appearances. This presumption can be deceptive and it is, perhaps, the result of perspectival illusion just as when we falsely take a painting to be a three-dimensional representation. The more sensations, from different distances, seen through various media, that come together in a representation, the more certain will be our conviction in its actual existence. The ground of our presumption can no longer rest on the narrowness of a single sensation. Agreement among sensations, however, leads to a common ground. But a doubt remains whether the limited sphere of knowledge offered by our sensations upon which this common ground is built may not as a whole be an illusion. Perhaps the condition I find myself in is that I see and hear and feel things, and take them to be real, but they only are processes in me and outside me they have no object. But the more people agree with me about these things, find them to be as I do, the more will be the certainty that the ground of my belief does not lie in my particular condition. (*Morning Hours* 6:54)

Humans share a common world of objects. They do not demand certainty that everything in that world is real, nor does the reality of the entire world collapse if it is shown to them that every perception, taken singly, is merely a representation of an object that does not necessarily have any connection with the object it seems to present. Humans build their common world through agreements about what they find there.

What allows humans to do this common work of world-building? We have seen that for Rosenzweig it is language. Rosenzweig resists the idealist temptation to search for an "essence" of things that makes them part of the common world. Mendelssohn also resists this temptation. Mendelssohn says that there is an "Urbild," an "archetype" or "fundamental picture," that is discernible in the background of the constantly changing common world of humans. This Urbild is of things moving in space, the world as Newtonian physics pictures it. Kant thought he had to posit the mind itself as constructor of this Urbild in order to answer the charge of the skeptics that perceptions do not offer secure access to objects. Mendelssohn also thinks that the Urbild is constructed, but not by single minds working apart from each other. Finite minds construct the common world within the framework of a fundamental picture, an Urbild, of reality that is the overarching vision of the ultimate *oneness* of the world. The Urbild keeps the world together as a unity. Not resting in any one mind or even in all finite minds together, the Urbild, Mendelssohn argues, must be held by an infinite Mind. We do not know the Urbild—it is infinite—but we may recognize its effects. The Urbild is the infinite horizon of the common world we inhabit. Because the Urbild remains in principle unknowable, it is a profound mistake to ask after its "in itself" identity. Showing that he has taken in Kant's basic message and can outdo Kant on his own turf of critique, Mendelssohn writes:

> We want to know, however, what this Urbild is in itself, not what it does. Friend, if this is your serious intent, I answer: it appears to me that you are demanding to know something that is absolutely not a possible object of knowledge. We are standing at the limits not only of what is humanly knowable, but of all knowability in general, and we want to proceed beyond without knowing where. When I say what a thing does or suffers, do not ask me what it is . . . This is what the atheist does. He asks, What is God *actually* ["eigentlich"]? Show him what God has done . . . and he asks, "What, however, is God in Himself?" (*Morning Hours* 59–60)

Mendelssohn insists that the commonness of the world is all the evidence we can have of an Urbild and of God, the fashioner of the Urbild. The commonness of the world is, however, given its firmest evidence in language itself, in the common terms that we use for things. The materialist would dissolve language into private names for private perceptions; the idealist seeks to transcend language by getting at the "essence" of God. Dualists somehow try to bridge the gap between the two by invoking special correlations between the private worlds of human minds and the public world of things in space. But the entire dispute is fruitless. Language must be trusted to provide evidence of a common world or no common world will be found. In one of the most remarkable passages of *Morning Hours*, Mendelssohn puts the case for dismissing metaphysical disputes as "word quarrels":

> I fear that in the end the famous quarrel ["Zwist"] of the materialists, idealists, and dualists might turn out to be a mere word quarrel that is more the province of linguists than of speculative deep thinkers. This would hardly surprise me. It would not be the first famous quarrelsome question which divided men from one

another, indeed had led them to hate and persecute one another, which in the end turned out to be a feud over words ["Wortfehde"]. Speech is the element in which our disparate concepts live and move. They can exchange one [language] for another and thereby suffer alteration, but they cannot leave it without endangering their life. (*Morning Hours* 7:61)

Mendelssohn is no less critical of metaphysical speculation than is Kant. Unlike Kant, he does not hope to escape from the language-bound conditions of the common world. One could say that Mendelssohn is not interested in living in a sublime world beyond this one, or in living in a world beyond the contingencies of speech. As Jeffrey Librett puts it in his comments on this passage from *Morning Hours*, "The point, then, is not that the materialists, idealists, and dualists should not fight because they may be saying the same thing in different ways, but rather that they should not fight because none of them can actually, completely or finally, know what it is they are saying: they will all always be saying something different from what they mean to say" (Librett 2000: 88). This is the point that Mendelssohn stressed in *Jerusalem* when he declared that no one should be compelled to swear allegiance to a creed; here the issue is carried over to speculative theses. Swearing allegiance to materialism or idealism or dualism sets the scene for persecutorial "word feuds." To make peace among the warring factions of philosophy requires that one make one's peace with language itself as an unfinalizable conversation.

Mendelssohn, however, is not content with the commonness of the common world, either. He understands that speech is the medium in which such truths as humans can find together can be expressed, but he also knows that language is the medium of poetic fiction. "What is the significance of the fact," he asks in *Morning Hours*, "that humans love both truth and fiction?" (7:64). The answer for Mendelssohn resides in the different attitudes humans may have toward the common world. Humans may either be driven to secure its *truthfulness*, that is, to bring their separate views of it into conformity with a more encompassing view. This is the *truth drive* ("Wahrheitstrieb") (*Morning Hours* 7:59ff.). Another attitude humans have toward the common world is to make the world conform to their private view of what it *might* be, what they imagine it might become. This attitude corresponds to the "power of approbation [Billigungskraft]" which has what Mendelssohn calls an *approbation drive* ("Billigungstrieb"),[1] the drive to perfect the common world by making it more beautiful. The truth drive and the approbation drive are not separate "faculties," but rather are "expressions of one and the same power of the soul, although they differ in respect of the goal of their effort" (*Morning Hours* 7:63–64).

The approbation drive seeks to bring the common world into greater harmony with one's sense of beauty. What is beauty? It is not a sublime vision that has no relation to this common world, but is rather this very world in so far as it is lovable, the object of *desire*. We love the beauty of this world when we love the world as the site of love, the place where love builds upward from private desires to lives shared in common. The truth drive, says Mendelssohn, "wants to remodel [umbilden] humans in accordance with the nature of things"; but the approbation drive—we might even call it *the beauty drive*—wants to "remodel things in accordance with the nature of humans" (*Morning Hours* 7:64).

A common world built up out of love for the world will not answer the demands of the truth drive. The truth drive wants only to accept personal judgments about the present state of the world that can be tested against what everyone else can and does know of the world; the beauty drive wants the future world to conform to its present desire. Our love for the world does not rest upon proofs of its lovability, but upon our desire to bring more love into it. Othello's love for Desdemona, Mendelssohn explains, is destroyed once Iago insinuates a doubt about the reality of Desdemona's faithfulness. Othello loses the object of his love when she becomes an object of his truth drive:

> In the midst of the strongest emotion he recognizes that his peace depends entirely upon an opinion and that his happiness depends upon his maintaining himself in the illusion of his beloved's faithfulness. But he feels that this is impossible. His drive is for reality, not opinion. The goal of his [Othello's] wish is outside him, it lies in the object. Desdemona should not only seem innocent, she should be innocent. (*Morning Hours* 7:65)

Being and seeming cannot coincide except under the regime of truth, the regime of the truth drive. The approbation drive exists precisely in the gap between being (what is real) and seeming (what is desired to be real). Or, put differently, the approbation drive exists in the gap between actuality and possibility.

The common world is one of actualities and possibilities. Its possibilities are presented as greater perfections of its actualities, as an increase of what binds humans together as it binds them to this common world. But there are possibilities as well for disunity, for greater divisions and partialities within the common world. But such divisions do not correspond to some destructive drive in humanity. They result from the confusion of the truth drive and the beauty drive, as when Othello becomes persuaded that his happiness rests not upon what the world can become but rather upon what the world presently is. Othello cannot bear the gap between actuality and possibility, and his murder of Desdemona is symbolic of all attempts to *force* reality to conform to one's private truth drive. Rather than put one's private vision of what is true to the test of common sense, one decides that the common world must be compelled to find one's private vision to be true. Rather than work to create a shared world of love, the "falsehood" of the world is condemned to destruction. The regime of truth and the regime of beauty can never be forced together this way. One must accept that the common world of objects is built up together, by an additive process in which no single perspective prevails over all the others. Then one can imagine a widening of this common world, an enlargement of what it finds to be true. One adds to this common world a new possibility, a new perspective, that does not cancel the world as it stands, but extends its boundaries. This is what poetry does: It uses language in new ways to conjure new worlds.

Another way of putting the point of the last paragraph is to say that only God can unite truth and approbation through a *single* will; finite beings can do so only by combining their wills. Since God works though finite beings to realize and perfect the common world, the coming together of finite wills is the only way that humanity can realize God's will. Mendelssohn claims in *Morning Hours* that this conception of God is exactly what his friend Lessing was driving at in one of his unpublished manuscripts, entitled "The Christianity of Reason." Mendelssohn quotes it at some length, but we perhaps can capture the import of this text with two passages. The first is paragraph 13: "God thought his own completeness as divided up, i.e., he created beings which each possessed a part of his perfection since, to repeat once more, for God every thought is also an act of creation." Paragraph 14 reads: "All these beings together is called the world" (*Morning Hours* 15:134). Lessing goes on to argue that to overcome the partiality of one's being by conforming one's acts to a sense of the greater completeness of the world is to act as a moral being.

Mendelssohn's invocation of Lessing's moral law—"act in accordance with one's particular completeness" (*Morning Hours* 15:136)—takes me back to the beginning of this discussion, to Kant and to the scene from *Pirates of the Caribbean*. Kant has lost his faith that this common world is able to provide an incentive to moral action. The world has simply dissolved into objects with no inherent relations to one another. The mind constructs the grid of space and time and constrains any object that appears on the grid to be determined in its position by prior causes. This mechanical world is like the land of the dead. To find one's way into the land of the living it is necessary to entirely reorient oneself in relation to the horizon of this common world. Neither Lessing nor Mendelssohn would find such radical reorientation to be called for. The common world is the site where one works out one's moral identity, precisely by enhancing the beauty of this world.

I said at the beginning of this epilogue that I wanted to show how Mendelssohn and Kant could complement one another. I think that Mendelssohn is pointing toward a recuperation of the beauty of the common world as the basis of moral action. It is not at all accidental that the two philosophers who helped me imagine an "immigrant Rosenzweig"—Arendt and Cavell—admit their indebtedness primarily to Kant's *Critique of the Power of Judgment*. Until his *Critique of the Power of Judgment*, Kant stressed the radical separation of the common world from the moral world. Such separation makes it difficult if not impossible to envision, as Arendt and Cavell do, a democratic politics. Arendt has actually claimed that Kant himself recognized this fact, and offered the lineaments of a democratic political theory in the *Critique of the Power of Judgment*. To pursue this would take me too far afield, but Kant's own turn toward the beauty of the common world does lead to the question, what can we preserve from Kant's "sublime religion of reason"? I think that what Kant emphasized in his vision of a sublime horizon of hope is important and must not be dismissed.

I take this sublime horizon to be Kant's response to the unredeemed nature of the common world. The common world, when looked at in all honesty, seems to give the lie to Mendelssohn's faith, a Leibnizian faith that he never abandoned, that this world is the *best of all possible worlds*. This faith is expressed in the final lines of *Morning Hours*:

> It is no immodesty on the part of the earthbound human if he dares to connect his finitude with the being of the Infinite, or his narrowness with the reality of

> the most complete being. It suits the immortal soul of the human quite well that he believes himself so connected to God that in every one of his thoughts there is a path to finding Him. Despite his limited vision, it is still granted him to see the larger truth, that he himself depends upon God in two relations: as an idea and as a real thing: as an idea he is an object of divine knowledge from eternity; and as a real thing, he in addition possesses actuality insofar as the conditions of time and space made him a worthy object of God's judgment that he *at a certain place* and *at a certain time*, because he belonged to the Best One, himself became the best. (*Morning Hours* 17:156–57)

There is in the final words a suggestion that the spatio-temporal actuality of the finite human being gives her a purchase on divinity. This is almost entirely the opposite of Kant's picture of how the human gains a purchase on divinity.

I think that we need not choose between either Kant's sublime vision of the noumenal horizon of the human being's freedom (her God-like identity) or the this-worldly vision of Mendelssohn's faith in the common world as able to become the best world. I believe that Kant and Mendelssohn complement one another. Indeed, Kant himself came to recognize the need to find a connection between the finite, contingent reality of the human being and the noumenal horizon of her freedom. He saw, like Mendelssohn before him, that the common world's beauty was evidence that the noumenal horizon of hope touched the common horizon of this world's temporality. But, perhaps more clearly than Mendelssohn, Kant maintained an awareness that this intersection was itself only a matter of hope, never of knowledge. Mendelssohn knew that the greatest danger confronted humanity when it sought to build its aspiration for beauty upon the certainty of knowledge. This was Othello's tragic error. But Mendelssohn was unwilling to conclude that Othello's error is due to radical evil, and that, perhaps, in this world radical evil has the last word. Perhaps his difference from Kant is to be explained by the fact that Mendelssohn's faith remained unshaken that, *at a certain place and at a certain time*, namely, at Mt. Sinai, God's sublime horizon and the common world's horizon had, in fact, intersected. Kant, however, no longer believed that the historical Jesus was the Best One in human flesh. History for Kant was not oriented in relation to the "critical moment" (*kairos*) of the Christ event; the sublime horizon of history—the achievement of perpetual peace—was infinitely distant from every moment in time. For Kant, the eternal and the historical can never intersect.[2]

In the end, we need both Mendelssohn and Kant. Kant, too, understood that the common world cannot simply be abandoned as the unredeemable site of radical evil. The scene in *Pirates of the Caribbean* shows what it takes to turn from the land of the dead to the land of the living, to reorient oneself in relation to a sublime horizon of hope. It will not happen by itself, nor by any single will acting alone. But the recovery of a new horizon is not the end of the story. One must find a way to continue to live in the everyday world, the common world where radical evil remains a threat. Here Mendelssohn's emphasis upon the task of creating beauty in the common world is important. This is the side of the story that Kant will tell in his *Critique of the Power of Judgment* where he speaks about the sense of beauty as evidence of the human drive to create a common world:

> If one judges objects merely in accordance with concepts [Mendelssohn calls this the "truth drive"], then all representation of beauty is lost. Thus there can also be no rule in accordance with which someone could be compelled to acknowledge something as beautiful. Whether a garment, a house, a flower is beautiful: no one allows himself to be talked into his judgment about that by means of any grounds or fundamental principles [or dogmas, Mendelssohn would add]. One wants to submit the object to his own eyes, just as if his satisfaction depended on sensation; and yet, if one then calls the object beautiful, *one believes oneself to have a universal voice, and lays claim to the consent of everyone*, whereas any private sensation would be decisive only for him alone and his satisfaction. (Kant 1996a: 101; italics mine)

Kant would agree with Mendelssohn that the "approbation drive" (or the "beauty drive," as I have called it) wants to create a common world through the *consent* of others. That consent is grounded in no concept which could "compel" consent. In a certain way, Mendelssohn is even more radical than Kant. Mendelssohn does not even believe that *truth* can "compel" through concepts. Rather, truth, too, is the product of human consent about what one finds in the world. The "beauty drive" seeks to win consent for what has not yet been found in the world. Kant calls this "genius." For Mendelssohn, every human has a "genius" that realizes the "best" that each individual is capable of in the here and now of the common world.

There will always be times when humans lose faith that history has any meaningful orientation, when the "best" or "beauty" seems to be a lie. The manic presumption of Hegel in 1800, who sought to replace Kant's sublime hope for an ever-deferred cosmopolitan peace with the dream of an aesthetic and ethical perfecting of the nation-state, is one answer to this loss of faith. To abandon the world to despair and the sheer errancy of the arbitrary will is another answer. Between these extremes is, as Rosenzweig would insist, the world of *hope*. In the world of hope, love takes one step at a time, risking and recreating itself each time anew. After the *Black Pearl* is returned to the land of the living, the task of orienting oneself in relation to one's heart's desire—he has not yet followed the needle of his mystic compass to its goal—begins anew. Captain Jack Sparrow, though he has found his way back to the land of the living, has not yet found his love, or he at least has not yet acknowledged the one whom he loves. Stanley Cavell makes a similar distinction between returning to the land of the living and continuing to live in the common world with others who may not yet fully share one's new horizon in his analysis of another story about a sailor who has entered the frozen realm of the dead, Coleridge's *The Rime of the Ancient Mariner*. Cavell, without using the term "radical evil," describes the Mariner's killing of the albatross as symbolic of the motivelessness (radical evil arises from the "inscrutable" subjective ground of freedom, according to Kant) that is not the absence of motive but the "horror of being human itself," i.e., the horror of one's freedom to choose to be human. The Mariner's return to the land of the living is not followed by his rejoining the common world. Rather, he carries his tale from place to place, and the first mentioned is the site of a wedding. At the opening of the poem, the Mariner leads the Wedding-Guest away "from the round of life," as Cavell puts it (Cavell, "Texts of Recovery," 63, in Cavell 1988). Call this Coleridge's appeal to the Wedding-Guest to "walk together to the kirk" of Kant's sublime religion of reason. But the passage back to common life must come after one has set one's sights on sublime horizon of hope. In Cavell's words, "letting yourself be loved devotedly and reciprocating the devotion (as if love were a ring)" is "the poem's hope" ("Texts of Recovery" 65).

The last word belongs to Franz Rosenzweig. *The Star of Redemption* brings together the sublime horizon of hope with the common world's horizon of lived experience and love for the next one in a way that I find powerfully compelling, although yet incomplete. I have tried to imagine an "immigrant Rosenzweig" who might embrace the common life-world of democratic sociality that was Mendelssohn's political aspiration and that informs the work of Arendt and Cavell. I do not think I have wrested Rosenzweig too far out of his context in drawing him into the common ambit of Mendelssohn, Arendt, and Cavell. I have quoted the final words of Mendelssohn's *Morning Hours*, in which Mendelssohn affirms that each human may, in God, find both his *truth* and his *goal*: to actualize *the best* that one's specific place and time makes possible, to make the world more perfect in the here and now. For Mendelssohn, this seemed to be a matter of following one's loving nature and allowing the truth drive to be guided by rather than to replace one's "beauty drive." It meant loving Desdemona rather than demanding proofs of her faithfulness as a condition of one's love.

Rosenzweig knows that in order to love Desdemona one must step outside one's defensive self-armoring against loss and pain. One must become vulnerable. To risk exposure to the loss of one's love, Rosenzweig knows that more is required than a vision of the beauty of the world, however much love it may inspire. What is required is a vision of the sublime horizon of hope, the horizon of the world's redemption. What is required is the hope that love itself will outlast one's death, that love is "stronger than death." There are many points of similarity between Mendelssohn's closing words to *Morning Hours* that I quoted above and Rosenzweig's closing words to *The Star of Redemption*, but what divides them, finally, is that, like Kant, Rosenzweig no longer begins his thinking with a secure orientation within history, with a conviction that God's sublime horizon and our common world *once before, at a specific place and a specific time*, intersected. If 1800 means anything, it means an end to one's belief in the evidence of history as evidence of revelation. Critical reason—playing Iago to the faith of Othello—insinuated an insurmountable doubt about the truth of God's word. After 1800, revelation must be *present* if it is to be real. But revelation—if it is to open the horizon of freedom rather than forced obedience—cannot (must not) win its case in the court of the *Wahrheitstrieb*, the truth drive. One's trust in the truth and the goal of history and of one's place within it must rest, after 1800, upon the sublime horizon of hope intersecting with the here and now of the individual. Then, oriented by a revelation that is not commensurate with any form of knowledge, one may join in the unending task—I have spoken of it as the task of a democratic redemptive politics—of raising this common world from death into life. "Radical evil" names the choice to sail in the realm of living death. It is the choice put by

Davy Jones to those captured by his *Flying Dutchman*: the postponement of death by slowly fusing with the deathless materiality of the sea and the ship.

The year 1800, Rosenzweig believed, is the moment when the choice between life and death—between *Glauben* and *Wissen*, faith and knowledge—is both revealed and occluded. Rosenzweig's *Star* unveils the choice once more and articulates the biblical words of hope: "May you choose life." Placing the reader before this choice, Rosenzweig repeats the rhetorical strategy that shapes the final book of the Pentateuch, the book of Deuteronomy, Moses's farewell address. Rosenzweig asks the reader to place herself together with all those who stood at Mt. Sinai. He asks her to choose life and enter the promised land. But the promised land as Deuteronomy presents it does not need to be conquered by an invading army. It is just one step away. To step into it, it is necessary only to take a step, to replace aimless wandering with a *salto mortale* into the future. To choose life is to enter life, or, better put, to return to life. It is to assume the burden of natality, the burden of migrancy, the burden of *sharing* life in all its conjugations and declensions: departing (from habituated routines), partaking (in praise of the beauty of the world), parting (from the world). Here, then, is the conclusion to *The Star of Redemption*:

> To walk humbly with your God—nothing more is asked for here than a wholly present trust. But trust is a great word. It is the seed from which faith, hope and love grow, and the fruit that ripens from it. It is the easiest of all and just for that reason the hardest. It dares at every moment to say Truly to Truth. To walk humbly with your God—the words are above the gate, the gate that leads out from the mysterious, wonderful illumination of the divine sanctuary where no man can remain alive. But whither do the wings of the gate open? You do not know?
> INTO
> LIFE.

NOTES

INTRODUCTION: MENDELSSOHN AND ROSENZWEIG BEYOND 1800

1. After indicating that the poem was composed in 1800 by placing the date after the poem's title, Rosenzweig includes the date 1909 on a second line followed by a colon and then, on the following line, the verse is quoted. The date 1909 is the year Rosenzweig began work on the Hegel book. Following the verse, after skipping a line, the year 1919, the year of the book's completion, is followed by a colon and then another verse from the poem, this time expressing the brevity of life and the impossibility of seeing into the future of a whole people's life ("But the years of the peoples, / These what mortal man's eye has seen? [Doch die Jahre der Völker / Sah ein stirbliches Auge sie?]"). For the text of *Hegel und der Staat*, I rely upon the one-volume facsimile edition in Rosenzweig 1962. Translations from *Hegel und der Staat*, hereafter *Hegel-Staat*, are mine throughout. The translation of the verses is taken from Hölderlin 1998: 45, 47.

2. For Rosenzweig's reflections on this famous quotation from the preface to Hegel's *Philosophy of Right*, see *Hegel-Staat* 2:79–82.

3. Rosenzweig recurs frequently in *Hegel-Staat* to the theme of Hegel's "Vereinigung mit der Zeit." See, for example, *Hegel-Staat* 1:99ff.; 2:82. "Vereinigung" is a key Hegelian term, recurring frequently in the early theological writings.

4. I will discuss the significance of 1800 in greater detail in Chapter 3. Paul W. Franks and Michael L. Morgan have laid the foundations for a proper understanding of 1800 in Rosenzweig's thinking in their introductory essays in Franz Rosenzweig, *Philosophical and Theological Writings* (Rosenzweig 2000, see esp. pp. 39–43). As they put it, 1800 marks the moment when "the world and history are prepared for fulfillment but are unfulfillable by themselves. Hence, revelation is both necessary and possible" (41).

5. I have relied on the German text in Rosenzweig 1976 and, for translations throughout, the Barbara Galli version in Rosenzweig 2005. All quotations from

The Star of Redemption offer a page reference to the translation followed by a page reference to the German text.

6. There are now three important editions available of the German text. The first, published in 1983, is the *Jubiläumsausgabe* volume prepared by Alexander Altmann, band 8 in Mendelssohn 1971–90. Although Altmann's introduction and notes remain an invaluable resource, problems with the text of the German exist. More reliable are the texts found in David Martyn's edition in Mendelssohn 2001 and in Michael Albrecht's edition in Mendelssohn 2005. I will use the Arkush translation in Mendelssohn 1983, with page references to the translation followed by section and page reference to the 1783 German edition (indicated in the header of the Altmann edition and in the outside margin of the Albrecht edition).

7. Batnitzky 2000: 33–40.

8. The essay, published originally in 1929, is collected in *Zweistromland: Kleinere Schriften zu Glauben und Denken* (Rosenzweig 1984: 801–16). It is translated in Buber and Rosenzweig 1994: 99–113.

9. Rosenzweig 1984, *Zweistromland*: 804.

10. Buber and Rosenzweig 1994: 102.

11. Ex 3:14 in Mendelssohn, *Das Zweite Buch Moses*; reprinted in band 16 of the *Gesammelte Schriften Jubiläumsausgabe* (Mendelssohn 1971–90, hereafter *JubA*). I have slightly altered the English translation offered in Buber and Rosenzweig 1994: 102.

12. *Du* in this context is more commonly translated as *Thou*. *I and Thou* is, of course, familiar as the title of Buber's most well-known book. On Jacobi and those who later used his "I-you" motif, see Buber's "The History of the Dialogical Principle" in Buber 2002: 250–52. Rosenzweig reveals his knowledge of Jacobi at many points throughout his writings. Paul W. Franks points out one such place in a note to his and Michael L. Morgan's translation of Rosenzweig's "The New Thinking" (Rosenzweig 2000: 118n18).

13. References will be to the English translation of George di Giovanni in Jacobi 1994: 173–251; hereafter *Spinoza-Letters*. When citing *Spinoza-Letters*, I will provide the pagination to the English translation followed by the original pagination as provided in the translation. The German text of the first edition of *Spinoza-Letters* (1785), with an *apparatus criticus* indicating changes made in the second (1789) and third (1819) editions, is presented in Jacobi 2000.

14. For a succinct discussion of these months, see Paul W. Franks's introductory essay, "From 1908 to 1914" in Rosenzweig 2000: esp. p. 2.

15. I have added the word *preach* to the translation because Arkush for some reason does not translate the word *predige* in this passage. See below, Chapter 5 (first section) for a discussion of the word's resonance in a 1919 essay of Rosenzweig's where the Jew is identified as an eternal "Prediger" of the word "Hope" "through his mere existence." See also note 16, below.

16. Given the contexts in which both phrases appear and the similarities of both the words and the thoughts, it is difficult to believe that we are looking at

a coincidence. Rosenzweig's detailed study of Mendelssohn's *Jerusalem* is apparent in *Hegel-Staat*, and it is likely that this passage in *Jerusalem* resonated so deeply with his own conception of the Jewish people that he adopted one of its most daring formulations—"through its mere existence [durch ihr bloßes Dasein]"—without his conscious awareness.

17. I will argue in Chapter 6 that Rosenzweig seems to have been influenced by an early book of Carl Schmitt's, *Der Wert des Staates* (1917) that joins the political philosophies of Hobbes and Hegel.

18. Rosenzweig's interpretation of Hegel's concept of the state is not uncontroversial. For a representative sample of the variety of contemporary views, see Bubner, Rüdiger and Mesch 2001.

19. One of the many important achievements of Peter Eli Gordon's *Rosenzweig and Heidegger* is to have drawn attention to the importance of considering Rosenzweig's profound engagement with Hegel when in search of any understanding of *The Star of Redemption*. See Gordon 2003: 82–118. I will return to this topic in Chapters 5 and 6.

20. I take it that Rosenzweig means that this "society of peoples" lacks any visible identity as a church, since its visibility is that of the separate states. Therefore, to call it "invisible" seems, according to Rosenzweig at least, to be "nearly ironic" because there is no visible difference between the populations of the Christian states and population of the "society of peoples."

21. Recently, Bonnie Honig has attempted to find in Rosenzweig's philosophy the resources to "think about how sovereignty postulates not just power or imposition of governance, but also, subtly, receptivity, openness, and a future" (Honig 2007: 80). Honig undertakes this attempt in the effort to define a "limitedly sovereign democratic politic" (83). Like Honig, I will draw from Hannah Arendt's political philosophy to assist me in reconceptualizing Rosenzweig's political theology. Also like Honig, I will argue that this reconceptualized democratic political theology directly contests the political theology of Carl Schmitt. Where I differ from Honig is in my reading of Rosenzweig's explicit treatment of the state and sovereignty as indebted to Hegel and quite possibly also to Carl Schmitt's early work, *Der Wert des Staates* (1917). Also, I look to Mendelssohn to find the resources with which to undo the equation of sovereignty with "power" and "imposition of governance."

22. While Rosenzweig did not deliberately set out to resolve the Mendelssohn-Jacobi quarrel, Leo Strauss, who dedicated his book on Spinoza (Strauss 1965) to the memory of Rosenzweig, aimed precisely and with full self-awareness at discovering a way to reconcile Jacobi's assault on Enlightenment reason with Mendelssohn's defense of Judaism as a revealed legislation. Strauss saw it as his task to recover the full seriousness of the Jacobi-Lessing-Mendelssohn moment in the German Enlightenment. For a brilliant study of Strauss in general and of his relation to Jacobi more particularly, see now Benjamin Lazier's *God Interrupted: Heresy and the European Imagination Between the World Wars*

(2008, see esp. ch. 6). Just as I do, Lazier finds Jacobi to be an advocate of a gnostic theology to which Strauss is partially drawn (Lazier 2008: 96). My reading of Rosenzweig places him squarely within the group of German-Jewish thinkers of the interwar years that Lazier examines (Hans Jonas, Leo Strauss, and Gershom Scholem) who in different ways sought to overcome the world-denying gnosticism that had taken hold in the contemporary "crisis theology" of Barth, Gogarten, and others. For a very fine discussion of Strauss's indebtedness to Jacobi's concept of experiential revelation and his eventual rejection of it, see Moyn 2007. Paul W. Franks has insisted on placing Rosenzweig first and foremost in the philosophical context of the Spinoza Quarrel, although, unlike Strauss, Franks seems uninterested in Mendelssohn's place in the quarrel. See Franks's remarks in Rosenzweig 2000: 32–34, and also his discussion of the Spinoza Quarrel as "Rosenzweig's context" in Franks 2006.

23. Seyla Benhabib speaks of this recovenanting as constituting a logic of "democratic iteration," and she precisely locates the immigrant or foreigner as the primary agent behind this logic (Benyhabib et al. 2006: 45ff.). Benhabib draws significantly from Hannah Arendt in formulating her notion of democratic iteration. Bonnie Honig also argues for the role of the immigrant (or "foreigner-founder") in the reconstitution of democratic sociality in *Democracy and the Foreigner* (2003). My effort at formulating a democratic and redemptive political theology using the resources of an "immigrant Rosenzweig" in conversation with Arendt and Cavell seeks to contribute to the (broadly construed) Arendtian project of both Benhabib and Honig. (I am, of course, aware of the many and salient differences between the two thinkers. For an ample demonstration of their conflicting interpretations of how democratic recovenanting functions, see Honig's response to Benhabib and Benhabib's rejoinder in Benhabib et al. 2006: 102–27, 155–65.)

24. "On the Possibility of Experiencing Wonder" is the title of the introduction to part 2 of *The Star of Redemption*. The word I have translated as "wonder" ("Wunder") is (more appropriately) rendered in Galli's translation as "miracle." I only use "wonder" here in order to capture the connection with the Platonic dictum (*Theaetetus* 155d2–3) that "philosophy begins in wonder."

I. PERFORMING REASON: MENDELSSOHN ON JUDAISM AND ENLIGHTENMENT

1. Moses Mendelssohn, "Ueber die Frage: was heißt aufklären?" *Berlinische Monatschrift*, Neuntes Stük, (1784): 193–200. A facsimile of the original text is available through *Zeitschriften der Aufklärung: Retrospektive Digitalisierung wissenschaftlicher Rezensionsorgane und Literaturzeitschriften des 18. und 19. Jahrhunderts aus dem deutschen Sprachraum* (http://www.ub.uni-bielefeld.de/diglib/aufklaerung/index.htm). The essay is translated in Mendelssohn 1997: 313–17. For a discussion of the historical background to the journal editor's call for an answer to the question, "What is Enlightenment?" see Schmidt 1989.

2. Moses Mendelssohn, *Morgenstunden; oder Vorlesungen über das Daseyn Gottes* in *JubA* 3.2:1–175; hereafter *Morning Hours*. In references to *Morning Hours*, I will refer to the chapter, followed by the page reference in *JubA* 3.2. The entire text is also available online through *Zeno.org* (http://www.zeno.org/Philosophie/M/Mendelssohn,+Moses). Translations from *Morning Hours* are mine throughout.

3. German text in Hamann 1949–57; 3:291–320; hereafter *Golgotha*. For a translation and full commentary on the work, see Dunning 1979. All citations will refer to the translation in Dunning 1979 followed by a page reference to the German text. I return to Hamann's critique in Chapter 4 (in "Overview: Reinhold, Kant, and Hegel Before 1800."). A good brief introduction to Hamann (and also Jacobi) may be found in Milbank 1999.

4. For more on Mendelssohn's views regarding common sense, see the further discussion of *Morning Hours* in my "Epilogue." A very fine discussion of the importance of common sense for Mendelssohn is found in Hütter 1990.

5. Rosenzweig wrote this book in 1921, but it was first published in an English translation entitled *Understanding the Sick and the Healthy: A View of God, Man, and World* prepared by Nahum Glatzer, then republished with a new introduction by Hilary Putnam in Rosenzweig 1999. Putnam's introduction draws attention to the similarities between Rosenzweig and Wittgenstein, especially Wittgenstein as Cavell reads him. See also the chapter "Rosenzweig and Wittgenstein" in Putnam 2008. I will speak more about *Little Book* in Chapter 7 (in "Rosenzweig and Cavell on Revelation").

6. I rely upon the text in Dohm 1781–83 for Dohm's *Improvement* (published in 1781) and also for the "Beurtheilung" of Michaelis (published in Part Two of the work in 1783). In references to Dohm's 1781 text I give the abbreviation *Improvement* followed by a page number; in referring to Michaelis's 1783 commentary, I give the page number preceded by a "2." Page facsimiles of both parts (1781, 1783) are conveniently available at http://www.ub.uni-bielefeld.de/diglib/dohm/ueber/. Translations throughout are mine.

7. Menasseh ben Israel, *Rettung der Juden, Aus dem Englischen übersetzt. Nebst: Einer Vorrede von Moses Mendelssohn. Als ein Anhang zu des Hrn. Kriegsraths Dohm Abhandlung: "Ueber die bürgerliche Verbesserung der Juden."* (*The Salvation of the Jews, translated from the English. Together with a Preface by Moses Mendelssohn. An Appendix to Herr Kriegsrath Dohm's Treatise "On the Civil Improvement of the Jews"*) (Berlin/Stettin, 1782). The translation and Vorrede are found in *JubA* 8:1–96. Citations will refer to the page number in *JubA* 8, followed by the page number of the 1782 edition.

8. Michaelis's remarks were published in 1783 as an appendix in Dohm 1781–83 vol. 2. For comments on Michaelis, see Bourke 1999: 47.

9. This account is found in Mendelssohn's Vorrede 19–20. Mendelssohn does not speak about a formal agreement among individuals that creates the social contract. He considers the social condition of humans to be an actualization of a natural potential rather than an artifice of human design.

10. J. G. Herder, "Litterarischer Briefwechsel," in *Der Teutsche Merkur*, 1782, no. 3, 169–92; online at *Zeitschriften der Aufklärung* (http://www.ub.uni-bielefeld.de/diglib/aufklaerung/).

11. August Friedrich Cranz, *Das Forschen nach Licht und Recht in einem Schreiben an Herrn Moses Mendelssohn* (Berlin: Friedrich Maurer, 1782) in *JubA* 8:72–87. For a discussion of Cranz's anonymous letter, see Alexander Altmann's introduction in *JubA* 8:7–10

12. In his 1764 prizewinning essay, "On Evidence in Metaphysical Sciences," Mendelssohn identifies the quest for unanimity and consistency as the despotic enemy of philosophy. People should rather follow their own "meagre insights than to recognize and blindly follow some philosophical pope," and anyone who complains about the confusion caused by the variety of philosophical opinions "cultivates despotic intentions and is a dangerous citizen in the republic of philosophy" (Mendelssohn 1997: 278).

13. In his prizewinning essay, Mendelssohn speaks about the resistance to philosophy: "Most of humanity embark on the journey of life with delusion and superstition and with the firm resolve to complete that journey with them" (Mendelssohn 1997: 277).

14. *JubA* 2:267–330; translated in Mendelssohn 1997: 253–306.

15. One such harmonization would place both opposed wills at a point of equilibrium, but in most cases the owner of surplus goods will not need to drop to the threshold of survival in order to bring the other person up to it. Mendelssohn does not envision the conflict of imperfect rights and duties to be a zero-sum game, but rather it is an unstable (he calls it "fluctuating," "schwankende") situation whose ideal outcome is the betterment of all parties.

16. Willi Goetschel nicely captures Mendelssohn's concept of perfection when he describes it as a "continual, pulsating dynamic in the nature of the universe" (Goetschel 2004: 95).

17. Carola Hilfrich has compared Mendelssohn's rejection of the unification of faiths with Arendt's conception of the "irreducible singularity of each human" (Hilfrich 2000: 161–62.)

18. Nancy K. Levene, in her very fine book on Spinoza, *Spinoza's Revelations*, puts the point about dynamic tension this way: "No state is permanent, but a repressive one much less so than a democratic one. As with the individual in the *Ethics*, political enlightenment is not about the achievement of some rational moment of stasis or balance. It is just the opposite. The perfection of the state implies that it is a breathing entity, one that, like any organism, naturally and inevitably comes to an end and one whose endurance is therefore an *achievement*, a function of effort" (Levene 2004).

19. For another Derridean reading of Mendelssohn's theory of language, see also Hilfrich 2000. I am sympathetic to the Derridean approaches of Martyn and Hilfrich, but I believe that Wittgenstein's philosophy of language, especially as it has been presented in the work of Stanley Cavell, offers a closer fit to Mendelssohn's theory of language.

20. Derrida has developed the performativity of the promise of language in a number of works, including *Monolingualism of the Other* and *Sovereignties in Question*. For a fuller discussion of Derrida's notion of the "I promise a language" behind every utterance, and also some reflections on its relation to Rosenzweig's philosophy of language, see Rosenstock 2007: 258–62.

21. Michaelis, *Orientalische Bibliothek*, 22 Teil, 326 and 332; Mendelssohn's response is found in *Über die 39 Artikel der englischen Kirche und deren Beschwörung, Berlinische Monatschrift* 1784, pp. 24–41 Both texts are reproduced in *JubA* 8:205–24; also online through *Zeitschriften der Aufklärung* (http://www.ub.uni-bielefeld.de/diglib/aufklaerung/suche.htm).

22. For a discussion of Mendelssohn's philosophy of history, see Erlin 2002.

23. Gotthold Ephraim Lessing 2005: 184–240. Mendelssohn had certainly read *Ernst and Falk*. Lessing had first sent the manuscript to Mendelssohn to read; see Schneider 1948: 1227.

24. Lessing intends with the words "ad extra" ("towards the outside") to refer to the outwardly observable deeds of the brotherhood; see Lessing 2005: 189.

25. The need to indicate a tooth in order to identify the pain is a point that Mendelssohn makes in *Morning Hours* 1:3 There, Mendelssohn makes the point that without such ability to identify an observable site of pain, we cannot be sure about the identity of the pain. That is why "children, who have not yet established a sufficiently firm connection [between observable source of pain and the inner experience of pain], rarely are able to say correctly what hurts or where it hurts."

26. Cavell's entire philosophical project is devoted to exploring the moral dimension of Wittgenstein's thinking, as well its significance for a political philosophy of democratic sociality. For the moral dimension, see, for example, Cavell 1979: 326–478. For the political implications, see Cavell 1979: 20–28. Cavell's development of a Wittgensteinian political philosophy is especially the concern of his readings of Thoreau and Emerson in such texts as Cavell 1992 and Cavell 1989.

27. I will return to this point in Chapter 5 (in "The Last Supper Once More").

28. I would like to draw attention to the fascinating comparison that Peter Fenves makes between this conception of Judaism as a living script that constantly inspires speech and the Platonic representation of the person of Socrates—someone Mendelssohn himself had sought inspiration from in his *Phädon*. See Fenves 2001: 92–93. Judaism, one might say, shows that—with God's help—a people might learn to embrace rather than kill Socrates. Another point one might make is that Mendelssohn is seeking to replace Christ with Socrates/Moses as the model figuration of love.

29. Jeffrey Librett makes the same point when he says that Mendelssohn, "maintaining a maximally discreet appearance," has shown that "Judaism is, in rational terms, *superior* to Christianity" (Librett 2000: 63).

332 Notes

30. Carola Hilfrich has quite insightfully linked Mendelssohn's invocation of the multiplicity of human faces with the passage in the Mishnah Tractate Sanhedrin (*b. Sanh* 37a–38b) that treats this fact as a sign of the irreplaceability of each single human created in God's image. Hilfrich also suggests a connection between Mendelssohn's evocation of the human face and Rosenzweig's concept of the Face. See Hilfrich 2000: 160–172. Hilfrich's book on *Repräsentation und Idolatrie in Moses Mendelssohns Philosophie* (its subtitle) can profitably be read in conjunction with Batnitzky's book on Rosenzweig, *Idolatry and Representation* (2000).

2. JACOBI AND MENDELSSOHN: THE TRAGEDY OF A MESSIANIC FRIENDSHIP

1. Rosenzweig 1984: 45.

2. Hereafter *Spinoza-Letters*, with page references to the translation in Jacobi 1994, followed by pagination of the 1785 edition. The authoritative republication of the texts of all three editions of the text (1785, 1789, 1819) is offered in Jacobi 2000. The most important recent discussions of the work and the controversy that led up to it can be found in George di Giovanni's introduction in Jacobi 1994: 3–167, esp. 67–90 and in Beiser 1987: chap. 2, "Jacobi and the Pantheism Controversy," 44–49. Also quite useful is Zammito 1992: chap. 11, "The Pantheism Controversy and the *Third Critique*," 228–47. Still one of the best and most wide-ranging examinations of the "Spinoza Quarrel" and its historical and philosophical importance is Thomas McFarland's *Coleridge and the Pantheist Tradition* (1969: 53–106, 289–97).

3. The letter from Jacobi to Elise Raimarus and her letter to Mendelssohn, dated August 4, 1783, is letter 607 in Moses Mendelssohn, *Briefwechsel* 3, *JubA* 13. Translations are mine unless otherwise noted.

4. A more extended discussion of the argument is offered in di Giovanni 1994: 73–86. For a brief but quite informative discussion of Lessing's relation to the Spinozism and pantheism of his day, see Zammito 1997: 115–17. Zammito also places the Jacobi-Mendelssohn quarrel over Spinoza into the broader context of the rise of German idealism.

5. Although di Giovanni is right to date the first conversation between Lessing and Jacobi to 1779, *Spinoza-Letters* reports only the conversations that took place the following year, in the summer of 1780, as di Giovanni more accurately recounts in his introduction in Jacobi 1994: 59. For a detailed history of the conversations, see Jacobi 2000: 330.

6. Jacobi calls the first the "principium compositionis" and the second the "principium generationis" (see Jacobi 1994: 287–88).

7. There are a number ways of formulating Jacobi's interpretation of Spinozism and his objections to it, although all of them focus on the confusion of conditions of explanation and existence. Besides di Giovanni's, one of the clearest is that of Paul W. Franks, who says that Jacobi claims that Spinozism is

"a system that meets two conditions: the *holistic condition* that every particular (object, fact, or judgment) be determined through its role within the whole and not through any intrinsic properties; and the *monistic condition* that the whole be grounded in an absolute principle that is immanent and not transcendent" (Franks 2005: 9–10). Such a system, according to Jacobi, *explains* everything with rational consistency, or as Franks says, offers a "genuine justification" for everything. However, Jacobi resists the logical attraction of Spinozism because "such a system would not only be unable to account for the individuality of persons and everyday objects, it would also tend to annihilate the individuality of any person who actually came to believe it and live according to it" (Franks 2005: 9). "Individuality" is the result of the inner power that brings the object into being and holds its manifold parts together as a unity. Franks develops this interpretation of Jacobi's position in a later chapter of his book (Franks 2005: esp. 84–145). Besides di Giovanni and Franks, I have also found quite helpful the discussion in Manfred Frank 2004: 58–75.

8. Cf. *Spinoza-Letters* 195; 34.

9. For a general discussion of Jacobi's influence, see Beiser 1987: chap. 2, and passim; for a more specific discussion of Jacobi's influence on Hegel, see Inwood 1998: 213–14; for Schleiermacher, see Lamm 1994; for Jacobi's influence on Schelling, see Wirth 2003: 33–53, and passim; for a collection of essays dealing with Fichte's relation to Jacobi, see Hammacher 1994; on Jacobi and Hölderlin, see Frank 2004: 77–96.

10. Jacobi 1994: 497–536.

11. I am aware that one needs to define rather precisely what one means by *gnostic* in order to give historical and philosophical clarity to a claim that there is a gnostic strain in German idealism, and I am indebted to the careful work of Cyril O'Regan in his *Gnostic Return in Modernity* for having accomplished a much-needed housecleaning in the critical literature on "modern gnosticism." I believe that O'Regan has persuasively shown the existence of a "gnostic return" in modernity, extending from Jacob Boehme to Hegel. I would simply argue that Jacobi occupies a significant place in this return. O'Regan also points out that to the extent that the gnostic turn makes use of Kabbalistic material, it does so in a decidedly anti-Jewish manner (see pp. 84–85). Benjamin Lazier (2008) has recently devoted much of his superb book on the intellectual history of Weimar Germany (*God Interrupted: Heresy and the European Imagination between the World Wars*) to the "Gnostic Return" in Christian theology, especially in the work of Karl Barth. He is, I believe, spot on in identifying a profound resistance to this gnostic theology on the part of many Weimar Jewish intellectuals, especially Hans Jonas. In the next chapter I will offer a reading of Rosenzweig as another of the combatants against the gnostic return. Unlike Lazier, I read this resistance to gnosticism within the framework of gnosticism's fundamental antagonism, in both its ancient and modern forms, to the God of the Hebrew Bible. But Lazier's wider contextualization of thinkers like Hans Jonas,

Gershom Scholem, and Leo Strauss is, I would argue, fully compatible with my own more Jewishly-focused framing. In the end, the Jewish Question is, as I have said at the end of the introduction, exemplary of the human question, the question about how to inhabit the world with a respect for its inescapable heterogeneity. Gnosticism seeks to escape from the strangeness of the world to a "home" beyond it; Rosenzweig and thinkers like Wittgenstein, Arendt, and Cavell (and Hans Jonas, as Lazier so ably demonstrates) embrace this strangeness as the condition of experiencing the miraculousness and unpredictability of existence.

12. That Germany is the nation which will provide the world with a philosophical rather than a political revolution is a part of German intellectual self-understanding early on. For example, Karl Leonhard Reinhold, then thirty-three years old, writes in 1790: "Among all other European states, Germany is the most disposed toward revolutions of spirit and the least disposed toward political revolutions" (Reinhold 2005: 133).

13. Supp. 2 to the second edition of *Jacobi to Fichte*, published in Jacobi 1812–25: 2:313–23; translation in Jacobi 1994: 528–33. The passage is found on p. 530 of the translation, p. 314 of the German text.

14. It is one of the great merits of Willi Goetschel's book *Spinoza's Modernity* to show how Heine was unique in resisting the "spiritualization" of Spinoza. Goetschel makes it clear how Heine's brand of Spinozism amounted to a "declaration of Jewish independence" (Goetschel 2004: 263).

15. For an overview of Wachter's intellectual odyssey from anti-Spinozist to Germany's most influential Spinozist, see Israel 2001: 645–52.

16. For a slightly longer discussion of Hamann, see Chapter 4 (in "Overview: Reinhold, Kant, and Hegel Before 1800").

17. *Jacobi to Fichte* is translated in Jacobi 1994: 497–536. Citations are from this translation, with page references followed by the pagination of the 1799 edition.

18. Jeffrey Librett has argued that for Jacobi "Enlightenment reason is Jewish" (1999: 236). Librett follows out to its extreme conclusion Jacobi's hatred of hyper-rational abstraction, what I am calling his "gnostic" rejection of the Jewish God, when he writes that the "transcendence of formalism that he [Jacobi] proposed could be achieved only through the (sacrificial) identification of certain restricted forms with particular populations, all of which would have to be kept out of the human community" (242). While I am sympathetic to Librett's point, I am not as willing as he is in this essay to reduce Jacobi to a "radical antirationalist" who laid the groundwork for late nineteenth-century racism.

19. I rely upon the 1816 edition in Jacobi 1812–25: 3:245–460; hereafter, *On Things Divine*. Translations of this text are mine.

20. Somewhat confusingly (Jacobi was often indifferent to consistency), Jacobi contrasts the self-deifying *I* with the "sovereign declaration," Machtspruch, "I am, who I am" that "founds everything" and whose "echo in the

human soul is the revelation of God within it" (418). That there is a revelation of a divine voice within the soul that awakens the soul to freedom is central to Rosenzweig's understanding of revelation.

21. German text in Jacobi 1812–25: 2:3–123; English translation in Jacobi 1994: 537–90. Citations are to the English translation followed by pagination of the 1815 text.

22. The quotation is on page 154 of supp. 7 to the 1789 edition of *Spinoza-Letters*, republished in Jacobi 1812–25: 4.2:1–276; English translation from Jacobi 1994: 376.

23. Citations will be to the English translation in Jacobi 1994: 253–338, followed by the pagination of 1787 text as provided in the English translation.

24. This same sort of perceptual realism, with its emphasis upon the experience of continuous extension and duration, will become a central feature of Bergson's philosophy from the very first, as Lévy-Bruhl had long ago pointed out in his book on Jacobi (Lévy-Bruhl 1894: 160).

25. Moses Mendelssohn, at age 56, died on Wednesday, January 4, 1786. On the preceding Sunday, in the midst of a severe winter storm, Mendelssohn had carried the manuscript of his new book, *An die Freunde Lessings* (*To the Friends of Lessing*), to the home of his publisher, C. F. Voss. (Moses Mendelssohn, *An Die Freunde Lessings. Ein Anhang zu Herrn Jacobi Briefwechsel über die Lehre des Spinoza*, Berlin: Christian Friedrich Voß und Sohn, 1786; *JubA* 3.2:177–218.) After returning home, Mendelssohn became feverish and in the ensuing days he grew weaker, finally dying in the arms of his oldest daughter. Those who were close to Mendelssohn said that Jacobi had brought about his untimely death. See, for example, the letters of Sophie Reimarus and Sophie Becker excerpted in *JubA* 22.1, (letters 293 and 295). Sophie Reimarus writes: "I would not want for anything in the world to be in Jacobi's place," and Sophie Becker speaks of the "Streit" ("quarrel") with Jacobi as the "Ursache seines Todes" ("cause of his [Mendelssohn's] death").

26. Even an inanimate object is perceived to have a certain unity of parts that cannot be reduced to a mere assemblage of parts with purely external relations to one another: "In corporeal extension we generally perceive something analogous to individuality, for extended being cannot be divided *as such* but everywhere exhibits the same kind of unity that inseparably joins together a multiplicity within itself" (*David Hume* 295; 116).

27. This side of Jacobi is the focus of Librett 1999.

28. Stanley Cavell, "The Avoidance of Love," 323; the essay is in Cavell 1969, 1976.

29. It is telling that the 1785 edition of *Spinoza-Letters* has a frontispiece showing a portrait of Spinoza, whereas the 1789 edition has a frontispiece with a portrait in profile of Jacobi superimposed over a similar portrait of Mendelssohn. Jacobi's classically sculpted features (he was widely reputed for his handsomeness) stand out in sharp contrast with the irregular (and unmistakably

Jewish) features of Mendelssohn. The viewer is forced to make a nearly visceral response to Mendelssohn's face as, in comparison with Jacobi's, ugly.

30. It is interesting to note that at the exact time when Mendelssohn and Jacobi were in correspondence, Mendelssohn was visited by the brilliant young Polish rabbi and philosophical autodidact, Salomon Maimon. Mendelssohn managed to persuade the Berlin Jewish community to allow Maimon to reside, with the economic support of Mendelssohn and others of his circle, in Berlin. Maimon says in his *Autobiography* that Mendelssohn found his attempt to link Spinoza and the Kabbalah—it must have been the last straw to be assailed by first Jacobi, and then Maimon as a defender of an unmystical Spinoza—so disturbing that he was forced to leave Berlin in order to avoid a direct confrontation with a man whom he in fact respected a great deal. Maimon translated *Morning Hours* into Hebrew. For a very interesting study of Maimon's Spinozism and his encounter with Mendelssohn in Berlin, see Yitzhak Melamed 2004. For a brilliant study of Maimon's "radical Enlightenment," see Socher 2006.

31. Republished in *JubA* 3.2; translations throughout are mine.

32. Mendelssohn's contention that sensation is not only a certain quality but also a finitely determined intensity within a continuous range prefigures the fundamental presupposition upon which all nineteenth-century German experimental psychology is built, from Johann Friedrich Herbart (1776–1841) to Wilhelm Wundt (1832–1920). Wundt summarizes the presupposition this way: "For in every sensation we distinguish two properties—one which we name its strength or intensity, and another which we call its quality. Neither can exist in absence of the other" (Wundt 1896: 15). Herbart enunciates the principle of the continuous intensity of perception in "Über die Tonlehre" (1839) whose "First Fact" states: "From any given tone one can continue to progress to higher and lower tones without being able . . . to reach a certain highest or lowest tone" (Herbart 1906, band 11: 69; translation mine).

33. Mendelssohn's argument against what he calls "pantheistic idealism" is precisely repeated by William James in *A Pluralistic Universe*: "If the absolute makes us by knowing us, how can we exist otherwise than *as* it knows us? But it knows each of us indivisibly from everything else. Yet if to exist means nothing but to be experienced, as idealism affirms, we surely exist otherwise, for we experience *ourselves* ignorantly and in division" (James 1909: 192–93). James concludes that if God is understood to possess a consciousness of the whole universe, only a "theistic" God can perform this role "for the theistic God is a separate being" (195). This is exactly Mendelssohn's objection to Jacobi's insistence that Spinozism must reject the independent existence of finite beings. Mendelssohn agrees with Jacobi that Spinoza did in fact deny the independent existence of finite beings, but he disagrees with Jacobi that Spinoza offers a logically consistent position in doing so. Mendelssohn argues that Spinoza should have recognized that finite conscious beings are not simply reducible to

God's thoughts. The "purified" pantheism that Mendelssohn attributes to Lessing would therefore be a logically consistent version of Spinozism that recognizes the gap between divine infinitude and human finitude while claiming that human finitude has its being and ground within the infinite substance that is God.

34. Republished in Mendelssohn *JubA* 3.2.

35. See the discussion of the initial reaction by the Berlin philosophical establishment to Jacobi in di Giovanni's introduction to Jacobi 1994: 89.

36. It is interesting to note that fifteen years later, Jacobi, in *On Things Divine*, will make use of the same verses in order to defend his own conception of a personal God against the impersonal One and All of the new idealist Spinozism; see Jacobi 1812–25: 3:422.

37. On the Wednesday Society and Zöllner's role in the question that arose out of central concerns of the Wednesday Society, see Schmidt 1989: 271–75.

38. *To the Friends of Lessing* 205; the translation is di Giovanni's in Jacobi 1994: 355, from the reprint of the same letter in Jacobi's 1789 edition of *Spinoza-Letters*.

39. English translation in Immanuel Kant 1996b: 11–22. Kant took his title from a phrase of Mendelssohn's in *Morning Hours*: "Whenever my speculations seem to have led me too far from the main thoroughfare of common sense, I stand still and try to orient myself" (*Morning Hours* 10:82). He reiterates this point in *To the Friends of Lessing*: "When I have beaten about in the thorns and hedges of speculation for a long time, I try to orient myself with common sense and at least point myself in the direction where I once again can join up with it" (202–3).

3. IN THE YEAR OF THE LORD 1800: ROSENZWEIG AND THE SPINOZA QUARREL

1. The uniqueness of the revelation at Mt. Sinai guarantees the uniqueness of the Mosaic constitution as the perfect unification of church and state, their being "one" as Mendelssohn says in *Jerusalem* (128; 2:116). The Mosaic constitution, says Mendelssohn, is an "individual thing, which has no genus, which refuses to be stacked with anything, which cannot be put under the same rubric with anything else" (131; 2:123). Funkenstein (1993: 225) asks "Why only once, if it is beneficial?" about this unique constitution. "Neither does Mendelssohn raise the question, nor can I answer it for him," Funkenstein replies. But perhaps the answer is not so far to find: The unique *form* of the revelation (unity of church and state) is perfectly instantiated by a particular *content*, namely, a certain *legislation* that rejects idolatry as its fundamental principle and that fosters felicity for a people without the need for state coercion. Any other revelation would have to instantiate the same form but with a different (and equally perfect) content. Since Mendelssohn believes that the legislation revealed at Mt. Sinai is not limited to one geographic locale or time period and allows for anyone to join who wishes, why would God need to create more than one legislative

code in order to realize the same form? Willi Goetschel has argued for "an alternative universalism" based on Mendelssohn's concept of revelation as historically specific. Goetschel argues for Mendelssohn's willingness in *Jerusalem* to acknowledge the multiplicity of historical revelations made to many different peoples (see esp. Goetschel 2004: 165). The point that Mendelssohn makes about the Mosaic constitution as sui generis goes against Goetschel's reading. Although Goetschel has pushed Mendelssohn's position farther than Mendelssohn himself was willing to go, I am, however, entirely sympathetic with Goetschel's effort to find in Mendelssohn a model for rethinking tradition so that it remains both "open to the future" and open to pluralism (166).

2. In Chapter 7 I suggest how the marriage of the "hoofer" (Fred Astaire) and the classically trained ballerina (Cyd Charisse) in the movie *The Band Wagon* offers an allegory for a democratic redemptive praxis whose ideal is not consensus but the agreement to create the conditions for ever new forms of partnerings.

3. I will cite the Galli translation (Rosenzweig 2005). Citations will include page reference to the Galli translation followed by the page reference to the German edition of Rosenzweig 1976. This German text is reproduced with identical pagination in Rosenzweig 1988. It also freely available (identically paginated) as a digital text, published in 2002 by the Goethe Universität under the editorship of Albert Raffelt, at http://publikationen.ub.uni-frankfurt.de/volltexte/2005/1932/.

4. For an argument that Rosenzweig can most profitably be read in relation to Jacobi, see Franks 2006. Rosenzweig mentions the importance of Feuerbach in "Das Neue Denken" ("The New Thinking") (Rosenzweig 1984: 152).

5. There is a great deal of evidence in the "Paralipomena" (notes written during Rosenzweig's military deployment in 1916 before his arrival at the Macedonian front) that Rosenzweig saw his concept of revelation standing in opposition to what he called the "gnostic" idea that the God of Creation is other than the God who frees the human being. "The factual reality [Tatbestand] of the moral consciousness requires (1) the authority of the law (therefore God) and (2) freedom (therefore the human being), but it does not require straightaway the drawing *together* (*Zusammen*hang) of (1) and (2). (1) requires something that is free, but not necessarily the human, but somehow gnostically the world, and on the other hand (2) requires a law, but not necessarily God, but perhaps merely a private law" (Rosenzweig 1984: 84). In other words, the God of creation could be imagined, as he is in gnosticism, to lay down a law in order to enslave the created world, and the individual could seek a law that is already within himself, as gnosticism also teaches. In contrast with this gnostic division of Creator God and free human, Rosenzweig claims that "the drawing together of (1) and (2) is *revealed* [*offenbart*]" (84): "considered from one side (looking out from (2)) the law is the law of the *Creator* (that therefore my existence [Dasein] is my being *there* [*da* Sein], my being led from Egypt towards here at

Sinai is the work of the very same God who gives me the law of my freedom) and on the other side (looking out from (1)) the law seeks no other actualization except for the human being, God therefore created *only* for the sake of the Tora. These two things are *not logical* necessities; paganism asserts (and irrefutably) the opposite of both; it posits a God who is his own goal and a human being who is his own law" (84). In an earlier note, Rosenzweig writes that the church's battle against gnosticism is really its battle against "philosophical paganism" that had no place for any "real history" ("wirkliche Geschichte") in which anything meaningful might happen (62). In a later note, Rosenzweig says the battle between Christianity and gnosticism is rendered "welthistorisch" ("world-historical") when the new Johannine church confronts the return of gnosticism, namely, "in the moment when philosophy creates *out of itself* the thought of revelation" (108). Rosenzweig explains that he has Hegel in mind. Rosenzweig thus sees revelation as opening the possibility for history to be the site of redemptive activity involving both the creator God and the free human being, rather than something to be escaped from or theorized away (in a gnostic flight from the world). Rosenzweig clearly identifies paganism and also German idealism as gnostic; I have claimed that, despite his critique of German idealism, Jacobi is operating within the same gnostic ambit. His concept of revelation has not yet drawn together the God of creation and the God who reveals himself within history.

6. Mendelssohn seems here to have failed to distinguish possibility from virtuality. A line is not made up of infinitely many possible points, each therefore the object of an infinite mind's consciousness. A line is, rather, made up of virtual points whose actuality is *created* when the line stops, or when it is divided. The virtuality of the self as it moves through time and actualizes itself in certain actions is a key notion developed in James, Bergson, and Deleuze. Mendelssohn's commitment to the Leibnizian principle that this is the best of all possible worlds divides him from the evolutionary perspective of the later thinkers.

7. For a concise description of Rosenzweig's view of art as providing a model for Creation, Revelation, and Redemption, see Rubinstein 1999: 212–20. See also Batnitzky 2000: 92–99. In Chapter 5 (in "Rosenzweig's Children") I will discuss Rosenzweig's aesthetic theory as it relates to his interpretation of post-1800 "Johannine" Christianity.

8. Batnitzky 1997: 96.

9. I want to note here that the title I have taken for this chapter, "In the Year of the Lord 1800," may remind readers of a similar title, not of a chapter but a chapter's first section, in George di Giovanni's very fine book, *Freedom and Religion in Kant and His Immediate Successors* (2005). Section 7.1 of his book is entitled "Anno Domini 1799" (242). Di Giovanni's account of the importance of the year 1799 bears a very close resemblance to Rosenzweig's account of 1800. For di Giovanni, 1799 marked the year that the "idea of reason was on trial," with Jacobi the prosecuting attorney pressing the case of the personal

God of revelation and, more particularly, the incarnate God of Christian revelation. Rosenzweig and di Giovanni agree that Jacobi had little chance of succeeding with his prosecutorial case because by the end of the year 1799, reason itself—represented by the new system of Hegel—had assumed the role of supreme judge. Reason could hardly condemn *itself*.

10. It is possible that Rosenzweig has in mind the poem "Meine Göttin" that is dedicated to Hope. But that is hardly the only source of Rosenzweig's identification of *hope* as a quintessential Goethean word, as I will show in what follows.

11. In Chapter 5 I will explore in more detail Mendelssohn's resonance within the text of Rosenzweig. As I mentioned when I quoted Mendelssohn's text in the introduction, I think it is likely that Rosenzweig is recollecting a passage that struck a chord within him as he studied *Jerusalem* as part of his work on his Hegel book. In Chapter 5 I will show how Rosenzweig's recovery of Mendelssohn is profoundly shaped by his reading of Hegel.

12. See Schelling 1998: 212–13 and Schelling 1992: 210–12. For recent discussions of Rosenzweig's debt to Schelling, see the essay of Paul W. Franks, "From 1914 to 1917," in Rosenzweig 2000: esp. 31–37, and also Bienenstock 2003: 233–36.

13. The "Reichdeputation" edict redistributed lands—dismembering the Holy Roman Empire, in effect—in an attempt to placate German princes who had lost territory to France west of the Rhine as a result of the wars of the French Revolution.

14. I choose the phrase "What remains" deliberately in conjunction with *hope*; the phrase is the subject of a brilliant reading of Hölderlin's poem "*Andenken*" in Santner 2001: 140–46. I will talk more about Santner's reading in what follows.

15. Rosenzweig's edition and commentary on the manuscript is found in Rosenzweig 1984: 3–44. I discuss it further in Chapter 5 (in "Introduction: Reading through Hegel").

16. In Goethe 1894: 217–388. Unless otherwise noted, translations from Goethe's poem are mine.

17. I will have more to say about the notion that marriage can serve as symbol of revelation and redemption in the everyday world in Chapter 7 (in "Rosenzweig and Cavell on Revelation").

18. Peter Eli Gordon notes that Hölderlin's poem "An die Deutschen" was chosen as the epigraph for Rosenzweig's *Hegel und die Staat*. Gordon, however, while noting that Rosenzweig lost his pre-war confidence in history and thus renounced the optimism of the book and its chosen epigraph, does not mention the importance of Johannine Christianity for Rosenzweig, closely connected with the very late poetry of Hölderlin, *Patmos* most particularly. See Gordon 2003: 83.

19. See Stahmer 1984: 61–62.

20. For a fuller account of *Faktum*, see Paul W. Franks's note on the term, in Rosenzweig 2000: 68n47.

21. I am not claiming that Rosenzweig is necessarily drawing directly from Jacobi. However, even if he is relying upon F. W. J. von Schelling as his philosophical guide (Rosenzweig's use of "A = A" and other such formulas are taken from Schelling's *Weltalter* [*Ages of the World*] as well as his *Philosophie der Offenbarung* [*Philosophy of Revelation*]), this nonetheless shows that, indirectly, Rosenzweig is working within Jacobi's problematic. Schelling's lengthy response to Jacobi, the *Denkmal der Schrift von den göttlichen Dingen und ihre Offenbarung* (1812), shows the importance of Jacobi for Schelling, even if only as a major polemical target. In his *Philosophie der Offenbarung* lectures, Schelling sees the essential problem for philosophy to be the explication of "monotheism" as distinct from polytheism, pantheism, deism, or theism. The problem of monotheism is, he says, set by Jacobi: how to reconcile the reality of a personal God with the concept of a Creator God. "Jacobi had confessed," Schelling explains, "that in accordance with the concept of reason the thought of a personal God seems impossible to reconcile with the thought of the creator of the world" (Schelling 1992: 139–40; translation mine). No doubt, Rosenzweig drew significantly from Schelling in his explication of God as world creator, but the notion that revelation is a personal encounter between an *I* and a *Thou* he would have found in Jacobi. For Rosenzweig's indebtedness to Schelling's notion of God's identity *before* creation, see Kavka 2004: 136–44.

22. The idea that the God-human encounter is part of the unfolding of God's creation of the world is found in Schelling, who speaks of God's "Geduld und Langmut, die von Anfang bis jetzt eine *freiwillige* Umwendung—metanoia—gewollt hat, so daß sie den ganzen Erfolg der Schöpfung auf den freien Willen des Menschen gestellt hat" ("patience and long-suffering spirit which from the beginning has willed a turning—metanoia—so that he has placed the success of creation in the free will of humans") (Schelling 1992: 212).

23. Rosenzweig's account of what he calls "the grammar of the logos" in part 2, book 1 ("Creation") of the *Star* (135–51; 138–45) is certainly one of the denser portions of the work. I have found that the themes Rosenzweig addresses here—the limitations of mathematics, the nature of affirmation and negation, the priority of quality over state and adjectives over nouns—can profitably be read together with the opening pages of chapter 4 of Bergson's *Creative Evolution* (1911: 272–98), where the same themes are addressed. Indeed, many points in the Bergson chapter have parallels in the "Creation" book of the *Star*, namely, the "logic of creation," "idealistic logic," and the first part of the "idealistic metaphysics" sections (142–57; 146–61). It is possible that Bergson and Rosenzweig have a common source in Schelling, but Rosenzweig was no doubt familiar with Bergson's major work of philosophy. The connection between Bergson's and Rosenzweig's concept of creation has been noted by Emmanuel Levinas, who describes them (as well as Heidegger) as the foremost thinkers

of the modern period who sought to "deformalize time" and restore to it "a concreteness 'older' than the pure form of time" (Levinas 1998: 176). The connection between Bergson and Rosenzweig deserves further study.

24. Aristotle in his *Categories* distinguishes between "substance" and all other categories, and for him "substance" is the subject *in* which (as "man" is predicated of Socrates) or *of* which (as when "whiteness" is predicated of Socrates) all the other categories are predicated. In the *Categories*, substance is the particular, like Socrates, and so B = A represents the abstract shape of the simple declarative sentence ("Socrates is a man"). In his *Metaphysics*, however, Aristotle will declare that "substance" is really form or universal, the unchanging species-identity that provides the condition of possibility of a thing's being counted as an individual. Without the universal "man" that makes Socrates the kind of being he is, Socrates could not stand as the subject of any predication at all. This is the framework in which to understand Rosenzweig's claim that B = A is the form of language that reflects the logos of the world, in which the particular grows into its species identity, whereas A = B is the form of all propositions from the perspective of philosophy, in which the species identity logically precedes the particular: A refers to the species and B to the individuating properties. A is the universal, B is the particular. See esp. *Star* 58–60; 54–56.

25. I return to the theme of the proper name as offering a path beyond solitude in Chapter 7 (in "Rosenzweig and Cavell on Revelation"), where I discuss the common motif of Adam's naming of Eve in Rosenzweig and Cavell.

26. Jacobi's call for a "metacritique" shows the influence of his friend Hamann, who in 1784 had sent him a copy of a brief text called *Metakritik über den Purismum der Vernunft*. The text was never published in Hamann's lifetime. It is found in Hamann 1949–57: 2:281–89. Hamann offers an analysis of transcendental idealism's search for the formal conditions of experience as a misguided search for a pure, formal language without phonic matter. Language, Hamann insists, cannot be divided into matter and form without destroying its living reality. Interestingly, Hamann attributes idealism's quest for formal purity to a "gnostic hatred for matter" (285). Jacobi seems never to have understood Hamann's faith in the power of language itself to embody revelation, to be a "sacrament," as Hamann describes it (289). In his identification of language as the site of revelation, Hamann stands as an important precursor of Rosenzweig.

4. REINHOLD AND KANT: THE QUEST FOR A NEW RELIGION OF REASON

1. "Orientation," as I have discussed in Chapter 1, is a key term in *Morning Hours*. There, it is "common sense" that orients reason. In his essay, "What does 'orienting oneself' by reason mean?" Kant agreed with Mendelssohn against Jacobi that reason requires orientation via the common-sense assumption that God is a moral being, not via revealed faith (English translation in Kant 1998:3–14; AK8:133–146). (*AK* refers to the standard German—originally

Notes   343

Royal Prussian—Academy of Sciences edition of Kant's works in Kant 1969–.) Of course, Kant could not accept the idea that a divine moral being would provide laws for a particular people.

2. Kant 1996b: 269; AK5:16

3. See, for example, the addendum entitled "Über die Freiheit des Menschen" ("Concerning Man's Freedom") that is part of the new Vorrede to the 1789 edition of Jacobi's *Spinoza-Letters* (Jacobi 1994:341–49; xxii–xlviii). Jacobi attacks the Kantian categorical imperative as a syllogism that robs the human of real freedom; real freedom is only revealed "in the human heart" ("im Herzen des Menschen"), in the feeling of pure love ("reine Liebe") that is also God's Spirit and creative will. Jacobi's attempt to join God as Creator and God as a Revealed Person through the notion of pure love is admittedly rather vague, but it indicates clearly the contours of the contrast between Jacobi on the one side and Kant and Reinhold on the other. It draws Jacobi closer to Hegel, as I will explain in what follows.

4. Hegel very clearly positions himself in relation to Jacobi in *Glauben und Wissen* (*Faith and Knowledge*) (1977: 97–152). Hegel phrases the distinction between God the Creator and God the Revealer as the distinction between the God of Knowledge and the God of Faith. In *Faith and Knowledge*, Hegel tries to show how Kant, Jacobi, and Fichte all fail to show how Knowledge's God and Faith's God are one. Hegel's solution is to posit a God who comes to know himself and create himself as he reveals himself in nature and history.

5. Unless otherwise noted, the translation I use of the early theological texts is found in Hegel 1948. I will offer page references first to the English translation and then to the German text found in the Nohl edition.

6. I use the translation in Dunning, 1979: 210–28, offering page references to this translation, followed by page reference to the German text in Hamann 1949–57, vol. 3: 293–318. For a perceptive study of Hamann's response to Mendelssohn, see the (now undeseservedly forgotten) essay by Ludwig Feuchtwanger on the reception of Mendelssohn, "The Image of Mendelssohn among his Opponents" (1929). Feuchtwanger seeks to recover the contemporary impact of *Jerusalem* by contrasting it with the work of Hamann: "in *Jerusalem* and its opposed work *Golgatha* [sic] *und Scheblimini* one sees with complete clarity . . . the absolute lack of understanding on the part of Hamann and the Christian world of Mendelssohn's spiritual identity" (216).

7. In his brilliant study of Mendelssohn in *The Rhetoric of Cultural Dialogue*, Jeffrey Librett (2000) argues that Mendelssohn deliberately structured his defense of Judaism in terms that would reverse the letter/spirit dichotomy advanced by Paul, who first articulated the supersessionism of the "circumcision of the heart" as the spirit of Judaism's literal circumcision of the flesh. The fierce attack on Mendelssohn by Hamann is evidence of the rhetorical power of *Jerusalem*'s defense of Judaism, reversing the terms of the letter/spirit dichotomy and placing Christianity on the side of the (dead) letter.

8. Reinhold's *Hebrew Mysteries* was originally published as "Ueber die Mysterien der alten Hebräer" and "Ueber die größern Mysterien der Hebräer" in *Journal für Freymaurer* 3.1 (1786): 5–79 and 3.3 (1786): 5–98. In 1787 they were republished together as a booklet (Reinhold 1788). Page references will be to Jan Assmann's recent republication of *Hebrew Mysteries* (Reinhold 2006). Translations are mine. Assmann offers a valuable historical contextualization of the work in his "Nachwort" (Reinhold 2006: 156–204). Reinhold's *Kant Letters* appeared originally in four volumes of *Der Teutsche Merkur* from September 1786 to August 1787. Together with the additions found in the two later book editions of the serialized letters, *Kant Letters* is now available in English translation (Reinhold 2005). I will provide page references only to the English edition, from which translations are taken.

9. Both texts are translated in Lessing 2005: 184–240.

10. I cannot do justice in an endnote to Librett's brilliant reading of Schlegel and the way that the Jewish daughter of Moses Mendelssohn, Dorothea Veit, figures in his writing. Let me only say Schlegel's gesture is to become both father and lover of Dorothea (leading to her divorce from her Jewish husband, Simon Veit), thus replacing Moses (Mendelssohn, but also Moses as founder of Judaism) with Christ. Schlegel positions himself as brother in flesh to the Jewish Dorothea and one in spirit with Christ. Their love unites flesh and spirit, raising up (Librett does not use this expression, but it is apt) the "mystical body" of Christ. It seems a foregone conclusion, given this *corpus mysticum* gender theology, that Dorothea and Friedrich will convert to Catholicism together (where the Church itself is construed as Christ's *corpus mysticum*).

11. Karl Ameriks (2004) has admirably defended Reinhold against Hegel's critique of him as a mere dilettante in presenting the history of reason. For Ameriks, Reinhold deserves credit as the first to make the "historical turn" ("historische Wende") in which the history of philosophy becomes an essential problem for philosophy. Ameriks has a hard time explaining why Reinhold undertook the project of explicating philosophy as the history of reason, and why he undertook it at the time he did. I am suggesting that it would help to answer this question if we take our start from the question facing German thinkers after Lessing's death: Who is the true heir of Lessing's project (in his last writings) of explaining how the present moment in Germany is an epochal moment in the history of revelation? Is it Mendelssohn (expositor of Lessing's "refined Spinozism" and defender of Lessing's hope for a religiously tolerant society)? Is it Jacobi (expositor of Lessing's fatalistic Spinozism and preacher of the "*salto mortale*" back into faith)? Or is it Reinhold as expositor of Lessing's Freemasonic dream of universal enlightenment? Reinhold realizes that to establish his claim to be the authentic heir of Lessing, he can present Kant as the philosopher who alone can solve the Mendelssohn-Jacobi dispute and thus show the limitations of their respective claims to be Lessing's heir. Reinhold uses Kant to present himself as Lessing's true heir.

12. The text is reprinted in Assmann 2006: 129–156.

13. Citations throughout will be from the translation of Allen Wood and George di Giovanni in Kant 1998, with references to the standard German Academy edition (AK). Hereafter *Religion-Reason*.

14. Kant 1996b: 277–309; AK8:275–313; the critique of Mendelssohn is on pp. 304–9; AK8:307–13.

15. It seems that this is the source of Marx's famous dictum about tragedy turning to farce in the spectacle of history.

16. For the evidence of Reinhold's concern with the threat of despotism within Freemasonry, see Roehr 2004: 160–65.

17. The passage is found first in the 1790 edition of *Kant Letters*.

18. The essay was published in two parts in *Der Teutsche Merkur* (1784, 3. Viertelj): 3–22; 122–32. Page images of the text and the journal are accessible through the website "Zeitungen der Aufklärung" (http://www.ub.uni-bielefeld.de/diglib/aufklaerung/). Translation mine. The quotation is from p. 19.

19. We know from the collection of notes entitled "Paralipomena" that date from 1916 that Rosenzweig carried the Reclam edition of Kant's *Religion-Reason* with him during this time. Rosenzweig finds the work significant precisely because it anticipates the late Schelling's interest in beginning philosophy with scripture rather than reason (see Rosenzweig 1984: 69) and also because the concept of radical evil, which Rosenzweig identifies as the "root concept" of Kant's philosophy, stands outside the critical system itself (68, 70).

20. In the *Critique of the Power of Judgment*, Kant says explicitly that "the intellectual, intrinsically purposive (moral) good, judged aesthetically, must not be represented so much as beautiful, but rather as sublime, so that it more arouses the feeling of respect (which scorns charm) than that of love and intimate affection, since human nature does not agree with that good of its own accord, but only through the dominion that reason exercises over sensibility" (Kant 1996a: 153–54; AK5:271).

21. In the *Critique of the Power of Judgment*, Kant speaks of the "ideal of beauty" that can only be rendered in the human figure because it contains a reference to the realm of morality (1996a: 120; AK5:235). Christianity has not reached the point where it can recognize that Christ's beauty is only a symbol of the moral sublimity that humanity must strive towards.

22. My analysis of Kant's interpretation of Judaism as a negative sublime covers some of the same ground as does Yirmiyahu Yovel in *Dark Riddle: Hegel, Nietzsche, and the Jews* (Yovel 1998).

23. In the *Critique of the Power of Judgment* beauty is said to exclude utility or any end outside of the object itself (see Kant 1996a: 111–16; AK5:227–32).

24. These quotations are from Kant's essay, written two years after *Religion-Reason*, "Toward Perpetual Peace" (1795). See Kant 1996b: 340; AK8:372.

25. Kant of course includes the Jewish people themselves in this characterization, and for this reason they never embodied Judaism "taken in its purity"

(*Religion-Reason* 131; AK6:126). Kant admits that "Jews ... produced, each for himself, some sort of religious faith," that is, some sort of moral faith (*Religion-Reason* 131; AK6:126).

26. I am, of course, aware that what Kant sees (hallucinates) in Judaism does, in fact, offer an uncanny preview of National Socialist ideology. Hannah Arendt has rightly seen Kantian radical evil at work in the silencing of the conscience in Nazi Germany and has called this "the banality of evil." What this banal evil produces is what Arendt calls "hell on earth." Kant sees the Jews as living in hell because of their pure politics of animal-creaturely survival; the Nazis will reduce the Jews to "bare life" in their projection of radical evil upon them. I am certainly not claiming, nor would I ever wish to claim, that Kant would have approved of the Nazi genocide of the Jews. His negative conception of Judaism should be interpreted as in large measure driven by the tremendous anxiety within German culture connected with the secularizing (i.e., de-Christianization) of the state when the institutional and symbolic structures of the thousand-year-old Holy Roman Empire began to totter during the French Revolutionary and Napoleonic Wars. *Religion-Reason* was published in 1793.

27. Kant 1996a: 156; AK5:274.

28. Kant notes that his idea of the Kingdom of God is actually *not* messianic because it does not fulfill a promise made in a covenant between God and a people at a moment in history. Entrance into the Kingdom of God does not depend upon remembering or reenacting a covenant; it is "available to cognition through mere reason" (*Religion-Reason* 139n1; Ak6:136n1). We will see that this is precisely the point at which Hegel will attack Kant: "mere reason" cannot provide the grounds for any empirical community to constitute itself in relation to the Kingdom of God. A commemorative, covenantal ritual is required. Despite Kant's technical point about the use of "messianic," I will continue to use it for heuristic purposes.

29. There is an interesting passage close to the end of G. K. Chesterton's *Orthodoxy* that describes the life of the "pagan or agnostic"—the individual who has no inkling of what Kant would call the sublime hope for humankind's ultimate redemption—as the life of someone who takes pleasure in worldly things, but can only grieve about the fate of humankind. Such an individual is "born upside down":

> Yet, according to the apparent estate of man as seen by the pagan or the agnostic, this primary need of human nature can never be fulfilled. Joy ought to be expansive; but for the agnostic it must be contracted, it must cling to one corner of the world. Grief ought to be a concentration; but for the agnostic its desolation is spread through an unthinkable eternity. This is what I call being born upside down. The sceptic may truly be said to be topsy-turvy; for his feet are dancing upwards in idle ecstacies, while his brain is in the abyss. To the modern man the heavens are actually below the earth. The explanation is simple; he is standing on his head; which is a very weak pedestal to stand on. But when he has found

his feet again he knows it. Christianity satisfies suddenly and perfectly man's ancestral instinct for being the right way up; satisfies it supremely in this; that by its creed joy becomes something gigantic and sadness something special and small. (Chesterton 2004: 186)

5. BEAUTIFUL LIFE: MENDELSSOHN, HEGEL, AND ROSENZWEIG

1. For a general discussion of the nature of these early works and their relation to Reinhold's and Kant's religion of reason, see "Overview: Reinhold, Kant, and Hegel before 1800," in Chapter 4.

2. Rosenzweig's short book in which the manuscript is published and discussed was written in 1914 and appeared in print in 1917. It is republished in Rosenzweig 1984: 3–44. Rosenzweig believed that the manuscript was composed by Schelling, despite the fact that it is clearly written in the hand of Hegel. Rosenzweig based his argument on the primacy of aesthetics over philosophy in the text, but this, I think, is consonant with the temper of Hegel's other early writings. Nothing in my argument depends upon the Hegelian authorship of the "Earliest System-Program" manuscript.

3. "Letter-philosophers," in the "Earliest System-Program," is thus more likely a Hegelian neologism also indebted to Mendelssohn than a phrase of Schelling's.

4. In his *Rhapsody, or Additions to the Letters on Sentiments*, Mendelssohn says that the aesthetic sensibility is a form of "intuitive knowledge" that can be of significant ethical and religious value. "One should learn to consider every human action in connection with the ever-present lawgiver of nature and in relation to eternity. One should get used to having these considerations before one's eyes in every action one performs. If one does this, a wholesome enthusiasm for virtue will be awakened in us, and each reason motivating us to be virtuous will attain an ethical majesty . . ." (Mendelssohn 1997: 165). If one reads this passage together with the description of the Jewish ceremonial law that I discuss below, it becomes clear that for Mendelssohn Jewish ceremonial law is the revealed legislation of the "ever-present lawgiver" intended to make all of life a beautiful representation that is both an incitement to virtue and the medium of an intuitive knowledge of the divine.

5. Once again, as we have seen with Kant, the philosopher projects upon the Jewish people an anxiety about the descent of his own nation (*qua* "Holy Roman Empire of the German Nation") into dismemberment and secularization. The fear was that the end of the thousand-year Reich would turn the German people into a machinal aggregate rather than a coherent state. Rosenzweig in *Hegel und der Staat* puts Hegel's political philosophy at the time of the composition of the early theological writings this way: "The state can now no longer be anything holy . . . Much more is it the task of the state in the modern world to protect the human right to the sanctities of conviction, of belief, which lie completely outside its realm; in general the state must content itself with its own unholy

realm of power [mit seinem eigenen unheiligen Machtgebiet zu begnügen]" (*Hegel-Staat* I, 45). Hegel in effect projects the negative image of this "unholy realm of power" as a spiritless machine onto the Jewish people. The dream of rebuilding the thousand-year Reich will reactivate the same anxiety with fateful consequences.

6. This is the entire thrust of Hegel's critique in *Faith and Knowledge* (1802) of Jacobi's overemphasis on subjective finitude.

7. Hamacher 1998: 182. Hamacher's study acknowledges the importance of Mendelssohn's discussion of writing in *Jerusalem* for Hegel's project in *Spirit-Fate*, but Hamacher claims that Mendelssohn is not aware that writing suspends "the system of identity" and therefore cannot be controlled or fixed "in the appropriate place" within his ontology. Hamacher seems unwilling to recognize that Mendelssohn's theory of the living sign-system of Jewish peoplehood challenges, as he believes Hegel ultimately also does, the possibility of closing the living text of revelation. Hamacher brilliantly shows how Hegel sought to turn his philosophy into the infinitely self-regenerating life-blood of all future texts on/of revelation, but he pays too little attention to Hegel's initial gesture, namely, (to use Hamacher's alimentary metaphorics) the consumption and extrusion of Mendelssohn's text on revelation.

8. "Christianity is, once again, Judaism," as Hamacher puts it in his discussion of the relapse of Christianity into its fate (Hamacher 1998: 174).

9. I discussed Hölderlin's poem as capturing Rosenzweig's vision of a post-1800 Johannine Christianity of hope in Chapter 3 (in "Christianity and Paganism: 1800"). Ian Cooper in *Near and Distant God* reads *Patmos* as a response to Hegel's *Spirit of Christianity and its Fate*, but he does not stress, as I do here, that Hölderlin's poetic claim that "history provides signs of continued presence [of Christ], of life given meaning, rather than made derelict, by [Jesus's] death" runs counter to Hegel's view that Christianity has fallen victim to "fate" when it seeks for signs of Christ's presence in history (Cooper 2008, see esp. 38–40). Perhaps Cooper is gesturing toward Hölderlin's break with Hegel when he writes that "the insight that the labour of humanity is the work of God states exactly what the community in [Hegel's] *Der Geist des Christentums* cannot articulate to itself: that the communality of human experience is itself the continued presence of divinity in the world" (42).

10. There is a notable sexist bias in both Rosenzweig and in the Judaism he is describing. The male is the bearer of the covenantal continuity. I by no means wish to endorse or gloss over the gender bias at work in Rosenzweig's text. I will say, however, that in the blessings said after a meal, God is blessed as one "who has inscribed his covenant in our flesh," and, since recitation of the blessings is incumbent upon women as well as men, this phrase is traditionally interpreted as referring to the corporate flesh of the *entire* Jewish people, men and women together constituting one "flesh." Rosenzweig is certainly aware of this rabbinic interpretation, but he does not make use of it to mitigate the sexist bias of discussion of the eternality of the biological people.

11. Ernest Rubinstein rightly draws attention to the linkage between Rosenzweig's approach to art and Christianity in the *Star* and what he calls the "romantic religion" of the early German Romantics, especially the Schlegel brothers and Schelling. My argument has been that Hegel's *Spirit-Fate* and *Fragment* together offer a full instantiation of the "romantic religion" that sees religion as the fusion of infinitude and finitude. I have no interest in attempting a relative ranking of Hegel, Schelling, and Schlegel as influences upon Rosenzweig. It is absolutely certain that Rosenzweig read Nohl's collection of Hegel's early theological writings very closely. Nearly everything that comprises Rubinstein's notion of "romantic religion" can be found the late texts in this collection, especially *Spirit-Fate*. Although it is no doubt the case that Hegel, who published nothing in the 1790s, was hardly thought of as major figure in the period, the publication of his early theological writings in 1907 was, at least for Rosenzweig, of tremendous significance. Rosenzweig at that time was under the influence of the new picture of Hegel provided by Wilhelm Dilthey's *Jugendgeschichte Hegels* (1905), and Nohl's publication of new Hegel manuscripts gave further impetus to Rosenzweig's attempt to reinterpret Hegel as the historical embodiment of the great transformation in German politics and philosophy marked by the year 1800.

6. MENDELSSOHN, ROSENZWEIG, AND POLITICAL THEOLOGY: BEYOND SOVEREIGN VIOLENCE

1. Derrida offers an extended discussion of Rosenzweig's ideas about language and the relation between the Jewish people and their languages in *Monolingualisim of the Other* (1998: 79–84). David Dault, in "Derrida and Rosenzweig at Yom Kippur" (Dault 2004), offers an interesting comparative study of Derrida and Rosenzweig, especially their different understandings of what it means to be a member of a messianic community. For a fuller exposition of the convergences between the philosophies of Rosenzweig and Derrida, see Hollander 2008.

2. See, for example, Cavell 2003: 144, and Cavell 2005: 233.

3. For a discussion of the Berlin salons, and of Varnhagen's in particular, as sites of a sociability focused on the "joy of conversation" in which a new, egalitarian "ideal of humanity" was being tested, see Benhabib 1995. Benhabib's reflections develop the work of Arendt in her biography of Rachel Varnhagen (Arendt 1997).

4. The enmity Schmitt felt for Mendelssohn's political theology is briefly discussed in Goetschel 2007: 477.

5. See, for example, his remarks in *Political Romanticism* (Schmitt 1986: 27, 139–40).

6. See especially Santner 2001: 55–57.

7. See Agamben 2005: 52–53.

8. One of the closest verbal and conceptual parallels may be found between Schmitt's and Rosenzweig's comparisons of states to streams that run into the sea. Schmitt concludes his book with a discussion of two "times [Zeiten]": times of "mediation [Mittels]" in which the individual is seen as having his or her meaning in terms of the wider historical configuration of the state, and times of "immediacy [Unmittelbarkeit]" in which the value of the individual is seen as being independent of the state. From a reference Schmitt makes to Angelus Silesius's dictum about not wanting to have a wall interposed before the light (the full dictum, found in *Der cherubinische Wandersmann*, reads "Weg mit dem Mittelweg: soll ich mein Licht anschauen, / So muß man keine Wand vor mein Gesichte bauen [Away with the middle way: if I should gaze upon my light, / then no one must build a wall before my face]") (Silesius 1960: 63), it seems that Schmitt has in mind with these two "times," two ways in which to fulfill one's identity as God's creation. These two times and ways are not contradictory, Schmitt says, but rather are complementary. There is a "rhythm" to these two times that "stretches over the ages of humanity [Menschenalter] and to whose great swing the individual submits." Schmitt goes on to compare these two times to a wave that carries the world's peoples forward. "The advocate of mediation," Schmitt writes in the last lines of his book, "can point out how a small source that springs up far away from the sea and that must search out its path through many obstacles, can become a majestic river. The defender of immediacy only sees that all bodies of water [alle Gewässer], both the powerful rivers and the small streams, finally end in the sea in order to find their rest [Ruhe] in its infinity [Unendlichkeit]" (Schmitt 1917: 109–11). Rosenzweig adopts the language describing the perspective of the defender of immediacy in order to characterize the Jewish people as a self-contained body of water (ein einziges Gewässer) at rest within itself, and the many streams that are constantly flowing towards it he compares—exactly as does Schmitt—to the historical life of the peoples of the world: "For their streams," Rosenzweig says of these peoples, "all run into the sea, and the eternal circle of the waters beneath heaven is not completed in the riverbed alone. Only one single water on earth stays eternally circling within itself, that is to say with no inflow or outflow—a miracle and impropriety for all those who see it; for it escapes the duty of all waters to flow into the sea. The brooks do not suspect that there is set for them in its eternal circling an image of their universal future" (*Star* 401; 421). If Rosenzweig in fact has Schmitt's image in mind, he is in effect claiming for the Jewish people the role that Schmitt assigns to the restful sea in which God's infinity is reflected without mediation. Schmitt would have found such an identification wholly unacceptable (since for him, the Roman Catholic Church is the restful center of history).

9. See, for example, Schmitt's discussion of Hegel's grasp of the concept of the political as based upon the friend-foe distinction, where Schmitt quotes with approval Hegel's statement that the only true foe is another *Volk* (Schmitt 1932: 50).

10. The dilemma of how sovereignty constitutes itself is the subject of Antonio Negri's *Insurgencies: Constitutive Power and the State* (1999). For a discussion of the problem in the context of the American Revolution, see Edmund S. Morgan 1988.

11. The fact that Michel Foucault wrote the introduction to the 1966 republication of Canguilhem's work allows for a further connection to be drawn between Canguilhem and Schmitt via the concepts of biopolitics and sovereignty that Foucault later developed on the basis of the work of both earlier thinkers.

12. Rosenzweig in *Hegel und der Staat* spends a considerable amount of time explaining the notion of "self-organization" ("Selbstverwaltung") by which the state constitutes itself as both sovereign and legitimate. See Rosenzweig 1962: 2:141–153.

13. For a complete bibliographic discussion of Schmitt's use of the Restrainer concept, see Günter Maschke's Anmerkung to Carl Schmitt's first use of it in *Grossraum und Völkerrecht*, reprinted in Schmitt 1995: 438–40.

14. Arendt's critique does not explicitly invoke Schmitt as its target, but in *The Origins of Totalitarianism*, describing Schmitt's turn to Nazism as the "most interesting" example of the conversion of academics to the ideology, Arendt admits that his works contain "very ingenious theories" that "still make arresting reading" (Arendt 1973: 339n65).

15. Andreas Kalyvas 2004 offers a comparison of Schmitt's decisionism and Arendt's political theory and he argues persuasively that Arendt is deliberately targeting Schmitt in her anti-decisionist positions. I completely agree with the contrast he draws between the two positions. Kalyvas does not note the important place of promising and covenanting in providing the enduring power behind the authority of natality, the "miracle" of the new beginning of which the will is capable.

16. Although, as I have mentioned above, Arendt never refers to Schmitt in *On Revolution*, there are numerous places where she seems to be deploying some of Schmitt's views, for example in her discussion of the emergence of the political notion of sovereignty from the theological one (Arendt 1990: 159–62).

17. I have earlier spoken of Julia Reinhard Lupton's *Citizen-Saints* (2005) and her call in her epilogue (she dubs it a "Humanifesto") for a shared discourse, a "literature of citizenship." I read her call as sharing the identical impulse within Arendt's and Cavell's insistence that democratic sociality is ever-recreated through literary acts, through reauthorings and rereadings of the covenantal agreements that bind us.

18. There is some debate regarding the sources of Arendt's concept of natality. The best treatment of the subject is in Miguel Vatter 2006: 138–43. Vatter proposes Augustine's concept of the creation of the human as the creation of a new beginning within nature (Arendt refers to this frequently) as the ultimate source of the concept of natality, refracted through Benjamin's view that human revolutionary action in history is "the emancipation or redemption of nature."

I believe that Rosenzweig's place in the genealogy of Arendt's concept needs further exploration, even if only through the mediation of Benjamin, a very close reader of the *Star*. While it is possible that Arendt is drawing directly from Rosenzweig, it is also possible, given her use of the term "absolute" and her insistence that the "beginning" as the "absolute of temporality" has "a measure of complete arbitrariness" (*On Revolution* 206), that she is drawing from the same philosophical source as Rosenzweig, namely, Schelling. Schelling's *Weltalter Fragments* contains a discussion of the "absolute beginning" ("absoluter Anfang") that he connects with the "miracle" ("Wunder") of "the world's origin" ("die Herkunft der Welt") and also with messianic birth ("Geburt des Sohns") (Schelling 1993: 76–77). Schelling also identifies this absolute beginning with the groundless beginning of freedom, hence it is a beginning that has "a measure of complete arbitrariness."

19. Arendt herself links her concept of the beginning, or natality, with the concept of Creation: "The problem of beginning, of course, appears first in thought and speculation about the origin of the universe, and we know the Hebrew solution for its perplexities—the assumption of a Creator God who is outside of his creation in the same way as the fabricator is outside the fabricated object" (*On Revolution* 206). It is precisely this disconnected Creator God that Rosenzweig sought to overturn with his notion of creation as ever-renewed beginning, as if, in Arendt's terms, God were an archrevolutionary. Unlike Arendt, Rosenzweig sees no relationship between revolutionary beginning and the sphere of politics.

20. To the best of my knowledge, Mendelssohn does not use the phrase *politcal-theological* (*politischtheologish*), as his younger contemporary Karl Reinhold does, to describe the intersection of political and ecclesiastical powers in the state, but it is certainly not wrong to consider his *Jerusalem* to be devoted to an examination of the problems that arise from the misalignment of these two powers. Therefore, I do not think it is inappropriate to speak of Mendelssohn as advancing a form of political theology in *Jerusalem*.

21. My discussion of Spinoza in this chapter is indebted to several recent contributions to the study of Spinoza's political philosophy: Steven B. Smith's *Spinoza's Book of Life: Freedom and Redemption in the Ethics* (2003), Nancy K. Levene's *Spinoza's Revelation: Religion, Democracy, and Reason* (2004), and Willi Goetschel's *Spinoza's Modernity: Mendelssohn, Lessing, and Heine*, chaps. 1–6 (2004). Although a Spinoza revival has been going on for some time, these works seem to me to offer the most accessible reappraisal of Spinoza as a theorist of democratic sociality.

22. I am indebted here to Nancy K. Levene's interpretation of Spinoza's notion of *causa sui* as the perfect expression of God's freedom to begin Himself eternally without antecedent conditions, and that in so beginning God is also ever-again beginning (i.e., creating) the world. "God's creation of the world," Levene writes, "is simultaneously of himself" (2004: 56). Levene denies precisely that God for Spinoza is *uncaused*, and she draws out the implications in

her book of what it means for God to be self-creator and creator of the world at once. Singular beings are "in God" and are not self-caused, but the singular being called *human* can imagine herself within God, and this offers her a taste of freedom, to partake (part-take) in the self-causing activity of God by directing her love toward God. In so directing her love, the human partakes in the ongoing *revelation* of God in creation. Stephen B. Smith makes a similar point: "If there is no preexisting pattern" for humans to conform to as parts of nature, "then it is up to us to create one" (2003: 199). Levene's reading of Spinoza comes very close at certain points to Arendt (as also to Rosenzweig). Here, for example, Levene's Spinoza sounds very Arendtian: "What is at stake for Spinoza is, precisely, inauguration, beginning: again, revelation. What matters, for Spinoza, is that what will move human beings from bondage to freedom—conatus—is always already in the world because—as the *causa sui*—it has come into the world. Religion, democracy, and reason, then can be the substance of *libertas*, can be true eternally, because they are what we strive to originate. They are eternally true only as long we continue to do so" (235). I do not believe that Levene is anachronistically reading Arendt or Rosenzweig back into Spinoza. Rather, Rosenzweig, and quite possibly Arendt as well, is attuned to this dynamic Spinozism because of his reading of Schelling, whose own dynamic Spinozism is, first of all, a reaction against Jacobi's portrait of Spinoza's God as the very embodiment of unfreedom. Schelling, opposing Jacobi, aligns himself with Mendelssohn. What Levene offers is a portrait of Spinoza that beautifully complements the portrait offered by Willi Goetschel in *Spinoza's Modernity*: a Spinoza who wants above all to offer an ontology of freedom that can undergird a rational and democratic political theology. Goetschel argues, and I agree with him, that Mendelssohn, Lessing, and Heine are the heirs of this project. I would add that Rosenzweig and Arendt stand within this tradition as well. (Jacobi, as I hope to have made clear in Chapter 2, attacks Spinoza in the name of freedom, so his place among these heirs of Spinoza is quite ambiguous. Steven B. Smith finds another of Spinoza's heirs, Leo Strauss, to be also an heir of Jacobi [191].)

7. BEYOND 1800: AN IMMIGRANT ROSENZWEIG

1. The book that I will refer to as *Little Book* was written in 1921 but first published (in English translation under the title *Understanding the Sick and the Healthy*) in 1954; a revised edition with introduction by Hilary Putnam is found in Rosenzweig 1999.

2. I have spoken of this at much greater length in Chapter 3 (in "Christianity and Paganism: 1800").

3. Speaking about Thoreau's *Walden*, Cavell says that the text aims to "win back" the "possession of our words." "This requires," Cavell goes on to say, "replacing them into a reconceived human existence. That it requires a *literary*

redemption of language altogether has been a theme of remarks from the beginning" (*Senses of Walden* 92). Just as Rosenzweig insists that language's redemption is embodied in the ongoing task of translating the scriptures, so Cavell reads *Walden* as a "revising" of the New Testament (cf. *Senses of Walden* 111).

4. That this rejoining of mind and body in dance gives expression to joy might be construed as an exemplary instance of the definition of joy in Spinoza's *Ethics*. I mention this because another philosopher who found profundity in the dance number in *The Band Wagon*, Gilles Deleuze, explicitly articulates his claim about Vincente Minnelli's unique use of dance within a Spinozist ontology (or, perhaps more accurately, a Bergsonian-Spinozist ontology). Just as Cavell views the dance number in *The Band Wagon* as offering a utopian glimpse of a more capacious body politic, so too Deleuze argues that dance for Minnelli reveals a "passage from one world to another, entry into another world, breaking in and exploring" (Deleuze 1989: 63). For Deleuze, the worlds explored by Minnelli in dance are expressive of Spinoza's "common notions," defined succinctly by Deleuze in *Spinoza: Practical Philosophy* as "the effect on us of a body that agrees with ours" (1988: 58). The first "body that agrees" with Astaire's in *The Band Wagon* is that of the black shoeshine man, with whom he will dance a remarkable pas de deux. Although Cavell acknowledges only having read Deleuze and Guattari's book *A Thousand Plateaus* (Cavell 1984: 136), it is quite likely that Cavell was also familiar with Deleuze's *Cinema 1* and *Cinema 2*. I doubt very much, however, that Cavell had Deleuze in mind when he wrote about Minnelli's use of dance in *The Band Wagon*, but the convergence in their approaches demonstrates once more—we have seen in the last chapter how Spinoza and Arendt seem able to be drawn together—the extraordinary place of Spinoza in the formation of the questions at the heart of this book. It is as if modern philosophy were one long attempt to come to grips with Spinoza's radicality and also his "ordinariness," that is, his commitment to embodied human existence as expressed in the joys and sadnesses of human togetherness.

5. Robert Gooding-Williams argues, *pace* Cavell, that Minnelli is promoting the myth that blackness "is a potency needful to that [American] civilization as an adorning supplement" (Gooding-Williams 2006: 252). Cavell responds to this critique in "The Incessance and Absence of the Political" (Cavell 2006: 300–8).

6. In the extended commentary on the DVD of *The Band Wagon* offered by Liza Minnelli and the dancer/choreographer Tommy Tune, we are told that Astaire's question to a hot dog vendor when he enters the arcade, whether the site had previously housed the Ertigan Theater, was not entirely unmotivated: Although there never was such a theater on Forty-second Street, there was a famous transvestite performer on the street with that name. Vincente Minnelli's 1956 *Tea and Sympathy* deals with homosexuality with great sensitivity without ever using the term "homosexual." If the dance between Astaire and Daniels in *Band Wagon* is homoerotically suggestive, as I am arguing it is, it is a further

tribute to Minnelli's capacity to allude to a homoerotic subtext with only gestures and glances.

7. Perhaps it is not going too far to compare Astaire as he wanders in the Forty-second Street arcade to Benjamin's flâneur among the arcades of nineteenth-century Paris. Benjamin's project is to kick free the redemptive force hidden within the arcades.

EPILOGUE: *PIRATES OF THE CARIBBEAN* ONCE MORE

1. I borrow the translation of *"Billigungskraft"* as "power of approbation" from Librett 2000: 86.
2. Ian Cooper (2008) in his discussion of Kant's reconceptualization of salvation history in *Religion within the Boundaries of Mere Reason* puts it this way: "The emphatic orientation of man's moral being towards an idea rather than a historical actuality has hermeneutic implications. On the one hand there remains an absolute split between the sensuous world and the noumenal world, which not even Incarnation bridges. Kant's understanding of Christ clearly precludes the presence of interpretable signs in history, just as our moral journey cannot be read off from the empirical details of our phenomenal life" (14). Cooper's point about the hermeneutic implications of Kant's denial that revelation can have a historical embodiment bears directly upon Kant's complete rejection of Mendelssohn's claim that Judaism is the "living script" of the revealed legislation.

BIBLIOGRAPHY

Agamben, Giorgio. 2005. *State of Exception*, trans. Kevin Attell (Chicago: University of Chicago Press).
Ameriks, Karl. 2004. "Reinhold über Systematik, Popularität, und die 'historische Wende,'" in Bondeli and Lazzari (2004), 303–33.
Arendt, Hannah. 1973. *The Origins of Totalitarianism* (New York: Harcourt Brace Jovanovich).
———. 1978. *The Life of the Mind* (New York: Harcourt Brace Jovanovich).
———. 1990. *On Revolution* (New York: Penguin Books).
———. 1997. *Rahel Varnhagen: The Life of a Jewess*, ed. Liliane Weissberg, trans. Richard and Clara Winston (Baltimore: Johns Hopkins University Press).
Auerbach, Erich. 1953. *Mimesis: The Representation of Reality in Western Literature*, trans. Willard R. Trask (Princeton: Princeton University Press).
Batnitzky, Leora. 1997. "Translation as Transcendence: A Glimpse into the Workshop of the Buber-Rosenzweig Bible Translation," *New German Critique* (70): 87–116.
———. 2000. *Idolatry and Representation: The Philosophy of Franz Rosenzweig Reconsidered* (Princeton: Princeton University Press).
Beiser, Frederick. 1987. *The Fate of Reason: German Philosophy from Kant to Fichte* (Cambridge: Harvard University Press).
Benhabib, Seyla. 1995. "The Pariah and Her Shadow: Hannah Arendt's Biography of Rahel Varnhagen," *Political Theory* 23(1): 5–24.
Benhabib, Seyla, et al. 2006. *Another Cosmopolitanism*, ed. Robert Post (Oxford and New York: Oxford University Press).
Bergson, Henri. 1911. *Creative Evolution*, trans. Arthur Mitchell (New York: Henry Holt and Company).
Bienenstock, Myriam. 2003. "Recalling the Past in Rosenzweig's *Star of Redemption*," *Modern Judaism* 23(3): 226–42.

Bondeli, Martin, and Alessandro Lazzari. 2004. *Philosophie ohne Beynamen: System, Freiheit und Geschichte im Denken Karl Leonhard Reinholds* (Basel: Schwabe).

Bourke, Eoin. 1999. "Christian Wilhelm Dohm's Conception of the Civic Improvement of the Jews," in *The German-Jewish Dilemma: From the Enlightenment to the Shoah*, ed. Edward Timms and Andrea Hammel (Lewiston: The Edwin Mellen Press), 39–51.

Boyle, Nicholas. 2000. *Goethe, The Poet and the Age, Vol. II Revolution and Renunciation (1790–1803)* (Oxford: Oxford University Press).

Buber, Martin. 2002. *Between Man and Man*, trans. Ronald Gregor-Smith (London and New York: Routledge).

Buber, Martin, and Franz Rosenzweig. 1994. *Scripture and Translation*, trans. Lawrence Rosenwald and Everett Fox (Bloomington and Indianapolis: Indiana University Press).

Bubner, Rüdiger, and Walter Mesch, eds. 2001. *Die Weltgeschichte—das Weltgericht? Veröffentlichungnen der Internationalen Hegel-Vereinigung Band 22* (Stuttgart: Klett-Cotta).

Canguilhem, George. 1991. *The Normal and the Pathological*, trans. Carolyn R. Fawcett (New York: Zone Books).

Cavell, Stanley. 1969, 1976. *Must We Mean What We Say? A Book of Essays* (Cambridge: Cambridge University Press).

———. 1979. *The Claim of Reason: Wittgenstein, Skepticism, Morality, and Tragedy* (Oxford and New York: Oxford University Press).

———. 1981. *Pursuits of Happiness: The Hollywood Comedy of Remarriage* (Cambridge: Harvard University Press).

———. 1984. *Themes Out of School: Effects and Causes* (Chicago: University of Chicago Press).

———. 1988. *In Quest of the Ordinary: Lines of Skepticism and Romanticism* (Chicago: University of Chicago Press).

———. 1989. *This New Yet Unapproachable America: Lectures after Emerson and Wittgenstein* (Albuquerque, N.Mex.: Living Batch Press).

———. 1992. *The Senses of Walden, Expanded Edition* (Chicago: University of Chicago Press).

———. 1996. *Contesting Tears: The Hollywood Melodrama of the Unknown Woman* (Chicago: University of Chicago Press).

———. 2003. *A Pitch of Philosophy* (Cambridge: Harvard University Press).

———. 2005. *Philosophy the Day After Tomorrow* (Cambridge: Harvard University Press).

———. 2006. "The Incessance and Absence of the Political," in Norris 2006: 263–317.

Chesterton, G. K. 2004. *Orthodoxy* (Vancouver: Regent College Publishing).
Cooper, Ian. 2008. *The Near and Distant God: Poetry, Idealism, and Religious Thought from Hölderlin to Eliot* (London: Legenda).
Dault, David. 2004. "Derrida and Rosenzweig at Yom Kippur," in *Derrida and Religion: Other Testaments*, ed. Yvonne Sherwood and Kevin Hart (New York and London: Routledge), 97–110.
Deleuze, Gilles. 1988. *Spinoza: Practical Philosophy*, trans. Robert Hurley (San Francisco: City Lights).
———. 1989. *Cinema 2: The Time Image*, trans. Hugh Tomlinson and Robert Galeta (Minneapolis: University of Minnesota Press).
Derrida, Jacques. 1997. *Politics of Friendship*, trans. George Collins (London: Verso).
———. 1998. *Monolingualism of the Other; or, The Prosthesis of Origin*, trans. Patrick Mensah (Stanford: Stanford University Press).
———. 2005. *Rogues: Two Essays on Reason*, trans. Pascale-Anne Brault and Michael Naas (Stanford: Stanford University Press).
di Giovanni, George. 2005. *Freedom and Religion in Kant and His Immediate Successors: The Vocation of Humankind, 1774–1800* (Cambridge: Cambridge University Press).
Dohm, Christian Wilhelm. 1781–83. *Ueber die bürgerliche Verbesserung der Juden.* 2 vols. Vol. 2 (1783) contains Johann David Michaelis, "Herr Ritter Michaelis Beurtheilung" (Berlin/Stettin; available online at http://www.ub.uni-bielefeld.de/diglib/dohm/ueber/).
Dunning, Stephen D. 1979. *The Tongues of Men: Hegel and Hamann on Religious Language and History* (Missoula, Mont.: Scholars Press).
Eisen, Arnold. 1990. "Divine Legislation as 'Ceremonial Script': Mendelssohn on the Commandments," *Association of Jewish Studies Review* 15(2): 239–67.
Erlin, Matt. 2002. "Reluctant Modernism: Moses Mendelssohn's Philosophy of History," *Journal of the History of Ideas* 63(1): 83–104.
Fenves, Peter. 2001. *Arresting Language: From Leibniz to Benjamin* (Stanford: Stanford University Press).
Feuchtwanger, Ludwig. 1929. "Das Bild Mendelssohns bei seinen Gegnern bis zum Tode Hegels: Ein Beitrag zum Neuafbau der geistigen Gestalt Mendelssohns," *Zeitschrift für die Geschichte der Juden in Deutschland* 3: 213–32. (Reprinted in Ludwig Feuchtwanger, *Gesammelte Aufsätze zur jüdischen Geschichte*, ed. Rolf Rieß, [Berlin: Duncker and Humblot, 2003]).
Foucault, Michel. 1984. "What Is Enlightenment," in *The Foucault Reader*, ed. Paul Rabinow (New York: Pantheon Books), 32–50.
Frank, Manfred. 2004. *The Philosophical Foundations of Early German Romanticism* (Albany: State University of New York Press).

Franks, Paul W. 2005. *All or Nothing: Systematicity, Transcendental Arguments, and Skepticism in German Idealism* (Cambridge: Harvard University Press).

———. 2006. "What Is the Context?" *Jewish Quarterly Review* 93(3): 387–95.

Frye, Northrop. 1969. *Fearful Symmetry: A Study of William Blake*, 2nd ed. (Princeton: Princeton University Press).

Funkenstein, Amos. 1993. *Perceptions of Jewish History* (Berkeley: University of California Press).

Goetschel, Willi. 2004. *Spinoza's Modernity: Mendelssohn, Lessing, and Heine* (Madison: University of Wisconsin Press).

———. 2007. "Mendelssohn and the State," *Modern Language Notes* 122(3): 472–92.

Goethe, Johann Wolfgang von. 1894. *Goethes Sämtliche Werke, Bd. 11* (Stuttgart: J. G. Cotta'sche Buchhhandlung).

Gooding-Williams, Robert. 2006. "Aesthetics and Receptivity: Kant, Nietzsche, Cavell, and Astaire," in Norris (2006), 236–62.

Gordon, Peter Eli. 2003. *Rosenzweig and Heidegger: Between Judaism and German Philosophy* (Berkeley: University of California Press).

Hamacher, Werner. 1998. *Pleroma—Reading in Hegel*, trans. Nicholas Walker and Simon Jarvis (Stanford: Stanford University Press).

Hamann, Johann Georg. 1949–57. *Sämtliche Werke*. 6 vols., edited with historical and critical notes by Joseph Nadler (Vienna: Thoms-Morus-Presse im Verlag Herder).

Hammacher, Klaus, ed. 1994. *Fichte und Jacobi, Fichte-Studien* (Amsterdam: Editions Rodopi B. V.).

Hegel, Georg Wilhelm Friedrich. 1907. *Hegels Theologische Jugendschiften*, ed. Herman Nohl (Tübingen: J. C. B. Mohr).

———. 1948. *Early Theological Writings*, trans. T. M. Knox (Chicago: University of Chicago Press).

———. 1977. *Faith and Knowledge*, trans. Walter Cerf (New York: State University of New York Press).

Herbart, Johann Friedrich. 1906. *Sämtliche Werke in Chronologisher Reihenfolge*, ed. Karl Kehrbach and Otto Flügel (Langensalza: Beyer und Mann).

Hilfrich, Carola. 2000. *"Lebendige Schrift": Repräsentation und Idolotrie in Moses Mendelssohns Philosophie und Exegese des Judentums* (München: Wilhelm Fink).

Hölderlin, Friedrich. 1998. *Selected Poems and Fragments*, trans. Michael Hamburger (New York: Penguin Classics).

Hollander, Dana. 2008. *Exemplarity and Chosenness: Rosenzweig and Derrida on the Nation of Philosophy* (Stanford: Stanford University Press).

Honig, Bonnie. 2003. *Democracy and the Foreigner* (Princeton: Princeton University Press).

———. 2007. "The Miracle of Metaphor: Rethinking the State of Exception with Rosenzweig and Schmitt," *Diacritics* 37(2–3): 78–102.

Hütter, Anton. 1990. *Moses Mendelssohn: Philosophie zwischen gemeinem Menschenverstand und unnützer Spekulation* (Cuxhaven: Junghans-Verlag).

Hutto, Daniel D. 2003. *Wittgenstein and the End of Philosophy: Neither Theory nor Therapy* (New York: Palgrave Macmillan).

Inwood, M. J. 1998. *Hegel* (London: Routledge).

Israel, Jonathan I. 2001. *Radical Enlightenment: Philosophy and the Making of Modernity 1650–1750* (Oxford: Oxford University Press).

Jacobi, Friedrich Heinrich. 1812–25. *Werke*, ed. J. F. Köppen and C. J. F. Roth, vols. 1–6 (Leipzig: Gerhard Fleischer).

———. 1994. *The Main Philosophical Writings and the Novel Allwill*, trans. George di Giovanni (Montreal and Kingston: McGill-Queen's University Press).

———. 2000. *Über die Lehre des Spinoza in Briefen an den Herrn Moses Mendelssohn, Auf der Grundlage der Ausgabe von Klaus Hammacher und Imgard-Maria Piske*, bearbeitet von Marion Lauschke (Hamburg: Felix Meiner).

James, William. 1909. *A Pluralistic Universe* (London: Longman's, Green and Co.).

Kalyvas, Andreas. 2004. "From the Act to the Decision: Hannah Arendt and the Question of Decisionism," *Political Theory* 32(3): 320–46.

Kant, Immanuel. 1969–. *Gesammelte Schriften*. 29 vols., herausgegeben von der Königlich preussischen Akademie der Wissenschaften (Berlin: W. de Gruyter).

———. 1996a. *Critique of the Power of Judgment*, ed. Paul Guyer, trans. Paul Guyer and Eric Matthews (Cambridge: Cambridge University Press).

———. 1996b. *Practical Philosophy*, trans. and ed. Mary J. Gregor (Cambridge: Cambridge University Press).

———. 1998. *Religion within the Boundaries of Mere Reason, and Other Writings*, trans. and ed. Allen Wood and George di Giovanni (Cambridge: Cambridge University Press).

Kavka, Martin. 2004. *Jewish Messianism and the History of Philosophy* (Cambridge: Cambridge University Press).

Lamm, Julia A. 1994. "Schleiermacher's Post-Kantian Spinozism: The Early Essays on Spinoza, 1793–94," *The Journal of Religion* 74(4): 476–505.

Lazier, Benjamin. 2008. *God Interrupted: Heresy and the European Imagination Between the World Wars* (Princeton: Princeton University Press).

Lessing, Gotthold Ephraim. 2005. *Philosophical and Theological Writings*, trans. H. B. Nisbet (Cambridge: Cambridge University Press).

Levene, Nancy K. 2004. *Spinoza's Revelation: Religion, Democracy, and Reason* (Cambridge: Cambridge University Press).

Levinas, Emmanuel. 1998. *Entre Nous: On Thinking-of-the-Other*, trans. Michael B. Smith and Barbara Harshav (New York: Columbia University Press).

Lévy-Bruhl, Lucien. 1894. *La Philosophie de Jacobi* (Paris: Fëlix Alcan).
Librett, Jeffrey. 1999. "Humanist Antiformalism as a Theopolitics of Race: F. H. Jacobi on Friend and Enemy," *Eighteenth-Century Studies* 32(2): 233–45
———. 2000. *The Rhetoric of Cultural Dialogue: Jews and Germans from Moses Mendelssohn to Richard Wagner and Beyond* (Stanford: Stanford University Press).
Lilla, Mark. 2007. *The Stillborn God: Religion, Politics, and the Modern West* (New York: Alfred A. Knopf).
Lupton, Julia Reinhard. 2005. *Citizen-Saints: Shakespeare and Political Theology* (Chicago: University of Chicago Press).
Martyn, David. 2002. "Der Geist, der Buchstabe, und der Löwe: Zur Medialität des Lesens bei Paulus und Mendelssohn," in *Transkribieren: Medien/Lektüre*, ed. Ludwig Jäger and Georg Stanitzek (München: Wilhelm Fink), 43–71.
Marx, Karl, and Friedrich Engels, 1998. *The German Ideology* (Amherst, N.Y.: Prometheus Books).
McFarland, Thomas. 1969. *Coleridge and the Pantheist Tradition* (Oxford: Clarendon Press).
Meinecke, Friedrich. 1972. *Historism: The Rise of a New Historical Outlook*, trans. J. E. Anderson (London: Routledge and Kegan Paul).
Melamed, Yitzhak Y. 2004. "Solomon Maimon and the Rise of Spinozism in German Idealism," *Journal of the History of Philosophy* 42(1): 67–96.
Mendelssohn, Moses. 1971–90. *Gesammelte Schriften, Jubiläumsausgabe*, ed. Alexander Altmann et al. (Stuttgart: Frieidrich Frommann Verlag).
———. 1979. *Briefwechsel der Letzen Lebensjahre* (Stuttgart: Friedrich Frommann Verlag).
———. 1983. *Jerusalem, or, On Religious Power and Judaism*, trans. Allan Arkush, intro. and comm. Alexander Altmann (Hanover, N.H.: University Press of New England).
———. 1997. *Philosophical Writings*, trans. and ed. Daniel O. Dahlstrom (Cambridge: Cambridge University Press).
———. 2001. *Jerusalem, oder über religiöse Macht und Judentum; Vorrede zu Manasseh ben Israels "Rettung der Juden,"* ed. David Martyn (Bielefeld: Aisthesis).
———. 2005. *Jerusalem, oder über religiöse Macht und Judentum; mit dem Vorwort zu Menasseh ben Israels Rettung der Juden und dem Entwurf zu Jerusalem*, ed. Michael Albrecht (Hamburg: Felix Meiner).
Michaelis, Johann David. 1771. *A Dissertation on the Influence of Opinions on Language and of Language on Opinions*, 2nd ed. (London: W. Owen, J. Johnson, and W. Bingley). Available on the internet through "Eighteenth Century Collections Online" (galenet.galegroup.com).
Milbank, John. 1999. "The Theological Critique of Philosophy in Hamann and Jacobi," in *Radical Orthodoxy: A New Theology*, ed. Catherine Pickstock, John Milbank, and Graham Ward (New York: Routledge), 21–37.

Morgan, Edmund S. 1988. *Inventing the People: The Rise of Popular Sovereignty in England and America* (New York: W. W. Norton and Company).
Moyn, Samuel. 2007. "From Experience to Law: Leo Strauss and the Weimar Crisis of the Philosophy of Religion," *History of European Ideas* 33(2): 174–94.
Negri, Antonio. 1999. *Insurgencies: Constituent Power and the Modern State*, trans. Maurizia Boscagli (Minneapolis: University of Minnesota Press).
Norris, Andrew, ed. 2006. *The Claim to Community: Essays on Stanley Cavell and Political Philosophy* (Stanford: Stanford University Press).
O'Regan, Cyril. 2001. *Gnostic Return in Modernity* (Albany: State University of New York Press).
Putnam, Hilary. 2008. *Jewish Philosophy as a Guide to Life: Rosenzweig, Buber, Levinas, Wittgenstein* (Bloomington: Indiana University Press).
Reinhold, Karl Leonhard. 1788. *Die Hebräischen Mysterien oder die älteste religiöse Freymaurerey* (Leipzig: Georg Joachim Göschen).
———. 2005. *Letters on the Kantian Philosophy*, ed. Karl Ameriks, trans. James Hebbeler (Cambridge: Cambridge University Press).
———. 2006. *Die Hebräischen Mysterien, oder die älteste religiöse Freymaurerey*, 2nd Auflage, ed. Jan Assmann (Neckargemünd: Edition Mnemosyne).
Roehr, Sabine. 2004. "Reinholds *Hebräische Mysterien oder die älteste religiöse Freymaurerey*: Eine Apologie des Freimauertums," in Bondeli and Lazzari (2004), 147–65.
Rosenstock, Bruce. 2007. "Leo Spitzer and the Poetics of Monotheism," *Comparative Literature Studies* 44(3): 254–78.
Rosenzweig, Franz. 1962. *Hegel und der Staat, Neudruck der Ausgabe 1920* (Aalen: Scientia Verlag).
———. 1976. *Der Stern der Erlösung*, ed. R. Mayer, bd. 2 of *Der Mensch und sein Werk: Gesammelte Schriften*, 4th ed. (The Hague: Martinus Nijhoff).
———. 1984. *Zweistromland: Kleinere Schrfiten zu Glauben und Denken*, ed. Reinhold Meyer and Annemarie Mayer, bd. 3 of *Der Mensch und sein Werk: Gesammelte Schriften* (Dordrecht: Martinus Nijhoff).
———. 1988. *Der Stern der Erlösung* (Frankfurt am Main: Suhrkamp Verlag).
———. 1999. *Understanding the Sick and the Healthy: A View of World, Man, and God*, trans. Nahum Glatzer, intro. Hillary Putnam (Cambridge: Harvard University Press).
———. 2000. *Philosophical and Theological Writings*, trans. and ed. Paul W. Franks and Michael L. Morgan (Indianapolis and Cambridge: Hackett).
———. 2005. *The Star of Redemption*, trans. Barbara E. Galli (Madison: University of Wisconsin Press).
Rubinstein, Ernest. 1999. *An Episode of Jewish Romanticism: Franz Rosenzweig's Star of Redemption* (Albany: State University of New York Press).

Santner, Eric L. 2001. *On the Psychotheology of Everyday Life: Reflections on Freud and Rosenzweig* (Chicago: University of Chicago Press).

Schelling, Friedrich Wilhelm Joseph von. 1992. *Urfassung der Philosophie der Offenbarung*, ed. W. E. Erhardt (Hamburg: Felix Meiner).

———. 1993. *Die Weltalter: Fragmente*, ed. Manfred Schröter (München: Beck).

———. 1998. *System der Weltalter: Münchener Vorlesung 1827/8 in einer Nachschrift von Ernst von Lasaulx*, ed. Siegbert Peetz (Frankfurt am Main: Vittorio Klostermann).

Schmidt, James. 1989. "The Question of Enlightenment: Kant, Mendelssohn, and the *Mittwochsgesellschaft*," *Journal of the History of Ideas* 50(2): 269–91.

Schmitt, Carl. 1917. *Der Wert des Staates und die Bedeutung des Einzelnen* (Hellerau: Hellerauer Verlag).

———. 1932. *Der Begriff des Politschen, mit einer Rede über das Zeitalter der Neutralisierungnen und Entpolitisierungen; neu herausgegeben* (Berlin: Duncker and Humblot).

———. 1976. *The Concept of the Political*, trans. George Schwab (New Brunswick, N.J.: Rutgers University Press).

———. 1986. *Political Romanticism*, trans. Guy Oakes (Cambridge, Mass.: MIT Press).

———. 1995. *Staat, Grossraum, Nomos: Arbeiten aus den Jahren 1916–1969*, ed. Günter Maschke (Berlin: Duncker and Humblot).

Schneider, Heinrich. 1948. "Die Entstehungsgeschichte von Lessings beiden letzten Prosaschriften," *Proceedings of the Modern Language Association* 63(4): 1205–44.

Shaffer, E. S. 1975. *"Kubla Khan" and the Fall of Jerusalem: The Mythological School in Biblical Criticism and Secular Literature, 1770–1880* (Cambridge: Cambridge University Press).

Shakespeare, William. 1965. *The Merchant of Venice*, ed. Kenneth Myrick (New York: Signet Classic).

Silesius, Angelus. 1960. *Der cherubinische Wandersmann*, ed. Charles Waldemar (Goldman).

Smith, Steven B. 2003. *Spinoza's Book of Life: Freedom and Redemption in the Ethics* (New Haven, Conn.: Yale University Press).

Socher, Abraham P. 2006. *The Radical Enlightenment of Solomon Maimon* (Stanford: Stanford University Press).

Stahmer, Harold M. 1984. "'Speech-Letters' and 'Speech-Thinking': Franz Rosenzweig and Eugen Rosenstock-Huessy," *Modern Judaism* 4(1): 57–81

Strauss, Leo. 1965. *Spinoza's Critique of Religion*, trans. E. M. Sinclair (New York: Schocken Books).

Sutcliffe, Adam. 2004. "Quarelling over Spinoza: Moses Mendelssohn and the Fashioning of Jewish Philosophical Heroism," in *Renewing the Past, Reconfiguring Jewish Culture: From Al-Andalus to the Haskalah*, ed. Ross Brann and Adam Sutcliffe (Philadelphia: University of Pennsylvania Press), 167–88.

Taubes, Jacob. 1993. *Die politische Theologie des Paulus* (München: Wilhelm Fink Verlag).
Taylor, Charles. 1979. *Hegel and Modern Society* (Cambridge: Cambridge University Press).
Vatter, Miguel. 2006. "Natality and Biopolitics in Hannah Arendt," *Revista de Ciencia Política* 26(2): 137–59.
Weber, Max. 1958. "Politics as a Vocation," in *From Max Weber: Essays in Sociology*, ed. H. H. Gerth and C. W. Mills (New York: Oxford University Press), 77–128.
Wirth, Jason M. 2003. *Conspiracy of Life: Meditations on Schelling and his Time* (Albany: State University of New York Press).
Wittgenstein, Ludwig. 1958. *Philosophical Investigations*, 3rd ed., trans. G. E. M. Anscombe (New York: Macmillan Publishing Co.).
Wordsworth, William. 1933. *The Prelude or Growth of a Poet's Mind (Text of 1805)*, ed. Ernst de Selincourt (London: Oxford University Press).
Wundt, Wilhelm. 1896. *Lectures on Human and Animal Psychology*, trans. J. B. Creighton and E. B. Titchener (London: Swan Sonnenschein).
Yovel, Yirmiyahu. 1998. *Dark Riddle: Hegel, Nietzsche, and the Jews* (University Park: Pennsylvania State University Press).
Zammito, John H. 1992. *The Genesis of Kant's Critique of Judgment* (Chicago: University of Chicago Press).
———. 1997. "Herder, Kant, Spinoza und die Ursprünge des deutschen Idealismus," in *Herder und die Philosophie des Deutschen Idealismus*, Fichte-Studien Supplementa, ed. Marion Heinz (Amsterdam: Editions Rodopi B. V.), 107–44.
Zöllner, Friedrich Johann. 1786. "Ueber eine Stelle in Moses Mendelssohn's Schrift an die Freunde Lessings," *Berlinische Monatschrift*: 271–75 (page images available online at *Zeitschriften der Aufklärung*, http://www.ub.uni-bielefeld.de/diglib/aufklaerung/).

INDEX

Agamben, Giorgio, 248, 349n7
Almodóvar, Pedro, 306
Altmann, Alexander, 247, 306, 326n6, 330n11
Ameriks, Karl, 344n11
Arendt, Hannah, 27, 43, 44, 246, 270, 277, 278, 280, 318, 322, 327n21, 328n23, 330n17, 334n11, 346n26, 351n14, 351n15, 351n16, 351n17, 351n18, 352n18, 352n19, 353n22, 354n4
  on the life of the mind, 67–68
  on natality, 26, 151, 245, 250, 266–68, 276, 351n18
  political theory of, 246, 250–51, 263–69, 271–73, 279
Assmann, Jan, 171, 344n8, 345n12
Astaire, Fred (*The Band Wagon*), 27, 280, 295–97, 301, 303, 304–6, 309, 338n2, 354n4, 354n6, 355n7
Auerbach, Erich, 240, 241, 242
Austin, John, 49, 75

Band Wagon, The. See Astaire, Fred
Barth, Karl, 139, 253, 254, 328n22, 333n11
Batnitzky, Leora, 5, 9, 11, 124, 131, 254–55, 256, 326n7, 332n30, 339n7, 339n8
Bauer, Bruno, 90
Beiser, Frederik, 322n2, 333n9
Benhabib, Seyla, 328n23, 349n3

Benjamin, Walter, 248, 256, 351n18, 352n18, 355n7
Bergson, Henri, 335n24, 339n6, 341n23, 354n4
Bible. *See* Hebrew Bible
Bienenstock, Myriam, 340n12
Blake, William, 90–91
Bourke, Eoine, 329n8
Boyle, Nicholas, 136, 137, 138
Buber, Martin, 4, 6, 8, 326n8, 326n10, 326n11, 326n12
Bubner, Rüdiger,, 327n18

Canguilhem, Georges, 258–59, 351n11
Capra, Frank, 291, 294
Cavell, Stanley, 26, 27, 251, 262, 263, 265, 268, 275, 276, 307, 308, 309, 318, 321, 322, 328n23, 329n5, 330n19, 331n26, 334n11, 335n28, 340n17, 342n25, 349n2, 351n17, 353n3, 354n4, 354n5
  on acknowledgment, 20–21, 63–64, 277–78, 285–88, 300
  on festive existence, 289–94, 301–9
  on ordinary language and skepticism, 30, 65, 105, 280–84
  political theory of, 246, 266, 278–80, 288–89, 294–98, 300–5, 331n26, 338n2, 351n17
  on *The Band Wagon*, 295–97, 304–6
  See also marriage/remarriage; redemption

367

368   Index

Charisse, Cyd, 304, 305, 338n2
Chesterton, G. K., 346n29
Coleridge, Samuel Taylor, 91, 104, 321, 322n2
Cooper, Ian, 139, 348n9, 355n2
common sense (*gesunde Menschenverstand*), 30–31, 116, 117, 119, 281–83, 311–13, 329n4, 337n39, 342n1
Cranz, August Friedrich, 38, 68, 72, 330n11

Daniels, Leroy, 304, 305, 354n6
Dault, David, 349n1
Deleuze, Gilles, 339n6, 354n4
democracy/democratic redemptive politics, 5, 15, 18, 19, 20, 26, 27, 43–44, 242, 244, 245–46, 247–48, 250–51, 257, 274–76, 278–80, 288–89, 291, 294–98, 301–9, 322, 327n21, 328n23, 331n26, 338n2, 352n22
  and Arendt's concept of natality, 26, 245, 250, 265, 268–69
  in Spinoza, 250–51, 271–72
  See also Arendt, Hannah: political theory of; Cavell, Stanley: political theory of; natality; political theology; redemption; state/sovereignty
Depp, Johnny, 200, 310
Derrida, Jacques, 47, 48, 50, 331n20, 349n1
  relation to Rosenzweig, 246
Descartes, René, 98, 99, 116, 126, 281, 285
di Giovanni, George, 80, 112, 326n13, 332n2, 332n4, 332n5, 332n7, 337n35, 337n38, 339n9, 345n13
Dohm, Christian Wilhelm, 20, 31–33, 34, 35, 78, 118, 329n6, 329n7, 329n8
Dunne, Irene, 303
Dunning, Stephen, 329n3, 343n6

Eisen, Arnold, 68
Ehrenberg, Hans, 139
Ehrenberg, Rudolf, 139
Emerson, Ralph Waldo, 266, 267, 291, 298, 303, 331n26

enlightenment: Kant's and Mendelssohn's essays on, 28–29
  and Freemasonry, 23, 56–58, 179
  Judaism as embodiment of (Mendelssohn), 20, 21, 48, 66, 68, 76, 77–78, 117
  Kant's theory of, 172–73
  Lessing's theory of, 56–59
  Mendelssohn's theory of, 29, 56–58
  and the unrepresentable God (Reinhold), 23, 175–77
  See also Freemasonry; rational theology
Erlin, Matt, 331n22

Fenves, Peter, 60, 62–63, 66, 331n28
Feuchtwanger, Ludwig, 343n6
Feuerbach, Ludwig, 90, 125, 338n4
Fichte, Johann Gottlieb, 87, 89, 90, 92, 95, 96, 101, 102, 103, 106, 126, 158, 159, 160, 166, 205, 220, 221, 333n9, 334n13, 334n17, 343n4
Fonda, Henry, 287
Foucault, Michel, 28, 29, 31, 351n11
Frank, Manfred, 333n9
Franks, Paul W., 159, 325n4, 326n12, 326n14, 328n22, 332n7, 333n7, 338n4, 340n12, 341n20
Freemasonry, 23, 56, 169, 171, 174–75, 176, 178, 179, 180, 182, 186, 196, 345n16
  Lessing's writings on, 56–59, 170, 344n11
  See also Lessing, Gotthold Ephraim; Reinhold, Karl Leonhard; Schiller, Friedrich
Freud, Sigmund, 101
Frye, Northrop, 90, 91
Funkenstein, Amos, 50, 337n1
  on German-Jewish philosophy, 1, 5, 9, 209

German-Jewish philosophy. *See* philosophy
gnosticism, 87
  in English Romanticism, 90–91

Jacobi's turn to, 81, 84–86, 95, 103, 147–48
in post-Kantian idealism, 89–90, 92
Rosenzweig's overcoming of, 125, 338n5
Goethe, Johann Wolfgang von, 130, 133, 134, 140, 142, 156, 157, 203, 340n10, 340n16
as "first Christian" (Rosenzweig), 135–36, 143–46, 145, 239–40, 242
renunciation and hope in *The Natural Daughter*, 136–38
Goetschel, Willi, 12–13, 43–44, 73, 75, 76–77, 257, 269, 274–75, 330n16, 334n14, 338n1, 349n4, 352n21, 353n22
Gooding-Williams, Robert, 354n5
Gordon, Peter Eli, 19, 208, 232, 255–56, 327n19, 340n18
Grant, Cary, 303

Hamacher, Werner, 222, 348n7, 348n8
Hamann, Johann Georg, 8, 29, 94, 95, 111, 169, 207, 329n3, 334n16, 342n26, 343n6, 343n7
critique of Mendelssohn (*Golgotha*), 167–68
Hammacher, Klaus, 333n9
Hebrew Bible, 20, 71, 73, 75, 114, 124, 125, 127, 158, 163, 167, 189, 192, 206, 333n11
as bearer of revelation in history, 9, 22, 26, 83, 128–29, 131–33
categories of creation, revelation, and redemption in, 129–30, 158, 233
Rosenzweig-Buber translation of, 4
story of Adam and Eve in, 285–88
Hegel, Georg Wilhelm Friedrich, 1, 2, 3, 7, 26, 87, 89, 90, 91, 92, 124, 133, 134, 135, 136, 142, 143, 144, 146, 151, 156, 159, 161, 162, 163, 167, 169, 187, 204, 249, 251, 252, 254, 255, 256, 257, 259, 260, 263, 308, 320, 325n1, 325n2, 325n3, 327n16, 327n17, 327n18, 327n19, 327n21, 329n3, 333n9, 333n11, 334n16, 339n5, 340n9, 340n11, 340n15, 340n18, 343n3, 343n4, 343n5, 344n11, 345n22, 346n28, 347n1, 347n2, 347n3, 347n5, 348n6, 348n9, 349n11, 350n9, 351n12
critique of Mendelssohn, 25
debt to Mendelssohn, 209–14
on the fate of Christianity, 25, 166, 222, 224–25
influence on Rosenzweig, 25, 205, 207–8, 231–33, 235, 237, 238, 250
on Jacobi, 206
on Judaism, 205–7, 215, 219–20
on the Last Supper, 25, 166, 206, 210–11, 222–25
on the philosophical religion of Infinite Life, 165–66, 216–19, 221–22, 225–30
theory of the state, 15–19, 256
Helvétius, Claude Adrien, 52, 55
Herbart, Johann Friedrich, 336n32
Herder, Johann Gottfried, 37, 53, 78, 330n10
Hesiod (*Theogony*), 149
Hilfrich, Carola, 330n17, 330n19, 332n30
Hobbes, Thomas, 12, 13, 14, 15, 43, 54, 77, 250, 254, 257, 259, 269, 270, 275, 327n17
contract theory of, 43, 50
Hölderlin, Friedrich, 1, 87, 91, 136, 137, 240, 325n1, 333n9, 340n14, 340n18, 348n9
renunciation and hope in *Patmos*, 138–44, 229–30, 255, 256
Hollander, Dana, 48, 349n1
Honig, Bonnie, 245–46, 327n21, 328n23
Hume, David, 55, 64, 98, 99, 100, 101, 103, 106, 156, 282, 311, 335n26
Hütter, Anton, 329n4
Hutto, Daniel D., 62

Inwood, M. J., 333n9
Israel, Menassah ben, 32, 35, 329n7
I-Thou, 326n12
in Jacobi, 7, 25, 99, 101, 102, 125, 158

in Rosenzwieg, 7, 125, 147, 152–53, 158, 161, 341n21

Jacobi, Friedrich Heinrich, 82, 83, 104, 106, 107, 108, 120, 121, 132, 150, 156, 157, 161, 162, 167, 168, 169, 173, 174, 186, 233, 309, 326n12, 326n13, 327n21, 328n22, 329n3, 332n2, 332n3, 332n4, 332n5, 332n6, 337n35, 339n9, 341n21, 342n26, 342n1, 344n11, 353n22
  critique of idealism, 95–99, 157, 159–60, 165, 166
  critique of nihilism, 96–103, 105, 337n36, 338n4, 343n3
  critique of Spinoza, 79–81, 88–89, 92, 93–95, 97–98, 163–64, 332n7, 333n9, 333n10, 333n11, 334n13, 334n17, 334n18, 334n19, 334n20, 335n21, 335n24, 335n25, 335n27, 335n29, 336n30
  on experiential revelation, 21, 84–85, 97, 99, 123–28, 158
  gnosticism of, 22, 85–87, 90–92, 95, 103, 147–48, 333n11, 334n18, 339n5
  Hegel's response to, 205–6, 221–22, 343n4, 348n6
  Mendelssohn's response to, 111–19, 122, 336n33
  realism of, 99–101
  See also I-Thou: in Jacobi; Lessing, Gotthold Ephraim: Jacobi's conversations with; Spinoza Quarrel
James, William, 336n33, 339n6
Jewish people. See Rosenzweig, Franz; Mendelssohn, Moses
Jewish Question, 9, 27, 40, 92, 170, 334n11
  Dohm on, 31–33, 34
  Michaelis on, 34
Judaism. See Hegel, Georg Wilhelm Friedrich; Kant, Immanuel; Mendelssohn, Moses; Reinhold, Karl Leonhard; Rosenzweig, Franz

Kabbalah, 57, 86, 87, 88, 91, 96, 336n30
  Wachter on, 93–94

Kalyvas, Andreas, 351n15
Kant, Immanuel, 3, 4, 7, 23, 26, 28, 29, 90, 102, 107, 120, 143, 159, 160, 161, 162, 163, 165, 166, 167, 169, 171, 174, 176, 177, 182, 185, 186, 207, 209, 210, 215, 311, 312, 313, 314, 315, 319, 322, 329n3, 334n16, 337n39, 342n1, 343n3, 344n11, 345n19, 345n20, 345n24, 346n28, 346n29, 347n1, 347n5
  on Judaism and radical evil, 186–97, 206, 220, 279, 288, 345n22, 345n25, 346n26
  on organic life, 216–17
  on the "sublime" religion of reason, 24–25, 88–89, 164, 172–73, 197–203, 309–10, 318–20, 321, 345n21, 355n2
  and the Spinoza Quarrel, 121
  See also Mendelssohn, Moses: critique of Kant; radical evil; Reinhold, Karl Leonhard: on Kant's *Critique*
Kavka, Martin, 341n21
Kierkegaard, Søren, 98, 125, 144, 293

Lamm, Julia A., 333n9
Lavater, Johann Casper, 8, 118, 120
Lazier, Benjamin, 108, 327n22, 333n11
Leibniz, Gottfried Wilhelm, 8, 95, 110, 126, 273, 274, 318, 339n6
Lessing, Gotthold Ephraim, 22, 28, 31, 51, 56, 66, 76, 79, 88, 99, 107, 112, 113, 118, 136, 162, 163, 170, 327n22, 331n23, 331n24, 353n21
  on Freemasonry, 56–59
  Jacobi's conversations with (Spinoza Quarrel), 21, 79–80, 82, 83, 86–87, 91, 93, 94, 160, 332n4, 332n5
  and purified Spinozism, 81, 108–10, 317–18, 337n33
  struggle over inheritance of, 89, 163, 170–73, 344n11
  See also Mendelssohn, Moses: critique of Lessing; Mendelssohn, Moses: friendship with Lessing

Levene, Nancy, 330n18, 352n21, 352–53n22
Levinas, Emmanuel, 285, 288, 341n23
Lévy-Bruhl, Lucien, 335n24
Librett, Jeffrey, 48, 70, 95, 170, 315, 331n29, 334n18, 335n27, 343n7, 344n10, 355n1
Lilla, Mark, 253–54, 255
"living script." *See* Mendelssohn, Moses
Lupton, Julia Reinhard, 247–48, 306–07, 351n17

Maimon, Salomon, 336n30
marriage/remarriage, 17, 277–79, 283–84, 285–88, 291–95, 303–8. *See also* Cavell, Stanley; Lupton, Julia Reinhard
Martyn, David, 50, 326n6, 330n19
Marx, Karl, 90, 345n15
McFarland, Thomas, 91, 332n2
Meinecke, Friedrich, 143
Melamed, Yitzhak Y., 336n30
Mendelssohn, Moses, 1, 5, 8, 18, 19, 22, 24, 26, 27, 79, 95, 97, 100, 105, 125, 154, 161, 162, 168, 170, 171, 172, 173, 174, 177, 178, 179, 181, 182, 184, 186, 191, 195, 196, 205, 206, 207, 208, 209, 210, 211, 215, 222, 228, 244, 246, 250, 251, 262, 263, 268, 308, 309, 310, 320, 321, 322, 327n16, 327n21, 327n22, 328n22, 328n1, 329n9, 330n15, 330n16, 330n17, 331n21, 331n28, 331n29, 332n30, 332n3, 332n4, 335n29, 336n26, 336n32, 337n39
  on church and state, 12–14, 36–37, 39–41, 44–46, 48, 214–15, 246, 257, 273–74, 337n1, 339n6, 340n11, 342n1, 343n6, 343n7, 344n10, 344n11, 345n14, 347n3, 349n4, 353n22, 355n2
  on civil rights and religious toleration, 32, 37, 38, 41–43, 44, 45, 47, 58–59, 70, 71, 74, 76, 77, 78, 214, 247, 248
  on common sense and metaphysics, 311–19, 329n4, 330n12, 330n13
  contract theory of, 15, 35–36, 41–44
  critique of Kant, 313–15, 318–19
  critique of Lessing's Freemasonry and progressivism, 22, 56–59, 76, 317–18, 331n22, 331n23
  death of, 335n25
  defense of purified Spinozism, 107–11, 116–17, 336n33
  on enlightenment, 28–29, 56–58, 68–69
  ("too messianic") friendship with Lessing, 21, 31, 66, 79, 81–83, 94
  on idolatry (of written signs), 10–11, 54–56, 59, 68–69, 76–77, 127, 211–13, 348n7
  on Jewish election, 47–48, 59, 77–78, 227–28
  on Jewish people as "living script," 9–11, 21, 25, 59, 73–76, 127, 130, 132, 134, 167, 168, 212–13, 243, 244
  on Judaism as embodying enlightenment, 20, 21, 48, 66, 68, 69–70, 76–77, 117, 119, 134, 167, 169, 227, 245
  on Judaism as revealed legislation, 23, 70–74, 115–16, 123–26, 163, 337n1, 347n4
  on oaths, 36, 46–47, 60–61
  political theology of, 269–75, 352n20
  on the religion of reason, 55, 111, 113–14, 126–28, 163, 310–19
  response to Jacobi (Spinoza Quarrel), 106–22
  theory of language as forerunner to Wittgenstein's, 30, 31, 38–39, 40–41, 49, 50–54, 59–68, 154, 330n19, 331n25
  on translating the name of God, 6–7
  See also Hegel, Georg Wilhelm Friedrich: critique of Mendelssohn, debt to Mendelssohn, on Judaism; Kant, Immanuel: on Judaism and radical evil; political theology: Mendelssohn's; Reinhold, Karl Leonhard: on Judaism; Spinoza Quarrel: Jacobi's initiation of; state/sovereignty: Mendelssohn's contract theory of
Mendes-Flohr, Paul, 139

372   Index

Mesch, Walter, 327n18
Michaelis, Johann David, 33, 35, 63, 64, 78, 329n6, 329n8, 331n21
  on Jewish oaths, 34, 63
  theory of language, 50–52, 59, 60, 120
Milbank, John, 329n3
Minnelli, Vincente, 180, 280, 304, 354n4, 354n5, 354n6
Morgan, Edmund S., 351n10
Morgan, Michael L., 325n4, 326n12
Moyn, Samuel, 328n22

natality
  compared to Rosenzweig's category of creation, 26, 151, 250, 267–68, 270, 275–77, 279, 323, 51n19
  as foundation of the political (Arendt), 245, 263–69, 271–72, 273, 351n15, 351n18
  See also Arendt, Hannah
Negri, Antonio, 351n10
Nicolai, Christoph Friedrich, 51
Nietzsche, Friedrich, 98, 144, 298
1800, epochal significance of (Rosenzweig): 1–5, 89, 133–46, 156–57, 322, 323, 339n9
  and the modern state, 16
  and the Spinoza Quarrel, 8, 92, 157–61

ordinary language, 31, 38–40, 65, 154–56, 280–83
O'Regan, Cyril, 85, 333n11

paganism. See Rosenzweig, Franz
philosophy
  and common sense, 281–83, 311–13
  and the condition of Jews in modernity, 27
  end of (with Hegel in 1800), 2, 26, 134–35, 143
  German-Jewish, 5, 9, 11
  Jacobi's critique of, 81, 96–97
  and ordinary language, 30–31, 38–40, 154–57
  and ordinary life, 26, 104–5

  task of (Rosenzweig and Cavell), 26, 246, 280–83
  See also revelation
Pirates of the Caribbean, 199, 200, 310, 318, 320
political theology, 20, 247, 248, 250, 251, 253, 254, 276, 306, 327n27, 328n23, 349n4, 353n22
  Arendt's, 263–68
  Hegel's, 16–17, 19
  Mendelssohn's, 12, 15, 18–19, 247–48, 257, 269–75, 352n20
  Rosenzweig's, 12, 14, 16–18, 19, 248–49, 261–62
  Schmitt's, 248–49, 257
  See also democracy/democratic redemptive politics; state/sovereignty
Putnam, Hilary, 154, 290, , 329n5, 353n1

radical evil, 191, 198–200, 321, 322, 349n3
  epitomized by Judaism (Kant), 24, 188–96, 346n26
  and the subjective ground of freedom (Kant), 24, 187, 310
rational theology:
  Jacobi's critique of, 8, 81, 84–85
  Kant's critique of, 3, 7, 8
  in Mendelssohn, 6–7, 74, 106–7, 163
redemption, 4, 5, 279
  and the art of dance, 301–6
  celebrated in communities of praise, 27, 279–80, 291–98
  as festive existence, 291–301
  of language, 290–91, 294
  See also Cavell, Stanley; Rosenzweig, Franz
redemptive politics. See democracy/democratic redemptive politics
Reinhold, Karl Leonhard, 26, 161, 162, 163, 166, 173, 187, 192, 195, 202, 205, 311, 329n3, 334n12, 334n16, 343n3, 344n8, 347n1, 352n20
  on the Egyptian mysteries, 23, 170, 181
  on Freemasonry, 23, 172, 174–75, 178–79, 345n16

on Judaism, 174–75, 177–80, 181–82, 185–86, 196
on Kant's *Critique*, 23–24, 170, 171, 173–78, 182, 185–86, 344n11
on the religion of reason, 164, 165, 167, 169–71, 177, 182–86
religion of reason. *See* Hegel, Georg Wilhelm Friedrich: on the religion of reason; Kant, Immanuel: on the religion of reason; Mendelssohn, Moses: on the religion of reason; Reinhold, Karl Leonhard: on the religion of reason
revelation
and the everyday world, 104–5, 138, 283, 285
vs. idealist philosophy, 26, 156–57, 338n5
and I-Thou, 7–8, 21
Jacobi's and Mendelssohn's views of compared, 122, 123, 125–28
in language (Rosenzweig), 23, 125, 132, 144, 147–52, 154–56, 283–84
as living experience (Jacobi), 21, 84–85, 99–101, 126–27
as Mosaic legislation (Mendelssohn), 10–11, 123,
vs. paganism, 3–4, 22, 128, 132, 133–34, 143–44, 148–52
See also Hebrew Bible
Roehr, Sabine, 345n16
Rosenstock, Bruce, 331n20
Rosenstock, Eugen, 83, 139
Rosenzweig, Franz, 204, 244, 329n5, 331n20, 332n30, 338n4, 340n11, 340n12, 340n18, 341n21, 341n23, 342n26, 345n19, 347n2, 347n5, 348n10, 349n1, 352n18, 352n19, 353n22, 354n3
on the Christian liturgical year and world history, 131, 132, 135, 146, 234–36, 237–38, 241, 260–61, 279, 302
on the epochal significance of 1800, 1–5, 143–45, 156–57, 158, 323
on gnosticism, 333–34n11, 345n19

on Goethe as "first Christian," 135, 143, 239–40, 242, 340n10
on Hegel's philosophy, 2–3, 15–19, 134–35, 142–44, 166, 252, 339n5
on holy days of redemption, 298–300
on Jewish and Christian commensality, 235–36
on the Jewish liturgical year as image of eternity, 130, 131, 146, 233–34, 262, 279, 302
on the Jewish people as outside history, 11, 14, 19, 130, 131–32, 232–33, 236–37, 242–43, 255, 260
on Johannine Christianity, 133–34, 135–36, 161, 242, 255, 348n9
on language as the site of revelation, 125, 128, 132, 144, 146–57
on lover and beloved (revelation), 277–78, 302, 335n20
on Mendelssohn's friendship with Lessing, 21
on Mendelssohn's rational theology, 5–7
on natural versus spiritual birth as the basis of covenantal community, 231–33
on the paganism of Greek myth and philosophy, 132, 146–47, 149–52
on the paganism of Greek tragedy, 153–54
on the paganism of idealist philosophy, 152, 156–57, 158–60, 252, 338n5
on the singularity of the created being ("B" term), 150–54, 158–59, 161, 233, 267, 342n24
on the state, 14–18, 19, 238–39, 351n12
on the translation of the Hebrew Bible, 4, 8, 129, 130–31, 290–91
views on the state, compared to Schmitt's, 249–63, 350n8
on the work of art, 130, 145, 157, 238, 240–42, 349n11
See also Hebrew Bible: as bearer of revelation in history; Hebrew Bible: categories of creation, revelation,

374   *Index*

redemption in; Hegel, Georg Wilhelm Friedrich: influence on Rosenzweig; I-Thou; philosophy; political theology: Rosenzweig's; redemption; revelation
Rousseau, Jean-Jacques, 56
Rubinstein, Ernest, 339n7, 349n11

Santner, Eric, 138, 39, 152, 203, 248, 340n14, 349n6
Schelling, Friedrich Wilhelm Joseph von, 87, 91, 92, 136, 159, 160, 165, 333n9, 340n12, 341n21, 341n22, 341n23, 345n19, 347n2, 347n3, 349n11, 352n18, 353n22
Schiller, Friedrich, 136, 140, 171–72, 173
Schlegel, Dorothea, 344n10
Schlegel, Friedrich, 344n10
Schleiermacher, Friedrich Daniel Ernst, 88, 91, 333n9
Schmidt, James, 328n1, 337n37
Schmitt, Carl, 26, 245, 327n17, 327n21, 349n4, 350n8, 350n9, 351n11, 351n13, 351n14, 351n15, 351n16
  on the violent foundation of the state, 248–63
  See also political theology: Schmitt's; Rosenzweig, Franz: views on the violence of the state, compared to Schmitt's
Schneider, Heinrich, 331n23
Shaffer, E. S., 91
Shakespeare, William, 147, 280, 284, 285, 292, 306, 307
Shylock (*Merchant of Venice*), 21, 64
Silesius, Angelus, 350n8
Smith, Stephen B., 44, 352n21, 353n22
Socher, Abraham, 336n30
Spinoza, Baruch, 8, 11, 13, 21, 22, 79, 80, 81, 82, 86, 87, 88, 89, 92, 95, 97, 99, 106, 107, 110, 113, 116, 117, 118, 119, 169, 162, 203, 246, 248, 251, 269, 327n22, 332n4, 334n14, 335n29, 336n33, 352n21, 354n4
  influence on post-Kantian idealism, 88–89

  as Kabbalistic pantheist, 93–94, 336n30
  theory of the state as expression of power, 43–44, 250, 257, 263, 269–72, 273, 274, 330n18, 352–53n22
  See also Jacobi, Friedrich Heinrich: critique of Spinoza; Spinoza Quarrel
Spinoza Quarrel, 8, 11, 12, 18, 21, 22, 23, 24, 157, 160, 174, 209, 244, 250, 328n22, 332n2
  influence of, 88–92
  Jacobi's initiation of, 21, 79–81, 92–95, 97, 112, 335n25
  Kant's response to, 121
  Mendelssohn's response to, 106–22
Stahmer, Harold M., 340n19
Stanwyck, Barbara, 287
state/sovereignty, 12, 307, 308
  Arendt's theory of, 250
  Arendt's and Schmitt's theories contrasted, 263–69
  Mendelssohn's contract theory of, 35–36, 41–44, 273–75, 308
  Mendelssohn as critical of, 12–14
  Rosenzweig and Hegel on violence of, 14–18, 19, 252
  Rosenzweig's theory of, 245, 248–49, 251–57, 260–62
  Schmitt on violent foundation of, 26, 245, 248, 257–60
  Spinoza's theory of, 43, 250
Stirner, Max, 90
Strauss, Leo, 108, 327n22, 334n11, 353n22
Sutcliffe, Adam, 119

Taubes, Jacob, 254
Taylor, Charles, 53
Thoreau, Henry David, 266, 280, 282, 291, 300, 301, 331n26, 353n3

Varnhagen, Rachel, 247, 349n3
Vatter, Miguel, 267, 268, 351n18
violence. *See* state/sovereignty
vochedik/yontovdik, 292–94, 302. *See also* redemption

Wachter, Johann Georg, 93, 94, 106, 117, 334n15
Weber, Max, 253, 254
Wirth, Jason M., 333n9
Wittgenstein, Ludwig, 20, 27, 28, 30, 31, 38, 39, 40, 50, 63, 64, 68, 154, 280, 290, 329n5, 330n19, 331n26, 334n11
  critique of private language, 62
  on language games, 67
  response to skepticism, 30, 65
  See also Cavell, Stanley: on ordinary language and skepticism

Wolff, Christian, 8, 95, 126, 273
Woolf, Virginia, 240, 241, 242
Wordsworth, William, 2, 104–5
Wundt, Wilhelm, 336n32

Yovel, Yirmiyahu, 345n22

Zammito, John H., 332n2, 332n4
Zöllner, Friedrich Johann, 120, 121, 337n37